Georgiana Fullerton

A Stormy Life: A novel

Georgiana Fullerton

A Stormy Life: A novel

ISBN/EAN: 9783741164064

Manufactured in Europe, USA, Canada, Australia, Japa

Cover: Foto ©Andreas Hilbeck / pixelio.de

Manufactured and distributed by brebook publishing software (www.brebook.com)

Georgiana Fullerton

A Stormy Life: A novel

STORMY LIFE

QUEEN MARGARET'S JOURNAL

A NOVEL

BY

LADY GEORGIANA FULLERTON

NEW EDITION

LONDON
BURNS AND OATES
GRANVILLE MANSIONS W
1885

HAVERSTOCK HILL NW
.
PRINTED BY THE SOCIETY OF ST ANNE

CONTENTS.

CHAP.		PAGE
I.	The Goddeshouse of Portsmouth	1
II.	What the Maids of Honour thought of the Queen	13
III.	A Conversation	21
IV.	The Dawn	33
V.	The early Morn	42
VI.	King René	47
VII.	Sorrow and Joy	58
VIII.	The Palace de Carrière	75
IX.	A Vow	83
X.	An Ending and a Beginning	92
XI.	Floreat Etona	104
XII.	Clouds at Home and Abroad	118
XIII.	Françoise de Dinant	129
XIV.	The Cloud of the Size of a Man's Hand	145
XV.	News from Brittany	157
XVI.	A King's Prophecy	164
XVII.	The Maids of Honour again	174
XVIII.	The Red Rose	183
XIX.	A Gleam from the South	193
XX.	A Visit to the Country	204
XXI.	At the Gray Friars	210
XXII.	The French Friar's Story	217
XXIII.	The Queen at Norwich	227
XXIV.	A new Joy and a new Anguish	233

CHAP.		PAGE
XXV.	Harlech Castle	244
XXVI.	Evil Tidings	256
XXVII.	Pages from the Queen's Journal	261
XXVIII.	Meeting with old Friends	272
XXIX.	Sir Pierce de Bracy	286
XXX.	A Chapter of Letters	298
XXXI.	A wilful Woman maun have her Way	316
XXXII.	A Week at St. Pol	333
XXXIII.	The Dead Man's Ground	346
XXXIV.	A Robber's Cave	358
XXXV.	The Queen's Lady in England	374
XXXVI.	Dame Catharine Bugdon	388
XXXVII.	Warwick-lane	401
XXXVIII.	An Arrival and a Departure	415
XXXIX.	The Comte de Queniez	431
XL.	The Struggle	445
XLI.	Love's Victory	459
XLII.	An Idyl of Anjou	475
XLIII.	The Abyss	489
XLIV.	"Out of the depths I have cried unto Thee"	502
XLV.	Per Crucem ad Lucem	517

[The following words were prefixed to the manuscript from which the ensuing narrative has been printed: "In an age not less perilous and replete with troubles than that in which this piece of writing was originally penned, one into whose hands chance or Providence ordained it should fall, in the year 1651, has produced a faithful transcript of its contents; only using, for the sake of conveniency and the better understanding thereof by unlearned readers, the style of language at present in use in this country rather than that which is now obsolete and barbarous. At a time when through rebellions and civil wars, many noble and virtuous persons in England are heavily afflicted, some drop of comfort may be tasted and hope of future peace derived, from a knowledge of the strifes which have convulsed this kingdom in times past."]

A STORMY LIFE.

CHAPTER I.

The Goddeshouse at Portsmouth.

On the 10th day of the month of April of the year 1445, the maids of honour of the Queen, of which she who writeth this was one, were conducted by their mistress, the Lady de Scales, to the Goddeshouse at Portsmouth, there to await her majesty's landing—a goodly set of maidens, of which only one, in her own thinking at least, was a disparagement to the rest. The Queen's arrival was somewhat delayed by reason of a foul wind, which such as were not well pleased that the king's majesty should wed the French king's niece called a good English breeze; but we her grace's servants turned bedeswomen in those days, and said many hundred Aves for it to change; and with a yet greater fervour when we beheld our lodgings at the hospital, the chambers of which were built only with planks, very homely, and not clean, and the pallets we had to lie on and the cheer provided for us exceeding mean. Verily the religious house where we had slept the night before at Holy Cross was a palace to this one. The cold was likewise so sharp, that some of our company shivered as if they had the ague, until a large brasier was set in the midst of the hall, around which we gathered like moths about a candle.

When the pleasant warmth had comforted their frozen limbs, the wits of the damsels began to brighten also, and their tongues to wag; mostly at first touching the groans of the roaring wind, and the rain, which was falling through the chimney and wetting the floor. One said that a vessel had been seen not very far off the coast which was thought to be the Queen's ship; but that it was not like to come into port that day, the gale being too strong.

"There are folks so unmannerly as to praise this ill-natured weather which keeps the French Queen from landing," said Mistress Allianor Daubeney, shaping her small mouth as if she feared her words should issue from it too fast.

"For the which speech they should be hung by the neck," cried Lady Isabel Butler, one of the ladies of the court which the most of us misliked for her haughty stomach and proud carriage.

"Heavens! how that wind doth moan, like unto a soul in jeopardy!" quoth Elisabeth de Scales, stopping her ears.

"Methinks," said Mary Beaumont, "we should say some prayers for her majesty, for the storm waxeth more fierce every moment. See how the white edges of the great waves betoken a rough and dangerous sea."

"Is this the first time you have bethought yourself of praying for the Queen, Mistress Beaumont?" asked Lady Isabel, in that jeering fashion which she often used, to the no small discomfort of timid persons. "I ween there are some, it may be not so forward to counsel others, which nevertheless have not neglected that duty."

"For my part," sighed Joan Dacre, "I forgot to say

my prayers this morn; I was so sick with early rising and the bad fare at Holy Cross."

One little Winefred Booth, the daughter of the Queen's chancellor, Master John Wenlock, which albeit only four years of age, because of her mother's death, who was the King's foster sister, was numbered amongst the maids of honour, slipt off my lap when she heard the others talk of prayers, and straightway kneeling on the floor, said a Pater Noster out loud, and then with a great bound exclaimed, "Winefred hath prayed. Is the Queen come?" which made us merry.

"I warrant you," sighed Elisabeth Beauchamp, "that, laughing or no laughing, I shall die of this Goddeshouse, if so be we must abide many days waiting for this 'pearl,' as the Duke Charles of Orleans styleth her majesty."

"A costly pearl she doth prove," Lady Isabel replied. "The King, like the merchant in the gospel, hath sold all he hath to buy it. His jewels he hath parted with, and pawned the third part of the collar of St. George, whereof two parts are already engaged to my lord the cardinal, for to raise money for the Queen's journey, and the wedding and the crowning, which are yet to come. I admire that kings should be so poor, when some of their subjects have so much wealth. If I were his majesty, beshrew me if I would not lay my hands on the cardinal's coffers, or impose round taxes on the greasy citizens of London."

"The king's majesty would not reign long an he followed your counsel," Mary Beaumont cried. "The saints deliver us from your queenship, Lady Isabel!"

"To my thinking," said Elisabeth Beauchamp, "that is as leal a prayer as any of the King's subjects could frame."

Lady Isabel's eyes flashed with anger; and drawing up her long neck, like an angry bird, she exclaimed, "There are subjects which should have brought the King, an he had wedded them, a richer dower than this French pearl; and then Maine and Anjou, those fair jewels of his crown, should not have been lost."

After a pause, Joan Dacre said: "Methinks the new Queen should be very fair, sith she has no tocher. But, I pray you, is not her father the King of Jerusalem? I ween the pilgrims which go thither are like to take him presents, and so he should be rich. I admire that he gives his daughter no dower, and taketh from us Maine and Anjou, when he hath Jerusalem, which Friar Bradley of Norwich said, in a sermon I heard last Sunday, was built of gold and precious stones."

We could not choose but laugh a little at this speech; and Lady Isabel broke forth: "I' faith, Mistress Dacre, I am astonished at your learning and good memory, and I hope you will interpret this praise as charity doth warrant. But if there be any here present not so well informed as yourself, I can learn them that King René hath a better title to the name of Lackland than ever had our King John; for he holdeth not one foot of ground in Judea, nor yet now in Naples or Sicily; and even a great part of Lorraine he is reft of, for the Duke of Burgundy, his sworn foe, is leagued with the Vaudémonts to despoil him of it."

"He is a prince," said Lady Ann de la Pole, "of great parts, and a very sweet poet. The music he composes is so delectable, that none like unto it can be heard."

"And M. Champchévrier says a more brave knight and pious and generous King can nowhere be found, not in all Christendom," Mary Beaumont added.

"Who is M. de Champchévrier?" asked Elisabeth

Woodville, the Duchess of Bedford's daughter, then for the first time opening her lips.

Mary answered: "He was a prisoner of Sir John Fastolf's since the battle of Agincourt; and I promise you, ladies, but that for the cunning dealings of this gentleman Bonne d'Armagnac should have been queen of this realm."

Lady Isabel lifted up her eyes, and then half closed them, so much as to say: "Mercy on us! what new tale is this! how that young damsel's tongue doth wag!"

But taking no heed of her grimaces, Mary went on: "The chevalier, who is a knight of Anjou, was the first to speak to his majesty of Madame Marguerite, and by his praises to set him thinking on her."

"Nay," quoth Lady Isabel; "if report speaketh truly, that should have been the doing of my lord the cardinal, to spite his grace of Gloucester."

"And I have heard it said," Lady Ann timidly uttered, "that my father was the cause of that change in the King's mind."

"I cry you mercy, ladies," Mary replied. "But my knowledge in this matter cannot be gainsayed, as you shall presently see. When this gentleman was Sir John's prisoner on parole at Caistor, I used often to meet him at Master Paston's house, whither he went for hawking and such-like diversions. He often conversed with me, because I could speak French, and told me little tales, chiefly about King René's children, which he said were the most beautiful ever seen, and the fairest of all Madame Marguerite, which although then only a bud, was like to prove the most perfect flower in the whole world; and that her wit was so great, that if King Solomon had been alive, he alone would have been worthy of her. This always made me laugh, and was a jest between us; so that whensoever I saw him I was wont to say—for in those days I had a nimble tongue for my years—"

"Nay," interrupted my Lady Peacock, for by this name we called that vain Isabel Butler, "this should seem now an incredible thing!"

"Go on, go on, good Moll," we all cried, not well pleased that she should be jeered at; and so unheeding that remark, she continued:

"I was wont to say to him, 'Well, Monsieur, how fares it with the wife of King Solomon?' At which question he smiled, and sometimes answered that the Comte de St. Pol should be Solomon, or else that there was no prince on earth so great and excellent as to be worthy of the pearl of Anjou. But one day he came to our house in as gleesome a mood as can be thought of. 'The King,' he said, 'had sent for him to Windsor.' He was a very curious limner of emblems and devices, and had painted a Missal so rarely ornamented with scrolls and minute pictures, that Master Westbury greatly desired his majesty should see it; and hence this summons to the court. We bade him God speed, and thought no more of it, until a short time afterwards, my father going to Caistor, touching some lands he had sold to Sir John, he found that good knight in so fierce a rage that nothing could be greater. He raved and stormed anent the French like unto a demented person, and swore, by the white beard and the black beard, he should have his revenge, for that the Chevalier had broken his parole and left England, without so much as one word touching his ransom, and that he should sue the Duke of Gloucester, who was a very good lord to him and his friend, to demand of the King of France that this caitiff be arrested and sent in chains to this country; and he went on in this manner for more than an hour, interspersing his speech with oaths not a few. A few weeks later we went to London; and when we had been there only two days, and had heard talk ministered for the first time of the King's marriage with Madame Marguerite, who should visit us at our lodgings but this false chevalier, with as gay a visage and bold carriage as if he had been one of the knights of the round-table? A less confused gentleman I never beheld. He then disclosed to us the cause of his absence, and described in a lively manner, as only Frenchmen know how to do, his first interview with the King, and the cunning praises he bestowed on Madame Marguerite, whose charms and excellences he portrayed so as to inspire his majesty with a passion for this unseen Princess, and an ardent desire to judge himself of her beauty; so that after three or four interviews with the knight, he charged him to travel with speed and secrecy to France, under cover of a safe-conduct in his own hand, and to confer with my Lord Suffolk, his plenipotentiary at Paris, touching the likeness of the Princess, which he would have painted by the best limner which could be procured, in her simple kirtle, and as like as if she was seen. My lord was nothing loth to aid in this matter; and betwixt them they despatched a very cunning painter to Nancy, which in an incredible short time achieved his work; and the chevalier, with equal diligence, hastened with it to England. But as he passes through Paris, lo and behold he is arrested for his breach of parole, and thrust into prison; but Lord Suffolk being apprised of it, dealt with the King of France to release him, and to grant him an interview. Methinks I can see the messenger's sly visage when, kneeling before his majesty, he drew from his breast in the one hand the King of England's safe-conduct, and n the other the portrait of Madame Marguerite.

"'By our Lady of Liesse,' the French King exclaimed, 'this is verily a surprise! We listed not the wind had set that way. I' faith, sir knight, if you have had a hand in this matter, we commend you. It had been reported to us that our fair nephew, the King of England, moved by the Dukes of Gloucester and Burgundy, was sueing for the hand of one of the Comte d'Armagnac's daughters, and that one Hans had been employed to portray the three damsels, for the better guidance of his choice. But he should have been a cunning limner to have painted them in such guise as to rival *this* lovely face!'

"'Sire,' quoth the knight, 'the Duke of Gloucester did verily send his favourite painter to the count's court on this message; but Hans, an it please your majesty, is a Dutchman.'

"'And you, sir knight, a Frenchman!' the King exclaimed, laughing, 'and so suffered not the grass to grow under your feet, like the good Hollander. Go to, go to, M. de Champchévrier: we commend your speed and your good service; and albeit our treasury is scantily replenished at this time, we will ourselves satisfy the Chevalier Fastolf touching your ransom, and you shall find us in the future well disposed to show you favour.'

"Whereupon the knight departed, well pleased to have served both his masters and his own fortunes also, which is not often found to be possible. And thus ended his recital, if I except—"

"O, I pray you, except nothing," cried Lady Isabel, with an unmannerly yawn, which behaviour on her part cut short Mary's discourse, who said in a good-humoured voice: "I crave your pardon, ladies, for this overlong tale; which, nevertheless, I thought to have some curiosity in it."

"Yea, and much pleasantness also," we most of us answered; but Lady Isabel could not restrain her ill temper.

"For all that chevalier's boasting," she cried, "I misdoubt his being the first mover of the King's marriage. I'll warrant you the Cardinal had the chiefest hand in it, and used him as his tool. Men can always make women believe what they like, howsoever shallow fools they be."

Then we all waxed dull and sleepy; and silence ensued, until the sound of a horse galloping, and then the jingling of spurs, and a quick tread along the cloisters, with much shuffling and noise of footsteps, waked us up.

The Lady de Scales was loudly called for, and her daughter, Mistress Elisabeth, said she should go and see if her mother had need of her; a piece of dutifulness which I ween served her turn very well at that moment.

"Think you there are tidings of the Queen?" we all asked of one another. In a little space of time the door opened; and who should come in with Lady de Scales but one concerning which my pen is somewhat loth to write, for more reasons than I can easily relate.

O Monseigneur Gilles, what sunlight of youthful days, what darkening shades of sad night, your name doth recall! And how shall I paint you, whose very name at the end of so many years doth yet stir up my soul with thoughts more bitter than sweet, and yet with some kind of sweetness in them! for since the days when I played with you at Havering Bower, when I was your grandam's little damsel, and you a merry princely wight, and a sore trouble to her ladies through your wantonness and mischiefs, I had a humble and tender, not worldly or ambitious, love for you, which made me think it an honour to sit and watch your sports, and listen to your tales of the court and the King, whose playfellow you then were, as since his friend. You had always a spirit, which neither Lord Warwick's severity nor the Queen your grandam's frowns could subdue; no, nor yet later the prospect of death itself, as I shall hereafter describe. It would have been better for me, I ween, not to have known you, my prince; my life should have been a different one if we had never met. But God knoweth. It may be that what is for some a cause of lightness worked in me, contrariwise, a gravity beyond my years, and a marked indifferency to the vanities of the world. An affection which soareth high, and for that reason meeteth with no return, must needs, I think, either disgrace or exalt her who doth entertain it; for if she is not modest, and her behaviour is light, it is a shame to her womanhood; but if she concealeth it in her heart, and feel it only by prayers said in secret for one she loves, and would be contented to see happy if she should be herself ever so miserable, then the pent-up tenderness, like an ascending flame, consumes the gross and more selfish materials whereof it is composed, and purifies the heart wherein it dwells. But how now, my pen! whither art thou straying? I gave thee license to chronicle the doings of others, not the seely dreams of thine own by-gone days. Return to thy duty, or I will cast thee aside for ever.

When the door of the hall opened, after all the confusion without, Lady de Scales came in with the Prince Gilles de Bretagne, whose dripping-wet attire and the broken feather in his bonnet betokened a hard ride through wind and rain.

"The Queen hath landed," her ladyship announced. "Monseigneur bringeth the tidings."

"Long live the King!—long live the Queen!" we all cried out with one heart and one voice.

Lady Ann de la Pole, filial love conquering natural timidity, ran forward towards the Prince, and said, "Ah, Monseigneur! are my dear parents also landed?"

"Fair damoiselle," he replied, smiling, "I am no sorcerer. How can I then divine who should be the happy wights who call you daughter?"

"This is the Lady Ann de la Pole," said Lady de Scales. "Lord and Lady Suffolk are her parents."

"I crave your pardon, Lady Ann," replied Monseigneur Gilles. "The great earl and his lady are arrived. It was my Lord Suffolk which carried the Queen in his arms from the boat to the shore, amidst the rough dashing waves. Heavens! how it did blow and rain, as if twenty thousand devils raised a storm to drive one angel away! Despite the lightenings and the rain, the good men of Porchester stood lining the shore, and roared out, louder than the thunder, welcomes to Madame. O, this Queen is a pearl of matchless beauty—a very phantom of delight! Pardon, fair ladies, if, in the presence of so much loveliness, I call any other beauty matchless; but your loyalty will not deny that title to this sovereign lady when you see her. I would you had all beheld her when she first set her foot, the smallest nature could frame, on English ground. Though pale and cold as a stone image, she raised her head with so noble an aspect, and smiling on the crowd, did bear herself in so right royal and gracious a fashion, that all the people shouted, 'A Queen! a Queen!' Verily, her eyes are globes of living light, fit to set the world on fire! and now, fair damoiselles, that I have paid you this my brief devoir, and cheered you by this good news, I must bid you farewell, and commend myself to your prayers. For neither mine horse nor I shall rest until we reach Southwicke. By Sainte Anne d'Auray, I would as soon never set eyes on a lady again, as fail to be the first to tell the King of the Queen's landing, and hear him say, 'Gramercy for these joyful tidings, my fair cousin!' and then see him raise his comely eyes to heaven, with the God-thanking look which doth become him so well."

So saying, Monseigneur took his leave; but noticing me as he went out, he doffed his bonnet with great courtesy, and kissed his hand as to a friend. I often think of the lines which the Trouvère Marie wrote of the Comte de Longue Epée, the son of the Fair Rosamond, whose bower was not fairer in her eyes than that of Havering in mine:

> "Pour Amour du Comte Guillaume,
> Le plus vaillant du royaume,
> Qui fleur est de chevalerie,
> D'enseignement et de courtoisie,
> M'entrepris ce livre faire."

And so I too write a book. Howsoever, not with the same intent as this Trouvère; for the love which possessed my heart was not of the same sort as hers, and hath been now a long time buried in a cold grave beyond the seas.

CHAPTER II.

What the Maids of Honour thought of the Queen.

WHEN the prince was gone, the Queen's household hurried to the cloisters, and stood there to wait her coming, which was not till two hours later. Cries of "La Royne! la Royne!" were heard without from the officers of the guard; and then she entered the walls of the Goddeshouse, led by my Lord Suffolk, and followed by her suite. Then was my first sight of this great queen; and as each knee was bent as she passed by, so gracious was her smile and the cognisance she took of the homage paid to her, that nothing, methought, could exceed the gracefulness of her carriage.

"Gramercy, mesdames," and the like pretty French words, uttered in a dulcet voice, which made them sound like music, ravished the hearers. Weariness from long travel had driven the roses from her cheeks; but every feature of her matchless visage was perfect, and her eyes more beautiful than any eyes I ever beheld. She went into her lodgings with her ladies, where she dressed, and refreshments were carried to her. Then, after supper, we were summoned to attend her majesty to the church, whither she went to give thanks and make an offering.

On the morrow the Queen and all her household were rowed in great state to Southampton. The sun, which had been churlish on the previous day, hiding his face behind the clouds, now, like unto a gracious monarch, gladdening the sea and land with his shining. The wind, his vassal, lowered his boisterous voice in that royal presence; and the waves, unchafed by rude stirrings, grew gentle also, and played like sportive lambs about the vessel's side. Many thousand persons stood on the shore; and little boats darted to and fro, like gleesome seabirds, between the land and the barge in which we were. Sounds of shouting from the crowd of spectators came wafted on the breeze; and lovely was the sheen of the Queen's eyes as she gazed on the coast, which verily seemed alive with welcomes.

I heard her say to Lord Suffolk, "I perceive that your English sky, my lord, though not so brilliant as that of Naples or Provence, can be of a very soft and lovely blue. Yesterday it seemed as if the inhabitants of the infernal regions had been let loose to impede my landing. I think I was the Jonas of Cocklejohn; for verily, as soon as you had carried me ashore, the storm abated. O, what a *Deo gratias* I uttered when my feet touched the ground at last!"

"Not a more fervent one, I'll warrant it, madame, than did your poor servant," answered the earl. "And yet there is a sadness in the discharge of these my last offices of duty to your majesty."

"Ah! believe me, good my lord," the Queen exclaimed, "Marguerite, the Queen of England, shall never forget the good services of Lord Suffolk to Marguerite d'Anjou."

Then she bade the earl present to her his daughter and with many fair speeches and smiles she greeted the Lady Ann. One by one she learned the names of all her ladies and damsels. When my turn came, she pleasantly said, "Then we are both daisies, for so, I think, you call marguerites in English."

When Mistress Woodville approached, she whispered to the earl,

"A very fair flower this, my lord. Is she not a true English beauty?"

"Not wholly English, madame," he replied. "The Duchess of Bedford is her mother."

"O, the beautiful Jacquette, of Flanders!" she answered, smiling.

And so, questioning of their lineage and studying their visages, she passed her household in review.

As we rowed past the Italian galleys moored at the mouth of the river, harmonious sounds of most sweet music came floating on the breeze. The Queen quickly asked whence they proceeded; and when she heard it was from the Genoese ships, a look of pleasure lighted up her face.

"God prosper the merchant princes!" she exclaimed. "They and their doge, the good Fregosi, have ever been true friends to the house of Anjou."

Then, as her eyes wandered along the coast, she said to Lord Suffolk, "Where are the white cliffs of Albion, my lord, which Alain Chartier speaks of in his description of England? I have seen nought but a smooth shore since we left Portsmouth."

The earl replied, "They are found on the coast more to the east, madame, nigh unto the port of Dover, the nearest point to France, whence they may be at times discerned."

"Nay, nay, my Lord," she answered pleasantly, "I think rather that you are an enchanter, and by a rare stroke of witchcraft do make that appear smooth to mine eyes which nature created rugged."

"Fain would I always have so good a power,

madame," quoth the earl. "And I pray God your majesty may never meet in this land with aught less smiling than these fair shores and still waters."

Thus discoursing with her noble guide and her ladies, the Queen whiled away the time, and when we landed rode through the town to the Goddeshouse, amidst the cheerings of the crowd.

We tarried some time in this hospital at Southampton, to the no small discontent of the Queen's household. It was bruited about that the delay was caused by her majesty's lack of apparel—her gear was so mean and scanty, that it did not befit a queen to put it on. Lady Suffolk would have it that the packages which held her clothes had been lost on board the ship, but others reported that King René was too poor to furnish his daughter with royal habiliments; and this caused impertinent language to be held amongst some of the attendants, which it misliked me to hear. Howsoever, Lady Suffolk resolved to send to London one John Pole, with three horses, for to fetch thence Margaret Chamberlayne, a renowned tire-woman in the city, to make gowns for the Queen. She gave him one pound for his expenses, and bade him ride fast, and lose no time on the way. I saw some of the letters which this messenger carried from the maids of honour to their friends in London. Like unthinking wenches, they suffered others to read what they wrote, so that they enjoyed the like privilege in their turn. This was Mistress Woodville's letter to her mother:

"*To my right worshipful Mother, her Grace the Duchess of Bedford.*

"MADAME,—I, your grace's humble daughter and servant, commend myself to your goodness, and crave

your grace's blessing. The Queen came to Portsmouth
three days ago, and now we are at Southampton. She
is very fair spoken, and hath showed me great favour,
though I am the youngest of her maids except little
Winefred Wenlock. She inquired of your grace's
health, with many tokens of her good will, and much
hopeth to see you soon. Her Majesty cannot yet
travel, by reason of her gear, which is lost, albeit some
declare she never had any fit for her to wear; not so
much as one gown well trimmed or costly, such as
your grace hath in your wardrobe. The people at
Portsmouth and here did very much shout at her
landing, and greeted her heartily. She doth not speak
much English yet. In the barge which brought us
here she conversed all the time in French with Lord
Suffolk. She holds her head very high, and looks
older than fifteen. But as regardeth beauty, your
grace, in my poor judgment, doth as much surpass
the Queen as a full-blown rose exceedeth a pale bud.—
Your grace's loving daughter and servant to command,
  "ELISABETH WOODVILLE."

Then Mary Beaumont wrote as followeth to Mistress
Alice Botley, which was his majesty's nurse and her
own kinswoman:

"MY WELL-BELOVED MISTRESS ALICE,—I would have
you to know as soon as I can tell you of it of the
Queen's coming, for methinks your very great love of
the king's majesty shall make you impatient for these
tidings. Her highness landed the day before yesterday. She is a most fair and winsome lady, with so
noble a carriage, and gracious behaviour that the
world cannot, I think, have seen her like since the
days when the Queen of Sheba visited King Solomon.
Sith his majesty was so well pleased, as is reported,

with her picture, the sight of her real beauty must needs make him the most contented person in the world. It is said we are to tarry eight days in this town, owing to the Queen's lack of fine gear. In my poor thinking, the meanest gown that could be seen would borrow so great a lustre from her majesty's wearing of it, that none would mark its defects. But my Lady Suffolk is resolved that her grace shall not travel till Mrs. Chamberlayne hath made her clothes most rich, and, as she says, befitting her present greatness. The Holy Trinity have you in His keeping, dear Mistress Alice ; so prayeth your loving friend and kinswoman,   MARY BEAUMONT."

Lady Isabel Butler wrote to her brother, Lord Ormond, this letter, which she showed in secret to Mistress Daubeny, who treacherously, when her ladyship was called out of the parlour, read it aloud to the other ladies :

" MY WORSHIPFUL BROTHER,—I hope your poor sister's writing shall be more welcome to your lordship at this time than it hath been afore now. For I remember your malicious speech touching ladies' letters, the bad writing of which you declared to yield more trouble to the reader than the contents were worth ; which I take to be high treason against womanhood, and what none of our sex should forgive. But, lo, now the Queen is come, and you, with all the gaping world, are, I doubt not, asking, ' Is she fair or foul ? black or white ? curt or kind ? merry or sad ? ' And none can tell you, except such as are shut up with her majesty in this Goddeshouse, which is the worst house I have slept in, and in my thinking should be aptly styled the devil's house, if truth should be spoken, it is so dark and uncleanly. Well, then, shall a woman's letter be worth the reading now, I pray you, if it be ever so ill written with the worst pen in the world, and no time to think of any right spelling? Ah, my good lord, methinks I see you stroke your chin, caress your beard, and sniff the air like unto a snorting palfrey, the while you call out, 'A plague on that shrewish Bella! Why cannot the foolish wench write her tidings, and forbear from teasing?' Ah, sweet Lord, how can a woman abstain from teasing, when so rare a privilege cometh in her way as the withholding of news which manly curiosity pineth to learn? But, come, I will be merciful, and in a few words portray this paragon, this pearl, which the French do brag of as if the world had not her like. Well, she is a black pearl. Men say such are the most costly. This should be true, for she hath cost us Maine and Anjou. She hath eyes which will, I promise you, set the world on fire. 'How so?' you ask. 'Marry, sir, read me that riddle. Let it be with love, if it please you; with hate, if you like it. But I pray you now, will fire and water agree together? Methinks water will quench fire, or else fire dry up water.' 'Is she fair?' you demand. 'Yea, passing fair, if the lightning is fair.' 'Is she queen-like?' Yea, more than queen-like—king-like, I mean, and yet a woman, for she can weep, by the same token that her tears fell like rain on the cushion when she was making her offering in church after her landing. But, I pray you, what a wife for a king is this, that hath neither lands nor gold, yea, not one silver penny for her dower, or so much as a gown to her back, and must needs be clothed by her good man, like the fair Grisel in Master Chaucer's tales! But I warrant you this shall be no patient Grisel, if the flash of her black eye, and the curl of her lip, and the sweep of her carriage belie her not. Fare ye well, good my lord and sweet brother.

"Written in haste at the Goddeshouse, Southampton, on the 12th day of April.

"ISABEL BUTLER."

Before the tirewoman had arrived the Queen fell sick. The first day she fought against the malady, and would not see a leech; but on the morrow she was very much disordered, and could not raise her head one whit. The report was spread that she had caught the small-pox, and most of her ladies were afraid to go near her chamber, so great was their terror of this disease, which threatens life and beauty. Some forthwith craved license to depart; others withdrew to another part of the building. Lady Suffolk wisely ordered the departure of such as were most affrighted, and shut herself up with the Queen. Lady de Scales, who knew I had no home at that time, by reason of my father being engaged in his majesty's service in France, wished me to go to the convent at Winchester with Mary Beaumont, whose aunt was the abbess of that house. I prayed her to intercede for me with Lady Suffolk, that I might remain with the Queen, for I had been diseased with the small-pox two years before, and had no fear of contracting it again, howsoever close should be my attendance on her majesty, the meanest offices in whose chamber I should be contented to perform. Shortly afterwards Lady Suffolk sent for me, and with a pleased countenance received me at the door of the Queen's lodgings.

"If it be true, Lady Margaret," she said, "that you have had the small-pox, and are not afraid of contracting it, then, in God's name, remain with us, and your service shall be welcome. When her majesty is able to sit up, it should be a cheering thing to her to have the company of one of her own age."

So saying she led me into the sick chamber, which was poor and meanly furnished for so great a guest.

CHAPTER III.

A Conversation.

FOR some days the Queen continued very sick; but her disease proved, howsoever, light of its sort, and she mended quickly. The time of recovery oftentimes needs more patience than that of sickness. We began to discern that this was not her majesty's chiefest virtue, and the little of it she possessed was sorely tried. The long delay she foresaw to her meeting with the King, who, when he had notice of the malady of his dear and best-beloved wife, was almost beside himself with grief and fear; the apprehension lest her face should suffer, and seem less fair to him when he should see it, than her picture; the sad aspect of her lodgings, the soreness in her limbs, and frequent pain in the head she suffered,—made her often sad and not a little impatient. One day, at last, I found her in better cheer, and inclined to talk. She was sitting in an armed chair by the closed window, with a cushion to rest her head, and held tablets in her hand on which she had been writing. As I could speak French with ease, it pleased her grace to converse with me: and on that morning she thus began:

"Madame de Roos, truth, poets say, lives at the bottom of a well, but I will not credit that it is not found elsewhere also. I think I see it in your eyes; so now, I pray you, tell me the truth, the naked truth, as clothesless as if it came out of a well. Is my face very sorely changed since first you saw it? My tiring glass is broken, and Madame de Suffolk will not procure me another."

"Your majesty's visage," I replied, "hath sundry red blotches on it, and your features are somewhat swollen; but it hath no holes or seams in it which should produce any lasting disfigurement."

"Think you so?" her grace answered musingly. "Madame de Suffolk showed me yesterday a letter she had written to the King. I could scarce keep from smiling at the similes it contained. She said my face was beautiful, like the moon, which hath also spots in it."

"Her ladyship," I said, "is the grand-daughter of Master Geoffrey Chaucer, and hath, I doubt not, inherited his poetic genius. But, madame, I speak only the truth when I say that your majesty need not fear to have lost your beauty. I would not flatter even a queen; but God hath bestowed upon you so much of it that even temporary disadvantages cannot greatly mar the perfect gifts of nature."

Her grace smiled, as one used to hear such commendations of her loveliness; not so much with a vain complacency as a kind of indifference, resulting from the assured possession of attractions which others covet with solicitude. She then asked me how I had learned to speak French with so great fluency, and I answered:

"At the court of the Queen Joan, the King's grandam, madame. I was there brought up with French gentlewomen, and acquired their language; but report declares that your majesty converses with ease in five diverse languages."

"Five?" her grace replied. "Nay, four—Latin, French, Italian, and Spanish; ay, and in mine own dear Provençal tongue also—the language of poesy and love, whose flowing accents glide from the lips like a stream of bewitching music."

"I have heard it said," I rejoined, "that this dialect is so soft and melodious, that none but singers should use it."

"Or poets," her majesty quickly added—" the singers of the soul."

"I fear, madame, your ears being so accustomed to those harmonious languages, that the rough accents of our English tongue must needs very much offend them."

"Ah," she said, with a smile, "English speaking is rough, but withal strong, and I doubt not, a meet channel for the utterance of deep thought. I mislike it not. The sea on these northern coasts is likewise ruder and more boisterous than at Naples, or on the shores of Provence; but it had a nobler aspect and more of grandeur in it, which pleaseth me."

"The waves gave your majesty a rude welcome to this shore."

"Ah, envious spirits—jealous of my great fortunes—raised, I think, a storm to drive me from England, and having failed in that intent sent this malicious disease to mar my visage and delay my joy!"

"Methinks, madame," I replied, in a grave manner, "it was rather God our Lord, Who, knowing your majesty to be possessed of more rare gifts in yourself, and of more love and admiration and praise from others, and in greater renown of beauty, genius, and wit than any other princess in the world, ordained these accidents as His ministers to ask back at your hands for one moment His own bestowings, even as a sovereign demands from a vassal the lands he holds from him, which, when he hath done homage for them, he straightway restores to him."

"Ah, my good Miladi de Roos," the Queen cried, laughing, "that speech savours somewhat of the great order of St. Dominic, the friars preachers. But, believe me, you will please me very much if you love God and are devout, for then you shall pray for me, who have great need of it; and I mislike not sermons if they are short and pithy, and delivered in good language; but romances and plays, and all the lore of the gai savoir, is my chief delight. My lord the King is much taken up with praying, I hear?"

"Madame, his majesty is reported to be exceedingly religious, and so virtuous in all his actions, that since the days of King Edward the Confessor so pious a monarch hath not reigned in England."

"The English are a very grave people. I sometimes fear that the gay spirits, which in mine own country I thought not to restrain, may beget in their eyes a suspicion of light behaviour."

"The English, madame, have seen so many French princesses of great virtue married to their kings, that they must needs honour the ladies of France."

"Ay, there was my aunt Isabel, who died before I was born, but her memory will be as long as her life was short; it lives in the poems of her last husband, Charles d'Orleans. The first verses, I think, I ever read were those which begin, '*J'ai fait l'obsèque de madame.*' Why do you smile, Miladi de Roos?"

Thus questioned, I told her majesty that I had done into English that fair piece of poetry.

"Ah!" cried her grace, "do you then possess the book of Duke Charles' writings?"

"No, madame," I replied. "I learnt these verses by heart some years ago, from hearing Monseigneur Gilles de Bretagne repeat them."

"What!" the Queen exclaimed, "is that fair young

prince, who greeted me on my landing, a lover of the gai savoir? But let me hear in English my favourite lay. Nay, do not blush so deeply to own yourself a member of the confraternity of which the Muses are the patron saints."

I doubt not that I blushed, as her majesty said, but not for the reason she supposed. Howsoever, I recited at her bidding this piece of poetry.

> "To make my lady's obsequies, my love a minster wrought,
> And in the chauntry service there was sung by doleful thought;
> The tapers were of burning sighs that life and odour gave,
> And grief illumined by tears irradiated her grave;
>   And round about in quaintest guise
>   Was carved, 'Within this tomb there lies
>   The fairest thing to mortal eyes.'
>
> Above her lieth spread a tomb, of gold and sapphire blue;
> The gold doth show her blessedness, the sapphires mark her true
> For blessedness and truth in her were livelily portrayed, [made.
> When gracious God with both His hands her wondrous beauty
>   She was, to speak without disguise,
>   The fairest thing to mortal eyes.
>
> No more, no more my heart doth faint, when I the life recall
> Of her who lived so free from taint, so virtuous deemed by all;
> Who in herself was so complete, I think that she was ta'en
> By God to deck His paradise, and with His saints to reign,
>   Whom while on earth each one did prize
>   The fairest thing to mortal eyes." [1]

"Good! very good!" cried her majesty, clapping her hands. "I thank the saints that I have found among my ladies a no mean trouvère, whose ingenious talent, in this instance exercised on a sorrowful theme, is able also, I doubt not, to smile as well as mourn in harmonious verse; one who can read and write as well as spin. There is something in your visage and grave carriage—nay, do not laugh—which calls to my mind

---

[1] This translation is from the pen of Mr. Carey.

my sister Yolande. I should like to make you my secretary, Miladi de Roos."

"Ah, madame," I exclaimed, "that would be too great an honour for your poor servant. But Lady Isabel is, I fear, named to that office."

"What! that long-necked damsel, whose obeisance hath in it more of defiance than of homage? From such a one *libera nos, Domine*. But I will then create an office for you, Miladi de Roos. You shall be the keeper of the queen's journal." As she said this her majesty took up the tablets she had been writing on, and held them in her hand. "But more of that anon," she added. "Now let us return to the French queens, my predecessors. 'The fairest thing to mortal eyes' you were not worthy of, for England slew her lord, King Richard, and cast her back penniless on her native shore."

"Pardon me, madame; King Henry the Fourth would fain have worn that fair lily in his bosom, or have decked his son's crown with it."

"Yea, yea," retorted her majesty, laughing; "but the lily would not be handed from one English king to another. She was younger by one year than I am now —only fourteen; but was yet old enough to be firmly resolved against such a marriage. I think the women of our lineage have stronger wills than the men. But France gave you another of its royal flowers,—my other aunt, Queen Katharine, my lord, the King's mother."

"Yea," I replied, "and also his majesty's grandmother, Jeanne la Bonne, as the Bretons called her."

"Ah, Jeanne de Navarre! Well, Miladi de Roos, if not *la mauvaise*, like her brother, I doubt her being quite *la bonne*."

"Madame, that Queen had a thousand great and noble qualities, which slander strove to hide."

"Did she not deal a little with the devil, to destroy her stepson?"

"Nay, nay, madame," I cried, most pained and angry that so great a falsehood should have been reported to the Queen; "that was a false calumny, invented by her enemies."

"Lord Suffolk told me that the day Queen Johanna died all the lions in the Tower died also; 'the which,' he added, 'was naught seen the like in no man's time before; and that this was set down in the Chronicle of London;' which made me laugh. I think a lion should have been born in England the day I landed, for the cognisance of our house is a lion. One is always maintained at the King my father's expense at Arles; and I have often heard him describe a fierce combat which took place between this his pensioner and other wild beasts which entered the lists with him. But, I pray you, is it true that the king's mother, my aunt Katharine the fair, wedded in a secret manner, after her husband's death, a poor knight of mean birth, and had children by that marriage? One of the English ladies which came to Nancy told me this."

I assured her majesty this was well known to be true, and that the gentleman was Owen Tudor, a Welsh esquire of no mean extraction, but yet not one which should have dared so much as to think on marrying the daughter, widow, and mother of a king. I added, that some time before she died the Duke of Gloucester took from her her children, and gave them into the keeping of Lord Suffolk's sister, the Abbess of Barking, and that this separation, it was said, had shortened the queen's life.

"I blush for my kinswoman," the Queen exclaimed.

"How could a queen so debase herself as to become a wife and a mother by stealth? Shame on Katharine of Valois! Would she had been no kin or kith of mine! If nobility hath its obligations, which a French saying declares, how much more so should royalty constrain a woman to scorn the weakness of amorous follies!"

Then she fixed her eyes on a portrait of the King which was affixed to the wall, and asked me if it was like, and if his majesty's visage was as beautiful as this picture showed it to be, and as had been reported to her.

"His countenance, madame," I replied, "hath almost a heavenly beauty, and every feature is as perfect as if a cunning imager had framed it."

She mused a little, smiled, then said, "I will make him love me."

"Ah, madame," I cried, kneeling down at her feet, for I dared not caress her except by an act of homage, "that will be no hard matter, I promise you, to make him, which should be most inclined to it, do that which those most reluctant thereunto could with difficulty keep from."

"What, then, you think it should be an easy matter to love me, petite Marguerite," she said, the while with her small hand she stroked my cheek. "Then you shall be my friend."

"Your loving servant, madame," I cried, passionately kissing her hand. When I did so some tears fell from her eyes upon it. "Ah, my liege lady," I could not refrain from saying, "'tis hard to leave a father's house and the old loves of childhood for new and untried affections."

"Even in my cradle," she replied, "I learnt that the world is full of changes and partings. The first thing I can remember is my mother catching me up in her arms at Nancy, and the terrible cry she gave when the news came of the loss of the battle of Bulgneville, and then her frantic queries, 'Alas, where is René? where is my lord? He is ta'en; he is slain!' She would not be persuaded he was yet alive, till Théophanie, who had been my father's nurse and was then mine, swore to her on the cross that he was a prisoner. 'Then all is not lost,' she cried, falling on her knees, Yolande and my brothers clinging to her, and returned fervent thanks. From that day I can call to mind almost all which befell us. The brain expands more quickly, I think, in some children than in others; and the apprehension of important matters awakens observation, and works an early ripeness which forestalls age. Soon after that great mishap my mother went to my uncle, the King of France, to crave his protection, and that he should deal with the Duke of Burgundy, whose prisoner my father was. She carried me in her arms, and my sister and my brothers followed, holding her robe.

"Ah, Miladi de Roos, it hath been said that on that day England lost France. The valiant sword of Jeanne la Pucelle would have been drawn in vain, perhaps, but for the eyes of Agnes Sorel, who was my mother's maid of honour and with us on that day."

"Madame," I replied, "albeit Jeanne was the curse of England, and some have reputed her not to be free from the suspicion of witchcraft—"

The moment after I had uttered those words I was trembling like an aspen leaf, for the Queen's eyes suddenly flashed with so great anger that I could not brook their aspect, and cast mine on the ground.

"I pray your grace to forgive," I falteringly said, "an error bred in this country by the natural resentments of a worsted nation. I did but mention the common credence amongst the English, which my poor thinking hath not shared."

"Nay, then, I commend rather than pardon you," quoth her majesty; "for to resist a current of false belief is more honourable than to float indifferently with the stream of a true one. Jeanne, in my grandam's thinking, and that of the most virtuous ladies in France, was as good as she was brave; and the sword of Charlemagne was not disgraced in her pure hands. My father fought by her side in many combats; and when counsels adverse to her prevailed at the French court, he befriended her cause, which was that of France. But may be," the Queen added, with a smile, "you think my warmth betrayeth an unseemly regard for France ill becoming an English queen."

"Nay, madame," I answered; "memory is more slow in changing sides than the heart. I ween yours is now wholly English."

Then I inquired of her majesty if the King of France had befriended the Queen, her mother, in the straits she had described. She replied, that the power, not the will, to do it had been wanting; and one who was born to command and reign was forced to sue in a like manner to her proud cousin Antoine de Vaudémont, who had robbed her of most of her inheritance and waged war on her lord. He could not choose but pity the royal lady at his feet, and consented to a truce.

"But what think you," quoth the Queen, "were the conditions he extorted? Nothing less than that Yolande should marry his son Ferry, with the lands my parents yet held in Lorraine for her dower; and what I think was the most hard, nothing would satisfy him but that she should forthwith be sent to the countess, his wife, to be reared in their house. I was likewise at that time betrothed to Pierre de Luxembourg, the son of the Count de St. Pol, who cut down my father at Bulgneville. But by reason of my tender years I was not taken from my mother. Jean and Louis were sent as hostages to the Duke of Burgundy for the fulfilment of this hard treaty, which deprived my father of his lands, his pelf, and his dear children. The day when he came to Nancy from Dijon to meet and then to part with three out of his four infants is one which even now I cannot think of without tears. When he saw me weeping in Yolande's arms, who was but five years old then and I not three, he laid his hand on my head, and said: 'Ah, petite creature, hath reason so soon appeared in thee, only to teach thee how to grieve!' Yolande hath told me that when she was taken to her mother-in-law, she should have died of sorrow, but that Ferry was brought to play with her. She would not take heed of him at first, which made him cry. Then she went to him, and wiped his eyes with her kerchief; and afterwards they always loved each other. My father could not then redeem his pledge to the Duke of Burgundy, and was forced to yield himself again a prisoner, and Jean stayed with him at the Tour de la Bar. Louis came back to us, and we both went with our mother to Provence."

Then the Queen closed her beautiful eyes, and either from fatigue of long speaking or the thoughts of early griefs working in her soul, she waxed for a few moments very pale.

"Well, my good Marguerite," the Queen said, after a time, "if you would know more of my past life,—not a long one indeed, if years are counted, but seeming so from the strange and varied fortunes which have attended it,—I give you free license to read this book, of which I make you the keeper. It begins where my recital ended—when, my uncle Louis dying, my father though a prisoner, became King of Provence, and soon afterwards of Naples. For the space of nine years I have written in it, not daily, nor yet every week or every month, but only when inclination, leisure, or increasing ease in the use of the pen moved me to it. I would not willingly part with these pages. Sometimes, when I have travelled, it has been my wont to send for a flower from a hedge or piece of turf, or even in Alpine regions from the snow alongside the road; and these were, I often think, the fairest of all. I placed them in a book which hung at my saddlebow. Albeit dry and withered now, they yet speak of the mountains, the fields, and the green valleys, where once they grew. And these poor buds of youthful thinking, preserved in parchment leaves, discourse also of the varied scenes which gave them birth. Take, then, this book with you; but let no other eyes but yours pry into its pages. The Queen's secrets are in your keeping, and I think I read in your eyes, sweet lady, the warrant of their safety."

I became that day the keeper of the Queen's journal.

CHAPTER IV.

The Dawn.

HERE beginneth the Queen's Journal.

Tarascon in Provence, 1435.

I, Madame l'Infante d'Anjou, am six years old to-day. Messire Antoine de la Salle has given me this fair book, and painted that garland of daisies which you see in the first page, and my name, *Marguerite*, in fine blue and red letters and much gold. Monseigneur Louis is jealous; but when he writes as well as I do, then Messire Antoine will give him also a book, and instead of daisies he will paint for him a laurel wreath, which doth become a soldier. I wish I was a prince, for then when I was tall enough I should be knighted like Monseigneur Jean, who kept watch by the side of his arms all night at Dijon, though he is only three years older than I am. It would like me to put on armour and fight against the caitiff Duke of Burgundy, who keeps my father-king in prison. But as I cannot be a man, I will be like Jeanne la Pucelle, and ride a fine white horse, and wear the sword of Charlemagne, and be called the Maid of Anjou. Of all the stories I have heard, none pleases me so well as that of Jeanne. I wish Monseigneur St. Michel would speak to me. But Théophanie never leaves me alone in the garden. I think that is the reason why Angels do not talk to me.

When we go abroad here the people throw flowers

on the road, and build green arches and fair bowers wherever we pass. This liketh me well, but yet more to hear them sing the lays of King René, my dear father. When they play on their instruments the "Sacre d'Angers," my heart beats in my breast like a little bird in its cage. The Provençals love us very much. They cry out that Louis and I are the most beautiful and excellent creatures in the whole world, and like unto God's Angels in the sky. But Théophanie says they do not know how naughty Monseigneur and Madame are at home, and not at all like unto Angels.

When we were on the terrace with the Queen to-day a crowd came to look at us. I saw ugly faces which scared me. When Agathe was undressing me she said that two witches had been caught, which sometimes turn into cats, and by means of a purse made out of a cat's skin work many devilries and charms, which cause lovers to hate each other and many dreadful things. They came from Hyères, and now they are taken to Aix, where the judges will cause them, she hopes to be burnt alive.

Last night I could not sleep for thinking of those witches; so Théophanie came and sat by my bedside, and talked of my dear father and my aunt Marie, whom she took care of when they were little, as she now takes care of me.

"Ah, petite, madame," she said, you must indeed be a very virtuous princess, for where can be found in one family so many great examples of piety as in your race? Your grandams, Madame Marguerite de Bavière and Madame Yolande d'Arragon, are the most esteemed princesses in Europe, and every one calleth them saints. Your aunt Marie, my sweet nurseling, is a paragon of virtue. The late King Louis and his queen, your great uncle Monseigneur de Bar, and your royal parents, have not their like in this age for nobility of soul and towardness in serving God."

"But I am too little to serve God," I answered.

Then Théophanie said,

"There is in Brittany a princess married to the Duke Pierre, your uncle Francis's brother, who, when she was but five years old, was called the little saint."

"What is her name?" I asked, for I liked to talk more than to sleep.

"Madame Françoise d'Amboise," she answered, "When she was only three years old she always said her prayers, and was never so happy as when in the church. One winter day after Mass her nurse, who was chafing her cold little feet, saw her shed tears. 'O good nurse,' she cried, 'didst thou not see my good patron Messire St. François in his chapel with his stone feet all cold and bare? Prithee carry him my stockings to put on.' When she was five, the good duchess took her one day on her knees, and said, 'Sweetheart, what aileth thee, that thou dost often weep?' 'Madame,' quoth the wise infant, 'I see you and Monseigneur and all your court go to the altar, and the good Jesus comes into your hearts. I weep because he comes not to me.' 'Comfort thee, little Françoise,' quoth the duchess. 'If the Bishop hearkens to my prayer, on All Saints' day the good Jesus shall also come to thee.' And so it came about that at All Hallows Madame Françoise, albeit only five years of age, received the good God into her heart."

"And how old is she now?" I asked.

"About twenty-five years of age," said Théophanie.

"And hath she been good ever since?"

"Yea," she said. "More good every day."

"Then methinks she must be very tired now," I cried; "for I am tired if I am good only one day."

And then I fell asleep, for I had forgot about the witches.

I have been a little sick to-day, and could not go out. To pass the time, I had a pack of cards to play with. I spread them all on the table, and made armies of them. Barbe told me those with faces are portraits. The Queen with the shamrocks is my aunt Marie; the one with hearts the late Queen Isabel; she with the lance the Pucelle Jeanne; and the other with the squares Agnes Sorel. I marvel she should be one of them. She is no queen, nor yet a brave soldier like Jeanne. The kings, Barbe said, were King Charles, and the King of England, who is dead, and the King of Spain, I think, and Monseigneur de Bourgogne, whom I hate. I tore that card into little bits, which Barbe thought was a pity. I like the knaves. They are Messire la Hire, and Dunois, and Hector de Galard, and the brave Barbazon, who died at Bulgneville.

To-night they have kindled great fires before the castle gate. Louis thought they were bonfires, and clapped his hands for joy. It was like the Eve of St. John, and Agathe hoped it would drive away all witches and fairies; but Messire Antoine told me it was done to chase the plague from us — the black death, which killeth many persons in the town.

They have lighted fires every night, but the black death will not cease. We are going to Marseilles in a few days, and then in a ship across the sea to my

father's new kingdom in Italy. The good Provençals
have given my mother soldiers, who will fight for us
against the Spaniards. Farewell, sweet Provence,
where every one loves us so well. Farewell, blue
river Rhone, which will carry us swiftly to the sea,
and then we shall see you no more. Farewell, Yolande;
farewell, Monseigneur Jean de Calabre. I wish I was
like you, in prison with my father. I wish I was a
blossom on a branch near to his window. I wish the
wind would blow me through the bars into his
arms. . . . . O, I am tired of wishing and of writing.

Messire Marie de St. André hath been this day
portraying the castle for a love-token from my mother
to my father. He hath made it so like to what we see,
that he will have methinks, much contentment in this
piece of painting. The queen stood a long time looking
on it, and then said,
"Ah Messire Andrè, my lord will recompense you
for this work. He hath a great heart toward skilled
persons such as you, and is no mean limner himself."
Then they talked of the chapel which shall be built
here underground, and the fair terrace above the river
to be added to the battlements. When the queen was
gone, Messire Antoine said to the painter,
"My master's passion for your art is so great, that
even the news of his advent to a new kingdom did not
suffice to make him lay down his brush."
"How so?" quoth Messire Marie; and M. Antoine
replied,
"The Sieur Vidal Cabanis came from Naples with
those tidings, and found his majesty portraying our
Lady's image on glass, who never so much as looked up
or stopped to say, 'Why or wherefore are you come?'
The envoy, weary of waiting, said, 'Monseigneur, God

hath called to Himself your sister-in-law Queen Joan, who hath made you her heir.' 'God rest her soul!' quoth the king and crossed himself. Then straightway took up his brush again, which angered the envoy, who was constrained to force his majesty to listen to the message by which the crown of Naples was tendered to him."

I admire that my father likes to paint more than to hear of a kingdom. It would please me to be told I should be a queen.

Marseilles, April 21st.

The sea is as blue as the Rhone, and so wide that it should be most like God, I think, of any thing else in the world, for it hath no beginning and no end that I can see. We have been to pray to our Lady of La Garde, at a chapel on a hill. When we were there, I saw the galleys which are to take us to Naples. Théophanie is not afraid now to cross the sea, since we have made a vow to our Lady. I have promised to give my little silver harp to buy bread for the poor, if we reach Naples in safety.

Capua, May 5th.

I think this land is Paradise. The people love us, if possible, yet more than those of Provence. No sooner did they see the ship than they came in boats, waving flags and crying "Evviva!" They carried us through the streets in a great chair like unto a throne, and a canopy of gold and red velvet over our heads. Wherever we passed, the shouts were so loud that it seemed as if they could be heard in the skies. Gold and silver cloths and pieces of tapestry, with imaged figures, hung from all the windows. The great street, which is called the Via di Toledo, was decked with flowers, and the bells of all the churches rung. Shots were fired, which frighted us at first, though I would not show it, but I looked at Messire Antoine, and he whispered to me it was a token of joy in this country to fire little guns. The Count de Nola and sixteen lords complimented the Queen. I counted them whilst he made his speech. She answered them in Italian, and then they cried "Evviva" again. Louis laughed at the men which ran screaming by our side. He took from the Queen her nosegay, and threw flowers to them, which they caught in their hands and pressed to their hearts. It liketh me well to be the daughter of a king. I will not marry a count, or a duke, no, nor any one but a king. Agathe says I was promised to Pierre de Luxembourg, and that he should have been a fitting husband for me when my father was Duke of Lorraine, but not now when he is the King of Naples. I will not wed him, and be only the Countess of St. Pol. I am too tired to write any more.

I fell asleep last night with my pen in my hand, and woke up crying " Evviva."

June 15th.

The black death, which was at Tarascon, is now at Naples; I hope it will not come to Capua, for I do not want to die, but to live in this fine palace, of which all the walls are painted, so that we need no other pastime but to look at them. The gardens are full of figures of beasts and birds, and sometimes persons, which appear all of a sudden; and if you set your foot in one place, a fountain springeth up and sprinkles you with perfume. It should seem as if fairies lived in these green alleys, and played us tricks. But Queen Joan was the fairy which made this palace. I asked Barbe if she was good. "Good insomuch, madame,' she answered, "that she left this kingdom to your royal father." Théophanie sighed when I spoke of the good Queen Joan. She sighs often now, and is not so merry as in France. I wonder she can be sad here, where each day is like a festival, and the sun always shines.

Last night, when Agathe was combing my hair, she said, "Ah! how well a crown will become this lovely head!" I asked her which king I should marry. "O, well-a-day!" she replied, "report says that the King your father shall soon be set free, and that the Duke of Burgundy, if he releases him, will have madame to wed her cousin the King of England." I snatched my hair out of her hands, and cried in great anger, "I will not be the Queen of England—no, not if the Duke of Burgundy should cut my head off." "And wherefore not?" said Agathe, laughing; "the English King is reported to be already more handsome than any other prince in Europe, and so puissant a monarch that his wife shall be the greatest queen on the earth."

I care not for what Agathe says. I hate the English, who burnt to death the brave Pucelle. I would kill every one of them if I could. I would crush them with my foot, as I did the wasp which stung Louis to-day. I would tie the Duke of Bedford to a post, and burn him to death, as he burnt Jeanne. She was not a witch, and he is, I am sure, a wicked devil.

I looked at the map this morning, to see if England is as large as France or Spain. It is smaller than France, but bigger than Lorraine or Provence, or even Naples, I think. Agathe told Théophanie, and Théophanie told the Queen, that I said I would not marry the King of England; upon which she commanded her to chastise me, because it is not seemly for a princess to speak of marriage, and to say she will

or will not marry any prince. Her parents do choose
her a husband, and she hath only to obey. I loathe to
be chastised, not for the pain, but the shame of it.
Alizon, who was maid to Queen Katharine in England,
says that when King Henry was a child he was made
to sign a warrant for his nurse, and afterwards for his
governor, to whip him, or it should have been high
treason to lay hands on his majesty. If I had been in
his place, they should never have had that warrant
from me.

I do not often write in this book now, for I learn
Italian and Latin, and read all the books I can. I
heard yesterday Jean Manget, one of my brother's
tutors, say to the Count of Nicastro, who was commending my face, " Ah, signore! Madame Marguerite
hath all her father's wit and ingenuity, and her
mother's strength of will. This young princess's
praise goeth beyond the reach of my describing. In
her eighth year she hath more learning and reflection,
and a greater aptness in conversing, than most women
at fifteen. Her beauty, which you praise, is the worse
half of her merit." Well, sith God hath given me
beauty and wit, I will acquire knowledge, which will
teach me to use them. I will be the most excellent
princess in the world, and famed for it at an age when
others are content with playthings. I have thrown all
mine into the sea. One fair doll I would fain have
kept, but I kissed her once, and then cast her away,
for I have resolved that books and the gittern and
limning shall be my only pleasures now.

CHAPTER V.

The Early Morn.

Naples, 1436.

SIX months have passed away since that last page was written. The child Marguerite is no more. Like the little worm which turneth into a butterfly, she is now changed into a young princess, not yet very tall, but wise for her years. She cares not now for toys, nor much for sweetmeats. She studies with her brother's tutors, and is much commended by them for diligence and quickness in learning.

This day I went with the ladies of the court, Enrico d'Auna the seneschal, and Messire Antoine, to see the paintings on the walls of the church of Santa Chiara, which were designed by one Giotto, whose real name was Angiolotto, which did become him well; for those who by their thinking and their hands do work the fairest things on earth must, I think, most resemble the Angels in heaven. Messire Antoine told us the designs in that church were wrought by the hand of this great painter, who was once a little shepherd boy, and with chalk drew so cunningly on a stone the likeness of one of his sheep, that Master Cimabue, when he saw it in a lone place in the Apennines, carried him to Florence, to teach him to paint. But it was Dante Alighieri, Giotto's friend, and the greatest poet the world hath seen, who imagined what the other wrought. Messire Antoine will not suffer me yet to read the Divine Comedy. "When madame is older," he says; which displeases me, for it takes a long time to grow old. To pacify me, as we walked in the convent garden, he told me this little tale:

"Madame must know," he said, "that in Florence they have a pretty custom of keeping a festival in honour of the Spring. On the first of May the citizens assemble their friends, and entertain them in their houses. One Folco Portinari, about one hundred years ago, invited all his acquaintances to his villa, and among the rest, Signor Alighieri, who carried thither his little son, Durante, for briefness called Dante, who was then only nine years old. There were many girls and boys at play under the trees, and after he had feasted at one of the tables on such dainties as befitted his age, he joined in their sports. Amongst that crowd of children was Folco's little daughter, Beatrice, a maiden of eight years. Her fairness and her heavenly modesty were so great that none could look on her without wonder. In her speech and her behaviour there was a wisdom, gravity, and suavity beyond her age. Each of her features was perfect in itself, and an incomparable harmony reigned in her face, so that she was thought by some to be an angel. The little boy, who was one day to be the great poet, saw her in the midst of her companions, and though he was so young, and she also, he loved her from that time, and loved her for ever after. In a few days he met her walking between two other maidens in a lane, dressed all in white. He was afraid to speak to her; but she smiled in so holy and courteous a wise, and her looks and her words were so sweet, that he went and shut himself in a room to think of her, and, falling asleep, he had a beautiful vision."

"What vision?" I asked.

M. Antoine smiled, and did not answer. Then I said:

"Was Beatrice a real maiden, or is this little tale an allegory?"

"Ah! madame," he replied, "some do maintain that the Beatrice which the poet writes of in his great poem is Folco's daughter, who died young; but others, that she is only a name for Heavenly Wisdom guiding the soul to Paradise."

Last night I was lying awake, looking at the stars, and thinking they should be the houses where the saints live, and I began to consider if I would be a great queen or a saint. Anna, who comes from Viterbo, has told me that St. Rose, when she was only nine years old, which is now mine age, went into the streets to preach to the people that they should do penance, and fight for the Pope against the wicked Emperor Frederic. I would like to be such a saint as this St. Rose. I said so to Brother James della Marca when I went to shrift to-day, and he told me this story:

"Once upon a time there stood a crowd of poor people at the gate of heaven, waiting for it to open. Then cometh St. Peter, with his keys in his hand, and crieth, 'Make room, make room, all you poor people. Here is a princess about to enter into heaven.' Then the poor people said, 'Marry, good St. Peter, we thought on this side of the grave princesses should not be of more account than beggars.' 'Ay,' quoth St. Peter, 'but you see we have so many beggars and poor persons coming this way every day, that we think nothing of them; but when a princess entereth heaven, it is so rare a sight we must needs make much of her.'"

I like Brother James, and I will be one of those rare princesses which go into Paradise.

Yesterday many young lords and ladies came to spend the day with us, because it was Monseigneur Louis's birthday. There was a banquet, and pastimes and plays in the garden. At night cunning carvers came to entertain us, which caused things to appear which were not, as flying dragons in the air; and they threw balls of fire at each other's heads, which burst with a sound like thunder. We danced the Capello, and Ciarletto Carracciolo was my partner. He danceth not so well as the Conte di Malatesta, but he hath more wit. He told me a story of two young lovers at Verona, Romeo Montecchi and Giulietta Capuletti, which fell in love with each other at a ball in the house of Giulietta's father. He said, when he heard it, he could not believe love should be so sudden; but that since he had come into the palace that day, he had become so enamoured of a lady, that nothing could exceed it, though he dared not whisper her name. He asked me if I had loved any one yet. I said that when I was at Nancy, Pierre de Luxembourg had said he would be my knight, and fight against all such as should deny me to be the fairest princess in the whole world. This made me love him very much; for I liked to have a chevalier which would kill all those who said I was not fair. Then Ciarletto said he would fight for me, and die for me, if I would love him. But I said I would not, for that he was not a king; which made him so angry, he would not dance with me any more.

This day the Queen gave me a long rosary of costly beads set in gold, which belonged to her mother, and my dear brother a fair copy of a sweet book, "The Little Flowers of St. Francis." I would fain go to Assisi, and to our Lady of the Angels, and to the mountain of Alvernia, which, after Jerusalem and Rome, should be, I think, the most sacred spot in the world. I read to Théophanie the story of the peace the saint made betwixt the city of Gubbio and the wolf; and she liked it well, for she would have every one be at peace with one another.

I am ten years old; and this morn I received, for the first time, the good God into my heart, with a restful, delectable, overpassing joy. After I had left the chapel I craved to be awhile alone, which is not often granted me, but was not then denied; and, with mine head resting on my hands, I sat at a window which looketh on the bay; my breast as tranquil as the smooth deep sea, and thoughts passing through my mind without troubling it, like the white birds on the surface of that blue water. When I had been there well-nigh an hour, I felt a hand on my shoulder, and, looking up, saw my mother, the Queen, standing by my side. She gazed on my face meekly and urgently, with a look of endless love.

"Marguerite," she said at last, "this life is full of troubles, mostly for such as are born nigh unto thrones, and, which is worse, with many temptations. We may not stand so long a space as the twinkling of an eye without the keeping of God's grace; and when royal persons offend, it is like the failing of the house of which the Gospel saith, 'great was the fall thereof.'"

Then she, who was not wont to speak of herself, but seemed moved to it in a sudden manner that day, took me on her knees, and conversed with me a long time, disclosing the nobility and greatness of her soul, and showing forth the mightful help she had had from God in her great straits. O, brave heart of my mother, first known this day — (a meet one for this lesson) — heart which fears God, and hath no other fear, I would fain resemble thee in thy great griefs, if in virtue I may also liken thee!

CHAPTER VI.

King René.

Naples, 19th of May 1438.

My hand is trembling for joy, and the gladness I feel exceedeth what my pen can describe. The King, my fair and noble father, is come. I have seen him ride through the city on his white charger, with a gold crown on his head and a sceptre in his hand, my two comely brothers by his side. When he passed, the people knelt, as if he had been a god come to reign over them. And is not the likest thing to God on earth a monarch which to his exalted rank and royal greatness doth add beauty of outward form and a natural majesty tempered by sweetness? When a great shout rises from thousands of hearts at once, it stops my breathing, and from my head to my feet there thrills a quivering passion, which ends in tears. If any should wish to paint a demigod, let them look at King René; or if a hero, study his actions. If they would describe a perfect man wearing virtue in his face, grace in his aspect, towardness in his behaviour, let them scan his visage, copy his gestures, list to his speech. If some great limner should desire to represent on wood or canvas Hector or Achilles, let them use King René's semblance, and all the world shall applaud. If

St. Sebastian or St. Maurice, draw his likeness when he prayeth. If a sage, the King when he is reading. If a poet, when he museth. If Apollo, when he playeth the viol. If a father, still the King when he encircles his children in his arms, and says so pleasantly, "The fairest fortune a prince can bequeath his heirs is the love of faithful subjects."

If there is happiness on earth, it should now reign in this land and in our hearts. For the spring with pleasure leads forward every passing hour, and the air which breathes delight, and the sunshine gilding the flowers, and the sparkling waves kissing the shore, join in one choir of gleesome harmony. Each day in the King's company I learn more of the story of this country in past ages, and of what poets have written, and skilled men of all times invented to adorn yet further, and extol this piece of earth which God Himself hath made beautiful, colouring it with hues which no painter can match, or he shall be supposed to exceed nature. "O, that I were not a king!" my father sometimes exclaims; "and that in these bounteous groves, and on those blue seas, amidst ruined temples and Christian sanctuaries, I might live for God, for prayer, thought, poesy, and art."

"Would you then be a monk of St. Benedict, sire?" my mother once replied. "For if this should be your pleasure, I will gladly be enrolled amidst the daughters of St. Scholastica."

"Nay, nay," cried the King; "jeer me not thus, sweet Isabel. Thou shouldst be a meet postulant for the cloister, who art never seduced by earthly enticements; but, alas! a passion for war's grim pageantries and the likeness of them in the tournament, the bewitchments of varied scenes, the passion of scenic

lore and music's wild enchantment, will abide with
me as long as I live."

"O, wayward prince!" she fondly answered; "to
sigh for peace, and cling to unrest!"

"Thou wouldst not forsake the throne, Isabel?" he
asked; and then she answered,

"Yea, my lord, very readily, if God so willed it.
But His vicegerents should not fly from the posts He
assigns. Our subjects, like unto our children, are
committed to us by the Supreme King, who at our
hands will demand an account of so great a trust."

When this people see the King, they madly worship
him. There are some who say he is too good, too
débonnaire. When the provinces revolt, moved by
Alphonso's emissaries, he conquers them; only afterwards to forgive and favour them. Some Calabrian
peasants, which would have murdered him some time
ago, he straightway pardoned, and gave them safe-
conducts to their homes. If I had been in his place,
I should have punished those wicked wretches. But
he goes and sits in the country people's huts, eats of
their poor fare, learns their savage songs, and plays
them on the gittern. When he is in Naples, not
St. Januarius himself, if he came to life again, should
be more honoured than the King; but if he turns his
back awhile, even to fight for them, this people are
shaken in their allegiance, like poor weak rootless trees
when a foul wind bloweth. They are as perfidious
as the sea, and as fickle as the wind. I begin to hate
them. I told Ciarletto Caracciolo I despised the
Neapolitans, and I am glad I did so; albeit he looked
as if he would have killed me.

I have not written in this book for a long time. I
like not to note in it troubles and griefs, but rather
triumphs. To-day I heard my father harangue the

E

people in the Piazza San Salvatore. The famine hath been dreadful; and he said he could no longer see them starve and perish for his sake. His heart is breaking, and the tears flowed down his visage. He said he must needs release them all from their allegiance, and would return to France. It pained and angered me to hear these words. I would starve and die sooner than yield to the Spaniards; and wherefore should not these mean common dastards starve and die too? They are as mutable as a weather-cock; for when he said he would go, then they fell to weeping and shouting they would not part with him. But I liked not their evvivas, as I was wont to do.

To-night I have great content in writing what I have seen. When the light declined, the King gathered round him in the court of the palace all the nobles of the city, and from the window I beheld them gathered round him. He stood by his horse with a drawn sword in his hand, Monseigneur de Calabre and forty French knights on each side. This time his words rang in mine ears like the sound of a trumpet. He said he was going forth to die or to conquer; that as long as Naples was faithful, he would shed the last drop of his blood in her defence. That to his noble lieges he commended his most precious treasures, his queen and his children, the while he went to meet their enemies and his. They all shouted, "Tarry, tarry with us, our king, our Rinaldo. Long live the King of Naples!" But he sprang on his horse and darted forward out of the town with so great speed, that his knights could hardly keep up with him. Then Raymondo di Bartello cried, "To horse! to horse! Let us follow our king!" and like one man the Neapolitan lords rode after their monarch.

Now Naples is besieged! The king of Aragon is encamped nigh unto the walls. My father is away conquering province after province by his valour, and hearts by his clemency; but food cannot enter. The people are waxing desperate. They starve and go mad with hunger. I have given my gold and silver ornaments and my only costly ring, to be exchanged for bread; and my mother all her jewels. But soon there will be no bread to buy, and then what shall happen? I see her weep when she eateth; and the sight of pale haggard faces when we ride abroad almost breaketh her heart, for the women hold up their famishing children in their arms when we pass, which is a sight of dreadful pity. A thought came into my mind this morning; a great thought, if I can do it. I will steal out in the night, and like that brave Judith, of which the Holy Scriptures say there was not such another woman upon earth in look, in beauty, and in sense of words, I will secretly repair to the enemy's camp and cut King Alphonso's head off; and then all his army will be filled with fear and run away, and I shall have delivered the city. I shall be renowned in all Europe as the bravest princess in the world, and the starving people shall have bread, and bless me all their days. I must have one of my maids to go with me. Agathe says she should be too affrighted. Barbe made me angry, for she pretends it would be a sin. "That is not possible," I answered; "for the Holy Scriptures do commend Judith for a like action." Then she urged we should perhaps be killed. "I heed not that," I replied, "for then we should go to heaven." She said she was not sure of that, for that to kill any one, and mostly a king, was a doubtful action if he was ever so wicked. And besides that, she added, "the gates of the city are shut, and we cannot get out, and madame has no weapon wherewith to cut the king's head off." "I can take Louis's sword with me," I said, "which he hath left behind him, and I will deal with the warders so that they will let me pass. Then will you come?" But still she said, yea and nay, and would not promise. At last, quoth she, "Madame, I will follow you, if your confessor commends this project." Then I was glad; and I have promised to go to shrift to-day, for I do not doubt that Fra Jacopo will urge me to fulfil it; for he doth nothing but pray for this starving people, and says it is a poor dole to give our jewels to feed them; that we should be ready to sacrifice our life's blood for their sakes.

I went with Théophanie to the church where Fra Jacopo comes to shrive me, but I told her naught of my intent; and I am glad I did not, for I think Fra Jacopo smiled when I spoke of it. I could see he did, though he covered his mouth with his hand. He says it is not lawful to kill any one in that wise since our Lord hath come into the world; and above all not a Christian prince, albeit he should be our greatest enemy. I said, displeased, "Then I am not to be like Judith, and save Naples?" "Nay," he said. "But I will tell you how you may resemble her. You can make yourself a chapel in your palace, yea, in your own chamber, and wear hair-cloth and fast, and ask the Lord, with tears, that according to His will He will show mercy to us, and humble your soul before Him." I must needs remain contented with this advice, for now Barbe will not go with me; and I should be afraid to go alone and unshriven to do that thing.

Corn hath come into the town, and great droves of

oxen and sheep; and the citizens are beside themselves with joy. For by a wise stratagem the king my father procured the entrance of these provisions into the town; and he now marches to our rescue.

Tidings have arrived from the Capitanate. The King of Spain is sick at Lucera, and the fight is begun. King René is about to fall like unto a lion on the Spaniards. Yet a few hours more and Alphonso shall be his prisoner, and Naples free! O God, I would fain pray; but my heart beats too fast. Minutes seem hours! hours days! O, that I could fly, like yonder bird, and see the battle! O, that I were a man, and had my spurs to win this day! I cannot sit nor yet stand still. I take my pen and lay it down. The least noise makes me start. I hate to wait; 'tis the curse of woman's lot.

Victory! victory! the news hath been brought by one from the battle! Naples and France have won the day. King René hath driven the Aragonese before him like the wind doth the leaves in autumn. Alphonso is surrounded; he cannot now escape. Ah! they are shouting in the streets. They have heard the glad news. They call for the Queen. Evviva! evviva! The sailors far out at sea shall hear that cry, and marvel at its might.

When they saw us the shouts waxed deafening. I waved one of Louis's flags. Methought they would have scaled the balcony, so great were their transports.

If there is a hotter place in hell than any other, or a more fearful torment than any Dante doth paint, shall it not be awarded to traitors? The pain I feel is worse than grief, worse than extreme pain of body. I am too much angered to weep, and my temples throb with a terrible pulsation. Caldora, I hate you. Caldora, your treason is so black that I have not words to describe it. You, whom my father loved and trusted; you, the King's friend—once honoured by that name, now most shamed by it, for highest honours breed deepest disgrace when caitiffs usurp them. O, cruel, unkind friend—friend worse than the bitterest foe—to snatch victory from his hand whom victory so well becomes. To stay his brave troops with a false order, and play the most foul traitor's part. My Lord Constable, but yesterday I should have scorned the man which had dared to call you false. O, I am sick with grief and trouble, and somewhat wroth (which most aileth me) with my father; for I have heard the Queen exclaim: "Alas, alas! what hath he done? René, my lord, is frank to a fault, and merciful to excess. What can serve him worse than to charge the traitor roundly with his guilt, and then, after a brief confinement, quickly forgive him, nay, restore him to his favour! My lord hath the courage of a lion and the gentleness of a dove, but he sorely lacketh the needful wisdom of the serpent." But a king should be wise. I would my mother were the king, and my father the queen!

I like not to look back at that last page, albeit my father hath returned to Naples, and there is peace for a brief time. I am yet troubled when I think of Alphonso's escape and Caldora's treason, who has now openly joined the Spaniards, though the King's forgiveness should have heaped coals of fire on his head. But for his vile perfidy, this fearful contest would now be ended. But Hope smileth again—God defend it should be a Siren's smile—on the House of

Anjou, and the good King's presence, like unto a loadstone, draweth all affections towards him. Festivals and rejoicings do again occur, and at this time in Castel Nuovo there is gathered together the noblest and fairest company imaginable. In the palace-yard are enacted allegories which please the eye and exercise an attentive mind. Now that I am twelve years of age, I assist at these pastimes, and often converse with the courtiers and lords most famed for their wit. I was most pleased to-day with an ingenious piece of acting, wherein the three greatest heroes of antiquity, Alexander, Scipio, and Hannibal, contended before Minos, the monarch of the infernal regions, for the foremost rank in the annals of fame, each in turn setting forth the merit of his actions. Minos, who was a learned lord, somewhat enamoured of me, inquired beforehand which of these great men I preferred. I answered, Scipio, for that he was more virtuous and equally brave with the others. Alexander should come next, and Hannibal the last; for I hated Rome's enemy, which, of all ancient nations, was the greatest, and most, I thought, to be admired. At the end of the play, Cyprian de Mero, who enacted Scipio, made a long speech, in which he likened King René to that great Roman, and the King of Spain to Hannibal. "For," he said, "Alphonso being old, cunning, crafty, and treacherous, doth resemble the Carthaginian; but you, sire, like Scipio, are young, just, prudent and truthful. Murder, rapine, and bloodshed followed Hannibal's steps; and your enemy, sire, hath spread famine, slaughter, and desolation in this land. Scipio defended Rome, and you, sire, are the shield of the Church, which hath its centre in the Eternal City. Brief prosperity lifted up the soul of the proud African. Transient successes swell the pride of your arrogant rival. You, sire, like Scipio, are brave, firm, and patient in adversity, and your final triumph shall surpass his. Go on, sire, reign and prosper. Advance from virtue to virtue, and then, not in the court of Minos, but in the realm of God most high, you will for ever reign with the saints and the blest."

I misliked not this discourse; but methinks I have sometimes written a more artful one in my lessons of history.

O, how brief are earthly joys! The joyous pastimes of last year are exchanged for so great disasters that the King is well-nigh distraught. Naples is now beset again, almost on every side, and the famine so fearful that the women throw their children under the feet of the King's horse when he rides, and cry to him to feed or destroy them. He, who hath the tenderest heart in the world, must see his subjects perish, for there is none to help them. A triple curse, war, famine, and pestilence, doth scourge this land. If it had not been for a letter of the Doge of Genoa, which raised a little his drooping soul, he had almost died of sadness. He can endure the extremity of suffering which only touches himself; but others' pangs move him so deeply, that a woman's sorrow doth not approach to his. Nothing will serve him now but to send my mother and me back to France, whither he will follow us when the last ray of hope shall have passed away for the House of Anjou. How like unto a dream do now show the few last years! Stormy ones, I ween, to those old enough, which I was not, to study the clouds, and mistrust fitful gleams of deceiving brightness. Farewell, Italy! Farewell, Naples! The common people here have a saying, "See Naples, and die." Shall this be my fate? What lieth before me, whose

life is only lately begun? God knoweth. When I
open this book again, I shall behold another sea, another sky, another land, other faces. 'Tis a taste of
dying, methinks, to leave any place long known and
early loved, never to return to it. O, my father King,
the old yearning to be a man cometh back to me in
this hour, when a kingdom vanishes in thy grasp like a
morning vision fled. If Marguerite had been a son of
thine, not a seely daughter, then she had fought with
thee for Naples, watered its soil with the best blood of
Anjou, conquered, or, at the worst, died.

After writing this, I sought my father, and found
him stringing beads, whilst the colours on the canvas
on which he paints were drying. I marvel he can be
limning and making rosaries when he is losing a fair
realm. He says the work of the hand and the eyes
stays painful thinking. My hand and my eye could
never so cheat my mind.

I have bade farewell to Fra Jacopo, who prayed God
to bless me. He said he hoped we should meet in
heaven. I must needs strive to forgive Caldora the
traitor, but none knoweth how hard it is.

On board the galley, in the bay of Naples. "Towers
and spires of fair Naples, for the last time I gaze on
you. Most beautiful handiwork of the good God—bay
which hath not, men say, its like on earth; mountain
from which liquid fire floweth; sea, only matched by
the sky which it mirrors, farewell. Good-bye, Naples
—good-bye, all."

CHAPTER VII.

Sorrow and Joy.

Poictiers, 1444.

How doth ambitious pain vanish when heart-sorrows arise! Death hath loosed his shaft and killed my sweetest joy. It chose for its prey the most beauteous flowers on Anjou's stem. Monseigneur Louis is dead! Alas! alas! How lovely was his life! how glorious, though brief! Hath it ever been heard of in these times, that one of twelve years of age, like unto a young David fighting with many Goliaths, should vanquish bearded men of renown! Ah! Monseigneur Antoine de Vaudémont, you were not afraid of the young Lieutenant of Lorraine, you and your friend the Damoisel de Commercy, that always perfidious and most lying knave, but he yet compelled you to raise the siege of Bar, and to surrender your own proud citadel. Louis, my fair brother, the most graceful prince God ever made, I loved you with so great a passion that when the tidings of your death came, I fell sick with grief, and well-nigh expired. For a long time I could neither read or write, my brain was so oppressed with sorrow. Nor would I even speak, but sat alone in the dark, refusing to be comforted even by my father and my mother. Then one came to my chamber, charming wisely my melancholy by the picture of his own. This was the Duke Charles of Orleans, so long a captive in England. He cheated

his grief for his dead wife, the matchless Isabel, by
turning mourning into worship, and building up a fair
shrine of poesy, in which memory took refuge with
right of sanctuary, and none dared to molest her.
Naught untender or less delicate than befitted so
sweet a theme there mingled with her name. At first
I listened to his similes and mournful rhymes solely to
solace my woe; for what he said of Isabel, my love
applied to Louis. But afterwards a new pleasure
supplanted grief. Each subject he discoursed on
derived a radiance from his mind, as natural objects
reflect the brightness of the sun. My father and this
prince are newly linked in such close friendship that
nothing can exceed it. There is a parity between
them of tastes and of talents, but yet a notable
dissemblance. The Duke's mind is, to my thinking
most like a cathedral full of melancholy beauty and
sad serenity, wherein the light shines through violet
and crimson hues, and pierces without flouting the
shades of sacred retirement. King René's is a temple
where fancy plays unchecked, and brightens each
object alike. Music is the twin sister of his muse, but
philosophy is married with poesy in the Duke's capa-
cious soul.

Tours, September 1444.

The court of the King of France is the most merry
which can be thought of, and some of his courtiers
the most pleasant persons in the world. He is himself
winsome, débonnaire, and, and to his niece Margaret a
most loving and indulgent lord. He saith his pearls
are his most costly jewels—Madame Marguerite of
Scotland, and his little one of Anjou. O, what a face
is that of the Scotch princess! I speak not of its
fairness, but of the tale it telleth of genius and woe.
I will write more of her anon. We have conversed

together often, and spoke of Alain Chartier. Some time ago she was passing in a gallery where the poet was asleep. She stooped down and kissed his lips, at the which her ladies exclaimed that she should confer so great an honour on one so foul-visaged. "Ah! mesdames," she answered, with her most speaking smile, "think you it is the *man* I honour, and not solely the divine sayings those ill-shaped lips have uttered?" There are men I would fain kill if I could. The Dauphin, if I had my will, should not long live. That so sweet a princess should be wedded to that caitiff, who hates and ill-uses her, doth work in me such desires of revenge that I could thrust a dagger in his breast.

Wit and jollity pervade this part of France like a subtle perfume, and men of great renown in arms and in council are as frolicsome as children. Light behaviour and light discourses are the fashion here, and even virtue is not morose. All things in turn take the form of a jest. Morality, love, vice, anger, goodness put on cap-and-bells. None are grave but fools, of which few are to be met with, at least in outward semblance and ordinary speech. I have now seen men the names of which have been famous for many years, such as the Count of Dunois, the Baron de la Trémouille, De Chabannes, and many others. But of all I have conversed with, none equal, I think, the Duke of Orleans, except young Pierre d'Aubusson. He is a young man in so great favour with the king, and of so great valour, which he showed at Montereau, that his praise is in every mouth. His mode of discourse hath in it some singularity. He pays no homage in speech to those he most admires, but if one utters a thought which pleases him, there is a more true flattery in the quick flash of his responsive eye than in any compliments the lips can frame. He said yesterday, as he rode by my side from the chase in the Forest of Marmoutier, that no beauty of any sort he had seen could equal what his fancy pictured.

"If this be so," I answered, "describe, I pray you, what you see on the canvas of your mind."

"I must then be a poet," he replied; "which I am not. But hath not your own thinking, madame, over-passed earthly beauty, greatness, and joy, and soared beyond this visible world, which at most appears to me as the antechamber of a divine palace, or a bridge to be traversed betwixt past nothingness and future perfection, the shadow only of a coming reality, like the visions of the Scottish seers which Madame la Dauphine speaks of?"

I told him that the future of this world so much filled my thoughts that they soared not often beyond it, except in brief times of prayer. Greatness, I owned, was my desire.

"Ay," he said laughing, "greatness is also my dream. It will be thrust on your highness. I shall have to seek it. Pleasures abound in this court; but how think you, madame? doth not the creeper, pleasure, kill happiness at last, like the enwreathing ivy the oak it covers?"

"Is that your experience, Messire Pierre?" I asked with a smile.

"No," he answered; "only my misdoubt, madame, which future trial must dissolve or confirm."

After so many years' absence and long delays since we returned to France, the false Vaudémonts have been forced to restore Yolande to her parents. They protest she is betrothed to their son, and that to marry her to another should be unlawful. She came here to-day under an escort of some of the King's troops, and is now delivered into her father's hands- She is a sweet, mild-visaged maiden, very like an image of our Lady in one of Giotto's paintings at Santa Chiara. Her behaviour is sedate, serious, and equable. Her speech very modest, each word uttered in low tones, as if wrung from reluctant lips.

When we retired last night to the turret where we sleep, the night being fair and warm, we sat on a balcony which overhangs the river. I kissed her and spake in jest, for I longed to see her smile. She answered timidly, as one who forces speech but would fain be silent. As the light declined, she waxed more bold, if to exhibit grief can be called boldness. Tears began to fall gently and sadly on her bosom, like unto droppings of an overcharged fountain. Then this dialogue took place betwixt us:

"What aileth thee, Yolande?"

"I dare not say it."

"Dare!" I exclaimed; "my motto is to dare all things except sin."

Then she, in a yet lower voice, leaning against the railing:

"I wish it were not a sin to leap into the river and so to die."

"Is it possible, Yolande, that you love the Vaudémonts, who have so long kept you a captive, more than your noble parents? Their castle was your prison."

"Sweet prison! more delectable than any palace!"

"Have you then ceased to love your kindred?"

"I must love Ferry, my betrothed lord."

"He shall never be your lord. Your father hath sworn that no Vaudémont shall ever wed his daughter."

I was affrighted when I saw her look like a scared

dove, the blue veins in her forehead swelling, and her eyes strangely dilated.

"I am Ferry's betrothed. Not my father or any king can break a knot the Church hath blessed. Ferry said so."

"The Pope can loose it."

"I would throw myself from these battlements sooner than marry any one but Ferry."

"Ferry! I hate his name. He hath stolen your heart from us."

"Nay, when I was a little child, I gave it to him. He never stole it."

"You have a resolved will, I see, like a true daughter of Lorraine."

"Lorraine! yes, I love Lorraine. Anjou I care not for."

"Shame on you, Yolande! you, the daughter of King René!"

"I love my father, but I care not for kings. If Ferry was a peasant, I would be one also."

"A peasant! I would sooner be bound hand and foot, and cast into the Loire, than not marry a king."

"What! will you not wed Pierre de Luxembourg, Ferry's friend, and, except my lord, the most comely prince I have seen?"

"No, not for all that the world contains."

She would not talk any more after this. In the night when I awoke, I looked on her sleeping, with tears yet on her cheeks, like a child which hath cried itself to sleep.

Ah, me! I love that gentle sister, but I would fain she cared for reading, or painting, or some kind of study. She sits all day and spins, with her eyes fixed on the river. 'Tis a marvel to me that any one can be so still in mind and in body. My father vows she shall never marry Ferry, but an Italian prince; and thinks she is so mild he fears not her disobedience. Methinks he counts without his host, as the proverb saith. I heard him say last night, "I thank God I have not to constrain my daughter Marguerite's liking; that should be a very desperate encounter; but I fear not Yolande should prove a rebel." Perhaps he may yet discover the chafing torrent is more easily turned from its course than the placid stream. "Oneness hath great power," is a saying of the Comte de Dunois. "If a man or a woman willeth but one thing only, the Lord deliver me from opposing them." I will a great many things; to be great, and to have weath; to be admired, and in renown of virtue : to be a puissante queen, and a saintly one to boot. But Yolande willeth nothing, I ween, but to be Ferry's wife. See if she compass it not. I think she is bewitched with the river. At morn and noon and night she doth stand and gaze at the running water, till I pull her by the arm to make her eat, sleep, or pray.

Whilst Agathe was dressing me this morning she said, "Madame, when we were at Nancy, three months ago, did not madame sit to a limner to be painted by him?"

"Yea," I replied; "you very well know I did."

"It is reported," she said, "that this limner, and the gentleman of Anjou which brought him there, came not as they pretended from the Duchesse Jeanne de Bretagne, but from England."

"Wherefore from England? Who should send them?"

"Ah, madame! who in England but the King should most desire to behold a visage the matchless beauty of which every prince of Europe would defend with his lance?"

"Tut, foolish maiden," I replied. "The King of England is about to wed the Comte d'Armagnac's daughter."

"As madame pleases," quoth the wench, submissively.

"It is not as I please," I impatiently answered, for it made me angry to see her smiling, as if she was wiser than others.

"Then it shall be as God pleases," she subjoined.

I had well-nigh said, "It should not be as God pleased," I was so vexed with her manner; but I forbore, and broke off the discourse.

There are daily diversions in this place and little happiness, if Pierre d'Aubusson's suspicion is true, that too much pleasure kills it; for naught but pleasure is thought of, and the day and the night seem too short for the pastimes which are on hand. For my part I would that sleep were no law of nature, for then I would talk with learned and pleasant men one-half of the night, and read and study the other. I perceive that some women are admired for beauty, some revered for goodness, some esteemed for ability. Now, if one was beautiful, virtuous, and witty; if she had withal a firm will and great courage, would she not rule all who approached her? The king, my uncle, showeth me exceeding favour, and will always have me in his company. My father charged me yesterday, which I rode out with his majesty, to move him to consent to a point in the treaty with England and Rome, which he demurs at; and neither himself, nor mine aunt the Queen, nor Madame de Beauté with all her art, can prevail on him to yield therein.

The king hath consented to my reasons. Little Marguerite d'Anjou hath brought to a good issue what princes and queens had in vain compassed. Doth she not then deserve to reign herself one day?

This is another dialogue betwixt Yolande and me.

"I marvel, sister, you never read!"

"Sweet Marguerite, I read my prayers in the Book of Hours the Countess gave me."

"But there are in this chamber our father's poems and Antoine de la Salle's tales, and many other fairly written volumes, which you should peruse."

"Wherefore?"

"For profit and good entertainment."

"The Countess saith it profits more to say one's prayers and spin than to be a scholar."

"For my part, I am of opinion it shutteth out one half of life to refrain from reading. What think you of all day as you sit spinning?"

"I have never thought of what I think about."

"Then you are like a flower which groweth without knowing it, or a bird singing without intent."

"But if the flower smelleth sweetly, and the bird singeth pleasantly, doth it matter they should know and intend it? Women which are scholars make not good wives, I have been told, and strive to rule their lords rather than be humble and obey."

"But if a woman is a king's daughter, should she not learn to be a worthy help-mate to a sovereign?"

"I ween sovereigns, as well as other men, love obedient wives. The Countess says that when the Duke of Brittany sent envoys to Scotland some years ago to judge of the Princess Isabel, they returned and said she was comely enough and well-shaped, but of wit they could not perceive she had any at all. 'Sirs,' quoth the duke, 'in my thinking, a woman hath wit enough if she can distinguish her husband's smock from his waistcoat.'"

"And that same princess hath been despised by her lord, and led a paltry poor life since her marriage, which I warrant you, Yolande, is the fate of witless women, whether on a throne or in a hovel. But I thank God you have sufficient wit yourself to defend with cunning a bad cause.'"

"O no, not with cunning. Ferry saith I have none."

"And no wit?"

She smiled and made no answer.

"Think you," I rejoined, "if the Queen, our mother, had been naught but a spinning housewife, she should have kept Naples for three years, with incredible skill and courage, whilst her lord, our father, was a prisoner?"

"But, methinks, if she had lost it then, the King should now be richer."

Then I was sent for to the Queen Marie, and had not time to answer this bad reasoning.

Life hath strange events, such as we read of in tales of chivalry. Yesterday there arrived in this town, which caused no small stir, an embassage from England, in no ways expected: my lord the Earl of Suffolk, the Dean of Salisbury, and many other English lords and gentlemen, the purport of whose coming no one heard. My father was straightway summoned to the King, and tarried a long time in the palace; whither we heard the envoys had likewise been invited. When he returned thence his face was inflamed, and seemed very much moved; but whether with anger or with joy did not at the first appear. He came and sat down by my mother's side and took her hand. She by a sign dismissed her ladies, and methinks, she thought it should be bad news, for the heart which hath often thus suffered is quick to presage woe. Yolande and I were working at one frame.

"Look at that petite madame," I heard my father say, directing his glance towards us. I raised mine eyes and smiled.

"Yea, Madame Marguerite, you may well smile," he continued. "For I doubt not you will deem a crown a becoming ornament for your audacious little head."

"A crown!" exclaimed my mother. "What doth my lord mean?"

I had already guessed the truth, and my heart was fast beating.

"I' faith, madame," the King said, turning again to the Queen, "the King of England is so enamoured of your daughter's picture, that he must needs despatch an embassage to sue for her hand. Say, Marguerite, wilt thou be Queen of England?"

"Yea, and of France too," I cried, throwing my arms around his neck. At the which he smilingly chid me, and said I was too vain-glorious to claim that title. Then he called Yolande, saying, "Come, my first-born flower! come and salute the Queen of England. If it please God, we shall soon have thee as royally mated as this daisy." Then he enfolded me with one arm, and her with the other. Yolande made no answer, but bowed her head on his bosom to meet mine, and so we embraced.

A Queen! The Queen of England and of France! My young desire fulfilled! I have seen men since I have been in France which I might have loved if they had been born on a throne. But I never yielded to the least tenderness for any living man, not even for Pierre d'Aubusson, though I admire his person and his

mind, and might have wished God had made him a
prince. But I thank Heaven my heart hath always
been equal to its high fortune; and it is a maiden
heart, unstained by any meaner love, I shall give to
King Henry. To-night I shall see Milord Suffolk and
his company. Is this a dream? No, I am not asleep
..... I went to the window to dispel the doubt. There
were the green fields, with the sun shining on them.
The poppies and the blue corn-flowers amidst the
waving wheat, the river, and the boats upon it. From
one of them a bird flew straight to the turret window
of the chamber. Yolande caught it in her arms. I
am certainly awake.

If King Henry is one-half so much my captive as
my Lord Suffolk, I shall be the most indulged princess
in the world. We conversed for two hours yestereve,
and he described the King's passion in such glowing
colours that I begin to be jealous of my picture.

"Ah, madame!" this gallant envoy exclaimed, when
I expressed this apprehension, "my only fear is, that
the King shall be so enamoured when he beholds the
reality of the semblance he now adores, that he shall
have no ears, no eyes, and no heart for the affairs of
the state, but live gazing on and worshipping his
Queen both night and day, and so fail in his duties
from excess of love and happiness."

"That shall never be," I replied; "for I will wed
his duties, his interests, and his people together with
himself. The cares of state should be the pastimes of
royal lovers, my lord; and, for my part, I would sooner
be the King's servant than only his toy."

"O, noble words for a monarch's bride!" Lord
Suffolk cried. "How will they rejoice the heart of
that virtuous prelate, Cardinal Beaufort!"

"Is his eminence, then, my friend?" I asked.

"So much so, madame," he answered, "that his last words to me were: 'Obtain the hand of the Princess of Anjou, my lord, for the King, and you shall not lack my poor prayers as long as I live. These are not days for virtue only in a queen. A king's consort in this realm should have wit, courage, and be of good counsel in the chamber, and, if needs be, on the field of battle.'"

Then he described some of King Henry's kinsmen. The Duke of Gloucester, he saith, will always hate me, for he had sworn to the Count d'Armagnac the King should wed his daughter.

Now it seems as if I lived for the first time. My pulse, methinks, beats quicker. Words pass more swiftly from my thoughts to my tongue. O, I had rather be a queen for one year, than a common princess for half a century!

Yolande hath cried all day, and naught will move her to tell her grief. Barbe, Agathe, and even Théophanie, think she is displeased and jealous that I should marry the King of England, and do pity her, I see. But I credit not their thinking. If she is not false, which is impossible, she loves Ferry, and weeps day and night that she cannot marry him. Her visage, which was at first calm, albeit sorrowful, is now often troubled. When her parents caress her, I see tears in her eyes. Yesterday she stood at the window a long time, kissing that stray pigeon which flew from the boat to our chamber. Then she let him fly, and watched him till he disappeared.

Yolande and I have quarrelled—that is, I quarrelled

with her. For there came to the court, two days ago, some envoys of the Duke of Burgundy, and with them, that false and ungracious knave, Robert de Sarrebruche, the Damoisel de Commercy. When I was a little child, I first heard that man's name coupled with so many treasons and vile cowardice, that I have since abhorred it. He was one of those who, before the battle of Bulgneville, dared to say to the brave Barbazan, that gray-headed hero and most valiant knight, because he counselled prudent delay, "Let those that fear stay at home;" and when the battle was engaged, himself fled with his troop like a vile recreant, so that to this day 'tis the custom to say of a craven knight, "He is brave like the Damoisel de Commercy." I have heard that when Barbazan lay dying on the bloody field, with his wound gaping, the coward passed him, spurring his horse. "Ah!" cried the expiring hero, "whither goes Robert de Sarrebruche? Is this your valour, young knight, so boasted of this morn?" The shameless truant answered curtly: "I promised my love a visit, and must needs pay it;" and rode on. 'Tis a foul disgrace this false knight should stand in the presence of two kings, and be invited to the court; but when I saw Yolande smile upon him with her soft and beaming eyes, and converse with him in a low voice, with a flushed cheek and eager countenance, I was so angered I could have wept. She chose him for her partner. It made me mad to see him hold her hand and whisper in her ear. When the brawl began, Pierre d'Aubusson and I fronted this ill-matched pair! and I should have touched his hand in the dance, but drawing mine away, I said in an audible voice, "Gramercy, Messire Robert, I have promised my love a visit, and I must needs pay it." He waxed pale with rage, and ground his teeth. When

Yolande and I were alone, I reproached her in the most stinging words I could think of for her courtesy to this wretch. She bore it silently awhile; but then broke forth suddenly in this manner:

"Sister, I cannot credit Robert should be so vile as you describe, for then he had never been Ferry's friend."

"Ah! if any thing had been needed," I cried, "to make me detest that man, it should be this friendship. Those who love the Vaudémonts are our foes."

Yolande took my hand, and with a strong pressure held it the while she said:

"Marguerite, I am Ferry de Lorraine's wife. I love the Vaudémonts, and if this must needs make my kindred hate me, why it must be so. If I must be the enemy of my lord or of my parents, God help me, for no more sad fate can befall a wife and daughter. But, O sister! have a little pity; for since I have set foot in my father's house, I have been sore troubled in mind and full of sorrow, robbed of peace, and much dejected. A sister should not add to a grief all too heavy to bear."

And then the sweet soul began to weep.

"You are happy," she added with deep sighs; "the whole world doth envy you. Who so admired, who so loved, who so praised as Marguerite? Should she not then compassion one so wretched as Yolande?"

I kissed her, and we withdrew to rest. In the night, when she thought I was sleeping, she stole from my side, and went to the casement, through which the moon was shining. She read a letter, which ever and anon I saw her press to her lips. Methinks the Damoisel must have brought her that missive from Ferry, whom she calls her lord. It is reported that the Duke of Burgundy hath partly sent these envoys to urge the fulfilment of that old contract. My father's brow was clouded last night. He says, the Vaudémonts may rob him of his lands, murther his subjects, and burn his towns, but that his daughter they shall not have, if his life depended on it. There are exceptions in all natures, and I perceive that most men in one point do differ, as it were, from their own selves. He who is so mild and *débonnaire* to all others, even to his enemies, is like an unshaken rock in his resentment against the Count Antoine and hatred of this alliance, as the worst disgrace which could befall him. He would as soon match Yolande with a poor troubadour, he says, as with Ferry de Lorraine. Yet report describeth this youth as a very paragon of beauty, virtue, and warlike gifts.

This day my father summoned Yolande to his presence, and with endearments and paternal caresses first, then with kingly majesty, and in the end exceeding passion, commanded her to think no more on Ferry.

" How should I not think on my lord ? " she answered.

And when he swore she should never marry him, still she replied, with downcast eyes, but firm, resolved. lips,

" Ferry is my affianced husband."

This moved him to more violent anger than I had ever witnessed in him before.

" Ungrateful, unnatural child!" he exclaimed, and appeared quite overwhelmed with grief.

In a few days we go to Angers, and afterwards to Nancy, where my Lord Suffolk will shortly arrive King Charles will be there, and more princes than I can count, albeit I heard all their names. The most beautiful and rare jousts will be held at that time. My father doth delight in such displays, and none shineth in the lists with more glory and magnificence, or ordereth with a like skill the pageants which accompany them. Yolande is of better cheer since he is thus employed. When talk is ministered of the grand tournament in the Place de Carrière, she stays to listen with an eager look in her sweet eyes, which mind me of Monseigneur Louis's; and she doth help my mother to embroider a scarf for the conqueror. Ah, many that day will break lances in mine honour. Many will weep that I go never to return. Is there always a drop of sadness in each earthly joy? I would not for the world not be Queen of England, and yet ... Ah! what should be that plashing of oars under the window? "Yolande, 'qui vive?' as the sentinels say." "Lorraine and Anjou," she answers from the next chamber. Ah! well-a-day! she has learnt the password from the guards.

CHAPTER VIII.

The Place de Carrière.

Nancy, November 1st, 1444.

THE Marquis of Suffolk hath exhibited to me this morn the letter of his master, King Henry, in which he says, "As you have lately, by the Divine favour and grace, in our name, and for us, engaged verbally and excellent, magnificent, and very bright Margaretta, the serene daughter of the King of Sicily, and sworn that we shall contract matrimony with her, we consent and will that she be conducted to us over seas, from her country and friends, at our expense."

I could not choose but smile at this missive. "Excellent, magnificent, bright, and serene!" Methinks I must study my actions and my words, and practise a very staid and gracious behaviour in future, to fulfil his majesty's expectations. Margaretta! That soundeth not like mine own name; and albeit mine ears have not been unused to praise, yet to be termed magnificent hath a novelty in it which I mislike not.

November 2nd.

A great company of English lords and ladies have arrived with my Lord Suffolk and his wife, to witness my nuptials, and assist at the feasts and pastimes which will follow. To-morrow and two successive days I will spend in close retirement at the Convent of St. Marie. This is the Feast of All Souls. I have carried a garland to the tomb of Monseigneur Louis, and prayed a long time in the chapel wherein he lies.

November 5th.

I am a queen! the wedded wife of King Henry, my yet unseen lord. St. Martin, in whose church my troth was plighted, pray for me! An English knight, who is also a poet, says in an ode I have seen, that I the bride of his sovereign,

> "Like to the rosy morning towards its rise,
> Cheered all the church, as it doth cheer the skies."

This is fair poesy; but she that cheered others then needed cheering herself. For when I stood at the altar by the side of the Marquis of Suffolk, to be espoused by him in the King's name, an unwonted fear chilled my heart, and I began to tremble, which I remember not to have done in any former haps. In eight days I shall be delivered up into the hands of the English. This hath an ominous sound; but this surrender is a loving, joyous, and triumphant one, which filleth every one with delight. I shall part with my kindred, than which none have loved a young princess with a more tender, passionate, and constant affection, or been more loved in return; but is it not said in Holy Writ that a bride must needs forget her father's house, and so the King shall take pleasure in her beauty? Some declare that my lord Henry is monkishly inclined, and overstudious for a lover; but my Lady Suffolk, with whom I conversed yestereve, assures me he is more like to dote on his wife than any other prince in the world. I look at his picture until the painted likeness seems to assume life, and almost speech. The youthful features, fair smooth brow, mild and most expressive eyes, appear to smile on me. Yet in them I perceive a melancholy beauty, which I think must needs exist in the royal visage. No limner would invent it.

November 8th.

I cannot sleep. 'Tis in vain I lie down and try to close my eyes. When the brain is crowded with varied images, it brooks not dull repose. I have lacked leisure to write. The days are all too short for the sports which each hour renews, the stately pageants which mimic war, and the long banquets and the dance which closes every night all other pastimes. The English envoys must needs marvel to see such frolics in this court, for they seem a race more grave than I have yet met with, and prone to melancholy, if I judge by their visages. Yet a true philosophy ruleth not, I ween, their gravity more than our glee; for if one steps an inch further than his rank warrants, or another boweth in a less lowly guise than court usage doth command, I' faith these English nobles fume and scowl as if the world should therefore come to an end.

November 9th.

The tournament which my father planned with so great pains hath begun, and verily 'tis a meet pastime for kings and nobles; but I wish all the brave knights here assembled formed an army marshalled in array to conquer Jerusalem and Naples. A most glorious yet soft sunshine, such as is seen in the summer of St. Martin, enlivened the field, than which a more befitting one cannot be found for such jousts than this one of Nancy. The flower of France's chivalry is here, and likewise of Brittany, Lorraine, and Allemayne. Also the English nobles are present, and churchmen and ladies not a few, to witness this famous passage of arms. At ten this morn, after dinner, which was one hour earlier than other days, my father rode into the lists with the knights of the attack; my brother with those of the defence. Every chevalier as he passed before the queens and the ladies made due obeisance; and smiles and whispers ensued as each passed by. For majesty and grace, methinks, none can be compared to King René; albeit the Counts of Maine, of Foix, and of Nevers, the Lords of Saintrailles, of Brézé, and of Beauveau, André of Laval, and young Louis de Luxembourg, and his brother Pierre Count of St. Pol, are fair and gallant knights. Pierre d'Aubusson, though so young, hath the semblance of an old soldier. He won his spurs in Hungary, fighting under the brave Hunniades. One knight had his vizor drawn, and no coat of arms on his shield save a black cross. If any in this field could have matched my father in form, figure, and martial carriage, it should have been this unknown knight. When he saluted the queens, he dismounted, which none of the others had done, and made so graceful an obeisance, bending on one knee, that a murmur of applause arose; and when he leaped into his saddle and rode on, every one cheered. Many conjectures were framed touching this knight. Some thought he was the Count of Anjou, others the King of France; but this was quickly disproved, for his majesty soon after rode into the lists bearing tne arms of Lusignan on his shield, the famed serpent of the fairy Melusina; and the Count of Anjou, who tilted with him, those of Aragon. The Dauphiness, who greatly affections Yolande and me, turned towards us with a smile and said:

"Mesdames, I will wager these two rings against two flowers out of your posies, that I guess who this knight is."

"Nay, madame," Yolande cried before I could speak,—she whose wont is to be speechless,—"hold us excused, I pray you."

"Nay," I exclaimed, "answer for yourself, fair sister. I accept the proffer, sweet princess. Who is the knight?"

"I' faith," the Dauphiness replied, "I warrant you 'tis the King of England in disguise. Ah! what a noble wooer he would prove which concealed royalty under the semblance of simple knighthood, and won in the same hour the love of his bride and the honours of the field!"

Lord Shrewsbury, who was standing nigh to the princess, said in bad French and a resentful tone, "'Tis not the custom, madam, for English monarchs to play at knight errantry, and act the part of mad troubadours."

The Dauphiness drew a ring from her finger and put it on mine, the while she replied,

"My lord, I take your word on this point as a final judgment; but methinks it should have been no disparagement to a monarch, howsoever puissant, to have encountered two kings in these lists, and that those eyes which we see had well excused a chivalrous folly, such as my poor thinking framed."

The English lord grumbled a few words betwixt his own rough language and French, which were, I ween, meant to excuse his sharp speech. These islanders have the proudest spirit imaginable, and take quick offence, for all their staid speaking and heavy aspect.

My Lord Suffolk sat by my side all the day, and discoursed of England and his King. If I so much as looked at any French prince, or spoke to him, he waxed uneasy. Methinks when I said the sky was fair and the air pleasant he was jealous, and misliked it. Poor my Lord Suffolk! I do pity him. To play the lover for another must needs be a sorry pastime. His grave visage almost moves me to laugh.

November 10th.

To-day at noon the trumpets sounded, and two kings entered the lists to tilt against each other,—King Charles and King René. O, then I held my breath, and my sight almost failed me; for this was no mean contest, no common encounter, and should have had the whole world for a spectator. It was a marvel to see these two crowned kinsmen jousting in such noble and ardent guise in the midst of a goodly crowd of valiant princes and lords. I would fain not have loved them both; for then my pleasure should have been greater when my father unhorsed my uncle, who at once turned to the ladies with a gracious frankness which beseemed a king, and cried aloud, "Je n'en peux mais," owning himself conquered; at the which so loud cries of cheering rose for the victor and the vanquished that the heralds' voices were drowned. Then the Comte de St. Pol tilted with Pierre d'Aubusson, and was unhorsed; albeit none had surpassed him the day before, and he had received the chief prize from the hands of the Queen Marie. Ah, my Lord Suffolk, you watched my visage with careful eyes during that contest, and seemed contented when I smiled at Pierre de Luxembourg's defeat. I ween that other Pierre had been the most like of the two to prove a Pierre d'achoppement to your king! The Knight of the Black Cross broke five lances in honour of a nameless beauty, and overthrew all his opponents; but when my father sent to challenge him, he replied that he had made a vow not to tilt against a monarch. A sudden thought comes into my mind.

Ah, Madame Yolande, peradventure your conscience forbade you to accept the Dauphiness's wager. I must needs clear this doubt before we sleep to-night. Now the banquet is at hand, and then the ball. If my life shall resemble my nuptials, it should prove a merry one; for pleasure treadeth on the heel of pleasure in these days, and pastimes never end. I marvel sometimes that so much glee should precede a long parting, and I wax a little sad. So doth my mother.

November 11th.

To-day Yolande and I sat with the Dauphiness in a bower of the garden, and conversed.

The princess said "Mesdames, of all the knights assembled in this famous tournament, and which wear garlands of daisies in honour of the Queen of England, which think you is the most like to break his heart when she departs?"

"Ah! without doubt," cried Yolande, "the Comte de Nevers; a more sad visage cannot be seen than his since my sister's betrothal."

Then the princess replied: "Yea, a more enamoured prince, methinks, never existed; and if your father, mesdames, hath recovered Maine and Anjou, Henri de Nevers is the cause."

"How so, madame?" I said, misliking her speech. "The King, my lord, freely yielded those provinces to my father's rightful claims."

"Freely!" quoth the lovely princess. "Ah, he had no greater freedom therein than a poor prisoner under the rack. The little blind tyrannic god holds him so tightly in his power since the day Madame Marguerite's image robbed him of his peace, that he hath no more liberty, this great king, than a caged bird. He may well thank God that Monseigneur René did not exact from him what King Herod promised his dancer—the one-half of his kingdom."

"But what share had the Comte de Nevers in this cession?" I again asked.

"This," answered the Dauphiness. "Monsieur de Suffolk wrote to his majesty that a very perilous and most enamoured suitor would obtain madame's hand if King René's demands were refused, and so worked on his fears that the provinces were promised and Monseigneur Henri reduced to despair."

"He is a brave soldier and a sweet poet," I said; "but one thing he lacketh."

"What?" asked the princess.

"Royalty," I answered.

"Royalty!" echoed the Dauphiness. "Ah, sweet heart, when life waneth, the glitter of that bauble, a crown, fadeth away as speedily as the hues about yonder setting sun."

"What know you, my fair cousin," I replied, "of life waning, when the morning of yours is only in its dawn?"

"Mine!" quoth she, with a look of scorn tempered by sadness, "Fi de la vie! ne m'en parlez plus." And her eyes fixed themselves on the sky, a moment before coloured with crimson and gold, but now beginning to wax gray. Then after a while musing, she abruptly said: "And the Lord of Varennes, the gallant Pierre de Brézé, was he not also one of your majesty's suitors?"

"Her knight," Yolande said, "not her suitor. Marguerite is too proud to have entertained less than a royal prince in her train of even hopeless lovers."

Then the Dauphiness said: "Messire de Brézé was appointed to negotiate the terms for the exchange of the Queen against Maine and Anjou."

Yolande exclaimed: "I would sooner be a peasant girl, and have a lover who should himself woo and wed me, than be exchanged in this royal fashion for lands and pelf. Methinks the King of England hath bought my sister."

This speech angered me not a little.

CHAPTER IX.

A Vow.

November 12th.

THIS night I have spoken for the last time, I ween, with Pierre d'Aubusson. It is not like I should set eyes on him again. What will the King, my uncle, say of his resolve, who was wont to declare that so great wisdom and so much fervour had never been seen together in one person? If the Dauphin, who mislikes most men, and yet likes him, did repent last year of his rebellion, and submitted to the King, Messire Pierre had the praise of it; and now the court shall see him no more.

I will set down the discourse I held with him when, after the banquet, we stood in a gallery which overlooked the dancers.

"Messire Pierre," I said, "you must be a contented person to-day, for none have excelled and few equalled you in the lists."

"Madame," he replied, "if each knight vanquished in that vain pageant had been an infidel foe, then verily I had rejoiced. But empty honours breed more confusion than contentment in a Christian when tales are ringing in his ears such as I have this day heard."

"What hath so strangely moved you, Messire

Pierre?" I asked. "What inflames your visage with so burning a flush?"

His clenched hand and fixed yet vacant gaze, as one looking on yet not seeing what lies before him, betokened an emotion which for a while impeded speech; then he slowly uttered the word "Warna." The blood now mounted to my face, for I was ashamed that the tidings which had awakened in him so deep a passion had not been present to my mind since I had heard them in the banquet-hall, and shuddered at their import.

"Is this a time," he broke forth, "for mimic fights, idle sports, and luxurious revelry? For mine own part I could as lief sit down to eat and rise up to play with the guilt of murther on my soul as dally here in shameful ease, when deeds are wrought by accursed hands which cry to God and man for vengeance; when Christian kings and priests die in torture, flayed alive by the Turks! O God, that Hunniades had been there!"

"I crave Christ's pardon," I cried, "that my unthinking mood dulled for a while the edge of indignant sorrow for these dire haps. But believe me, sir, I am not one whit less sensible of their horror than yourself. Methinks the name of 'Warna' should be a knell in every Christian ear, and the ghosts of King Vladislas and the holy prelate Cesarini haunt our beds and our feasts, until such time as the last infidel which slew them is destroyed."

"There spoke my noble princess," Pierre replied. "But it is not only the strong arm or the boastful courage of the natural man which must wage this war and avenge these martyrs. No, when the Cross is trodden under foot by its foes, it hath to be borne not by the hands alone but the hearts of its champions;

hence the vow which I now make in your hearing, young Queen, whom God hath, I think, sent to hear it, not without a gracious intent. Few in yonder crowd would commend the sudden resolve; but albeit nursed in pomp and pleasure, you have yet been familiar from your cradle with heroic thoughts, and from your lips I fear not dissuasive words. Some might deem a sanctuary and an altar a more befitting place for the utterance of this oath; but no, this is the place, this the time in which God hath called me....."

"To what?" I asked, somewhat moved; for if this man had been a king, I should perhaps have loved him.

"To the making of this vow," he replied; and then said in a firm, clear, and most impressive voice, albeit not a loud one, " I, Pierre d'Aubusson, do from this hour renounce the love of woman, the joys of home, the hopes of fortune; and I do moreover promise the Lord my God, His Blessed Mother, and St. John, to wage war against the infidels in the Order of St. John, and under its law to pray, fast, and fight, and obey all the days of my life. So help me God, who hears this vow."

"Amen!" I unconsciously said. It may be I misliked not to hear him renounce all other loves than that great one which had kindled this burning flame in his breast. "It is a noble vow," I said; "but have you counted its cost?"

"The cost!" he repeated with a smile the most beautiful I have ever seen. "Ah, daughter and bride of a king, I give God thanks in this solemn hour that you were born so far above me—you, the fairest of His handiworks—that no earthly dream of human happiness mingled with the reverent worship I have paid you, so that there hath been no need to weigh in the balance the cost, which alone should have been one."

He hesitated a moment, and then, as I still seemed to be listening, though I made no answer to his speech, he went on :

"And yet, methinks, I could wish I had been one who might have aspired to the hand of Marguerite d'Anjou ; one who might have been blessed with a love pure, mighty, and sweet as thine shall be for thy wedded husband, O royal maid! more royal in thy gifts than in thy birth, most royal in greatness of love ; for then I should have surrendered at the Lord's bidding a peerless joy, a perfect earthly contentment. This, this should have been a worthy sacrifice for a soldier of the Cross."

"And if it had been thus," I asked, "should you still have gone ?"

"Yea," he answered, "or I had been a recreant. And now, madame, if in after years the name of Pierre d'Aubusson reaches your majesty's ears, as of one living to defend the Church, or dying fighting for Christ, pray for such a one if he lives, yet more if he dies. If God's voice hath spoken to him in your hour of joy and triumph ; if in the midst of the splendours of an earthly court the tale of glory and of shame, which fell unheeded on a thousand careless ears, stirred but two hearts this day, yours and his—"

"Mine!" I exclaimed ; "mine was only moved by a sterile and impotent pity."

"Nay," he rejoined ; "no emotion is sterile which taketh its rise in a noble soul. Be it yours to awaken the spirit of true Christian chivalry in the realm of England, and by that power which many misuse, a queen's and a woman's, raise up new champions of the Cross."

Then he bade me farewell; and to-morrow he will take leave of the King and the Dauphin, and depart for Rhodes. 'Tis a strange thought! I thank God I never loved Pierre d'Aubusson; but I think I shall not often look on his like again. I told Yolande this hap. She said she hoped there should be no more Crusades; for which I chid her. Methinks love doth make a heart to lose the greatness which should dwell in royal breasts; and yet in my mother this effect is not seen. It may be that a wife's affection hath more nobility in its nature than a fond maiden's. If this is so, I thank God that I shall know none other than that more generous one.

November 13th.

I am troubled and sore perplexed. The doubt of yesterday hath grown into a certainty. The Knight of the Black Cross is no other than Ferry de Lorraine. I noticed signs exchanged between him and Yolande; and when his horse fell with him, she well nigh swooned. Heaven forgive me if I judge rashly, but I think some plot is in hand. She trembles as an aspen-leaf if a door doth but shut or open with a sudden noise, or a bird flies across the sky. Her eyes have an uneasy glance, as if ever expectant of a new hap. Last night, when I was in bed, and, as she thought, asleep, what did she do but cut off a lock of my hair! I caught her hand, and, laughing, said, "Halte là, sweet thief; give me back my hair. I will have it encased in gold and richly jewelled, for a parting gift to thee."

But she answered, "Nay." She must have it then, and would not let it go. Soon afterwards I heard her sob.

"Foolish one!" I cried, throwing my arm round her neck, for she was now lying by my side, "foolish one! still to grieve for that Ferry."

"Nay," she replied in a low voice; "I grieve not for him to-night."

"What! hast thou then found a new lover?" I jestingly asked.

She started up as if stung by this light word. "Fie on thee, sister," she said, "to mock me in this wise!"

"Prithee, pardon me," I whispered, caressing her.

"Yea, a greater offence I must have forgiven thee this night," quoth she, hiding her face in her pillow.

What shall I do? I must needs soon decide. Agathe hath discovered to me the plot I did suspect. In the midst of the tournament this day, if my father is not warned, Ferry de Lorraine will carry off Yolande under the eyes of the assembled kings and princes. He will enter the lists with twelve knights in his train, one of whom is Agathe's kinsman, and challenge the knights of Anjou. Then, when the combat is at its height, and all eyes fixed on the champions, he will rush, by a sudden action, to the pavilion wherein we sit; and Yolande, who hath been used in old days to leap on to his charger, which for fleetness is unmatched, shall be borne, like another Helen, to the fortress of our foes. If I reveal this plot to the King, his anger will know no bounds. He will send Yolande to a convent, as he once threatened, and perhaps slay Ferry. Shall I cause her this terrible grief? or shall I suffer my father to be thus wronged? No; that should be impossible. This will I do. I will charge her to her face with this unseemly and rebellious intent, and procure, by remonstrances and threats, if needs be, that she shall herself refuse to leave the palace to-day.

My God! this is yet worse. She hath knelt at my

feet, her hair hanging disordered about her face, her
eyes full of tears, and her plight so piteous that any
one must needs have had compassion on her. She
caught hold of my hands and kissed them as one who
sues for life. O, not for her own life would the poor
soul have pleaded with so great urgency. But she
fears for him whom he doth so idolise; this hope,
she says, hath kept her alive since she was parted
from him; and that she will now die if it fails. And
if my father should kill him, she then would lose her
senses, and perhaps her soul. When I tried to reproach her, the blood crimsoned in her cheek, and
she said with so much of pride as became her well,

"Sister, I am no truant daughter, or love-sick maiden
parted from a new lover, but an affianced wife, who will
never break her plighted troth."

Then relapsing into tears, she wrung her hands and
cried,

"You have seen his noble carriage; you have never
yet seen his comely visage. You have witnessed his
prowess; you have not known his tender heart. He
cherished me when I was a little child, and had no need
to woo me when I became a maiden; for the love of
the child changed not as years went on, but waxed
larger as the heart that held it."

Finally she clasped her hands together, and in a
mournful manner exclaimed,

"Marguerite, this is the first time one has sued to
thee in deep anguish. Peradventure thou wilt thyself
one day kneel and sue for like mercy at the feet of one
who shall hold thy weal and woe in his hands. O, be
merciful now, as thou wouldest then have mercy shown
on thee. If now thou breakest my heart, a dark
shadow shall fall on thy bridal."

These words pierced my heart, but shook not my

resolve. Never could I brook, not if she was to have died at my feet, that aught of shame and disgrace should rest on my father's house; so I left her and sought the King, and there fought a battle which hath left me weary, but exulting. This is the second great triumph I have obtained since my fourteenth birthday. O, with what impassioned vehemence I urged on my father that, as his parting benison on a child most loved, his favourite since her natal hour, he should yield his consent to Yolande's marriage with Ferry de Vaudémont! Refusal on refusal he uttered; and still I pleaded, urged; and at last, when imperious prayers, tender reproaches, and bursting tears, which most did move, but not yet conquered him, had been exhausted, I broke forth:

"Sire, I have in my keeping a secret which closely touches your honour, if unrevealed; and yet here I do swear that naught shall rend it from me if you grant not my suit."

At first he was angered at this threat; but methinks something in my eyes, which I ween flashed with no common fire, bewitched him, for he cried, half in passion, half in jest,

"Avaunt, thou resistless witch; avaunt!"

And then I threw my arms round his neck, and would not take off my eyes from his struggling face till he had smiled and consented.

Ah! who shall resist Marguerite d'Anjou?

'Tis a marvel to me that the victory of this day should have cost so much labour; for no sooner was it achieved than, with the pliable spirit and natural contentment which belongeth to my father's temper, he surrendered in one short hour the hatred which had seemed so fierce. Like a weed which hath no root, it was loosed from the soil of his heart. And, moreover, his fondness for romance changed as by a magic wand the whole colour of his thoughts. When he heard that Ferry de Lorraine was the unknown knight which had gained so great a repute in the lists, he commended the bold lover; and, methinks, would not then have exchanged this son-in-law for any sovereign in Europe. I admire that what seemed like an oak of firm resolve should prove a mere sapling. Ah me! what a change hath twelve hours wrought! There is Yolande, the most happy person in the whole world, beaming with smiles which sometimes turn to laughter, sometimes turn to laughter, sometimes from very excess of joy to tears; and I see my father from this window leaning on the arm of the hated Ferry, in as kinsmanslike, yea and paternal a fashion, as could be thought of. And she who hath procured this happiness for others, what aileth her to-day? Is she not so contented with her fate as some days ago? Hath the sight of Yolande's happiness made her misdoubt if to be a queen should be the greatest joy on earth? No; I love my kindred; I love France; I love youth's memories, but far more greatness.

CHAPTER X.

An Ending and a Beginning.

November 15th, 1444.

THREE leagues from Nancy! a short space to traverse; but how long in respect of the past and the future, which it seemeth to divide! Here, where we are halting to rest, my dear uncle the King of France hath parted with me. O sire, you embraced me many times with exceeding great affection, and your eyes were full of tears when you said, " I seem to have done nothing for you, my niece, in placing you on one of the first thrones of Europe; for it is hardly worthy of possessing you." O sweet uncle and most noble king, if I should forget your love and goodness, may none in this her native land remember Marguerite d'Anjou whilst she lives, or pray for her when she dies.

I cannot restrain my tears; grief overflows the limits set to it. I did not weep this morn when my mother kissed me for the last time; but now, like a surprised citadel, my courage surrenders.

Barr, November 16th.

Disseverance of hearts most tenderly attached, how doleful is the suffering you inflict! My father is gone! When he clasped me to his breast, he said nothing; nor could my lips utter the word farewell. But I know that in that final moment he commended me to God with as hearty a prayer as the most passionate paternal

love could frame. I followed him with my eyes as long
he was in sight, but he never once turned round to
look at me. Monseigneur de Calabre and the Duc
d'Alençon yet ride with me. Soon none but the English will have charge of their queen.

Mantes, March 18th, 1445.

Four months which it ill pleaseth me to think of,
have passed since I wrote in this book. Heavens!
that lack of money should prevent a monarch from
receiving his bride! Is this credible? and if credible,
honourable? What a stubborn, disloyal race these
islanders must be, that they lay not their wealth at
their sovereign's feet at such a time, and sue to him to
accept it! I admire that these proud lords should be
so mean as to withhold from their king what his
necessities demand. I have seen the brave Provençal
nobles and the lieges of Lorraine and Anjou, even
when their provinces have been ravaged and well-nigh
destroyed, force gold on King René, and sell their
jewels to aid him. It makes me mad to hear these
Englishmen say that King Henry writes letters to the
Goldsmith's Company, to *entreat* them, forsooth, to do
their devoir at the coming of his wife, and the like to
others of those mean companies to sue for money,
that he may have the means to espouse and crown his
consort as befits his royalty. If the King did not
himself grieve at my delayed coming, which I think
he does, I had ere now dispatched a messenger to the
Kings of France and Sicily, to crave to be restored to
their keeping and peradventure wedded to the Comte
de Nevers. But now we are at Mantes, and hopes
arise that in a few days we shall embark. The lord
regent, the Duke of York, is here. We sup with him
to-night, *at his own cost*, I heard from Monsieur

Brecknock, our treasurer, who informed me thereof, with no small glee. Verily that good man's *computus* is his religion: he sets more store, I ween, on a ducat than on an Agnus Dei.

Mantes, March 19th.

The Duke of York hath entertained me with exceeding great courtesy. He is noble in aspect, graceful in manner, pleasant in discourse. After supper yestereve, he sent for his son to kiss my hand. This little Earl of March, now three years of age, is a very fair child, of a white and pink complexion, such as is not seen in France. My Lord King Henry hath restored this prince to his rank and dignities, and from Earl of Cambridge made him Duke of York. He said at dinner to-day that he, Richard Plantagenet, owed so great a debt of gratitude to his king, that nothing could exceed it, nor life be long enough to give tokens thereof.

Vernon, March 21st.

Last evening Lady Suffolk conversed with me some time, and the theme of our discourse was her cousin, the Lord Cardinal Beaufort. She says he is a prelate, of great virtue, and so entirely attached to the King and contented with his marriage, that he will be ready on all occasions to aid me with his counsel. I answered to this speech that my best adviser should be the King himself. Whereupon she replied that albeit his majesty had an excellent wit and discretion, he was not always so resolved in his thinking as could be wished; or, if in thinking he excelled, in the doing thereof, he sometimes did hesitate. She added, that some of the English nobles, were so adverse to good government, so turbulent in their humours, and the Duke of Gloucester so great an enemy to me, that an experienced counsellor like unto my Lord Cardinal would be very needful to my young years, and assist me to defeat their machinations.

Rouen, March 23d.

I am forced to borrow money, which chafeth me not a little. It is an insupportable thing that I should be constrained to solicit of the English lords of my suite means wherewith to reward trifling services, which Monsieur Brecknock will not requite; like when the poor mariners which rowed us across the Seine to-day cried "largesse" as I passed, after he had paid them a niggardly fare. I have pledged my vessels of mock silver to the Duchess of Somerset for a few pieces of gold. I am not a little angered at the talk which is ministered amongst my attendants touching my expenditure. I bought at Mantes fourteen pairs of shoes, which I bestowed on poor bare-footed women on the road. Jean Brecknock misliked this purchase, and said it would be no easy matter to find money for the remainder of my journey. If I *am* a queen, I will noways brook this usage. Had poverty been my choice, I would have elected, like St. Isabel, the sister of St. Louis, to live a bare-footed nun of the Order of St. Francis; but to be styled your Majesty, and yet denied a few pieces of gold wherewith to give alms, is too base a condition for one of my house and heart.

Honfleurs, April 3d.

Day followeth day, and yet England's coast, like unto a delusive mirage, mocks my hopes. But patience, proud heart! Naught of greatness can be achieved without it.

Honfleurs, April 8th.

Now the ship is in sight. To-night we shall embark.

O sea most wild and rough, and all unlike the blue one which is seen at Naples and in Provence, prithee be merciful to day! Surge and roar, if thou wilt,— thy ups and downs I can endure; but let thy rude arms carry me to my husband and my kingdom. Winds, adverse and strong, abate your violence! Clouds, black and dense, disperse! Time, pass swiftly! To-morrow I shall see England.

Here the writing ended in the early portion of the Queen's journal, which she gave to me, Margaret de Roos, at Southampton. She ceased for some time to write on her tablets, fearing methinks to disclose in this wise her thoughts in England, lest any should by surprise discover them; or it may be she lacked leisure for this employment. I then took up the pen, being unwilling that her majesty's actions should be unrecorded, or those discourses forgotton which she at sundry times held with me in the first years of her marriage. Events which appertain to mine own history and that of persons I have known, both in mine own country and in France, are sometimes involved in this narrative. What through the course of time has thus been joined together, I find no reason to dissever; and it hath also happened that when letters have been written to me relative to these haps, and profitable for future history or present edification, I have likewise inserted them in this manuscript.

'THE LADY MARGARET DE ROOS'S NARRATIVE.

On the 21st of April the Queen rode from Southampton to Tichfield Abbey, where the King was to espouse her on the morrow. None but a cold and disloyal heart had been unmoved, I ween, when the cavalcade approached the convent-gate, and that long-looked-for meeting was at hand. I could not restrain my eyes from watching the Queen's visage as we drew nigh to the portal. Her colour came and went; but I saw she was resolved to preserve a composed demeanour. She beheld the King standing on the threshold, with my lord the Cardinal by his side. He came forward to receive her, and she bent the knee with a wifely reverence and so sweet a grace, that all who witnessed it must needs have admired that one so young should join so much dignity with humility in the same action. She was, I think, struck at once, less with any ordinary majesty (if two such opposite words can agree) in the King's countenance than by a subduing gentleness, which few can see unmoved. He quickly raised the lovely lady, saying, "St. John, this should not be!" and in a loving fashion saluted her. Then taking her by the hand, he led the way to the chapel through the cloisters, and those that were near them heard him say:

"Fair wife, God our Lord hath been so bountiful in the giving of thee to me, that I would fain offer up thanks to Him, if it please thee, before we further converse."

She assenting, they approached the altar, and the *Te Deum* was sung. The Lord Cardinal afterwards said some prayers; and I noticed that the King's eyes never wandered from the crucifix; but not the like of the Queen's, which sometimes glanced with curiosity at more objects than one. Afterwards they walked in the garden of the Abbey, and sat down on a bench in the pleasaunce, where all their suite could see them discoursing for an hour with great mutual contentment.

When the Queen had dismissed her women that evening, she sent for me to read to her, as I had been wont to do since her illness at Southampton; but before I had opened the book she said,

"I was thinking of Pope Gregory the Great."

"Truly, madame," I answered, "your majesty's thoughts do always, I well know, run on greatness; but what should bring that holy pontiff to your mind at this time I am ignorant to discern."

She laughed, and replied,

"Where hath your wit fled to? Did not St. Gregory cry, when he saw the British captives, 'Non Angli, sed angeli'?"

"Ah! even so," I exclaimed smiling, for now I perceived her drift. "The King's aspect is not English but angelic."

She bent her beautiful head assenting, and bade me read; but soon stopped me to ask if the King's eyes were not of a darker blue, in my thinking, than his picture had represented, and if he was not taller than she had been told. Then she broke forth in praises of my Lord Cardinal, and said she had found him most excellently disposed towards her; that he was, she doubted not, very wise and holy, and had an excellent understanding. He and the Duke of Somerset and my Lord Suffolk would always be her very good friends. The King, she thanked God, had greatly commended them as his well-beloved kinsmen and trusty counsellors. "He did not say one word of that hateful Duke of Gloucester," she added, who is my enemy."

The royal marriage was a fair sight; and for beauty, sweet piety, and mutual contentment, no wedded pair could surpass King Henry and his bride. The days which followed their union were as bright and blissful as the most loyal hearts could desire. Her majesty's loveliness enchants all beholders, and what her aspect promises, her speech fulfils. Even the Lady Isabel Butler is obliged to own she is fair, and the courtiers cry out that Marguerite is not Queen of England only, but also of love and beauty. Through her early majesty of mien and haviour girlhood sometimes pierces. She exclaims now and again, " Mesdames, I am more contented to be my lord Henry's wife than to be the Queen of England; but nevertheless I am most contented that he is a king, and I his queen."

His majesty wedded her with the ring with which he was sacre'd at Paris; a fine one, garnished with rubies, the Lord Cardinal's gift. She was pressing her lips on it one day as I was standing near her, and catching my eye at that moment, with a look of joy the most enchanting that could be seen, she exclaimed, " I have no reason now to envy Yolande. The most enamoured peasant youth dotes not on his bride more than my king on me; the most lovelorn knight of fairyland worships not the lady of his thoughts more than England's monarch his queen; and Ferry's passion of twelve years is surpassed by three days of King Henry's wedded love."

When it was my turn to ride by her side, she would point to the shady groves and verdant slopes, and say, " The colour of England is green; and poets say that signifies hope." When we passed a meadow starred with daisies, " The King," quoth she, " declares the fields do emulate his nobles and knights, which in their bonnets of estate do wear my emblem flower. These smiling meads, he agreeably says, display the same token of loyalty to his Marguerite."

It is true that there is now none of both sexes and all ranks which doth not delight to wear the daisy for her. From the towns on the way issue noble companies of lords and esquires to do homage to their sovereigns. Her majesty was a little angered on one of these occasions. Of all the gifts she had received since her coming to England the one which most pleased her was a young lion, which at Basingstoke, where we lay one night, a gentleman presented to her. She said it was the cognisance of her house, and a right princely gift, which she would fain retain in her household; and the royal beast, being yet young, would be tamed, she doubted not, and would prove in time as tractable as a dog. But none of her suite would take charge of this favourite, and it was carried to the Tower of London by two keepers.

Monsieur L'Escosse, a squire of the King of Sicily, who accompanies the Queen, quarrelled with Mr. Brecknock because he complained that he had to pay 2*l.* 5*s.* 3*d.* for the carriage and food of this lion. These Provençals take umbrage at the poverty of our King, as if their own sovereign was not the most needy prince in Europe. The Queen admires that his majesty should lack wealth when so great riches are to be found in England. When the rain compelled us to take refuge in a small hostelry between Basingstoke and Guildford, I heard her say to M. de Serrecourt, one of the French gentlemen in her suite, " Messire, see you not in this country a man, howsoever poor and humble he may be, serves his table with silver dishes and drinking-cups ? The vessels of silver in this parlour would not disgrace the house of a French noble."

" Yea, madame," the Frenchman replied, "and there is not a parish church, I perceive, nor a convent, no not one of mendicant friars, but possesses crucifixes, candlesticks, censers, and cups of gold and silver.

These English religious houses are more like baronial houses than monasteries."

The King and Queen attended Mass every morning, and each time made an offering for the poor of a gold angel. They say the office of Our Lady together in a low voice, and each time they pass a church dismount and pray for a short space.

At Greenwich their majesties lodged at the Duke of Gloucester's palace. His highness came to meet them with five hundred men wearing his livery and badge, and many watched with eager eyes the behaviour of the Queen and of the Duke when he saluted her. In the visage of the one was to be seen a defiant courtesy; in the other an undisguised haughtiness which it pained me to behold. The marked favour shown to the Beauforts by her Grace even in the Duke's own palace must needs offend him. Monseigneur Gilles de Bretagne, who conversed with me awhile that night, said he feared this would confirm the Duke in his ill-will to her majesty, and that a more dangerous enemy could not exist. When I saw the Queen afterwards, she said, "It mislikes me to sleep under this roof."

"Ah, madame," I had the boldness to answer, "would that your majesty exercised the witching power God hath given you to conjure hatred ere you depart! Methought I saw anger and admiration in the Duke's face struggling for mastery; and who can foresee the haps which may ensue if resentment is kept alive?"

"Be not afraid," her Grace replied; "I am already mistress of the King's heart, and fear neither duke nor earl." Then she gazed on the Thames, and a proud smile lighted up her face. "How majestic," she exclaimed, "is this broad river! and how noble these ships we see yonder! These are the bulwarks of our kingdom—the wooden fortresses of this mistress of the seas; this small island—small in size, but great in power. England is like me," she said, turning to a mirror; "not very large, but capable, I ween, of ruling the world if it lists."

"Madame," I replied, "M. de Serrecourt ascribes our country's greatness to a quality which, if I may stand excused for the thought, is not peradventure as eminent in your majesty as some others."

"I misdoubt there is a malicious intent in this speech, Madame de Roos," the Queen answered with a smile. "What is that good quality which is an element of greatness in that gentilhomme's thinking?"

"Madame, when we came from the cathedral at Winchester on Sunday this monsieur said to Monseigneur Gilles, who repeated it to me: 'Ah, my prince, I have now discovered why the English conquer our provinces, and are so puissant, though they are not more brave, and have less wit than the French.' 'What is your discovery?' quoth the prince. 'Alas, Monseigneur, their patience is so great. Monsieur de Wicestre preached one whole hour and half another, and they endured this long sermon without complaint. When hath it been heard of that a French preacher found so great fortitude in his hearers?'"

Her majesty laughed, and said she was somewhat of the same opinion as her countryman, and that also the long prayers of the English exceeded her ability.

From Greenwich to Westminster triumphal arches were erected, and various pageants performed, to the Queen's great comfort and that of such as came with her. She exclaimed several times, "I would my father could see these ingenious devices and scenic displays; for nothing would give him greater content than this ingenious welcome to his daughter." All the magistrates of London and the crafts of the same came riding on horseback in blue gowns, with embroidered sleeves and red hoods, to escort her into the City, which was beautified with fine hangings, and enlivened with sumptuous shows. Justice and Peace kissed each other at the bridge of Southwark. Noah's ship was on the river. At Leadenhall a speech was made by Madame Grace, the Chancellor of God. At the Cornhill St. Margaret recited an ode. At the great conduit at Cheapside the Wise and Foolish Virgins greeted the Queen; and at the Cross at Charing Cross the New Jerusalem was pictured. The French gentlemen smiled at some of these pageants. I could hear them commend in a low voice those of their own country, where, in their opinion, of late years more graceful and erudite fashions have prevailed, and heathen gods and goddesses are set forth in place of saints and angels, which methinks is a bad exchange, and very unchristian. Monsieur l'Escosse says all things are sad in England: the skies, the visages, and even the sports; and that these last seem duties rather than pastimes.

On the day the Queen arrived at the palace in Westminster the chief persons in the State and the Court came to pay her their devoirs; the Duchess of Bedford amongst others. She conversed some time with her majesty in a very agreeable fashion, and commended to her with many adroit speeches Mistress Woodville, her daughter. She said it was the greatest contentment to her in the world that this young lady was attached to the Queen's service, and that for this favour which had been shown to her she, the Duchess, was the most indebted person in England to her majesty's goodness. But I see that the Queen, albeit much entertained by this royal lady's pleasant conversation, mislikes so much her marriage as a degrading thing to one of her birth, that she is not, I think, favourably inclined to Mistress Elisabeth, who she says is neither fish nor fowl. The Lord Cardinal, the Bishop of Bath and Wells, and the Provost of Eton, discoursed with the King in the evening. Before their majesties retired to rest prayers were said in the chapel.

CHAPTER XI.

Floreat Etona!

"FLOREAT ETONA!" How sweetly those two fair words flowed from the lips of England's young Queen as she stood in front of the noble college which her lord the King built for the honour of God's holy name, the increase of virtue, the dilation of cunning, and the establishment of the Christian faith! A loud cry of greeting burst from the collegers and the crowd assembled to receive "La Belle Marguerite" on this her first visit to our Lady of Eton. The boys all wore daisies in their hats. The sky and the earth both seemed to smile on her. The ancient gray towers of Windsor, the newly-erected college's fane, the meadows studded with gold and yellow flowerets, the old trees of the playing-fields, the broad river, its little boats, and the glad faces of the young scholars, were all lighted up by the broad sunshine, and welcome writ on every countenance, every leaf, and every sail; each waving blade of grass looked to be cheering her as she passed, and I fancied I heard the words, "Long live the Queen!" resounding in the bells of the old church of St. Marie.

The most renowned and noble scholars surrounded

their majesties, and conversed with them in the cloisters of the college, paying their devoirs to the lady Queen, whose learning and ready wit they all marvelled at. When Lord Talbot approached, who a few days before had made the King and her an offering of the most finely painted missal yet seen in England, she said :

" My lord, this fair sky we see reminds me of your rare gift, wherein the blue of each oriel is of a like hue; but this natural roof above our heads lacketh at present the rich ornament of gold stars which stud your book."

Then to my Lord of Worcester, who hath been a pilgrim to the Holy Land, from whence he brought curious manuscripts to Oxford, she addressed this speech :

" My lord, you kiss our hand; methinks we should kiss your feet, which have touched the soil which Christ our Lord did tread on. As we cannot follow your example and become pilgrims to God's sepulchre, we will leastways crave such a recital of your pious travel as shall move us to devout envy. I have been told that Oxford owes precious treasures of Eastern lore to your munificence."

" Not one half so indebted is Oxford to me, madame," the Earl replied, " as to others now in your presence. My Lord of Gloucester hath endowed that seat of learning with not less than 264 volumes."

" Ah! a right royal gift," said the Queen; but on her face I saw a cloud rising, and without any compliment to the Duke, who was about to address her, she turned to Master Waynfleet, the Provost of Eton:

" Your name, Monsieur, is so often on the King's lips—from the abundance of the heart the mouth speaketh " (this she said in Latin)—" that if so evil a passion as jealousy should enter my heart, methinks you would be the object of it. When we visited Winton College, his majesty told me Master Waynfleet, its former master, was his most dearly beloved friend and helper in all things. This title I will no longer suffer your reverence to enjoy, or we shall be foes."

This was said with a playful smile, and in a truly gracious fashion. The holy man to whom these words were addressed, thus answered:

"I pray God, madame, his majesty shall find in your grace so great comfort that he shall never need any other for his worldly honour or his soul's health."

"But we both do need the friendship and aid of those who love us," the Queen replied, glancing round the circle which encompassed them, and fixing her dark orbs in turn on each person present; with almost filial affection on the Cardinal, with engaging confidence on the lords which she counted to be her friends, with a gracious winningness on those she had a scanty knowledge of, and with a defying lightning-like flash, which I have never seen in any eyes but hers, on the Duke of Gloucester's countenance, which had waxed each moment more lowering since her abrupt turning from him to Master Waynfleet. Whilst she looked at him she added these words to her speech, in a voice loud enough, I think, for him to hear, "Yea, of those who love us against those which hate us."

God save the Queen from making enemies! Even this Duke might be won to a liking for her, so matchless are her attractions, if she displayed not her girlish rancour unrestrainedly; lavishing in his presence marks of favour on his foes, not so much apparently to honour them as to goad him to anger. Like others, he had worn a daisy that day; but I saw him before long remove it from his breast, and casting it on the floor, set his foot on it.

As the royal train advanced towards the church, the Queen said to the King, "Sire, which is most dear to you—Oxford, or this new college?"

"Sweet wife," the King replied, "Oxford is my mother, at whose breasts I sucked learning under the nursing care of his Eminence my dear uncle, and his Grace of Bath and Wells" (the King turned to the two prelates with a grateful smile). "But Eton," he added, "is my child, whom I in turn nourish with the wholesome furnishing of devout instructions and profitable teaching."

"What did my lord of Warwick, the brave Lord Beauchamp, learn you, sire?" said the Queen.

"Endurance under heavy chastisement, sweetheart," answered the King, smiling. "His loyalty was evinced by many a severe lashing; loathed at the time, but now gratefully remembered. God rest his noble soul!"

The Queen sighed somewhat impatiently, I thought, and then said, "And when thought you first, sire, of building this church and college?"

"Before I was eighteen," replied the King. "At the commencement of my riper years, when I took in hand the government of both my kingdoms, I diligently considered after what fashion or by what kingly gift I might do fitting honour to our Lady, so that the great Head of the Church, her Son, might therein be pleased; and whilst I thought of these things with inward meditation, it became fixed in my heart to found this college."

"It was a great and good thought, sire," quoth the Queen, as they went into the church, the beauty of which, albeit unfinished, ravishes the eyes and draws the soul towards God. The orient colour and painted imagery of the windows, which are the work of the cunning artists of Southwark; the vaulted roof and the quaint carvings, the many altars, the fair stone image of Blessed Mary, the scutcheon of arms emblazoned everywhere with three silver lilies on sable ground, betokening constancy and purity, attracted the Queen's notice and moved her to admiration.

Before they left the church their majesties offered an alms for the support of the college buildings, and the expulsion of infidels, whereby those which visit our Lady of Eton may gain an indulgence. Then issuing from the church, they visited the large hall for reading and disputation, the goodly devised conduits in the midst of the quadrangle; and nothing would serve the King but to conduct the Queen also to the pantry and buttery, the bakehouse and the breadhouse, and the square court for wood and other such-like stuff, which he had with his own thinking provided for his dear scholars' comfort.

"For I would have all things," he said, "edified of the most substantial and best abiding stuff that can be had, clean and in large form, setting apart superfluity of too great curious works of entail and busy moulding."

At the collation, which was served in the college hall, talk was ministered of the great uses of this college; and the Bishop of Bath and Wells told the Queen how the King had laboured for them now many years to achieve this foundation, and spent many hours in the day and in the night in prayer on his knees, with sighs and tears, commending it to God; and ridden sundry times to Winton, there to confer with Master Waynfleet, and study the ordinances of the great Bishop Wykeham, and examine the boys one by one and the masters, till he had drawn up statutes for Eton.

The Queen said she liked well the device of the scutcheon everywhere to be seen on the walls, gates, and buttresses — a sable shield, with three fair silver lilies. She trusted that, like those of the knights in battle, it should ever excite these young students to most fair and valiant deeds.

"Yea," the Bishop replied, "if it please God, Eton shall always endure a memorial of the King's holy zeal. Its sable shield betokening endurance should move these young scholars to send up by their holy living a perpetual sweet savour before Angels and before men, and the white bright flower set thereupon engrave on their hearts the most fair image of Blessed Mary, their mother and mistress."

When the sun began to decline, their majesties descended to the playing-fields, where the scholars were making merry in honour of the King's bridal, and sundry sports were carried on, and boat-races not a few. A goodly company that evening assembled on the margin of the Thames, joylity seemed to prevail in all hearts. But some of those about the Court were not of very good cheer, I ween; the Duke of Gloucester had craved leave to return to London, for news had reached him of an embassage from France.

"St. John!" the King exclaimed, after he had departed, "this toucheth thee nearly, sweet wife. I would these ambassadors had arrived in time to witness thy crowning and the grand tournament at Westminster; but an old Saxon proverb teacheth that 'better is late than never;' and so these envoys of thy father and uncle shall be most welcome; and mine uncle of Gloucester will ordain that a meet reception be prepared for so worthy guests."

"Sire," quoth the queen hastily, "his Eminence the Lord Cardinal, or the Duke of Somerset, or even my Lord Suffolk, should be more fitly charged with this duty. If you love me, sire, let not the Duke of Gloucester have the ordering of this matter."

I heard not the King's answer, but the contentment visible on the Queen's face betokened consent. To be refused what she desires and to be contented, is an impossible thing to her majesty. Lady Isabel Butler is no friend to the Queen. She notices each cloud on her brow; and if it be as small a one even as a man's hand, like that the prophet saw in time of drought, straightway she draws omens therefrom of gloomy import. I would she was banished from the Court; but her friends are so powerful, it should be a dangerous thing to warn the Queen against her. She was angered at Eton because the Queen called me to her side in the playing-fields to make a chain of daisies for the cap of little John de la Pole, the youngest of the Oppidans.

Then there gathered round the throne, which had been erected for their majesties to witness the games, the sons of the noblemen and esquires which were known by name to the King—young Lord Robert de Hulme, Richard de la Warr, Simon Digby, Edward Beaufort, and many others. The Queen entertained herself by asking them questions, in not very good English always, but which, broken as it was, sounded pleasantly on her lips. Thus she catechised them. To one she said:

"At what o'clock rise you, messire?"

"At five in the morning, madame, the præpositor's *Surgite* resounds in the dormitory."

Then to another:

"What prayers do you say?"

"Before the time of the High Mass in the church we say the Lord's Prayer five times in the burial ground or the cloister; and after each prayer a decade of Angelic salutations, with a Credo in confession of the Christian faith. We recite every day the whole Psalter of the Blessed Virgin."

"What! fifteen Paters and one hundred and fifty Aves?"

"Yea, madame, unless we say the Little Office instead."

"Have you made your first Communion, my Lord Robert?"

"No, madame, but on next Thursday I shall, if it please God, and watch the Sepulchre that night."

Then Master Digby said,

"The scholars which have been to Communion sit at a table apart from the others, and have better fare that day, at the expense of the college."

"Wherefore is it thus ordained?" the Queen asked.

"To honour those," the boy quickly replied, "whom the Lord Himself hath honoured with a visit. They are also permitted to go and walk alone in the fields."

"Indeed!" said the Queen; "and for what purpose?"

"To entertain themselves, I ween, with the great Guest they have received in their hearts," was the ready answer. "On Easter Sunday morning we rise early to greet the day and see the sun rise."

Then the Queen said to young Beaufort,

"Art thou a diligent scholar, Master Edward?"

"Madame," the youth replied, "I have not once been flogged on Fridays for remissness in study; and I have won this year the second prize for Latin verses on All Souls' day."

"What was the theme, I pray you?"

"The blessedness of souls which depart in the faith of Christ. On the Feast of St. John the Baptist I made a song and a picture, which was hung in the dormitory framed with green boughs. Master Waynfleet showed it to the King."

"Can you speak Latin?"

"Yea, madame. For when the King cometh here he speaketh to all the boys he meets in Latin; and if they answer well, his majesty pats them on the head and says, *Sitis boni pueri, mites et docibiles, et servi Domini.* But I misdoubt, your majesty, being a woman, understands not Latin."

"Nay, nay," cried the Queen, laughing; "Antoine de la Salle hath not so ill-tutored me, that I should lack a certain knowledge thereof. But methinks your life at Eton is made up of prayers, Latin, and flogging; for naught else have you told me of."

"O, if your majesty careth for pastimes, she should come to Windsor Forest on a Holy Cross day, when we go out nutting; or on the Fast of St. Philip and St. James, when, if the weather be fair, we may rise at four and go and gather branches of May, so that we wet not our feet; and then we make the house odoriferous with green herbs, and adorn the windows with fair boughs. But mind you, madame, we must needs write verses before these playdays on the fertility of Autumn, or the sweet vernal time of May."

"Gramercy for the information," said the Queen, smiling. "And how keep you carnival time?"

"O, on Shrove Tuesday the cook fastens a pancake to an old crow, which is the rarest pastime imaginable; and on St. Peter's day we have bonfires."

"Will your majesty come to Eton on the next Shrove Tuesday?" a little boy asked; at which the Queen laughed, and said she would if the King pleased.

His majesty stood listening to this discourse with a pleased countenance, and he ended by calling to the foot of the throne some of the older students, which he presented to the Queen.

"These are the præpositors, madame," he said, "ordained by the provost to maintain order in the school. This is George Neville."

"What is your office, sir?" the Queen inquired.

"If it please your majesty, I keep watch in the dormitory."

"And thou, Anthony Woodville?" said the King.

"I in the school-hours," answered the boy.

"And thou, John Wenlock?" asked his majesty of a fair-haired youth of fifteen years of age.

"I am Moderator Aulæ," he replied, "and keep order in the refectory."

"And thou, Ralph Butler?"

"I inspect the face and hands of each scholar, as he enters, sire, to see they are clean."

"Ah, I commend this observance," exclaimed the Queen; "and I hope Eton College will ever prove a school famous for clean hands."

"And pure hearts," subjoined the King. And then he called several of the collegers, and spoke kindly to them, which was at all times his wont; for I have often heard that if he meets any of the students in Windsor Castle, whither they sometimes go to visit his servants whom they know, on ascertaining whom they are, he admonishes them to follow the paths of virtue, and gives them money to win over their goodwill.

When their majesties rose to depart, my little cousin William Paston came to my side, and whispered in mine ear; which the Queen observing, nothing would serve her but to learn what the youngster desired of me.

"An it please your majesty," I said, "he craveth

that I do despatch to him a box of figs and raisins by the next barge from London, and to remind his brother John, when I see him, to send him eighteenpence wherewith to buy a pair of slippers."

The Queen smiled, and said Master Paston should have from her the largest box of fruit and the fairest slippers London could show, as he was the kinsman of her sweet namesake—for so her goodness named her poor servant who writeth this.

The sun was setting when their majesties entered their barge. The sky was then more lovely than the earth; and the red crimson clouds beautified the river, which shone as if on fire with that reflected light. The King began to talk with the Queen in French, not knowing or else not heeding, that I understood this language.

"Sweetheart," he said, as the boat glided on the smooth water, "a river puts me always in mind of the voyage of life to the sea of eternity. Methinks our joint travel to that blissful ending is as like to be a happy one as any on earth."

"Yea," answered the Queen; "mutual love and the possession of one of the greatest thrones in the world promise happiness, if it is to be attained before Paradise is reached."

"I could be happy with thee in any place where I could save my soul and do God's will."

"God's will, sire, is undoubtedly that you should reign happily, and therefore firmly, in this your fair kingdom. O, my very good lord, 'tis well to pray and to study; 'tis well to build holy fanes and learned retreats; for common men, but one half of what you, sire, have already achieved would be sufficient for the glory of a lifetime. But the son of King Henry V., the crowned monarch of England and France, can never be satisfied with the praises of churchmen and the love of schoolboys."

"St. John!" sweet wife! thou wouldst not have the war with France renewed, and the new bond of unity whereof thou art the link dissolved?"

"Not now, sire, not now, when your treasure is exhausted, your council divided; this is not the time to attack—"

"Thine uncle, and mine, Marguerite?"

"O, my lord, the dearest bond of kindred must be forgotten where the welfare of your subjects is concerned. Royalty has a special obligation akin to that which the Gospel speaks of when it bids those whom God calls in a special manner to hate father and mother, if needs be, for His sake. A king's sacre is, like the vow of religion, a solemn consecration. His subjects are his children; his greatness his country's greatness. He shall answer on the Day of Judgment to the Great Supreme King if in aught he hath unfaithfully discharged his high commission."

"God and St. John knoweth that from the day when on my seely brow in Paris the crown was placed, and the holy chrism flowed on my head, I have daily prayed to fulfil a king's duty, day by day examining my conscience in that regard. I would not wilfully wrong one creature on this earth, how much less my own people!"

"And yet, sweet King—"

"And yet what?"

"O, my lord, see you not that your most devoted friends, your more than father, the Lord Cardinal, the good Lord Suffolk, the gallant Somerset, are sacrificed to—"

"To whom, Marguerite? My favour hath been constantly shown to those good lords, who are indeed most deserving of it."

"Ah, but your grace banisheth not from your councils the Duke of Gloucester, their bitter foe—and mine."

"Thine! Hath my uncle dared—"

"O sire, he yieldeth outward homage to your Queen —he weareth the daisy in his breast; but if looks do ever speak what the tongue dareth not to utter; if cutting speeches, expressive of hatred to Lord Suffolk for his share in your majesty's marriage; if fears confided to others that his dominion in this realm shall cease if your grace loves King Charles's niece; if insults daily renewed and studied injuries inflicted on the good Cardinal—newly increased since he hath showed parental goodness to my poor self—denote hatred, then my Lord of Gloucester's enmity to me is proved."

"If I thought so—" the King said, greatly moved. "I have borne much from my uncle Gloucester. My childhood reverenced in him the appointed guardian of this realm; I displeased him in nothing, and studied his wishes. But as years advanced, his ambitious, worldly, and not very religious spirit often grieved me, O, I have suffered, yea, wept over the exhibitions of his hatred to the Cardinal, my most generous, kind and loving father in God. Often have I been from one to the other in years past, and with tears besought them to be reconciled, and not wound my heart by their divisions. Both wish me well, I ween. But if the Duke of Gloucester shows himself to be *thy* foe—"

"My lord and husband," quoth the Queen, "I will submit to your guidance. If your majesty desires that I should turn a deaf ear to the Cardinal's counsels, and my back on Lord Suffolk, who hath been my very good friend for so long a time, and be ruled by my Lord of Gloucester, then I will obey your grace, and so, it may be, obtain his friendship."

"St. John forbid!" the King hastily cried. "The Lord Cardinal, and all who bear the name of Beaufort, are our true friends. But naught will I do against the Duke of Gloucester till it is proved to me he is false. He cannot pardon his wife's shame and sufferings, and his temper since those sad haps hath grown stern and morose. God forgive those who dealt hardly with the accused, if aught moved them thereunto besides loyalty and justice. I would give the collar of St. George, and every jewel I yet possess, that that trial had not taken place, and the Duchess's two associates had not perished."

"Yet if they practised against your majesty's life they were righteously condemned."

"God knoweth! I often pray for their souls, and I would my uncle's wife had not been put to open shame in this realm. Yet if she was guilty, the sentence was a just one; for royalty should not shield Christians from open penance when they have sinned. If—which God forbid—I should commit an offence which gave open scandal, I would go to St. Paul's Church as a penitent in the eyes of all the people."

"God forbid!" echoed the Queen. I fear she thought then of the penance at least as much as of the sin.

CHAPTER XII.

Clouds at Home and Abroad.

THE Queen came into my chamber where I was writing in this book; and as I stood up, she said, "Prithee rise not from thy good task, which it liketh me well to see thee prosecute. If thou art a faithful chronicler, thou wilt set down that this year hath been the happiest I have yet known—great thanks to St. John, as my dear King would say. Hast thou described the day we went to Eton for the first time?"

"Yea, madame."

"And hast thou made mention of the reception of the French ambassadors on the 16th of July, and that the King told M. de Presigny that he did not hold them to be strangers, insomuch that they belonged to the household of his uncle of France, whom of all persons in the world, after me his wife, he loved the best, and that he desired the continuance of peace beyond anything on earth; and that they all said, 'Amen'?"

"Yea, madame; and I have likewise related how the King was seated in a very high chair of state, covered with tapestry of blue diaper, and dressed in a long robe of vermilion cloth-of-gold."

"O, I'll warrant thee, good Meg," the Queen said laughing, "to record these details. I doubt not thou hast indifferently well described the hangings of gold of Damascus newly purchased by the Cardinal for my state chamber in his house at Waltham Forest, and the various costly furniture of my lodgings at Eltham, and Kew, and Windsor, not to speak of the Tower and this Palace of Westminster; but I often wish we were less magnificently lodged, and had more gold in our exchequer; for William Clive, the clerk of the works, says he has no money to pay the poor labourers their weekly wage, and has the utmost pain and difficulty to provide for them. If the Lord Cardinal was less generous, the King would have been, ay, and would still be, in exceeding great embarrassment. But, God be praised, his Eminence is as bountiful as he is rich."

"Ah, madame," I said, "his riches are often thrown in the teeth of his friends, as if it should be an unbecoming thing for a prelate to have so great wealth."

The Queen replied, "This great and good man is the most misjudged person in the world; for, I pray you, is it on himself he spends his wealth? Is not his own fare and his couch those of a poor man in the midst of his splendour? Doth he refuse at any time an alms to the poor? Doth he not adorn churches and found monasteries with his wealth? Doth he not assist the King in his necessities with a princely generosity? If he had not amassed gold, where, I pray you, would means have been found to save the dignity of the crown, to reward loyal services, to pension poor servitors? Ah, the greedy cormorants, the selfish spendthrifts! the King's false friends cry out against this our most loved friend and uncle; for they would fain clutch themselves what he holds but in trust for his King, for the poor, for the Church! The Duke of Gloucester would fain have kept the King in poverty; for then he would have ruled more absolutely in his stead, and abused his gentle nature by a rougher tyranny. I have no patience with that Duke. Each day yields to me some new knowledge of his old enmity to the Lord Cardinal, and his present one to me. He rivals the King in his people's affections; he displays opposite qualities to his. He maligns me in the minds of men. My happiness is great beyond my hopes; for when was a wife more supremely blessed by a husband's love, or a queen more esteemed by her consort, than I am, or blessed with more true friends? But the fabric of my joys would soon totter and fall if this Duke had his will. He burns with resentment that one of my young years thwarts his policy, checks his purposes, and humbles his pride. But not one inch will I yield to him; and his arrogant soul shall stoop to sue for pardon to the Lord Cardinal before this year is ended. Lady Suffolk and I often declare that should be the most happy day we could see."

"Madame and dear Mistress," I said, "if your goodness will suffer me to speak truly, I would fain conjure you to moderate the excess of your animosity against the Duke of Gloucester. God knoweth none of my kindred love the Duke; but he is powerful,—a favourite with the people."

"Therefore I hate him," exclaimed the Queen. "O, think you not, dear Meg, I perceive his cunning and the shrewd manner with which he throws the King in the shade? Whilst my lord Henry prays and reads, or rules his little kingdom of scholars at Eton, the Duke rides through London with a martial aspect and haughty carriage, which pleases the common people; and the cry, 'Long live the Duke of Gloucester!' reëchoes in the streets and pollutes the air I breathe, for I loathe his very name."

"No sovereign is more beloved," I said, "than the King."

"I know it," the Queen replied. "And who should

be more justly loved than he? Think you I worship not his holy virtues? the more reverently, I ween, because they are foreign to mine own too ardent nature. Heavens! is there on this earth a more saintly spirit, a more God-fearing prince, than King Henry? Those to whom his soul hath been an open book since the days of his infancy aver that no grave sin ever sullied his conscience. Like unto a pure lake which reflects no shadows, his mind receives no taint from evil examples; nor does an imperfect word escape his lips. And yet they are true words which the Cardinal said to me the last time I conversed with him alone at Waltham Forest. ' My niece, your husband has the virtues of a saint, and almost the nature of an angel; but the cunning which in these turbulent days is needful for a king he wholly lacks. Be it yours, to whom God hath given a manly understanding in a feminine garb, to supply this want, and to guard this saintly soul from the perils which excess of goodness conjures around you. On the stormy sea whereon you are embarked, be henceforward the pilot, and in your young hands take the helm which my aged ones must resign.' This is a solemn charge—the fate, the reign, the glory of the King committed to my inexperience! I must needs despair, if I possessed not devoted friends and counsellors with more of the world's knowledge than one of my sex and years can have attained. But Somerset, Suffolk, and Shrewsbury have sufficient wisdom and bravery to continue the Cardinal's long struggle with Gloucester, even if the Duke of York and the young Earl of Warwick espouse his interests."

Then the Queen left me, and I mused sorrowfully on her words; for I fear me the Lord Cardinal will no more come to court, and is not like to live long—

leastways this is the common report. He is shut up in his palace at Wolseley, and wholly given up to devout exercises, preparing for death. When he departs this life, alas! who shall counsel the Queen?

I have received a letter from Jeanne de Kersabiec, who was my bedchamber companion at Havering Bower, the contents of which have disturbed me not a little. After the death of the Queen Joan, our mistress, she returned to Brittany, and entered the household of her cousin, Madame Catherine de Rohan, wife of Messire Jacques de Dinant, the most wealthy lord in that province. She often writes to me, and absence hath noways diminished an affection which began when we were both little damsels and playmates of Monseigneur Gilles de Bretagne. I know not which loved him the most. When he was about ten years old he used to laugh at my English gravity and her French vivacity, and to call me "*Jean qui pleure*," and her "*Jean qui rit*." When he was a little older, he likened Jeanne to a sunny day, and me to a moonlight night. But I think we were more like unto two little planets revolving round one sun; for we had no brothers, and the affection young girls are accustomed to bestow on near relatives and close companions in childhood was wholly centred on this young prince. When we were alone together all our talk was of Monseigneur Gilles. We learnt little songs to please him when he came to Havering Bower. We decked his chamber with odoriferous herbs, and mingled thyme and lavender with the rushes on the floor. When he went hawking, Jeanne rode with him, and I sat by his side when he conned his lessons. If he was chastised, we both wept and offered to suffer in his place, and we loved one another the more because we both loved him so well. When afterwards he lived with the King at Windsor, only to hear his name or see it written was the greatest joy on earth to Jeanne and me. If one of us was in London, and only so much as once beheld him riding in the street, she forthwith wrote to the other how he was dressed, and the colour of his horse, and what favours he wore, and this would furnish a whole week's entertainment. A short time before his grandam's death he came to Havering Bower, and this was the last time we three were together, which had been so long playmates and friends. It was in September, and very hot for the time of year; too hot, Monseigneur thought, to shoot; but I knew this was an excuse, and that he liked best to sit in the shade in the garden and converse. It put him in mind, he said, of past pleasant days, and, "God knoweth," he added, "if in England we shall meet again." He took off his bonnet, and I fastened to it a piece of jessamine, which led him to discourse on flowers and their meanings. Poesy was always his delight, and when he repeated verses, his voice made the most indifferent lines sound musical. Hs asked Jeanne to sing with him one of the *Noëls* which the peasants in Brittany go about singing on Christmas nights. This air has a mournful cadence, which strangely tickles the ear. They had learnt it from their nurses, and in old years the Queen Joan often asked to hear it. When Jeanne had finished the last verse, and their joint voices sank into the dwindling final note, she sighed, and he said: "Ah, Jeanne! you are not '*Jean qui rit*' to-day."

This made her laugh, but the laugh ended in tears; only she hid her face in her kerchief. that he should not see she wept. We often disputed after that day which of us was the most like often to see Monseigneur Gilles again.

"Of a surety you," Jeanne said; "for when the Queen dies, and I go to Dinant to my cousin, I leave you to judge how like I shall then be to see the prince."

"Yea," I answered, "you will meet him at the Duke's court, whither he must one day return, and then you will speak together of England and poor Margaret de Roos."

This which I predicted may yet happen; for Jeanne is so great a favourite with Madame de Dinant that she parts not one day from her if she can help it, and has often carried her to Vannes; and this year to Guincamp, the castle of Monseigneur Pierre de Bretagne and Madame Françoise d'Amboise his wife; and this letter which I transcribe is partly written from that place:

Mademoiselle Jeanne de Kersabiec to the Lady Margaret de Roos.

"The Castle of Guincamp, 1446.

"SWEET MARGARET,—A merchant of Vannes who goes to Cherbourg will take this letter to a shipmaster, who will send it to London. My entirely beloved friend, among all earthly creatures I love you most; and to converse with you in this wise is the greatest earthly pleasure I can enjoy, since our sorrowful parting, seven years ago, after the silent and fearful conclusion of our Queen's long and grievous malady. Ah, how truly does her epitaph describe her as the joy of your land and the brightness of our own! But it is not of the dead but of the living I would now speak. My heart often reverts to England; but here, as you well know, new affections have arisen, which link themselves with those old ones by a thousand ties. Mostly dear to me is the little Françoise, my special charge and daily care. She is the most gracious creature in the world; and when she sits on the knees of her godmother Madame Françoise d'Amboise, you would think you saw St. Anne with the Blessed Mary on her lap.

"Heavens! how sweet and pleasant a home is this castle of Guincamp, and what rare lessons of virtue are here to be learned! Devotion excludes not joylity, nor piety wholesome diversions. A noble society of knights and ladies assemble here every day, of the most commendable in the neighbourhood. Whilst Monseigneur Pierre and his companions shoot and hunt, Madame Françoise, with their wives and daughters, sits spinning fine wool and making garments for the poor; and never so much as one wanton or malicious word is uttered in her presence. Then when the sun is setting, and the time approaches for her lord's return, the noble lady goes to the Porte de Rennes and there sits on a stone bench under the wall of the tower awaiting his coming. This seat is her audience-chamber. Thither flock the rich and the poor, nobles, artisans, and serfs, — all which have need of aid, counsel, or tenderness, and desire the sweet comfort of her benign words and gracious charity. This princess's good actions are so numerous, that time would fail if I tried to record them. The good Duchess Jeanne bequeathed naught to her when she died, except the beads, made of wood, of the holy man Vincent Ferrier. This heritage hath already prospered in her hands, and many, young as she is, hold her to be a saint."

"Dinant, February 5th.

"This letter, which I began to write three days ago to my well-beloved friend, I now continue in great trouble and sore grief. Alas! God our Lord hath suffered a mighty affliction to befall my poor cousin

Madame Catherine. Tidings have reached her of the mortal, 'tis to be feared, sickness of Messire Jacques her husband. She is all unfit to endure this great and sudden woe, for she never had much wit or courage, and she returned to Dinant almost beside herself with grief. All the way on horseback she lamented loudly her hard fate, and her tears fell like an abundant rain. 'Ah me!' she kept crying, 'what shall become of a hapless widow?' and with great demonstrations of grief tore her hair, and chid her little daughter if she said one word all the day.

"The end hath come. Messire Jacques is dead. God rest his soul! and from the paradise where soon it will ascend, may he watch over his child, which now slumbers by my side! Ah, poor unwitting damsel thou art now the most richly dowered maid in all Brittany, and peradventure in all France. No king's daughter now living will bring a husband so many towns and lands and money. Good Margaret, this leads me to seek thine aid in a weighty matter, wherein prudence is much needed. My cousin is almost distracted with the fear of a hap which would be to her the most grievous of all sorrows, and a disgrace to the houses of Dinant and Rohan. I have before this spoken in some of my letters of the duke's favourite, young Arthur de Montauban, than which there exists not one man in the whole world, I think, of more consummate art and more desperate wickedness. His greed for riches knows no limits; nor are there any bounds, I fear, to his influence over his master. If this hawk should pounce on our dove, —and that he hovers with evil intent over her nest is too evident,—God shield her! for no lesser power than His shall save her from his clutches. One human hope alone I can discern. If a noble eaglet

bars his approach and rescues this innocent prey, the
arch deceiver may yet be foiled. Monseigneur Pierre
conversed a few days before his death with Messire
Jacques, and spoke of the ill usage our Monseigneur
Gilles has experienced from his brother the duke.
The poor inheritance bequeathed to him, the domains
of Ingrande and Chantocé, are contested by the King
of France; and he is the poorest prince in Europe,
who, if justice existed, would be one of the richest.
Monseigneur Pierrè said he would fain see him re-
trieve his fortunes by marriage, or in any other lawful
manner. Whereupon Messire Jacques straightway
offered his daughter's hand to the prince for his
brother, who with gracious words thanked him, and
gave him many assurances that no marriage would
be so agreeable to his wife and himself as the one he
proposed, and that he would broach the matter to
the duke. Since her husband's death, my cousin has
secretly written to the Prince Pierre on this subject;
and in his answer he says that his liking for this
match is as great as ever, but that from some words
of his brother the Duke Francis, he perceives him to
be wholly averse to it, which is not credible, except
the arts of his favourite have poisoned his mind towards his brother. If Monseigneur Gilles was here,
then methinks Monseigneur Pierre would certainly befriend him, and the Constable de Richemont also. If
through the Queen of England, or by direct communi-
cation with the prince himself, thou canst move
him, good Margaret, to come here without delay,
there shall be hopes of a happy issue. In his absence
naught can be effected. The noblest love on earth
is that which forgets its own desires and private joys,
and only cares for the honour and the happiness of
the object of its affections. Bethink thee, dear friend,

how we were wont of yore to plan little surprises for Monseigneur. I saved sometimes the fruit which fell to my share, and laid it on green leaves in his favourite bower, to regale him. And thou didst often write his lessons for him to copy at night, when he returned from the chase, and had no mind to con them himself. Now that time has lapsed, other self-denying proofs of affection are required.. This fair little maiden, whom I school in pleasant knowledge and sweet behaviour, shall, if it please God, become his wife and enjoy his love. And if by thy means he is informed of this good fortune which awaits him if he is bold and active, thou mayst indeed forego his pleasant society; but how much dearer shall be the thought that he is happy, and partly by thy help! Procure, then, he uses no delays. Let not the love of English friends mar so great a good. Madame de Dinant is passionately bent on this alliance; but she is the most timid person in the world; and if time is allowed to Arthur de Montauban to mature his schemes, God help her and the little Françoise!—Thy humble loving friend,

"JEANNE DE KERSABIEC."

My God, my God! is mine a selfish love, or doth some dark presentiment oppress my soul? I would this letter had never reached my hands.

CHAPTER XIII.

Françoise de Dinant.

In the evening I met Monseigneur Gilles in the Queen's withdrawing room. (No cousins can love each other more than the King Henry and this prince, albeit their dispositions are very dissimilar.) As soon as he heard what Jeanne had written to me, his resolve was formed; he would go at once to Dinant.

For some time past I had observed that he was consumed by the desire to return to Brittany; and the injustice of his brother, who refused to repair the losses he had sustained from the King of France's dishonesty, and left him without any heritage, increased that desire. For he knew his uncle, the valiant Arthur de Richemont, loved him tenderly, and the people regarded him with no common affection.

" Too long, too long," he said, " I have been absent. Monseigneur my brother would have done me justice if I could have had speech with him. As to Arthur de Montauban, he is a caitiff, whom every virtuous person abhors. God knoweth, it is not the enmity only he bears me which moves me to oppose that man. From childhood he has been an evil spirit at the duke's side. His mother was a Visconti, and from her he inherits the crafty, lying, seducing spirit of that race. Francis never committed a fault but this childish companion applauded it. He had never a virtuous intent but with infernal art he nipped it in the bud. With the face of an angel, he has the vices of a demon; and since the ducal crown has rested on his master's brow, he has surrounded him with associates which are his own creatures. He distils poison in his mind against his kindred, and chiefly against me; and the poison is so disguised that its effects alone are visible. Pleasures he hath a marvellous skill in inventing; piety he scoffs at. The court of Vannes, once the most devout in Europe, groweth every day more licentious, and the sovereign more despised by a God-fearing people, the like of which doth not exist for loyalty, tempered by a generous freedom of soul. This message from the good demoiselle Jeanne confirms my resolve to return to Brittany, and the new hope it suggests I will not blight by unwholesome delays. The swiftest horse that can carry me to the coast, and the best sailing-vessel in which to cross the sea, shall now be my best helpers. I would be at Dinant before the duke or his favourite intercept my coming. Thou wilt pray for me, sweet Marguerite?"

"Yea, Monseigneur," I replied. And then, fearing he should rise, for I knew that I should never see him any more after that night, I added: "May God prosper your suit, and give you comfort in future years!"

He answered rather my thinking than my words when he said:

"Catherine de Rohan, her mother, is in greater repute of beauty than any lady in Brittany, and famed likewise for virtue; and Messire Jacques de Dinant was the most valiant and honourable lord of the whole province, except my uncle the Connétable."

"You will see Jeanne," I said; thinking I would fain be Jeanne, who would now enjoy the sight of him whom I should never more set eyes on.

"Good Jeanne!" he answered. "Our winsome *Jean*

qui rit. By St. Anne, Madame Marguerite, those were happy days at Havering Bower, and I shall never forget them. You and Jeanne are my very good friends. Ah, do not weep, Marguerite."

"*Jean qui pleure* was my name," I said, trying to smile through my tears.

"Prithee do not weep," he again kindly said.

"*Je n'en peux mais*," I answered, as he had taught us to do in our childish sports.

Then he kissed my hand, and said, "Adieu, Marguerite."

That night he took leave of the King and Queen, who parted with him with exceeding great grief. But what grief was like unto mine?

Monseigneur once told me that when he was about to be born, the duchess his mother said to the holy man Vincent Ferrier, "I beseech your reverence to pray that this my infant may live to be baptised." Whereupon the good saint (for such he was held to be) made the sign of the cross upon her, and answered: "Content thee, my daughter. This child shall live to be baptised, and moreover be a martyr." Alas, this prediction doth haunt me. He added that his mother was wont to remind him of it, when his passionate and vehement nature showed itself in childhood. "Ah, sweet son," she would say; "I ween that through much tribulation thou shalt reach heaven, if God does thee that good at the last; and so the holy man's words shall be fulfilled."

The days went by, and each that passed without tidings of his arrival at Dinant seemed long and heavy to me. At last I received this packet from Jeanne by the same hand as before, and these were its contents:

"MY ENTIRELY BELOVED FRIEND, — What hath

happened is so singular and so sudden, it involves so great fears and so great hopes, doubts and contentment mingled with uneasiness,— that I can ill describe the various emotions I have experienced, nor in my own thinking resolve which of these sentiments most prevail in me at this time. That which I most desired has come to pass, but in such wise as I should not have desired. I would not undo what is done, yet would fain it had not been done. I rejoice in trembling; I grieve, and yet am glad. But no longer will I keep thee in suspense, but plainly, and as shortly as I can, relate the haps of the last days which have worked in me these manifold and opposed sentiments.

Tuesday last week Dame Catherine sent for me, which she does often in the day, and always when anything disturbs her more than usual. She is the most dependent person on others that can be conceived—a very weathercock for changeableness, yet stubborn in her bent sometimes. I found her much vexed by a letter she had received from the Duke of Brittany, which expressed a hope—from a sovereign, it read like a command—that the hand of her daughter should be speedily bestowed on the Count Arthur de Montauban, than which a more honourable gentleman and leal subject did not exist. And that this marriage of the sole child of his well-beloved Messire Jacques de Dinant to one which he likewise held as one of his dearest friends would yield him so great contentment, that nothing should exceed the favour he would show to the count and his young wife. And much more in that strain.

"Jeanne, what shall I do?" quoth Madame Catherine. "Here is the duke resolved on this contract. I shall die if Françoise must espouse this man, which her father misliked more than any other person in the world; but if the duke and he are determined to compass it, what can I do?"

Then she began to weep and wring her hands in a piteous manner. The sight of great bursts of grief doth not work in me the compassion which some feel at these explosions. Over-softness in others works in me a singular hardness and excess of passion, a notable coldness; and my cousin's lamentations, howsoever well-founded, awaken in me—I cry mercy for it!—a greater resentment of her folly than pity for her grief. This uncharitableness is, I know, very wicked; but there are persons which seem created to tempt others to this sin; and if this was the end of Madame de Rohan's coming into the world, she hath then fulfilled her destiny as far as I am concerned.

When she had bewailed herself for some time, and cried out that she was the most miserable person in the world, and asked many times what she should do, yet never listened to an answer, I at last said, in the deliberate manner which commands a hearing, "Madame, you must needs act with courage: call to your aid the Connétable de Richemont; advise with Monseigneur Pierre and his holy consort. If it must be so, appeal to the Estates of Brittany and the King of France; but never yield an inch on a point wherein the weal of your child and your own honour are concerned."

But, alas, all the blowing in the world cannot elicit a spark of fire from damp wood; nor can any stirring evoke an effort of courage from a timid soul. I had as lief deal with lewd persons as with those in whom virtue hath no strength. Catherine de Rohan's merits are like the wheat which grows on the rock; fair for a while, but lacking the depth of soil which furnishes endurance when the heat of trial arises. She loves to be compassionated. She must needs be always caressed. Her blue eyes solicit pity—her tears flow in graceful showers. She was a fair and useless ornament in a brave man's home; and now its prop hath fallen, what stay shall she afford that house? Averse to yield, but afraid to oppose the duke, she spent two days in vain complaints; on the third the paper was spread before her, and she held her pen musingly, unresolved yet what to write, though she had kept the duke's messenger waiting two whole days and nights! Then she said she would go to Vannes to see him; that her tears would move him to desist from his request.

"Yea," I replied somewhat angrily, for I knew if she went what the upshot would be,—" yea, go to see him, and on the morrow Françoise will be betrothed to the miscreant whom Messire Jacques would have slain if he had dared only to think on her."

O, what an injured countenance she then assumed, exceedingly meek and pitiful, and cried that I little knew a mother's heart, which, when her child is concerned, will face a lion or a tiger!

"A painted lion," I answered, "or a caged tiger at a fair." These were, I know, unkind words; but, i'faith, I could not restrain them. It made me mad to hear her utter these fine speeches, and to see the while she had not more courage wherewith to defend her daughter than a mouse or a hare.

Whilst we were thus disputing, she with querulous complaints, and I with angry reproaches, of a sudden we heard the sound of horses' feet in the court beneath the windows; and as I was going to look what this arrival should be, Françoise ran into the chamber, and said,

"Madame maman, a beau sire, on a fine black horse, hath come to the front door. Who is he?"

There followed a brief suspense, during which a cold fear seized me. It is Arthur de Montauban, I thought, or it may be the duke to plead the cause of his favourite, and then all is lost. But when the constable of the castle announced Monseigneur Gilles de Bretagne, I was as near fainting as I ever was in my life, the surprise and joy was so sudden.

"Ah, Monseigneur, you are very welcome," Madame Catherine exclaimed, with one of her most sweet looks.

Mademoiselle de Dinant—Heaven bless her!—put out her little hand when he turned towards her, expecting he would kiss it, as many are wont to do. But kneeling before her, he said to her mother, "Do you permit me to embrace my little cousin, madame?"

"Yea, Monseigneur, you will greatly honour her," Madame Catherine replied.

Upon which he kisses Mademoiselle Françoise on both the cheeks; and she, as if she had conceived a sudden liking for the prince, threw her little arms round his neck, and kept him a while stooping to her height. Then rising, he took her by the hand (she nothing loth) and led her to her mother.

"You grant her to me?" he said, with his bewitching smile. "She is mine from this day forward?"

Madame Catherine did not gainsay him, but called him her fair son, and showed great contentment at his coming and at his suit.

Then the prince said, looking at me, "Is that my good friend Jeanne?" and greeted me as a sister. His visage is but little altered, and his heart not at all, since the days that we were all at Havering Bower.

By her mother's orders I led the little damoiselle into the garden, which stands, thou must know, between the palace and the court, which in its turn opens by one gate upon the town, and by the other on the open fields towards Rennes.

For an hour or more Monseigneur conversed with Madame Catherine. When he came out his brow was clouded, and his aspect changed.

"O beau sire," Françoise exclaimed, "see, they have led your horse to the gate. Let me ride with you once round the court, as I was wont to do with Messire Jacques, my good father."

"Yea, Mademoiselle Françoise," the prince replied, "so you shall, if it please you. But will you not be so gracious as first to gather for me a posy of yon sweet flowers to carry to my ladylove?"

The little damsel pouted her pretty lips, and said, "I will be your lady-love, and none other shall you have."

"So you shall, Ma Mie," he answered smiling. "You are my lady-love, and none other shall I have."

"Then," she cried, clapping her hands, "I will gather for you the most fair posy can be seen."

And like a butterfly she flew from one bush to another collecting roses.

Then Monseigneur said to me, "The noble lady yonder, Jeanne, will she match in cunning Arthur de Montauban?"

"Nay, Monseigneur; nor even one of his pigeons, I ween."

"Hath she the virtue of courage, or the courage of virtue?"

"Neither one nor the other. She cannot so much as conceive what courage signifies."

"But will not her love for her child furnish her with it when it comes to a struggle?"

"Monseigneur, in weak natures love partakes of the general feebleness."

"Does she verily detest Arthur de Montauban?"

"Her hatred is real, but persistency even in hatred implies some kind of strength."

"She says she desires above all, things a contract of marriage betwixt her daughter and me. Is this true?"

"Yea, true as the gospel at this time. More true to-day than it was yesterday, or than it shall be to-morrow, if your grace is out of sight. If she sees the duke and his minion, it may soon not be true at all."

"If an event is accomplished, will she long lament it?"

"Not long, unless she lacks a theme for lamentation; and then any hap will furnish it."

The prince sat down, and on his countenance anxious expressions flitted like clouds on a sunny sky. He held his head in his hands, then walked to and fro in a restless manner, his eyes glancing now towards the court, now over the fields which lie behind the palace, now on Françoise, as she wandered about the garden; and I marvel not that he should have gazed on the little damoiselle with pleasure and admiration. She is the most lovely child imaginable; her complexion fair and delicate, her eyes blue, but of a more dark blue than her mother's. Each vein in her temples is visible through the transparent whiteness of her skin. Her slender neck is most graceful, and her hair of the most beautiful golden hue that can be thought of. The parterre rang with her sweet laughter the while she was gathering flowers and conversing with herself half in speech and half in song; and when holding up her kirtle full of roses with both her hands, her cheeks flushed with running and her eyes beaming with joy, she came to us, I heard Monseigneur Gilles say in a loud voice, speaking between his teeth,

"No, forsooth and forsooth, this angel shall never belong to that caitiff!"

"Beau sire," the little maiden said, "I would that these roses would change into bread in my lap, like it happened to the good Madame St. Elisabeth, for then I would feed your black horse when he has carried us round the court."

"You are not afraid to ride with me, Mademoiselle Françoise?" the prince said.

"No, no, beau sire," she cried, "if you will hold me fast with one arm, as my father used to do."

"Never fear, petite madame," he answered, "I will hold thee fast, and never let thee go."

I was half afraid to let her ride, and urged she should not trouble Monseigneur; but neither he nor she would listen to me: she clung to his hand, jumping as they walked along. When we reached the gate, the constable of the castle was standing by the side of the prince's horse.

"Bon ami, I am going to ride," Françoise cried.

He shook his head, and said mademoiselle was too bold; but when Monseigneur Gilles was in the saddle, she stamped her foot and cried, "Lift me up to ride."

Then M. de Maulévrier placed her upon the horse before the prince, and all the roses she held in her hand fell to the ground. She exclaimed, "O, my roses!"

I stooped to pick them up. The next instant I heard her say, "Hold me fast, beau sire." I looked up, and saw Messire Gilles dash his spurs into his steed, and then like a flash of lightning pass through the portal out of the court.

In the presence of the old constable, the esquires, and serving men, and of me who stood rooted to the ground in speechless fear and amazement, he had carried off Françoise. I heard her mother scream— a rushing of persons to and fro, loud cries of alarm, and could not move, I was so wildered with this hap. No one, I ween, knew what to say or do, and least of all Madame Catherine. She was too much consternated to think of any fine speech then.

"Whither hath he carried her?" she kept crying. "What hath he done with my Françoise? You said he would befriend me, and he plays the part of a cruel enemy. He robs me of my child. Bid them pursue that wicked man. Where is the constable?"

"Madame," I said, "be calm;" but mine own heart beat so fast that I almost lacked the ability to speak. "Here is the constable to take your orders. Reassure him, I pray you. Tell your household . . . ." I stopped bewildered, for verily I knew not what to advise.

"Speak to them Jeanne," she cried, pointing to the attendants, who stood aghast, waiting for a sign of her will. I saw she was like to faint; so I collected my thoughts and said, "Good friends, the prince hath committed an unwarrantable action, but with no dishonourable intent, as you will, I doubt not, soon perceive. Your lady, Madame Catherine, promised this day to Monsieur Gilles the hand of Mademoiselle de Dinant."

"Nay, Jeanne!" my cousin exclaimed.

"Nay, madame," I interrupted; "I hold him not therefore excused."

"We are losing time," old Armand de Maulévrier cried, his pale visage flushing with indignant resentment; "whither shall we ride, mesdames? to Rennes, or to the coast?"

In sooth we could not tell; and at the mention of the coast, Madame de Rohan shrieked, and cried she should die if her daughter was carried beyond seas. The constable rode out with the garrison of Dinant, and scoured the country; but no tidings could be heard of the prince and the child, except that some peasants had seen one riding like the wind plunge into the forest behind the town, after which all clue to them was lost. The greatest fear she entertained was that Monseigneur Gilles should have carried Françoise to England, which she would have it was a barbarous country. Verily my disquiet equalled hers, for I apprehended many terrible results should ensue from so rash an action. It pierced my heart with a twofold anguish to hear this poor creature bemoan herself, and accuse the prince of cruelty and horrible craft in robbing her of her child, which he verily had done, albeit with no evil intent I felt assured; and of this I tried to persuade her. But she would take no comfort from anything I said; until on the morrow a messenger came from the castle of Gualdo with a letter addressed to " Haute et puissante dame Catherine de Rohan, the well-beloved mother of my most entirely loved wife Françoise de Dinant." This was what the prince wrote; and the while I transcribe his words I marvel that one so good and God-fearing, and of so tender a heart, should have done so great a wrong as this to steal a child from her mother; albeit I conceive some excuse can be found in the suddenness of the act, and the fear that he had that through weakness Madame Catherine should ruin his designs and her own, to the no small injury of them all. Be that as it may, this was his letter:

The Castle of Gualdo, 11th of January, 1445.

MADAME AND MOST WELL-BELOVED MOTHER,—In the humblest manner in my power (and verily I should wish to kneel at your feet to beseech this pardon) I entreat you to forgive your poor loving son and husband now of your most fair and gentille daughter Madame Françoise, for the fear, pain, and sorrow I have caused you, whom I most desire to love, honour, and serve as long as I live. Mother, I beseech you to command me in everything; and as you were most willing I should wed your daughter, so now be not angry with me that I have prevented long and dangerous delays by contracting marriage with her this day in the presence of many weighty and honourable persons. I ween this lady is not more meanly married than you should wish her to be: and I shall always and at all seasons be ready to accomplish, with God's grace, whatever shall most be for her advantage and yours, whom I hold to be, next to her, the dearest person to me on earth. It was full sore against my will that I so much offended you, as I must needs have done, in this matter; and I shall be more glad than any man alive if you will overlook the bad doing of that which you desired should be done, only not in this wise, and speedily come hither to my wife and your child, who says she would be the most contented little madame in the world if her lady mother and her good Jeanne were here. If you will do me this good, then I shall be absolved of any notable offence in this matter; for everyone then shall see that as you received me yestereve as your son with many gracious and endearing terms, so now you accept me for your daughter's husband and your most faithful and loving servant in all which you shall command me.

I have taken this paper whereon I write to Françoise, who is playing with a doll, which the majordomo's children have dressed to simulate a queen, and she stayed her playing awhile to write these words: "Madame maman, prithee come here. Gualdo is a very fair castle. I had a long and gleesome ride with

Monseigneur Gilles yestereve, and this morn we have been to church to be married. I like to be his wife, but I want my good mother and Jeanette."

Madame and dear mother, God seeth my heart. When last night I went into Madame Dorac's chamber to look at Françoise asleep, I knelt down by the side of the little bed wherein, like the fair image of a carved saint, she reposed, and made a vow, which He heard, that I would always worship her from this time forth, first as a tender, playful father, and then a loving husband, until death us do part; and in token thereof reverently kissed her little hand, which was resting on the bedclothes all beautiful and white. Now the small finger of that fair hand weareth the nuptial ring in token of plighted troth. I confess and deny not that her broad lands and much dowry allured my ambitious hopes; but trust me, lady, I would now liefer forego them all than possess them and yield Françoise to my brother's minion. Every thread of her golden hair is a sacred link about my heart. The sight of her moves me to pray. The thought of her brings heaven to my thinking, and chases evil from me like a good spell. God forgive me if, as I misdoubt, I committed a sin in the stealing of my promised bride; but now I will serve God, and be a meet guardian for this angel. If you come hither, all shall be well. I pray God to move you to do me and Françoise and yourself so great a good. Almighty God have you in His keeping!

Your loving humble son and servant,
GILLES DE BRETAGNE.

This letter changed the current of Dame Catherine's thoughts, and straightly reconciled her to Monseigneur Gilles. Now she forgave him more easily than I could do. She was both glad that Françoise was married to a royal prince, and greatly comforted that neither the duke nor any one else could reproach her with any complicity therein. If he is angered at it (which is almost incredible, for this marriage brings great estates into his family, and makes his brother rich and puissant without loss to himself), she can then plead that she has been compelled thereunto, and made, as the proverb says, virtue of necessity. So we went to Gualdo that day, and Françoise and her lord were, I ween, right glad to see us. She flew into her mother's arms, and he fell at her feet, shedding tears of joy. Methought the embracing and fine speeches would never end. Madame Françoise begged of me a holiday because she was married. I foresee I shall have some trouble with her royal highness. She pouts a little when I call her to her lessons; and when I said there were rods at Gualdo as well as at Dinant, she answered, Monseigneur her husband would order them all to be burnt if she asked him. I know not the thing he would not do at her request, he is so fond of the petite madame. So I use other ingenious methods to reduce her to obedience, exhorting her to be staid and reasonable, as befits a married princess; and she is so apt and toward a child, that these means suffice to move her to correct her faults. Ah, beloved Marguerite, 'tis strange, after so long a lapse of time, to live again under the same roof as Monseigneur Gilles! I had often said to the good God that I prayed Him to take from me all happiness in this world, if only I might one day serve this prince in some notable manner; and methinks if I can train his wife so that she shall be a comfort to him when she cometh to years of discretion, I shall have been heard therein. But I beseech you, good friend, cease not to be his bedeswoman, and to crave the like of other devout persons, so that no evil shall happen to him in consequence of this marriage, which I sometimes fear will bring no good with it. For doth not the holy Paul say, " Do not ill that good may come thereof"? and this saying troubles me not a little. Françoise was sitting on his knee one day, when I perceived her countenance waxed sad; and laying her soft cheek against his bearded one, she said, " Ah, my good prince—my poor prince!" and there was somewhat mournful in her utterance of these words which pained my heart very much. An old man who lives in a neighbouring forest, and has showings of the future, hath told me that once, when he was in prayer, he had a vision of Monseigneur's visage pale and livid, and like to one who gasps for breath. God help us all! At the last pardon, strange persons were seen lurking about the castle, which some took to be spies. I pray thee have a Mass said at the shrine of our Lady of Everingham for the prince and his little wife. The Holy Trinity have thee in His keeping!

" Thy loving friend and servant to command,
    JEANNE DE KERSABIEC."

CHAPTER XIV.

The Cloud of the Size of a Man's Hand.

JEANNE's letter filled me with manifold apprehensions, which would have wholly captured my thoughts, had they not been forcibly engaged at that period by events at home of grave and dire import. The Queen told me one day, as a great secret, that it was soon intended to summon Parliament to meet at Edmondsbury. When I inquired wherefore there sooner than in London, she laid her finger on her lip, as if to caution me not to speak freely on that point. But in another moment she said:

"Great events are at hand, Meg. In sooth, the old enemy's power is waxing too great."

"What, the devil's?" I said.

"Nay, nay," she replied, laughing. "Albeit I deny not that the enemy I speak of hath a diabolical spirit."

"Does your majesty speak of the Duke of Gloucester?"

"Yea, I do. York is horribly discontented because Somerset is regent of France in his stead, and letters and interviews have passed betwixt him and our uncle of Gloucester, which give reason to apprehend some treason to be hatching in the realm. Nay, not apprehensions only, but rather proofs of this exist."

"Good Lord! And what is then to be done?" I asked, dismayed.

"Much," the Queen answered. "But the first step is this Parliament at Bury."

"Hath the Cardinal advised this?"

"The Cardinal is no longer accessible to worldly thoughts. He still repeats, if spoken to by any one he cannot refuse to answer, that there shall be no safety for the King or for me, or for this realm, whilst the Duke hath power. This he will maintain with his last breath, and that if he has to appear to-day at God's judgment seat, he fears no condemnation for this part of his conduct, albeit many other sins he shall have to answer for; but otherwise he is absorbed in the expectation of death. Hast thou not heard how last week he rehearsed his own funeral, and lay on his coffin in the Cathedral at Winchester, his hands joined on his breast, whilst the clergy and the monks sung over him a funeral dirge, as though he had been already dead? Then afterwards his will was read, in which he bequeathes all he has to the poor, excepting two hundred pounds to the King, who will not, I know, accept it. When it was mentioned to him, he answered, 'that he would not touch his money, for he had ever been a most kind uncle to him, and all he left behind him should go to the poor, which was what would most benefit his soul, and he prayed to God to reward him.' The day after this solemn office a High Requiem Mass was said, and then the Cardinal took leave of all his friends, and was carried back to his chamber. But after we return from Bury I hope to go to Wolseley, for I would fain receive a final blessing from this dear friend, who hath been a father more than an uncle to me."

I did not accompany the Queen to Bury, whither she went a short time after this conversation, for it was not my turn then to wait upon her majesty; but her grace favoured me with a letter immediately after her arrival, in which she said that all the commonalty of Suffolk had assembled there in defensible array. The Parliament had met that day in the refectory of St. Edmund's Abbey, and the first matter brought forward was the exchange of her revenues of 4,666*l*. 13*s*. out of the customs for certain lands and hereditaments settled on her for life, which pleased her not a little.

The next day to the one on which I had received her majesty's favour, it happened that in the maids of honours' chamber at Westminster I was sitting with Lady Isabel Butler, Mary Beaumont, and some other persons. Tidings had reached England of Monseigneur Gilles's marriage and the manner of it; and the Lady Isabel, who hath always borne him ill-will, because he is a French prince, and their majesties' great affection to him, related the story in an ill-natured manner. She said common men had been hung for less crimes than the one this beau sire had committed. "For is not a man gibbeted," quoth she, "for stealing a horse or even a sheep,—sometimes for killing a deer or only a fox in a nobleman's park? but here is a prince which, in a forcible and brutal manner, robs a mother of her child—not for any affection which he entertains for the damsel—for I pray you, doth a man of more years than twenty care for a wench of seven years of age? —no, but for the lands and towns she owns, he forces a marriage with her against her mother's will, who is a widow, and therefore without defence. If this offence doth not cry to Heaven for vengeance, I know not what sin should do so."

I was opening my lips to defend the prince from this slanderous charge, yet feeling sorely wounded at heart that he should have been so rash as to commit an action which none could justify, albeit much may be advanced to excuse it; but before I could speak the door opened, and Mr. Cotton, one of the gentlemen of the Queen's household, burst into the room, and cried:

"Ladies, news have arrived from Bury at the which men hold their breath. What think you has happened?"

"Nought to the King or Queen?" several exclaimed at once.

"No, God be praised!" he cried; "but the Duke of Gloucester is arrested on the charge of high treason, and committed to close custody."

We stood speechless—some for one reason, some for another. I was seized with a great terror, for methought this looked like the beginning of an endless trouble. Thinking of the Queen's youth, her sway over the King, the uneasy state of the kingdom, which I heard of from persons outside the Court; and my Lord Cardinal on his death-bed, who had been the main stay of their majesties' councils up to that time, my heart misgave me. Even amongst the Queen's household there existed great disaffection to her favourite noblemen, if not to herself; and strong symptoms thereof were not lacking on this occasion. Lady Isabel's countenance grew as black as thunder, and she said with passion: "God forgive those which have done this foul wrong to a prince of the blood!"

This reminds me how often words are used which convey a different meaning than the poor words themselves should have. As one says to another, "Much good may it do thee!" or, like in this case, "God forgive you!" and all the while hath no desire good should ensue or mercy be shown to the offenders. Mary Beaumont's irascible spirit resented her companion's speech, and she exclaimed:

"God be praised, treason is discovered in time, and justice overcomes traitors!"

Her thanksgiving incensed Lady Isabel as much as

she herself had been angered at that lady's pious desire; and from the lips of both there flowed an abundance of retorting speeches touching the chief persons of the State, and even the King and Queen; which were very unseemly in that place.

In a few days I was sent for by the Queen to Bury. If my fancy erred not, her mien and behaviour had become somewhat different from what I had hitherto observed in her. Till then she had not indeed lacked decision of manner, but it was rather that of a petted child or indulged woman resolved to have her will, than the commanding aspect of a sovereign. Though only seventeen years of age and slight in form, the majesty of her countenance and carriage had noticeably increased. She looked like one who could bear on her young brow the whole weight of a crown.

"Meg," she said when I came in, "the battle is engaged—the gauntlet thrown down. Since my coming to England I have had to fight, as one might say, in the dark. I have been the object of shameful attacks from the duke's party, and, like one pinioned, could not return the blows. At last the King is convinced of their treachery, which he was very loth to credit. The coast is now clear, and I feel mine own power. When the act was done, and the warrant for Gloucester's arrest signed, I for the first time felt I was a queen."

I replied, "Madame, God send that this course proves safe and prosperous for this country; for men will surely lay it, if otherwise, to your majesty's charge."

"I care not what men say," she answered; "nor do I deny my part in this bold deed; but Somerset and Suffolk, Shrewsbury, Beaumont, and Worcester, all advised it. The proofs are indisputable that the duke has been corresponding with York. Because I have as yet no children, they plot as to who shall succeed the King, and without his knowledge devise his crown as they list. Ah! they counted without their host, as we say in France; without the Queen, as they shall find in England."

In this strain she talked whenever I saw her; and on the morning of the 7th of March, as she was sitting at her toilette-table, her maids dressing her hair, she spoke in French with me on the same theme. She looked at herself in the mirror, and, smiling, said, "Meg, I would give those black eyes, which men say are so beautiful, those features, which painters declare nothing can excel (here she shrugged her shoulders with a pretty indifference), for more ability, more patience, more cunning. Those qualities, I warrant you, I need; for even in his prison the duke is a powerful enemy. York and Warwick, that young baron for whom hundreds of Nevilles would fight and die, are at large. A party of turbulent nobles, the lewd burgesses of London, the wicked Lollards, which blaspheme and rebel, he secretly and from his durance leads and impels. O, my Lord of Gloucester, it is a *combat à la vie et à la mort* between you and Marguerite d'Anjou! Which shall conquer?"

She shook her head in defiance, and, with her raven hair hanging about her shoulders, and her countenance fired with passion, she looked very beautiful. At that moment the King entered her chamber paler than was his wont, with an inexpressible sorrowful look on his face; he walked up to her, and took her two hands in his own. "Good wife," he said in a faltering voice, "a miserable hap has befallen us,—mine uncle Gloucester is dead."

"How? where?" gasped the Queen.

"Found dead in his bed. O Jesu, have mercy on his soul!" the King exclaimed, and began to weep.

"He hath not been foully dealt with?" the Queen asked in a wild manner.

"There are no marks of violence on his body. But his soul! O God, his soul! would to God he had not thus died!"

The Queen was shivering; then she burst forth crying, "They will say he was murdered, and his death shall be more fatal to us than his life. Dead! O death, death; *this* is thy victory, *this* is thy sting. Hatred dies before a corpse. Heavens!" she exclaimed, starting up, "but wherefore do we delay to speak and to act at this crisis? Where is Lord Suffolk? Sire, the duke's body must be this instant carried to the Parliament chamber, and let all the world witness that no violence hath been committed. Yes, let the English gaze on their dead idol." Then she wrung her hands, and cried passionately, "O Duke of Gloucester, I would fain see you alive again; for I have wished your death, and when such wishes are granted they affright the soul." She turned to the King. He was sitting with one hand supporting his face, and the other resting on his knee. I noticed a strange fixity of expression in his gaze, as if he beheld something to us invisible, with no grief or horror, but an indescribable stedfastness of contemplation, which methought had in it somewhat either above or beside what was natural. The Queen looked anxiously upon him, and spoke to him twice or thrice before he answered her. At the last she said, "Sweet my lord, come to the chapel, where mass will be said for the repose of the duke's soul." Then he seemed to awake, and uttered the words, "*Requiem æternam dona eis, Domine*," and walked straight with her to the chapel.

Not long afterwards his Eminence the Cardinal died also, and the King and the Queen mourned long and bitterly for him. A more gentle spirit than I had yet observed in her showed itself at this time in her Majesty. Her fear that the Duke of Gloucester had met with foul play (it was bruited about that he had been murdered; without any warrantable grounds indeed, but with so much animosity and bold assertion that she herself was accused of being privy to it) tormented her very much. Master Waynfleet came then to Court. The very day of the Cardinal's death the King sent for him, and addressed these words to him: "Master William should you obtain a benefice by our favour, do you look to be able to retain it?" Master Waynfleet replied he would do with diligence whatever the King should order. "Then," quoth his Majesty, "our will and order is that you should be Bishop of Winchester;" and, without suffering him to speak any more, he sent the *congé-d'élire* to the chapter of the cathedral with an earnest commendation of his right trusty and well-beloved councillor, Master William Waynfleet, the provost of Eton. There was not one dissentient voice amongst the canons; and a deputation was sent to the new bishop, who had heard of his election with a very heavy heart, for he affectioned his college and the peacefulness thereof beyond any honours. This good prelate was of so humble and affable a disposition, that the most adverse persons of all parties set store by him. He was very devout to the Blessed Virgin, and his favourite prayer and chief study had ever been the hymn *Magnificat*. His life and behaviour proved, I ween, a true commentary on our Lady's words, and copy of her example. He hid himself for some hours from the deputies, and spent the time in fasting and prayer. At sunset, they found him lying prostrate before the altar of the college chapel. I think he must have said as he rose and followed them, "Behold the servant of the Lord; be it done unto me according to Thy word." To this prelate the Queen disclosed her conscience, and derived much comfort from his wholesome counsels. She thought more of religion than at any previous time of her life, and laboured hard to bring about the continuance of peace with France, and to promote in this country the establishment of useful trades and manufactures to benefit the poor people, and also commenced the foundation of Queen's College in Cambridge, which was dedicated to the honour of Almighty God, and placed under the tutelage of her patron St. Margaret and of St. Bernard. Sir John Wenlock laid the first stone thereof, with this inscription on it in Latin: "The Lord shall be a refuge to our sovereign lady Queen Margaret, and this stone shall be a token of the same."

She laboured very hard at that time to reconcile enmities and win over adverse persons. The gay spirits she had hitherto evinced were exchanged for a thoughtful demeanour, and her lightsome mood seldom returned after the Duke of Gloucester's death. Many persons noticed this change, and some, I think, ascribed it to some sort of remorse of conscience touching that mysterious event; but I am not of that opinion. Some other cause, I well know, worked that effect. She prayed more after that day, and began again to write on her tablets. Perceiving her to be thus employed, I said on one occasion, "Madame, may not the keeper of your journal transcribe what you have written?" She shook her head, and her eyes filled with tears. One by one she tore the leaves and cast them into the fire. "These are not pages," she said in a low voice," which any eyes, not even yours, good Meg, may see; but the old habit of writing relieves the pent-up heart."

She gazed silently at the parched and shrivelling scroll, and heaved so deep a sigh that, falling down on my knees, I said, " Oh, madame, discharge your soul of its burthen. Your majesty may trust one who loves you so entirely as your poor servant."

She answered, trying to smile, " I am vexed with those crabbed English mercers, who jalouse my silk weavers which I have sent for from the Low Countries. They say these poor creatures injure their trade, and that a like privilege was never before granted to women, which I misdoubt; and if it is true, why then methinks a bad custom should be no hindrance to a good work."

" Madame," I said again,— and indeed in the writing of it I am ashamed to have been so bold,—" I know it is not this quarrel which grieves you. I cry mercy for my foolishness; but I pray your majesty excuse the license of the tongue, which wags at the bidding of a leal heart."

" Meg," the Queen answered kindly, taking my hand, " if aught grieves me more than usual, it is only —" Then she stopped short. " It is only," she resumed, " what I never can so much as utter in any ear but his who shrives me. The Bishop of Winchester shall soon be here; and if he comforts me, all shall be well."

When the bishop came, her majesty confessed to him. Afterwards I thought her gravity, when she was alone, increased, as did also her application to State affairs. One or two other changes I also noticed. She had been wont till that time to express sometimes impatience when the King went often to Eton, or made

pilgrimages to holy places out of London; but now
she seemed well pleased he should follow his devout
bent, and procured him books from France of entertainment and devotion. When she was in his company,
she seemed the most happy person in the world, and as
merry as she had ever been; but when he went abroad
without her, I have seen her eyes follow him, as he
rode out, with a wistful expression; and then suddenly
breaking, as it were, from her thinkng, she sent for
the ministers, and held long conferences with them
touching questions of peace and war, and the internal
government of the kingdom. Sometimes she spent the
whole night in reading State papers and reports, which
I heard the King once with much tenderness reprove.
She smiled most sweetly, as was always her wont when
he spoke to her, but said she must needs employ some
hours in study, which in the day she had no leisure for,
or she should forget her learning. She tried in the
evenings to engage the King to play at chess with her,
and at prime, in which she excelled; but he had no
liking for these diversions. His chief entertainment
was to plan new colleges or hospitals for his poor subjects, or compute means for more abundant almsgiving
from his exhausted treasury. "Come, good wife," he
would say, "exercise thy great wit, which God our
Lord hath given thee, to devise help for these great
needs;" and then he showed her letters from destitute
persons, and compassed measures for their relief. And
on the days of his father's and mother's deaths, and
other members of his family, he made with her solemn
offerings for their souls. When the griefs which she
heard of at that time excelled human ability to assist,
or the Lollards committed sacrileges, which of all things
pained him the most, methinks she used ingenious
artifices to conceal the tidings as far as she was able

from his knowledge. Once when she refused to present to him a petition from some town wherein many had died of hunger and had lacked assistance, so that they had been almost distraught with suffering of body and soul, the Archbishop of Canterbury exclaimed,

"Madame, you enjoin silence, and would spare the King the recital of these woes; yet I doubt not his majesty would find some means to aid the sufferers, and would not desire to be ignorant of his subjects' dismal plight."

"O my lord," she quickly exclaimed, "the King's heart is too great for his ability." Then she seemed to fear to be misunderstood, for a crimson colour rushed into her cheeks, and she added, "for the ability of his purse, my lord, which ill matches that of his heart and of his head."

O Deus meus! Deus meus! I think I see a cloud of the size of a man's hand, which may one day obscure the whole sky of the Queen's life; but hardly in mine own thinking, much less on paper, dare I give the frightful phantom a defined shape. And, now I think of it, some of the Nevilles have uttered in my hearing words which, as I recal their sense by the light of this fear, cause me an inward sickness of heart.

CHAPTER XV.

News from Brittany.

IN the month of April of the same year I received the letter I now transcribe:

Jeanne de Kersabiec to the Lady Margaret de Roos.

"I recommend me unto you, my good friend, and write in great haste from Nantes, where I would to God we did not abide, but whence I can send you a letter with better convenience than from the Castle of Gualdo, where indeed it may easily happen we never return. Since I last wrote to you, very angry letters have passed betwixt Monseigneur Gilles and his brother the Duke of Brittany, wherein the latter charged him with many crimes besides the offence he committed in the enlèvement of Mademoiselle de Dinant, accusing him moreover of high treason against himself. The Connétable de Richemont and Monseigneur Pierre reasoned with the duke, and pacified him for a while with many assurances that Monseigneur Gilles had never so much as thought of any treason in this matter; that Dame Catharine de Rohan was well pleased he should marry her daughter; and that great mutual advantages would be derived from this union. Arthur de Montauban, when he found his master inclined to a reconcilement with his brother, now urged, I cannot choose but think with a cruel artifice, that an interview should take place betwixt them here at Nantes, where the Court was to remain at this time. He well knows that fire and water agree not more ill than those two brothers, and that the poisonous oil of his own discourse falling on the flame of kindred discord would easily cause it to burn fiercely. So nothing would serve him but to persuade the duke to invite Monseigneur Gilles to bring his young wife to the Court. My heart misgave me when this summons came, but I dared not to disclose my thoughts, and followed my little princess to this place. Her mother's mourning and weak health kept her at home, and Madame Françoise d'Amboise assumed the care of her young sister-in-law. In the midst of the feasts, tournaments, and diversions of the Court she leads a life so pure and holy, as if the palace was a cloister and the world a school of virtue. Though she is so beautiful that none can look on her without admiration, there is not so bold a gallant on earth which should dare to utter in her presence the least unseemly word. I saw her come into the duke's presence holding my little princess by the hand; and albeit so different in age, one looked not more pure and innocent than the other. All the nobles of Brittany were there assembled, and the ambassadors of France, Scotland, and Spain. All eyes were rivetted on the fair child, of whom all had heard and none had yet seen her. Like a guardian angel, her young noble god-mother led her to the duke's feet and presented her to him. 'Another Françoise,' he said smiling. 'Another sister,' she gently replied. 'Monseigneur, embrassez-la.' Then the duke saluted his little kinswoman, and a murmur of applause rose in the hall. I then saw a face which, if I was to live until doomsday, I should not lose the memory of. I divined whose it was, and I watched it with an admixture of fear and admiration. I have heard that in Naples there is an evil charm which some carry in their eye, and misfortune falls on whosoever these persons look upon. This Arthur de Montauban—for it was he—has, I think, this fatal spell in his gaze; the very beauty of his visage I misliked with no common aversion, and the lurking devilry in his smile made my blood run cold. I saw him and Monseigneur Gilles meet that day, and noticed the flush of the latter's cheek, and the deadly paleness of his foe. It was a wise scheme, alas, to launch an enemy on this uncertain sea of a court, and by false pilotry to mislead him amidst its shoals. This is the work which this son of an Italian woman with feminine malice pursues and succeeds in, I trow. O Marguerite! the rashness, the imprudence which marked the early years of Monseigneur Gilles doth but increase as life advances. The duke's suspicious resentful temper is like unto a heap of combustible material, upon which his brother's outbursts fall like sparks which would not kindle a fire, if an ever-ready enemy did not secretly fan the flame. The more the prince is loved and praised, the more renown he gains in the lists, the more the duke grows ill-disposed towards him. So much so, that a child's innocent speeches are reported to blacken his fame. The little wife said one day she wished her husband was as puissant as the Duke of Brittany, and lo and behold, a report is spread that the prince doth conspire to supplant the duke. I pray you, who can be safe where this spirit prevails, and the most horrible calumnies are believed by one brother of another? I shall soon leave this Court. God be praised that the young Françoise is in the hands of the Lady of Guincamp. It sorely grieves me to part with her; but Madame Catherine, my poor cousin, is dying, I fear, and hath sent for me. I have long ago abandoned all thoughts or hopes of earthly bliss, and every day detaches me more from the world, which, as Friar Brackley used to say, has no one joy full and perfect; for if a man be set at a board with delicate meats and drinks, and he sees a cauldron before him with pitch and brimstone, in the which he should be thrown as soon as he had dined, should he joy much in his delicious meats?

"I have but one passionate desire, which is to see those I affection on the path to Heaven. Scandals increase every day; dreadful crimes are committed. Indifferency to religion prevails, and talk is ministered concerning the Church by strangers from other lands— I thank God not by mine own people—which makes the blood run cold. Ah, methinks those that love God in these bad days should do penance, and afflict their bodies and souls to obtain mercy for others. I have a strange call sounding in mine ears, yea, knocking at the door of my heart sometimes; and God knoweth where it shall lead thy poor loving friend, for whom cease not to pray."

I have not heard from Jeanne for many months, but through some other persons mournful tidings from Brittany have reached this Court. Alas, Monseigneur Gilles has been thrown into prison. His enemies have so far compassed his ruin, and the duke's heart appears hopelessly closed against him. In vain did the Connétable entreat the King of France to use his good offices, as the uncle and sovereign lord of these princes. Albeit the Queen will not allow it, he hath, I ween, acted with treachery in this matter, and deceived Arthur de Richemont. Then, as a last resource, this good man, with Monseigneur Pierre and his wife,

forced the duke by their great urgency to grant an
audience to his brother in the presence of all their
kindred. The aged warrior fell on his knees before his
stubborn nephew, bowing down his gray hairs to this
humiliation for the love he bore to his sister's youngest
born, the fair son she loved so well. In vain did
Françoise d'Amboise, with streaming eyes, embrace
his knees and shed torrents of tears, which only seemed
the more to anger him, whose jealousy waxed more
bitter at every sign of affection for his young brother.
His visage waxed more fierce as these pleadings
became more urgent, and at last he broke forth in a
violent fury, and insulted his victim with savage up-
braidings and cruel taunts. The venom a lying tongue
had daily distilled into his soul now found vent in a
malice which knew no bounds. The lips of a sovereign and a brother poured forth the hatred of the
serpent coiled round his heart. For a while (an eye-
witness described the scene) Monseigneur Gilles listened in silence on his knees, his gaze fixed on the
ground. Then suddenly rising he exclaimed,

"No more tears, I pray you; no more prayers for
me. Messire le Connétable, and you all, my loving
and noble kindred, bear witness that I appeal this day
to the justice of my country. Let me be tried by the
Estates of Brittany. Now I return to custody, and
God judge betwixt thee and me, Monseigneur François,
and deal with me on His Doomsday as mercilessly as
you now do, if in aught I have deserved this treatment
at your hands."

Then he was hurried back to prison, and the Connétable left Nantes broken-hearted. Dame Françoise,
in season and out of season, plied the duke with remonstrances, ever calling to his mind his cruelty, and
beseeching him, for his soul's sake, if for no other

L

cause, to be pitiful to his brother. Then he grew weary of her reproaches, and banished her and her husband from the Court; and she took the little Françoise to Guincamp; and one who has been at that place has seen them often in the church. Monseigneur Gilles is soon to be tried by the Estates of Brittany, as he desired. O, God send they acquit him! I asked the same traveller if he had heard aught of Jeanne. He said Madame de Dinant was dead, and Mademoiselle de Kersabiec had disappeared the day of her funeral, after long prayer in the chapel, and naught since hath been seen of her.

The war with France is like to break out again, though the Queen hath laboured hard to prevent it. But the King her uncle is resolved, 'tis said, to reconquer Normandy, and the people here accuse the Queen, because she is French, of desiring ill success to our arms, which is a most false calumny. The friends of the Duke of York spread these reports, and because the Duke of Somerset is regent in France, foretell all manner of calamities to the realm. The Queen hath procured that the Duke of York should be charged with the government of Ireland. "Now," her grace says, "we are rid, for a time at least, of this plotter."

But some reckon this to be a very dangerous policy; for thus this prince has opportunities to strengthen himself in one part of his majesty's dominions; and my Lord of Salisbury, and his son Lord Warwick, take care his interests shall not suffer at home. Albeit they dare not attack the Queen directly, nothing can exceed their animosity against the Duke of Suffolk; and I hear talk even amongst such as come to the Court touching the King's incapacity for government, and that he is fitter for a cloister than a crown; and has in a manner deposed himself by leaving the affairs of the kingdom in the hands of a woman, who useth his name to conceal her usurpation, for that, according to the laws of this country, a queen consort hath no power, but title only. Though her majesty hath a firmer hand wherewith to steer the helm of the State than any other person of her sex and her years in Europe, she is nevertheless only nineteen, and her advisers, I fear, not often discreet, and more concerned to advance their fortunes than her interests. Once I told her the speeches I heard touching her ambitious designs in entertaining the King with everything except the affairs of the State and the cares of government. She rested her face on her hands, leaning her elbows on a table, and fixing her piercing eyes on mine, as if to divine my secret thoughts.

"Say they so?" she asked, with some bitterness of tone. "O, I admire how fools babble of what Angels would scarcely dare to speak of."

"Forgive me, madame," I said, in a faltering voice.

"Peace, peace, good Meg," she cried, half impatient, and yet kindly; "I meant not to reprove thy well-meant garrulity. I know thou lovest the King and me, and therefore I will tell thee that this vulgar blame condemns in me what it cannot—and God send it may never—comprehend. There are secret wires in stage-plays which spectators discern not, and in the conduct of men springs of action which none but the actors themselves can fathom."

"Will your majesty play at cards this evening with the King?" I asked; for it is my business to set the table for prime; and I wished to break off a dangerous discourse, in which I had almost angered the Queen, I thought.

She turned round with a fierceness which amazed me. Her lip quivered.

"You are too bold—or else stupid," she added; and verily I looked bewildered. Then she seized my arm, and said in a hurried manner, "Know you not when and where cards were invented?"

"No, madame, no," I answered with unfeigned surprise, her behaviour was so strange.

"O, then, go and set the table for prime," she said, with a half-relieved, half-dejected countenance.

CHAPTER XVI.

A King's Prophecy.

As I was one day with some other persons of the Queen's household in the ante-chamber which leadeth to our apartments, we listened to the speeches of various persons as they went in and came out. Lord Shrewsbury's visage was most sad, I thought, and he looked older by a great deal than when I had last seen him at court. This earl's affection for the Queen hath never altered; and in it is united a meet reverence for his sovereign and a paternal tenderness for one so young and lovely. 'Tis pretty to see him study her likings, and minister to her delights, in all honourable and pleasant ways; and she, with a winsome respect, regards his aged years with a cherishing affection. He is more pleased than any man alive in this country with her majesty's wit and learning, and he loveth to speak French with her, wherein he thinks he excels; but her grace sometime cannot refrain from smiling at the mistakes of the good lord, and says she talketh in English with less faults than he French, which he disallows, and thereupon they have friendly disputes. Not further than yesterday, her majesty had writ a letter for the recommendation of one dame in the Convent of Barking to be prioress, and used these words therein; "Wherefore we desire and pray you that in accomplissement of my lord's request and ours in this partie, ye will have the said dame in your next election right tenderly recommended, and choose her to be your prioress and governor, by consideration of her many virtues, religious governance, and good fame that she is renomed of." So when my Lord Shrewsbury, for whose contentment this letter was writ—for that dame was a kinswoman of his—read these sentences, he grimly smiled, and said, "Madame, I misdoubt if *accomplissement* and *renomed* should be English words." Upon which her majesty laughed, and answered they should be English if she pleased; "for," quoth she, "if a man speaketh amiss, 'tis the custom to say he doth clip the King's English. By that same token, I may do what I please with my lord's possessions; for what is his is mine." One only quarrel the Queen has had in these four years with Lord Shrewsbury. This was touching Joan of Arc, which he holds to have been a witch; and the Queen conceives she was a saint.

When he returned from the presence-chamber on the morn I speak of, Lady Elisabeth de Say met him with these words:

"My lord, it is bruited that the Duke of Suffolk is in the Tower. I pray you what is laid to his charge?"

"Madame," the old lord replied, "his father and three of his brethren have been slain in France. He has himself served in the wars thirty-and-four years. He has been of the Order of the Garter thirty years, and a councillor of the King fifteen years, and has once been seventeen years in the wars without once returning home. I pray God his enemies may serve the King one-half as well as this strange traitor hath done."

"Marry, my Lord Shrewsbury," cried that bird of evil omen Lady Isabel Butler, "he intended to wed his son John with little Margaret Beaufort, and, after murthering the King, to declare her to be heiress of the crown."

"Murther the King!" I exclaimed, amazed. Upon which she rejoined, with one of her malicious smiles:

"Mark, I said not *the Queen*."

If frowns could kill, then methinks the lady would then have died, if I judge by the scowl which darkened my Lord Shrewsbury's countenance.

"Madame," he cried, "you have to thank God that you are a woman. No man should have gone unscathed after he had uttered that speech in my hearing."

The lady turned away, feigning not to hear; and then talk was ministered concerning the bad news from France: and some persons said that the Duke of Somerset was losing all which the Dukes of Bedford and of York had preserved; and one Thomas Crawford, the Queen's herbman, reported that tidings had arrived from Portsmouth, where there had been very mischievous riots, and the Bishop of Chichester, who had gone there to pay the troops for the French expedition, had been killed by the mob. And presently Ralph Osborne brought news that William Taylboys, the outlaw, had been discovered with armed men near the council-chamber, and at the instance of Lord Cromwell committed to the Tower. Mary Beaumont came afterwards to my chamber; and when I said, "Ah, Moll, these new haps will cause further grief to the Queen," she answered, "In truth, she hath enough of it and to

spare. I warrant thee, Meg, there are not many
women with so brave a heart in their bosoms as this
lady. I have heard here and there a word fall from
her lips which betokeneth sore inward disturbance.
Sometimes when she is at Windsor she cometh to see
Dame Alice Botler, my kinswoman, which was the
King's governess, and now lives in a house in the Park.
She questions her touching his majesty's childhood,
and likes to hear her relate how he looked and behaved
when she had him in her charge. Once when I was
there she exclaimed, "Ah me, Mistress Alice, I love
this Windsor, because my liege lord and dear husband
was born here." Dame Alice replied: "Well, *his*
mother, Queen Katherine, shed many tears because of
that birth at Windsor," "And why so, I pray you?"
the Queen asked in great amazement. Then Dame
Alice related that when the late King departed for
France, after the death of the Duke of Clarence at
Beaugy, he charged her with many urgent enforcements
not to lie in at Windsor, for that if he had a son born
at that place he should be misfortunate all the days of
his life. The Queen (she said) smiled, and would have
it that to be born at the birthplace of Edward the
Third must needs prove a good omen for an English
prince, and Windsor the most comfortable palace for
her to be delivered in. But the King would in noways
alter his thinking, and left her with this strenuous
injunction. "And durst she disobey it?" the Queen
asked. Dame Alice replied, "She was wont to say
the King was too superstitious, and she should lie in
where she pleased, and no evil should come of it to
her child or herself. She had a playful and daring
spirit in those her young years, and would not be ruled
even by her lord. At last she resolved to remove to
Sheen, but was taken ill before her departure; and so

my lord the King was born at Windsor. I remember the bright smile on her pale fair face when she held him in her arms, who was the most beautiful infant that could be seen, and the glee with which she said, 'Nothing in this babe, methinks, doth betoken that misfortune should be his lot.' Yet when some time afterwards Lord Fitzhugh related to her how, when the King heard at Meaux of his son's birth, he had eagerly inquired where the child was born, and being told at Windsor, had exclaimed,

> "I, Henry, born at Monmouth,
> Shall small time reign and much get:
> But Henry of Windsor shall long reign and lose all;
> But as God will, so let it be."

The poor Queen shed some tears; and as years went on and disasters occurred, she thought more and more of those words, and sorrowed very much for her youthful stubbornness, and humbly confessed her fault when she was dying, and begged the King her lord to forgive her."

"What said my lord?"

"He bade her be of good comfort, for that misfortunes are no evils to a Christian soul; and if he should lose all on earth, he should hope to get the more in heaven."

"That is like his majesty," the Queen exclaimed. "Goodness is never lacking in his grace; and was he in childhood grave and *débonnaire* ?"

"He had always a sweet gravity in his countenance," my kinswoman replied, "and I have not seen the child which could be compared to his highness for towardness of disposition. Mrs. Joan Astley says that even in his infancy graciousness was noticeable in his looks and actions. When he passed through the streets of London, sitting on his mother's lap, he saluted the people, and conducted himself with much sadness; and those pretty hands, which could not yet feed himself, were made to wield a little sceptre. I mind the day when the Earl of Warwick showed him to the peers in Parliament, and one of the lords presented him with the orb. He put one little hand upon it and then the other, and seemed to doubt if it should be a thing to be afraid of or to play with."

"Ah, Dame Alice," the Queen said smiling, "you must needs have been in great renown for a very wise and expert person, since the King's council appointed you to teach him courtesy and nurture. No doubt you learnt him early to say his prayers."

"I promise your majesty the King could say his beads as soon as he could speak. And I warrant your grace, when he was only eighteen months of age he would not travel on the Sunday."

"Nay, nay, Dame Alice, this is not to be believed," the Queen exclaimed.

But my good kinswoman would not be gainsayed therein, and declared that it was written in the *Chronicle of London.*

"It happened upon the 13th of November," quoth she, "when the King and his mother were coming from Windsor to London. At night, on the Saturday, they lodged at Staines; and on the morrow, when the King was carried to his mother's car, he shrieked, and sprang, and cried in so lusty a fashion, the like of which had never been seen in him before, and they must needs carry him back to the inn; and there he abode all the day. But on the morrow, when he was borne to the car, he was glad and merry of cheer."

"Come, Dame Alice," cried the Queen, "I am a

misbeliever touching this early sanctity which showed itself by kicks and screams. And yet—O, I can well credit that the King had an earlier towardness to serve God than other children."

Then she kissed Dame Botler, who cried this was too great an honour for a poor woman.

"Nay," the Queen said; "surely you kissed the King many times, and so his wife may well kiss you."

"I must confess," Dame Botler replied, "that sometimes the sweet King's little arms were thrown about my neck, and then I could not forbear to kiss his fair cheek. God defend his grace, and you, madame, also!"

The Queen said to me afterwards that she liked to converse with Dame Alice, for she reminded her of her own good nurse, Théophanie. And then she harped on the words of the late King touching Henry born at Windsor, and let drop somewhat which showed me she hath fears which others little wot of, and so judge her wrongfully. Yea, Meg, as I said before, this Queen our sovereign lady hath as brave a heart as any woman alive.

I was not often with the Queen betwixt the time of the Duke of Suffolk's arrest and that of his departure from the Tower. But that day I stood by her side at a window in the palace at Westminster, and she said to me, with tears in her eyes, "Our most true and leal friend Suffolk is banished for five years. This sentence the King hath signed to save the duke's life, and I pray God this merciful intent succeeds; but I am of opinion that yielding an inch to save an ell in matters of justice on the one side and popular clamour on the other is an ill policy, as was shown forth when Pilate ordered the Lord Jesus to be scourged; the end of which was what we all know."

"'Tis reported," I replied, "that your majesty urged the King at the last to sign that order."

The Queen did not answer for a moment; then she fixed her eyes on me, and said, " Yea, I did so. God only knoweth the cause."

As she uttered those words, a noise beneath the windows of rushing footsteps was heard, and we saw crowds of ruffianly men hurrying towards the Tower, whence the Duke of Suffolk was to depart that morn. A rumour was spread shortly afterwards that his grace had been attacked and maltreated by the mob; but this proved to be false: only his servants had been intercepted and beaten. He himself escaped to his estates in Suffolk, whence he was to embark at Ipswich. The Queen had a bad headache in the evening; and as I was ministering to her, and chafing her brows with distilled water, she broke forth in this wise:

"Jesu, how will all this end? Discontent is at its height; the people starve. Their sufferings remind me of the famine in Naples some years ago. Then the pestilent teachers of Lollardry lurk about, poisoning men's minds, and teaching them to ascribe their sufferings to the sins of the clergy and the nobles. They provoke rebellion against the Church and the throne, and promise that the lands of the rich shall be divided amongst the poor. And there are none that I can see so good, or so wise, or so strong, that they can stem this torrent, which rises more and more, like the tide of the sea when it comes up. The Cardinal is dead, Suffolk is banished, Shrewsbury is old and feeble. Waynfleet and Beckington are holy men, I trow; but as was said of the few loaves when thousands hungered, ' what be they amongst so many?'"

"God be thanked," I said, "that the King is wise and good."

She pushed my hand away from her forehead in an impetuous manner, and, sitting in her bed with her fair white arms crossed on her bosom, and her hair falling disordered about her face, exclaimed:

"The King! Do you too accuse me of small esteem for him? I tell you there is not one alive that would rule a kingdom so beneficently as my lord if .... Ah, perhaps you are one of those who think that I desire to govern alone,—that I am pleased he should pray and study like a monk, so that I may throne it as an absolute sovereign? Yes, I am blamed on every side; enemies slander, and friends blindly advise. From France my kinsfolk send me letters which cause me to smile and weep in turn; they write so unwittingly of what happens here. One only in all the world knoweth what I suffer. God help me! if I disburthened not my soul in shrift, methinks my brain would give way. Those Lollards teach the damnable doctrine that none should confess. If the day should come when pent-up hearts are debarred this comfort, I promise you madness shall increase."

A short time passed, and then again I was sent for by the Queen. She was going abroad, and commanded me to accompany her. Her visage was pale, save one crimson spot on each cheek. She laid her cold hand on mine, and said,

"Suffolk is dead—murthered! I go to condole with the duchess. Would I could carry to her the head of Exeter! That should be her best comfort."

"The head of the Lord Admiral!" I exclaimed, affrighted. "Good God! what hath he done?"

"Done!" the Queen bitterly repeated. "This is what he hath done. He, the servant of the King, the minister of the Crown, gave vessels to the false lords, poor Suffolk's adversaries. They sent miscreants on board the Nicholas to pursue him on the seas. They bore down on his ship, snatched him from it, and hailed him on one of theirs, with the mocking cry, 'Welcome, traitor!' and the worse mockery of a feigned trial. Then they lowered him into a boat, and with an old rusty sword cut off his noble head. I tell thee, if I was his wife, I would die, or have their blood; and being his Queen, who owed him all and loved him well, I can only mourn for him with hot useless tears, which shame impotent royalty! Heavens, to be so used! To see the King raise to heaven his meek eyes with an anguish which words cannot express! And this poor soul I am about to see submerged in bottomless grief. What can I say to her?"

"O madame, tell her to pray, to be patient in her sorrow, to hope in God!" I cried.

"You might as lief bid the angry wind preach to the raging sea, as bid me exhort to patience the wife of murthered Suffolk. If the King sees her, then true comfort, heavenly wisdom, sweet hope, not of this earth, may perchance pass from his soul into hers. In his presence furious passions subside. I have seen this, yea, felt it at times."

Then we reached the house of the duchess, and the Queen went into her chamber. When she came out again, her eyes were red with weeping.

CHAPTER XVII.

The Maids of Honour again.

I REMEMBER that one day at Sheen, being sad because no tidings reached me from Jeanne, and only uncertain reports of Monseigneur Gilles's lengthened imprisonment and the ill usage he endured, I went into the garden and sat there on the grass in the shade with some of the Queen's maids. At first the merriment of these damsels sounded harshly in my ill-disposed ears, so I leant my head against a tree and feigned to be asleep. Whilst they were gayly devising, my thoughts were far away, picturing to myself a dungeon in France and a fair comely face grown wan with long captivity. Yet I noted their speeches, which, from the well-known sound of each one's voice, I easily distinguished. Albeit in no cheerful mood, their joylity little by little infected me with mirth. The buzzing tongues, light prattle, and gleesome bursts of laughter matched the music of the birds in that pretty grove. Partly from a natural heavy humour, and a pensive melancholy which early sorrows have engendered, I am not prone to merriment; but when others are gay around me, it lightens my heart; and this contagion is wholesome, for over-gravity breeds moroseness, and ill becomes youth.

Since I began to write, four years ago, many changes have come to pass in this young circle. One hath died, some have married, and new damsels fill their places. Ten little maidens of noble families, not yet twelve years of age, have also been taken into the Queen's household for nurture and instruction; but they do not company with the maids of honour. Only the Lady Margaret Beaufort, because the Queen shows her especial favour, is often to be seen in her majesty's private chambers. I thought that time, when we were sitting under the lime-tree at Sheen, that some of those to whose discourse I then lent a lazy ear would perchance one day play a part on life's stage; that the dawning loveliness of one would expand into beauty, entangling many in its meshes; the sprouting wit of another set the world gaping with wonder; a third leave behind her at death an admirable odour of sanctity; a fourth become perhaps an outcast or a heretic—which God defend! Life in its outset resembles a roll of parchment, which little by little unfolds its pages; and, to turn a grave thought into a merry one, I will relate what the Duchess of Bedford said to Lord Bonville when he boasted he was made of the stuff which heroes are fashioned of: "O, good my lord," her grace replied, "let us see one ell of that stuff, I pray you, that we may judge of the rest."

Then little Margaret Beaufort's voice first struck on mine ear. I heard her say, "What flower love you best, Mrs. Katherine Strange?" (This was one of the new maids of honour.)

"The rose," that damsel replied.

"And you, Isminia Scales?"

"Why, Peg, methinks I like the sweet-william most."

Then some one near me whispered to another, "'Tis pity there is no blossom called the sweet-henry." A laugh ensued; for it was well known this lady was like to wed Henry Bouchier, Lord Essex's second son, and was not a little fond of him.

Then in an aggrieved voice Mistress Isminia said, "Methinks persons which live in glass houses should not throw stones."

"Peradventure," said another, "Mistress Katherine thinketh the rose which she prefers if called by any other name would smell as sweet, and that an ill-sounding name is no disadvantage to a comely gentleman."

Then all laughed; for it had been bruited at court that Mistress Katherine had tormented the Queen to write for her a letter to Mr. Nicholas Strange, her father, to press him forthwith to consent to the fulfilment of her contract with Robert Bugdon; and I knew this to be true, for I had copied it myself; and methought her majesty was very peremptory with that gentleman, for she charged him, desired, prayed him, and on God's behalf exhorted and required him, to incline to the accomplishment of that marriage without delay or impediment.

Pretty Mistress Katherine waxed very red, and said one name was as good as another, but for her part she would as lief not marry a man called Bouchier, for in French that meant butcher.

Johanna Dacre then said that she liked no flower so well as a pansy.

"You should call it, 'heart's-ease,' Joan," cried Gwendoline Talbot, Lord Lisle's daughter; "'tis a more comfortable name."

"Nay, I see not that," quoth Johanna.

"O yes," rejoined the other, "for in French a pansy is a pensée, and that means thought; and thought, mesdames, is troublesome, and often robs folks of their rest."

"Come!" exclaimed some one,—Mary Beaumont, I think,—"there is a lady there which is a great thinker, and yet is not robbed of her sleep."

"Who said that?" I asked, opening mine eyes. They all laughed, and cried I should guess; but I would not—I was too sleepy. So after a pause one said,

"O, Maud Everingham! I ween you have had a letter this morn from Isabel Woodville."

"I pray you call her Elisabeth," said another.

"Nay, call her Bessy," little Margaret Beaufort cried. "Pretty winsome Bessy! but, mesdames, as the Queen says when she speaks to you, I am greatly displeased that none of you have chosen her majesty's flower and mine—the white and pink daisy; is it not a very fair one?"

"We all wear the daisy in our hearts," Lady Gwendoline Talbot said. "But now, Maud," she added, "prithee let us hear Bell or Bessy's letter. 'Tis a pity she was not called Jacquetta, like her mother; but when this was proposed, her grace exclaimed, 'Forsooth, no! These English would call her Jacket, which would be an unseemly name.'"

"Now, now, let Maud read," cried several voices; but Maud refused to read or show the letter, to the no small vexation of those damsels: for methinks such as live at court have a greater craving for any kind of news or reports touching the concerns of others than any other persons in the world. However, when they had dispersed, which happened soon, and they found Maud was resolved not to yield to their entreaties, she took the missive from her bosom and gave it into my hands, desiring my counsel thereon. As it seemeth to me a notable thing that two personages of great merit and nobility should address a young lady touching the suit of a private gentleman, I transcribe Mistress Woodville's epistle.

"WELL-BELOVED MAUD,—I thank you for your gentle letter, full tenderly written to me some time ago; and I doubt not you marvel that I have so long delayed to reply thereunto. I cry you mercy, sweet Maud, for this my slothful behaviour. Verily, I am a more hearty lover than a ready writer, and I have had to pen two letters this week; and to whom you would never guess—no, not if you exercised your wit from this time to doomsday. What think you, mistress? Should it not be a wonderful thing if the Duke of York and the great young Earl of Warwick should demean themselves to write with their own hands to simple Elisabeth Woodville, though indeed she hath a very noble princess for her mother! But methinks they might have employed their pens to a better purpose than to try to persuade a poor maiden to wed a landless knight, albeit a very excellent gentleman—I mean that long-patient, silent wooer you wot of, Sir Hugh John, who never could find courage to speak for himself. And so nothing will serve this humble man but that the Duke of York, forsooth, must turn suitor in his behalf; for, saith his grace, 'he is credibly informed that his well-beloved knight Sir Hugh John, for the great womanhood and gentleness approved in my person, hath wholly given unto me his heart. Howbeit, he adds, my disposition towards him is yet unknown. But he doth heartily pray me to be well willed to the performing of this his desire, and I shall therein do him pleasure; and further, also, he doubts not my great weal and worship in time to come.' Great weal, in sooth, it should prove to live in Wales and be a poor man's wife! I had as lief be a nun. Howsoever, the duke adds, that if I fulfil his intent in this matter, he will be to him and me such lord as shall be to both our great advantage. This caused me to reflect a little, for to precipitate in these matters showeth little prudence. John Gray also desires to do me worship in the way of marriage, and would be the best husband of the twain. But I would not suddenly deny the duke's wishing, and so wrote a humble letter to say the knight could come to Grafton, and I would civilly entertain him; which I did, to John Gray's no small discontent, who hath heard of it. But when Sir Hugh pressed his suit too warmly, I dismissed him with an obliging answer, neither wholly denying or allowing of his suit; which is what her grace my mother advised me. But yesterday I received a letter from the Earl of Warwick which I copy entire, that you may judge if I have need of good counsel, when I am so pressed by two such mighty advocates.

'Worshipful and well-beloved,—I greet you well. And forasmuch my right well-beloved Sir Hugh John, which now late was with you unto his full great joy, and had great cheer, as he saith (methinks the gentleman was easily contented), whereof I thank you, hath informed me now that he hath unto your person, as well as for the great seriousness and wisdom that he hath found and proved in you at that time, as for your great and praised beauty and womanly demeaning, he desireth with all haste to do you worship by the way of marriage, before any other creature living, as he saith. I, considering his said desire and the great worship that he had, which was made knight at Jerusalem, and after his coming home, for the great wisdom and manhood that he was renowned of, was made Knight Marshall of France, and after of England, with other his great virtues and deserts, and also the good and notable service that he hath done and daily doth to me, write unto you at this time and pray you affectuously that you will the rather at this my request and prayer condescend to this his lawful and honest desire, wherein you shall provide notably for yourself unto your weal and worship in time to come, and cause me to show you such good patronage as you by reason of it shall hold you content and pleased, with the grace of God, which everlastingly have you in bliss, protection, and governance.

'*Written by the* EARL OF WARWICK.'

"Now, well-beloved Maud, herein lieth my perplexity. Patronage is good, but lands are better. The good lordship of these two great peers is not lightly to be thought of; but what if, gaining their favour, I should lose the good opinion of her majesty? Sir Hugh John is a sightly person and a valiant soldier; but methinks the Duchess of Bedford's daughter should not be content to be called Lady John, and her fortunes to depend on a less person than the King. If I marry John Gray, then I wed the heir of the wealthy Lord Ferrers of Groby; and if you and Margaret de Roos will be my good friends in this matter, and speak to the Queen, so that she shall discern that out of loyalty to her majesty I have refused the Duke of York's and Lord Warwick's suitor, then she will, I doubt not, bestow on me an equal dowry to that which she hath granted to Isminia Scales and Joan Dacre, that is, 200*l.*; and then the Lord Ferrers shall be satisfied, for her grace my mother will give me the portion she hath promised, which you know; and if so, I shall be well content to marry John Gray: in good hour be it. I beseech God send you good health and greater joy in one year than you have had in seven.

"Your loving true friend,
ELISABETH WOODVILLE.

Written at Grafton Castle,
Tuesday, 14th of July 1449."

"What think you?" said Maud Everingham, when I returned to her this letter.

I smiled, and answered: "What I think is, that Mistress Elisabeth hath the most innocent countenance and the profoundest cunning of any maiden of her years alive."

"Some are of opinion," Maud answered, "that she is simple."

"Well," I replied, "there is maybe some simplicity in the plain unvarnished avowal this letter doth contain. Even to a friend some would have feigned to be more generous, and less careful of their own weal."

"She is the most gentle person on the earth, and of so sweet a disposition that one must needs like her," Maud replied. "It is not to be credited how many gentlemen are in love with Bessy, though she is so silent and reserved that none can affirm she favours their suit. And for all that she has little or no tocher, few damsels have had so many offers of marriage."

"It is a noticeable thing," I answered, "that these silent women, if they have beauty and prudence, are the most apt to inspire love. As they show no marked preference for any one, all which admire them are like each to suppose he is most favoured. And if the lady only once smiles, or lifts up her downcast eyes, or accepts a trifling service at his hands, my lord or master is straightway enraptured, and ready to fall at her feet. Then a sweet blush, and a 'Nay, nay, I pray your lordship,' or 'I beseech you, sir, forbear,' checks the presumptuous lover, and dismisses him for that time without more ado, but not quite in despair. O, I have watched these pretty tricks; and albeit two-thirds of the men in the world—yea, more perhaps—

are justly served when women make fools of them, it mislikes me to see a good and brave gentleman like Sir Hugh John caught in these smooth traps."

"Nay," cried Maud, "you are too severe."

"You are too good," I said. "There is none, be they so full of defects as an egg is of meat, but you defend them. If the devil had need of an advocate—"

"Nay," she interrupted, with a pained countenance, "say not so, dear Meg. But methinks our Lord God used not bitter words even to the devil, but only drove him away with words of holy writ. But prithee, sweet lady, wilt thou move the Queen to do that good to Elisabeth?"

"For thy sake, Maud, and none other," I replied. "But I would it had been thee, not she, that was to be married."

"Married!" she exclaimed. "I'll warrant thee I shall be more nobly wedded than poor Bessy."

"How so?" I asked, surprised.

"No meaner bridegroom than the King of kings can content my ambition," she said. And I then saw her intent was to be a nun. Well, the more I know and hear of courts and the ups and downs and dire haps of this toilsome world, the greater groweth in me an esteem of the life religious persons lead, albeit I never found in myself any calling thereunto.

The Queen was well pleased to give Mistress Woodville a portion; for she said John Gray was a leal gentleman of good renown, and his father a devoted friend of the late king.

CHAPTER XVIII.

The Red Rose.

A CHANGE hath come over the King. He shows more concern about the Duke of Suffolk's murther than he hath yet evinced at the ill-usage of his friends. The spark of fire in his nature which the Queen hath long laboured to kindle is at last elicited. The spirit of his father awakes. Now that tidings have reached London that one Jack Cade, a mean fellow which calls himself Mortimer, hath raised the mob in Kent,—instigated, many surmise, by the Duke of York,—and is marching towards the city, for the first time the King is roused to action, and takes the lead in his own council. With absolute and royal disdain he rejects the insolent petitions of Master Amendall, this common fellow, and new reformer of grievances; and nothing will serve his majesty but to command himself his forces against these turbulent aggressors. Methinks this is the most glad hour the Queen hath yet known. If I should live to be a hundred years old, I could not forget her looks. She watches with an inexpressible delight the King's actions, and seems to revive in the new light of his countenance. When she saw him put on his armour, convene his officers, and address them in words which caused them to start with a glad surprise, as if the victor of Agincourt had risen from the dead to lead them, she was well-nigh beside herself with joy.

"See," she whispered to me,—"see the new fire in my lord's eye. Angel-like as ever is his beauteous face; but now 'tis the avenging Archangel, the commissioner of the high God, we behold in him. At the last men will perceive the nobility of his wonderful soul, in which courage equals virtue, and a passionate love of God marshals all other merits befitting a king and a hero."

I saw her ride forth from the palace this morn by the side of her lord, apparelled in warlike guise, which became her well; the steed which carried her curvetting proudly, as if glorying in his burthen. Her face beamed with a radiant beauty. Thus the queen of Amazons should have looked, or the pictured goddess of war leading captive kings in her train. Her chest seemed to expand, and her slight form to dilate, with the chivalrous spirit which fired her dark eye. The smile with which she greeted the old Lord Shrewsbury when he came to her side was bright enough to illuminate the world with its shine. Ever and anon I saw her casting quick glances at the King, whose cheek was flushed with war-like ardour, and his eye sparkling with an unwonted vivacity.

Some hours' suspense have elapsed. I went into the Abbey to pray at St. Edward's tomb; for in prayer alone could I find strength to endure this waiting for news.

A messenger hath come. Joy, O, joy greater than can be thought of! The very sight of the royal troops, and the report of his majesty's presence, hath dissolved the rebel bands like snow melts in the sunshine. They have dispersed in disorder, and Jack Cade himself hath fled, 'tis reported, to the thickets behind Seven Oaks. An easy victory is at hand. A council, hastily gathered together on the field, is taking

measures for the pursuit and the final rout of these
miscreants by the King, who shall firmly settle his
glorious rule. O, my Queen, this joyful hour hath
come! What a glad return shall be thine!

The night hath come. Its dark veil is spread over
the sky; and how deep a shade of gloom hath fallen
on my heart! O God! O God! too well I foresee the
mournful hap. O God! to look on that face so glad
this morn, and see it as it will be this night when she
arrives! Henry Bouchier hath ridden from the field.
I met him on the stairs. "Is the King defeated?"
I cried, trembling. "No, not defeated," quoth he in
a surly tone; "I had as lief it was so." "Heavens!
what mean you?" I exclaimed. "This," he replied;
"that when victory was secure if he advanced, and his
name acting with more power than the report of 20,000
men, and every heart beating with joy and triumph
that he should prove a King at last, lo, a report goes
forth — God forgive me! I could swear, and curse,
and grind my teeth at the thought of it; and would it
were only a thought, not a miserable deed! — I say,
the report goes forth that the King hath resigned the
command to Sir Humphrey Stafford, and forthwith
returns to London with the Queen. I warrant you,
oaths and curses did then abound; for like a dismal
cloud on a fair sky, this sinister news dulled ardour,
checked loyalty, spread confusion amongst the troops;
and when those scattered tinkers hear of it, God
knoweth how their courage shall revive!" "Alas for
the Queen!" I cried; "I am much sorry for her."
"The Queen!" he exclaimed. "Why, nothing would
serve the Queen but to bring back the King in this
base manner. He would fain have advanced, 'tis
thought. He had declared he should not rest or sleep
till the last rebel had surrendered. She too was urging

—so I was told—a hot pursuit, and with kindling eye and eloquent words urging the lords not to delay one instant, when a panic seized her most strange and sudden. The colour at once forsook her cheeks, her lips quivered, a quaking anguish shook her limbs; she frantically prayed the King to leave the army, would listen to no arguments, but held his arm, and, with large tears streaming from her eyes, besought him to return with her to London. And when Lord Shrewsbury and others tried to speak to her, she would not heed, but dragged the King aside; and soon I received orders to ride to Westminster to announce their coming back. Heavens! what a poor feeble reed is courage in a woman! I deemed this Queen had been as brave as any man in Christendom; and now, by her cowardly fears, she hath ruined the King; for I tell you, Dame Margaret, the desertion of his troops this day shall never be forgot. This hath been an evil hap for the House of Lancaster!" He went sorrowfully away; and I am waiting in the Queen's chamber.

October 7th.

O, what a return was that on the 25th of September! I dared not lift mine eyes to the Queen's visage when she entered. "Shut the door," she said; and when we were alone fell into mine arms and hid her face in my bosom. The King was some days reported ill, and few went into his chamber. News came soon that the rebels had rallied, caught the royal troops in an ambush, slain Sir Humphrey Stafford and his brother, and encamped on Blackheath. His Grace of Canterbury and my Lord Buckingham went to parley with them, but that false varlet the pretended Sir John Mortimer would not treat with any, forsooth, but the King in person, and, like a stage-player, strutted about as a king himself in gilt armour. Seditious cries were heard in London, "Long live Mortimer! Long live the Duke of York!" The rebels marched on towards Westminster, and their majesties, with the court, fled to Kenilworth Castle, where I write this.

Last evening the Queen said to me, "Ah, then, Master Bouchier is of opinion that womanly fears moved me to carry back the King to London from the army. If so, he should do well to despise me, although I am a queen and his sovereign. And thou, Meg, dost thou think the same?"

"Madame," I replied, "I think that was the bravest action that your majesty shall ever have, I pray God, to perform."

"Yea," she said in a low voice; "and thou mayest say the like of my flying with my lord to this place when Cade approached London. The day may come when an easier sort of courage will be witnessed in Margaret of Anjou. Hast heard that vile impostor, the pretended knight, smote with his staff on London stone, and cried, 'Now is Mortimer lord of London?' York, the ungrateful duke, the false Plantagenet, is the spring of this vile rabble's rising. Horrors are enacted in London—murthers, robberies, and fighting day and night in the streets. But the burgesses are well nigh weary of these reformers. A general pardon will soon be proclaimed by the advice of Waynfleet; but I will have some exceptions made to it. There is one John Payn in prison, the servant of Sir John Falstolf, an obstinate knave, who will not impeach his master of treason; but I know that knight is a traitor, and I will have his head."

This was the first time I had heard the like words from my mistress's lips, and they fell on my ear with a grating, ominous sound.

"Yes," she repeated, " he is a partisan of York, and he ill-used my countryman, Champchévrier. I tell you I will have his head."

I heard a sigh, and turning round, saw the door of the King's chamber open. The Queen took me by the hand, and said:

"Come and see his majesty. He used to like thy playing on the gittern;" and she led me in.

When I saw his face, a sort of awe stole over me. It was so still, so calm, like a waveless sea. His eyes were raised to heaven, and his lips moving slowly. The Queen knelt by his side, striving to hear what he said, her eager intent eyes fixed on his motionless form. His voice was a little raised, and I caught these words; "Dimitte nobis debita nostra, sicut et nos dimittimus debitoribus nostris, et ne nos inducas in tentationem; sed libera nos a malo." Had he heard in his silent trance the fierce words she had uttered? Methinks this thought crossed her mind. She kissed his brow and withdrew.

"Meg," she said in a low voice, with an inexpressibly sorrowful countenance, "the sins of the fathers are visited on the children. But this is not "—she paused —"this is not madness; the mind is not distraught— only absent; far from this earth; in heaven, I sometimes think. But these intervals are short. Soon the King will be restored. I know when these clouds are rising, I discern when they are about to disperse. At Blackheath I saw that awful calm falling like a mist on his spirit, and snatched him from the wild scene. Now thou knowest the secret which, since the Duke of Gloucester's death, hath darkened my young years. There, in the horror of that sudden event, the cloud first showed. I dared not breathe the thought to any soul; even then the remembrance of King Charles

VI.'s malady darted across my brain. Under the seal of confession I disclosed it to the Bishop of Winchester. It was no new light to him. He tried to comfort me, as holy men are wont to do; but he dispelled not my fear. I took counsel from him, and found him wise as well as good; the love of the priest and the aged man for his young King well nigh equalled the passion of the wife poured forth at his feet in those hours when a queen forgets her crown. We have since often devised means for his entertainment, which none know the value of but I, which day by day watch every turn of his countenance. Books and paintings, the adornment of churches, quiet converse with God in prayer and learned men in privacy, almsgiving, too, compose the King's mind, and mend his health. Alas, in the first years of marriage I shook unwittingly the delicate fabric of that rare mind by impetuous excitations and impassioned leadings to uncongenial virtues; now, like one skilled in the notes of a fine sensitive instrument, I touch cautiously each chord, and watch the vibrations thereof." Then she said, with a gentleness of tone and look which I now always observe in her in the King's presence, or even in speaking of him, "May it please God I should so play upon this holy instrument that no jarring may ensue, but only sweet and peaceful music!" So saying she dismissed me.

When the rebellion was ended and the ringleaders slain, we returned to London; and I marvel, now that the Queen's secret is disclosed to me, at the rare prudence she evinced in the hiding thereof from any but the most leal attendants on the King. When news came before we left Kenilworth of Lord Say's execution by the rebels, she told his majesty this dire hap without apparent emotion, and in so religious and comfortable a manner that he was noways shaken, albeit grieved at it. Yet I had seen her in her chamber grind her teeth and clench her hands, like a fire-eyed fury, with an uncontrolled passion; but the moment she entered the King's chamber she was as calm and mild as if perfect peace reigned in her bosom. And in London this year I have witnessed the like wonderful governance of herself when the Duke of York marched thither from Ireland with four thousand men, to the great terror of the Court. The Duke of Somerset was not yet returned from France, on whom she builds her hopes; and with a patience and composure which would to God she did more often use at other times, she witnessed the interview between the King and the ungrateful duke, wherein he demanded that a parliament should be summoned; and his request was granted. Compressed lips and pale cheeks belied her outward calmness, but not one intemperate word or look betrayed it.

The King and Queen are overjoyed at the coming of the Duke of Somerset; and I see he will reign in their counsels as did the Duke of Suffolk, which causes no little uneasiness to their majesties' well-wishers. For this duke hath a most violent character, and is detested by the commons and disliked by the peers, because of the ill-success of his government in France and the loss of so many provinces to this country. He was committed to the Tower by the parliament a short time ago; but now the session is over he is released and favours showered on him. The Queen, alas, disguises not her hatred of his foes, and makes no choice betwixt the enemies of the crown and those of Edward Beaufort. To-day there is a banquet at Guildhall; and at her toilet-table I knelt to her, with many tears beseeching her not to wear a posy of red roses in her bosom, for my brother Edmund yester eve related to the gaping ladies of the court the hap at the Temple Gardens—the fierce quarrel betwixt the Duke of Somerset and my Lord Warwick, the seditious speeches of York's friends, the angry retorts of the Beauforts, and the Queen's name injuriously mixed up in the invectives of their enemies. O God! is there no honesty, no virtue, no innocency of life, no conjugal affection, which shall shield a royal lady from blaspheming tongues and false aspersions? Methinks a nation should resent as the most arrant injury accusations which if true should be its most loathsome shame, and visit with revenge these vile slanders on one whose name should be as sacred to every Englishman as his wife's or his daughter's. But, alas, alas! the Queen, by a misplaced chivalry and dangerous confidence, secure in her virtue, proud of her unsullied life, dares with headstrong wilfulness the malice of her enemies.

"Madame," I cried, with anguished supplications,—"Madame, for your own sake, for the King's, for God's, throw aside the bloody-coloured rose which disfigures your bosom. Pluck that fatal flower from your breast. Let not England see you wear the badge of Somerset."

"Of Lancaster, Meg," she exclaimed, looking down complacently on the ill-omened flower,—"of royal Lancaster! Red is the proper hue for the rose; white roses are pale mean counterfeits. See how sweetly the Reine Marguerite and the red rose match together!" As she said this, she joined together a pink and white daisy and a damask blossom.

"Madame," I cried, almost weeping, "is it thus you dally with a danger greater than can be well expressed?"

Then her eye gave one of their sudden flashes.

"Now," she cried, "Honi soit qui mal y pense! Dishonoured be the wretched who shall dare to call this flower the badge of Somerset! It is the rallying sign of every loyal heart, of which Somerset is only the chief. It is the mark by which friends shall be known from foes. It is the flower of those that love the King. I will wear it as I ride along the streets of London. I will plant it on the battlements of every fortress in the realm. None that hold by me shall fail to wear it in their breasts or their bonnets, or they shall be thought traitors. It shall grow on every inch of English ground; and if not red enough to please their English eyes, let them dye it in the blood of York!"

She went into the meek King's chamber, as was her wont, when adorned for the banquet, and she wore the red rose in her bosom. He smiled as he greeted her, and praised the perfume of her flowers. She took one from her posy and fastened it to his vesture. It made me sad to see it there. After that day all the ladies of the court fashioned badges of the like kind in ribbons and paper, and gave them to their friends. The die is cast. As God wills, so be it!

CHAPTER XIX.

A Gleam from the South.

ONE day at the Tower, when I was in waiting on the Queen, there was a heavy mist on the river, so that the opposite bank could not be seen: the air was chill and damp, and naught was to be seen under the windows save barges full of coal unloading on the bank. Her majesty was sitting at a little table with a lighted taper, for it was too dark to read without a candle even at noontide. She held two letters in her hand, and as she gazed upon them a heavy sigh escaped her.

"From the north and from the south," she said, as I looked the question I durst not ask. "The contents are dissimilar," she added; "yet both make me sad. This is from my kinswoman, Marie de Gueldres, the Queen of Scotland. Alas, the brave Lord Douglas is no more!"

"What! the noble chief whom your majesty entertained with such great cheer when he returned from his pilgrimage to Rome?" I exclaimed.

"Yea, and who had promised to bring an army to aid us against York, if he should take the field against us."

"Alas, is he dead?"

"Yes," she replied; "and what think you is reported? That King James slew him with his own hand! Is it not horrible? Methinks it is enough that I should look favourably on any one, and then misfortunes follow him. What a murtherous sky is this beneath the which we live! dark as if the day of doom was at hand! And list to the dull croaking voices of those men at work on the water!"

"Is your majesty's other letter sad, also?" I said, to turn her thoughts from the first.

"Sad!" she exclaimed. " You may read it, Meg. It should be a remedy for sadness, if the joylity of others could cure selfish dejection." Then she sighed again, and perusing that long letter which came from France, smiled once or twice, and then sighed again. It was from the Princess Yolande, her sister; and these were its contents:

"Ah, Madame Marguerite, queen of love and beauty, wherefore doth cruel fate so long divide us? Wherefore doth that most entirely beloved daughter and sister of our hearts never gladden by her sweet presence our longing eyes? Would that a fairy had spread her wings and flown to your great London, and from the midst of your fine palace snatched you like Jove did Europa from the flowery mead, where she did frolic, and carried your majesty across the sea and the land to this sweet field of Fornica, under the walls of Tarascon! O, how welcome should be the flying genius and its royal burthen! I' faith, sweet Marguerite, these have been days of so much joylity, pleasance, and entertainment, that the like hath not been seen for many years. Messire Rumurin, the pursuivant, proclaimed the tournament in all Provence, and many noble lords, knights, ladies, and damsels came from Aix, Nismes, Arles, Marseilles, and Montpellier, to this fair castle, which is the home of pleasure and delight. Banquets and plays, dances and masquerades, and sham fights of all kinds enliven the day and night. My lord and Louis de Beauveau have already in sport broken lances with so great skill and grace, that nothing could exceed the contentment of this noble company. But I would have thee to know that this is not a simple martial tournament, like the emprise of the dragon's mouth at Saumur, our father's fair and well-seated city, where Ferry won so many trophies some time ago, and the ladies' prize from the hands of Jeanne de Laval, who was then only thirteen years of age, and a kiss from her fair lips. I took from him that rare casket, which is studded with precious stones, for I said he had had a kiss from the dame Jeanne, and that should be enough for him. But he said, if I kept the box, I should pay him with as many kisses as there are pearls and brilliants on it. I warrant thee, dear sister, that Ferry, though a gay knight, and gallant in his devoirs to the ladies, esteems one hair of his poor wife's head more than all the dames of Lorraine and Provence together. But this Jeanne de Laval is a most wonderful young princess; the like of her hath not been seen since Madame Marguerite d'Anjou crossed the seas, leaving France behind her. The singularity of this little damsel lieth in this: she never laughs, nor scarcely smiles, yet in her countenance there is a winsomeness which ravishes all beholders. The King our father hath idolised her from her cradle. Messire Guy de Laval and Madame Isabelle de Bretagne, her parents, do not love her more, I ween, than the King and Queen of Sicily. Now he is reft of thee, he affections Jeanne with an almost excessive tenderness. She is the lady and the queen of all the sports he invents, the theme of his poems, and the little sovereign of the court. Our sweet mother, whose health daily declines, is never so contented as when this little damsel is with her, And I will tell thee a secret. A few nights since, when I was sitting by her side, on her favourite seat, which overlooks the Rhone, she said to me, 'Fair daughter, my life shall not last many years —nay, many months it may be; and God knoweth I should like to die and go to His Paradise when purged of my sins, whereunto thine and other good prayers shall, I hope, help me. But it causeth me annoy that my lord the King my entirely loved husband, will suffer so great sorrow when I depart, that his health shall suffer, and grief consume his heart. For we have been most dear and loving to each other through a life full of sad haps, yet sweetened by an extraordinary mutual affection. One used to the watchful tenderness of a wife can ill exist alone; and when I have been dead a little while, I would have your father marry—not ever to forget me, for where a great love hath filled the heart, the memory thereof can never die—but that he may find comfort, and cheerful company and consolation in trials from one who shall love him, if not with the passionate liking I had for him, and which yet endures as vivid as if age had heated rather than cooled its fervour, yet with the reverential, trustful and tender love which advanced years inspire when divested of defects and stamped with virtuous glory.' I kissed that dear mother's hand, and denied that she was like to die. Then she said, 'Now let not what I am about to utter pass your lips, Yolande, except the day shall come when the knowledge thereof shall shed a sweet comfort in thy father's heart. My prayer, my hope, and dear wish— think it not too strange— is this—' She looked at me so much as to inquire if I divined what she was about to say; and as I nothing spoke, she went on, 'I would that my lord should marry, when I am dead, Jeanne de Laval.' I started in amazement. 'Yea,' she rejoined, answering my unuttered thought, 'she is very young; but there is more thinking, I will warrant it, in that youthful head, as noble a purity in that young heart, as great valour in that high soul, as in any woman in France. I have watched her with this secret thought, and listened to her innocent conversation with a jealous, careful curiosity which cannot be deceived. I note that she despises youthful homage, spurns free gallantry, loathes unseemly discourse; and when I have seen her bestow the guerdon of prowess in the lists, she has offered her pretty blushing cheek to the victor with a modest shamefacedness and dignified behaviour which well became her noble birth and virtuous breeding. Her great love for the King, begun in childhood, will turn, if she is his wife, not so much into a flower of passion, but rather into the rich fruit of wifely affection. Ah, fair daughter, when in the night-watches I lie awake, forecasting my lord's grief when he is reft of me, ever I see before me rise, like a consoling vision, the sweet grave visage of Jeanne de Laval, which never laughs and rarely smiles, but like the sober shine of the moon, doth shed light and breathe peace. I shall die the happier for this hope.' 'Nay, live the longer for it,' I answered smiling, and, with a tender kiss, parted from her. I pray thee, dear Marguerite, when hath conjugal love been more disinterested than in this noble woman's heart?—when evinced by a more forecasting solicitude and unjealous regard for her lord's happiness? I fear my love for Ferry is a baser one; for if I were to die I should mislike him to be too quickly consoled, and I warrant thee I should grievously jalouse the lady who should replace me.

"Since this discourse with our mother the Queen, I have taken more heed of the singular affection of the demoiselle Jeanne for the King. If one says: 'The Comte de St. Pol is a valiant lord,' 'Passably so,' she answers; 'but not so brave as the King of Sicily.' Or if the Comte de Nevers' martial aspect is praised, she replies, 'he hath in sooth a fine carriage; but what is it in comparison with King René's?' If Poton de Saintrailles breaketh a lance with wondrous skill, she affirms Monseigneur the King can do it better; if any one exclaims (and I warrant thee this is a very frequent speech in the mouths of princes and ladies), 'Is there a knight, lord, or gentilhomme which for strength of arm, greatness of soul, beauty of face and person, can be likened to Ferry de Lorraine?' —then Mademoiselle de Laval says, 'He resembles his father-in-law, whom few can equal, none excel.' If the talk is of poesy, and others commend Monseigneur Charles d'Orléans or Messire Chastelain's verses, she shakes her head, and maintains that for her part she sees more philosophy, cunning, and beauty in the romance of *De très douce Mercy au Cœur d'Amour épris* than in any other poem in the world. She thinks Messire Van Eycke is a poorer limner than his pupil, and Antoine de la Salle a writer of less wit than his kingly master. When the Duchesse d'Alençon called Alain Chartier '*le bien disant*,' the petite demoiselle whispered in mine ear, 'I know a *meilleur disant* than even Messire Alain.'

"Now will it please thee to learn the style and fashion of this present passage of arms, the most quaint, dainty, and pleasurable that ever has been witnessed. Instead of the pavillon de joyeuse garde, all decked with cloth-of-gold and flags, there is at one end of the field a green flowery cabin, wherein a fair shepherdess tends her lambs. Instead of the haute et puissante demoiselle de Laval which guerdoned

the victors at Saumur, with two lions chained by her
side, here is the gentle pastourelle Jeanne, dressed in
a gray kirtle, wearing on her fair hair a crown of
roses, and holding in her hand a little silver crook.
Philibert de Laigues and Philippe de Lenoncourt, her
two brave champions and comely shepherds, stand
by her side. The knights which enter the lists touch
with their swords the black and white shields nigh to
the cabin, and this is the signal of defiance. The
victor's prize is a posy and a kiss from the fair
shepherdess; but other gifts she also bestows. On
the first day Pierre Carrion, the Sire de Beauveau,
Tanneguy du Chatel, and others, contended with much
skill and valiant ardour; but Ferry won the guerdon,
and on my finger I wear the victor's ring. When
Jeanne presented it to him, he gave her in return the
rich housings of his steed. Messire Honoré de Berre,
a very learned and honourable gentleman of Aix, but
little used to these combats, also entered the lists.
The king our father strove to dissuade him therefrom,
but nothing else would serve him; and, lo and behold,
before he ever encountered his adversary he rolled off
his horse, which swerved, and his great weight and
heavy armour impeded his rising, which caused much
diversion amongst the spectators. Louis de Beauveau
says that even the grave Pastourelle Jeanne laughed;
which, if true, should be almost a miracle. Gaspard
de Cossa for the first time tilted to-day. The king,
who singularly affections this youth, leaving his royal
seat, descended into the field to minister advice to
his inexperience, and furnish him with new lances
when his own were split. He thus often assists young
knights in their first essays; and these marks of goodness do marvellously endear his Majesty to his subjects.
When Messire Duguesclin was a prisoner, he said,

'There is not one spinner in France but would spin to ransom me.' And I say, There is not a woman or man in his dominions but would die for King René. I hope there is also not an Englishman that would not die for thee, sweet sister.

"Well, in the evenings pleasant poetry and gay music beguile the swiftly flying hours. Each knight and lady is constrained to furnish a poem or a song; and some steal away in the day to search in books for fair pearls of harmonious lore. If any one doth possess a copy of the Duke of Orléans' lays, or Alain Chartier's, or Messire Chastelain's, or Olivier de la Marche's poems, then he is envied. Such as possess the gift of poesy compose little pieces themselves, to the great contentment of the company. I would fain send thee some of these witty flowrets; but be content, madame, with this little conceit in your own praise:

> 'All other flowrets drop their leaves
> When blows the cold east wind;
> But steadfast daisies, pure and white,
> Still in their place you find.'

Now, who think you wrote this quatrain? Thereby hangs a little tale, which your Majesty shall hear. The king our father said yester eve that the poem was most to his liking which had yet been recited was the lay of Messire Olivier de la Marche, called *The Knight's Vesture for his Lady*, which runneth thus:

> 'Lady, I am no limner;
> My hand cannot portray
> The beauty of thy face;
> But my pen shall essay
> To frame for thee a vesture
> So perfect, so complete,
> So graceful and so fine,
> So virtuous and so sweet,

That in the eyes of God most high,
And men also I ween,
This habit shall surpass
The rarest ever seen.

Fair honesty shall be thy smock;
Thy slippers humble thoughts;
Thy shoes a spotless conscience;
Thy garters firm resolves;
Thy pincushion meek patience;
Thy rings nobility;
Thy knife impartial justice;
Thy kerchief modest haviour;
Thy ribbon duteous fear of God;
Thy comb contrition keen;
Thy stay-lace perfect charity;
Thy kirtle daily prayer;
And last of all thy mirror,
The wholesome thought of death.'

"When the King exceedingly commended this piece of verse, Ferry said, 'I warrant your Majesty I can write in one minute four lines which will please you more than Messire Olivier's ingenious poem.'

"The King smilingly defied him to do it. Then Ferry, holding the paper on his knee, penned in less than a minute the lines touching the steadfast daisy, and gave them to the King, who, when he read them, said quickly, with tears in his eyes, 'Fair son, je n'en peux mais. You have vanquished. The verses which praise Marguerite must needs content me the most.'

"What a good father we have, and what fine children God hath given me! and would it should please his Holy Majesty to give thee the like blessing! And now this is the last day of this great emprise, which shall be remembered as long, methinks, as France exists and memory endures of chivalry, poesy, and art—the gay savoir and King René's code.

"It was not till this eve that our father adjudged

the final prize of this magnificent passage of arms. I promise thee my heart beat very fast when, in the midst of all the court and the foreign ladies, his majesty rose to declare the victor; and it gave a great bound as if jumping for joy, when the cry rose 'Prégny! Prégny! Lorraine a le Prix!' Ferry received the golden wand, the posy, and a diamond worth one hundred pieces of gold, from the gentille Pastourelle. And what think you he did? He besought her to keep them all! Methinks this beau sire is something too generous. But it was soon bruited that nothing would serve Jeanne but that the diamond should be sold for the relief of the plague-stricken of Aix. After the dancing was over, the whole court was entertained in the pavilion of Louis de Beauveau; and the King sent there for the ladies sweet confections and rare fruits. The sky was so beautiful that the night seemed almost as bright as the day. The moonshine lighted the swift river with a soft radiance. The most entrancing lays, in which poesy is sweetly married to music, sounded in our ears; and nothing marred those gleesome hours, which only, like the fast-flowing Rhone, passed too quickly.

"The Dauphin hath come to this province since the death of his sweet wife. Her last words were those she often used towards the end of her brief life: 'Fi de la vie! ne m'en parlez plus.' Monseigneur our cousin maketh no end of pilgrimages, and hath visited la Sainte Beaume and many other sanctuaries, and he writeth to Rome touching the relics of the Maries disinterred lately on the coast. The good people of this country take him to be a saint, and cry out when he passes, 'Noël, Noël! Viva lou Daouphin!' Agnes, the dame de beauté, hath died at Rouen with great sorrow for her sins, and an exceeding great desire to atone for them, if time should have been afforded her. Fra Bernardino of Siena is also dead, and, as all believe, gone straight to heaven; for miracles have already been wrought by his invocation when his corpse was exposed in the church of Massa. Our father is sorely grieved at his decease, but hopeth much from his prayers now he is with God. And now no more, sweet sister. I recommend myself very humbly to your Majesty and to the King my good brother. We all pray to Jesu to have you in His keeping.

"Yolande d'Anjou."

"Ah, fair land!" exclaimed the Queen, who had followed with her eyes my reading of this letter. "Fair Provence! sweet skies, loving visages, chivalrous hearts, ye have passed away from me like a dream!"

"Alas, madame," I said, "do you grieve that you are England's queen?"

"Nay," she quickly replied; "now less then ever." The colour rose in her cheek.

"The day I am a mother," she added in a low voice, "I shall be as happy as Yolande."

That day came. O, my poor Queen!

CHAPTER XX.

A Visit to the Country.

BY reason of a sickness I had in the course of the year 1454, I was advised by the physicians to remove from London for a season; and therefore, released for the space of six months from my attendance at court, I went to the house of Mistress Elisabeth Clere, a kinswoman of my mother's, which lived near Norwich. The day before I left town, this letter came to me from my father. Its contents did but increase the heaviness I then endured, as will be seen by those who read it.

The Lord de Roos to his Daughter.

"I greet you well, my dear daughter, and send you God's blessing and mine; and touching the matter which by your means their majesties desire I should inform them of, and write them the truth thereof, I have discovered, through the reports of honourable spies, that Monseigneur Gilles is yet in prison; and that the letter which our sovereign lord the King sent by the hands of the King of France, or rather the French king I should say, and which was so noble and so reasonable that nothing more convincing could be thought of, failed of its effect because that king joined to it one from his own self, which weakened its urgency, and rather should incite the Duke of Brittany to persevere in his ill-usage of his brother than dissuade him from it. So greatly hath this ill-usage increased, that he is withdrawn from any care or charge of honourable men, and committed to the hands of one Olivier de Meêl, an extremely wicked man, the creature of the Maréchal de Montauban. These wretches have, it is said, shut up the prince in a dark dungeon, and cruelly maltreated him. Verily it seems they would kill him in this wise, whom no judges can be found to condemn. Contrariwise, the Estates of Brittany publicly absolved him, to the no small anger of the duke and his favourite. Then the prince found means from his prison to write to his liege lord the King of—I mean the French king—a narrative of the horrible sufferings he endured, and entreated to be released by his authority, and brought before him to confront his accusers. The same messenger also took letters from the Lady Françoise d'Amboise (who hath the keeping of the prince's little wife), and likewise from the Constable de Richemont, to the king, beseeching him with much liberty and urgency to procure his nephew's deliverance. And this time they succeeded; for the king sent the Admiral Coëtivy to the duke to enforce that demand, who under this pressure, yielded; and Monseigneur Gilles was informed that he was about to be set free, to the no small joy of his well-wishers. But the news thereof had hardly reached the ears of his friends, when the wicked malice of his enemies invented a foul stratagem whereby this fair dawn of hope was overcast. A herald appeared at court with a letter from our sovereign lord King Henry to the duke; wherein his majesty demanded, in very peremptory and haughty terms, the instant release of Monseigneur Gilles, by reason of his being Lord Constable of England and a knight of the most noble Order of the Garter. The duke's fury burst forth with a fresh violence. He recalled the order for his brother's release, and vowed revenge on the English. The French king's envoy withdrew; and then in a few days it was found that this famous herald was no other than one Pierre Larosse, a servant of Arthur de Montauban, who had forged the letter, and pretended to bring it from the King of England, on purpose to anger the duke and impede the prince's liberation; but the evil was now beyond remedy, and when the Lady Françoise of Amboise supplicated the duke to show mercy on his brother, she and her husband were banished from the court, and commanded to return to Guincamp. Now no one knoweth if the prince is alive or dead. This is all the tidings I can hear; and whilst this war lasts there is little hope of the mending of his fate, even if so be that he doth yet live. For the French king hath need of the duke's aid, and will not therefore offend him; and if his majesty stirs in the matter, it only addeth fuel to the flame, as men say, which was lately seen when that false herald came. So, good daughter, fare thee well; and the Holy Trinity have Thee in His keeping! When I return to England—and God alone He knoweth when that good shall befall me—I look not to be remembered by thee, or that thy present visage will be familiar to me until I have studied it well, which methinks I shall not be slow to do. I thank God that I do hear from time to time good reports of thy prudent behaviour and great favour with the Queen, which I pray may never be less than it now is. And so with my blessing I end this letter; and if some honest man, of sufficient rank and fortune, should sue thee in marriage again,—as many have done hitherto, but fared badly,—I would that thou shouldst hearken more readily to his desire than heretofore; for it should be for thy weal now to be settled in marriage, not having, as I understand, any calling to a religious life. I do heartily wish this letter had been a more comfortable one for their majesties, touching the Prince of Bretagne; but while there is life there is hope, as the leeches say; and so fare thee well."

"*Writ at the Camp of Guisnes,
in France, by the* LORD DE ROOS."

There was but poor comfort in the concluding words of this letter, for they are what physicians use in desperate cases; and the situation of Monseigneur Gilles was then, like to that of a dying man, all but despaired of by his friends. With a heavy heart I left London, but the sight of the green fields made me of better cheer, and yet more the agreeable conversation of Dame Elisabeth, to whom I disclosed some of my troubles. We were wont to walk on Sundays to the church of the Gray Friars, in Norwich, for to be present at Vespers; and as we went through the meadows on the way to it we discoursed on the events of the past, and the hopes and fears of the future, and admired that Providence had cast our lives in such dissimilar shapes: my chief cares relating to great personages,—kings, queens, princes, and royal dukes; and she the while concerned with the affairs of simple gentry and homely persons. But, alas, there is greater likeness in men's doings and grievings and rejoicings, whether they be of high or low degree, than is usually thought. The cruelty of the Duke of Brittany to his brother was one of my most sore griefs; and Elisabeth suffered a like great heartache because of Mrs. Paston's (our aunt's) unkindness to her daughter Ellen. This poor wench, a very comely and gracious young lady, was extremely used by her mother, because she would not break off her contract with Master Scrope, to whom, with her parents' consent at one time given, she had promised marriage. Mistress Paston is a very notable lady, of great ability in household matters and dealings touching money and lands, and an obedient and dutiful wife; but the obedience she yields herself to her husband she exacts from her children. No tutors, Elisabeth said, are severe enough to her liking. "Belash him well till he amend," is her commandment to their masters. And what she preaches she practises, for Elisabeth says that she beats her daughter once in the week, or twice, and sometimes twice in a day. Wherefore Nell Paston has sent to Elisabeth by Friar Newton's counsel, to pray her that she would write to her brother in London, and beseech him to be a good friend to her in this matter, and to assist her to to fulfil her contract without impediment or further ill-usage.

We laid a little plot together, that when the Queen came to Norwich, which she was like soon to do, we should move her to intercede with Mistress Paston in favour of these lovers, as she did with Mr. Strange in behalf of Mistress Katherine, who is now Mistress Bugdon. But, alas, who shall intercede for Monseigneur Gilles with any hope of success? One of my torments then was that Jeanne de Kersabiec had wholly ceased to write to me. I had no friend in the world which I affectioned one half so well as Jeanne. One day when we were passing through the lime-walk to the chapel, I said,

"Jeanne must be dead, or else hath ceased to love me."

"I am not of that opinion," Dame Elisabth answered. "Methinks she hath turned hermit."

"Hermit!" I answered, amazed.

"Yea, a hermit," she replied. "Now that the world is so wicked, the like of which was never seen in Christendom before, so much so that many are of opinion it is like soon to come to an end, there be many more women as well as men which retire to solitudes for their souls' health, and give themselves wholly to prayer, except some special call to a good deed withdraws them for a while from that manner of life."

"Do you know any such person?" I said.

"Yea," she replied. "My brother Henry, when he was only nineteen years of age, begged of me the gift of two garments from my wardrobe, and also a hood which our father used sometimes to wear. I did as he desired; and he cut off the hanging sleeves of my gown, and made with them a covering for the neck and arms. I was so affrighted when I saw him in this strange dress; I feared he was mad. But he went away, and lived in a cave at first, and afterwards in a cabin, serving God with exceeding great fervour and devout contemplation, yet sometimes going forth to instruct poor people, all for the love of our Lord; and he lived very hard, and performed many penances."

Elisabeth was very fond of reading, and mostly of a ghostly sort. She had copies of Richard Rolles' books, —his translation of the Psalms into English, his *Craft of Dying*, and the *Mirror of Sinners*,—and used to read them with a great delight ; also a poem called the *Handling of Sinn*, by one Robert Mannyng, a canon of Semperingham. She said Mistress Paston, who cares not for any book but such as she uses for accounts and receipts, hath accused her sometimes of a leaning to Lollardry, because once she found in her cupboard *Heaven opened*, which she said was writ by John Wickliffe; but if this was so, she herself knew nothing thereof, and would not for the world then have kept it, for he was a teacher of heresy, which she abhorred. And so she took the said book to Friar Newton, and never would read in it again.

CHAPTER XXI.

At the Gray Friars.

WHAT Elisabeth said touching hermits reminded me of something Jeanne had written in the last letter I had from her, which served, now that I thought of it, to confirm this suspicion. I mused on this as we walked on, and Elisabeth did not interrupt me; she was a great lover of silence, and took pleasure in looking at the trees and the flowrets; for the sight of God's works preached to her, she said, lovely sermons of His greatness and goodness. She was the most pleasant companion in the world: her kindly face, even when she did not speak, made me cheerful; and when she spoke, I did not tire of listening to her sad but agreeable discourse.

When we arrived at the chapel of the Gray Friars, one at the door told us that after Vespers Friar Brackley would preach, which pleased me not a little, for I had a curiosity to hear this holy and learned man, which is so famous in all England. And verily his sermon was pithy and instructive; for he taught us how we should pray to God by good working, rightful labouring, and in good deeds persevering; and that we ought to ask that our joy may be a full joy and a perfect one. And when he ended his discourse, he said this joy was to be found in one Name only; and thus broke forth in its praise: "Ah, that Name! that wonderful Name! that delectable Name! that Name that is above all names! Name the holiest, without which no man hopes salvation! This Name is in mine ear a heavenly sound; in my mouth honeyful sweetness. Therefore no wonder that I love that Name which gives comfort to me in all anguish. I cannot pray, I cannot meditate, but with the sound of the Name of Jesus. I can savour no joy that with Jesus is not mingled. Wherever I be, wherever I sit, whatever I do, the thought of the Name of Jesus departs not from my mind. *Gaudete quia nomina vestra scripta sunt in cælo; ut gaudium vestrum sit plenum.*"

After the semon was ended, we went to the monastery to speak to Friar Newton, Dame Elisabeth's ghostly father. He was very glad to see us, and greeted me with hearty goodwill and kindliness, and said he hoped I had come to Norwich to teach the damsels of that town to visit hospitals and poor sick persons, as it was reported the Queen, my mistress, was wont to do. I answered, that I was frightened her good example in that respect had not yet done me much good, for I had a niceness about the sight of wounds and lepers, which only once or twice I had overcome. Then he said, smiling, if I had *once* done it, that was worth a dozen times, for to begin was the weighty point in these matters; and then he asked us if we had heard the history of one Pers, which was a miser, and became afterwards a saint.

"No, Father Newton," said Elisabeth; "but methinks there is a likelihood in that transformation."

"Wherefore, Mistress Clere?" the good friar asked.

"Because," she replied, "both are bent on storing treasure, only the one on earth, and the other in heaven. Both be covetous, I ween, and the habits of the miser should serve the saint."

"How prove you that?" he said, amused at her talk.

"Well," she answered, "you Friars Minor dispense with linen and stockings and a hat, and many other things besides, for to lay up treasure in a good bank, the keeper of which is God. And misers likewise renounce their comforts and conveniences for to lay up gold and silver in a chest, or else lend it to needy persons for usurious interest; so that the habits of the one resemble those of the other."

"Ay, mistress," quoth Friar Newton; "but what answer you to this? Saints love to give alms. I say not friars; for, alas, they be not always saints, by the same token as this poor sinner" (this he said striking his breast) "is of their order, and moreover they are, or should be, poor themselves; but saints, friars or not, will give a beggar all they can; this is not a miser's habit."

"Yea, a miser will give," she cried, "if he hopes a great return for his gift, or else can oblige with it a great king, which shall bestow on him tenfold more for it."

"Ah, I yield you the point," quoth the good friar, laughing. "And this is the tale of Pers the miser. He would never give so much as a groat to any poor man; but a beggar one day made a wager with some other men that he would get an alms from him if he were ever so grim. So he went and stood near the door of Pers's house while an ass's load of bread was being discharged, and begged of him very piteously. The churlish man was so angered that he stooped for a stone; but not finding one, he flung a loaf to the man. Well, that night Pers had a vision or dream— he saw his own self standing at the judgment-seat, and all his sins dragging him down to hell; and he was about to sink, when his angel guardian pleaded 'he had once given a loaf to a beggar. The plea was admitted, and Pers yet had another chance for to save his soul. So when he awoke out of his trance, his first words were,

> 'Blessed be all poor men,
> For God Almighty loves them.'

And from that day he began to wax meek and kind, and give alms; and the liking to it so increased, that at the last, one day, when he had only ten pounds of all his pelf left, lo, he goes to a notary and gives it to him for to sell him into bondage. The notary takes him to a church, sells him to a reduced rich man called Yole, and gives the ten pounds to the poor, which makes me misdoubt the unjust saying, as if there should be no notaries in heaven. Pers's master offered to free him, but he would not, for now he had never enough of sufferings and labours."

"Yea, yea," cries Dame Elisabeth, clapping her hands, " a miser still! O good miser! O exceeding wise miser! God send we be all misers like him!"

Then they talked of Ellen Paston; and Friar Newton commended our scheme touching the Queen's intercession, and said Master Scrope was a worthy gentleman, and it would like him well they were married.

"But," quoth he, "until that can be, counsel your cousin that she bear patiently her good mother's correction; for by your own showing, Dame Elisabeth, she shall be the gainer thereby; and so, if she is a wise miser, she will rejoice in each stripe."

Then as we were craving his benison before departing, he suddenly said, " By the way, ladies, do you, the one or the other of ye, speak French, or at the least understand it?"

Dame Elisabeth said she did not know so much as one word of it, except some little sayings which are in every one's mouth, but that I spoke it like a French person.

"And better, peradventure," quoth Father Newton, smiling; "as one answered, to whom a pestilent Lollard said, 'One man is as good as another.' 'Yea, yea,' quoth the wily knave, 'and better also.'"

"Talking of Lollardry," said Elisabeth, "wot you, father, that Mary Beaumont keepeth a copy of Master Wickliffe's English Bible, which you let me from reading?"

"Is it so?" quoth the friar. "Alas, poor child, she poisons her soul with holy food, as Eve ruined her race by tasting of the fruit of the tree of Paradise. The Bible, when read by folks on their knees with a devout spirit and a docile mind, feeds the soul with heavenly truth; but as men do read it now, to foster proud disputings and overturn ancient teaching, it is perilous meat which sends many to hell. Master Wickliffe's English hath many doubtful words in it, which by varied meanings already changed in one hundred years should lead unwary persons from the right understanding thereof, and so into divers heresies. Go to, go to, my children. 'Be not wise in your own conceits,'— those words are from the Bible, as you know,—and think not that the readers of Wickliffe's book shall be holier, or wiser, or more loving towards God and man, or more burning with charity, or more fervent in prayer than St. Clare of Assisi or the holy Elisabeth of Hungary, or the Scotch Queen Margaret, which read not the Bible in their own tongue, but had its spirit in their hearts, and showed forth its received teachings in their lives."

"I thank God," said Dame Elisabeth, "that having

you, sir, for my ghostly father, I can be content; for
your actions accord with your preachments; and when
I hear persons speak of the sins of the clergy, I bethink
me of one in whose presence I may not speak out of
the abundance of my heart, or he would be angered
with me, hating his own praise; but methinks, sir, an
unvirtuous priest, or a worldly one, ruins many souls
in these days."

"To his own Master, my child, such a one must give
an account. But think you verily that St. Mary Magdalen should have been wise to quarrel with God's
Church because Judas filched, and St. Peter lied when
he was affrighted, and St. John and St. James disputed
along the way with the others, and all craved each one
to be the greatest? Nay, nay, there is but One which
is good, and that is God; but children should as lief
discard their parents, and despise those which gave
them life, because they be not perfect, as Catholic
Christians turn against their mother the Church, and
think to teach her, forsooth, whom the Lord God hath
set forth to instruct them. But enough on this theme;
and if it please you, I will now fetch to you one of our
brethren, who hath landed on this coast from France,
whence he came in a little fishing vessel, and was
driven northward by stress of weather. We cannot
understand his language, nor he ours; and his Latin,
which sounds like a strange whistling in our ears, is
not much more comprehensible than his French. He
seems to have escaped from some kind of danger. But
if your cousin will be a good lady to us and interpret
his speech, we shall know more thereof soon than we
have yet done."

Then Dame Elisabeth and I sat down in the cloister,
which was outside the enclosure, and Friar Newton
went to seek for the French friar, and in a short time

returned with him. He was of a middle size, rather tall than short, and his eyes were mostly bent towards the ground; but when he raised them, I saw that they gleamed with a fire which was sometimes veiled by a singular sweetness. His few hairs were tinged with gray, his forehead broad, and his eyebrows dark. Methought at first he looked stern, but when I greeted him in French, a beautiful smile illumined his whole face. He said,

"Mademoiselle, I am happy to meet with one who will comprehend me, and can explain to my good fathers and brothers, which have so hospitably entreated me, the events which have driven me to your country. Will you have patience to listen to this long recital?"

"Yea," I said, "and very gladly also."

I answered little witting what should be the subject of it. Then we all sat down, I with Dame Elisabeth on one bench, and the French friar with Father Newton on another. And here I will transcribe his story as I heard it, doing it into English like the Queen's journal.

CHAPTER XXII.

The French Friar's Story.

"My convent is in Brittany, not far from Moncontour. I have lived there many years in great contentment and peace, and never thought to have left it, far less to have crossed the seas. But some weeks ago I was saying my office in the chapel when one entered whom for four years I had seen coming there to hear Mass, and I had also sometimes shriven her. She was young, and wore a russet dress of a singular shape, and sandals to her feet. She told her scanty sins curtly and plainly, and often with tears, which fell so abundantly, that the place where she knelt to confess was oftentimes wet with this plentiful shower; but never added one word which should lead me to learn her name, or whence she came, or what manner of life she led; albeit I thought it should be a solitary one from the tenour of her confessions. But this day she approached me in the church, and in a low voice asked me to give her a piece of bread, for the love of God. I somewhat marvelled that one yet young should live alone and lack the necessaries of life, and said something of this kind to her. She then uttered these words in a low voice, with her eyes fixed on the ground: 'Good friar, there are devils which can be thrust out, our Lord saith, only by prayer and fasting. When one would save a soul against which wicked men and hell combine, he or she must become a victim, and by suffering obtain for it singular graces.'

"There was somewhat in this woman's countenance and manner of speaking which showed her to be no common person; so I pressed her that day with no further questions, but gave her a loaf of bread, which she thankfully received. When she returned again, she confessed, and then told me that I must needs go with her somewhere that night for to shrive a soul in danger of death. I refused to go if she did not tell me who this dying person was.

"'I said not a dying person,' she replied, 'but one in imminent danger of death.'

"This affrighted me yet more. I thought she might be a devil in the form of a woman, luring me to destruction. I again said I would not go if she did not tell me her name and who she would take me to. She was silent some moments—praying, I think; and then she said in a faltering voice,

"'Father, I will tell you all.'

"'Then, first,' I answered, 'tell me where you dwell and who you are.'

"Then she disclosed to me her name—"

"O, good friar," I (Margaret de Roos) exclaimed, "was it Jeanne de Kersabiec?"

He looked amazed.

"Holy Mary! how should you know it?"

"O, sir," I replied, "she was my bed-fellow and playmate for many years. For God's dear sake proceed."

Then he: "Yea, this was Jeanne de Kersabiec, who for four years had left the world and lived an anchorite in the forest of La Hardouinaie. She is a rare soul, and her vocation to this sort of life a singular one."

"How came she to embrace it?" I tremblingly asked.

He replied: "You have heard, it may be, of our poor prince which lived so long in this country, Monseigneur Gilles de Bretagne?"

"Heard of him! yea, more than heard of him, Father. Alas!" and then tears choked my utterance.

Father Newton and Dame Elisabeth looked at me surprised.

"What hath befallen him?" I cried. "Is he alive or dead?"

"Listen, lady, and you shall hear," he gravely answered.

And so I sat still as a stone, and he spoke thus:

"This Jeanne was the cousin and friend of Monseigneur Gilles' mother-in-law, Madame de Dinant: when that lady died, the prince was in prison already; and Jeanne told me that, kneeling in prayer one day in the chapel at Gualdo after her decease, the thought came into her mind that she had always asked God to do her that favour, that by her means some great good should happen to this Messire Gilles, and that, being too weak and too obscure to aid him by her acts, she should do so through prayer and suffering. She would not go into a convent; 'for,' quoth she, 'then if God willeth I should serve him in some other way, I should not have liberty for it.' But she went to the forest I named, which is nigh to one of his castles, and therein found a cave, where she hid herself, and lay on moss at nights, and in the day communed with God in prayer, and wrought with a knife little carved images of wood, which she exchanged for bread at some religious houses in the neighbourhood, walking sometimes many leagues to reach them. She had no company, she said, but one little squirrel and two little hares, which had grown to be tame, and frisked about her as she worked. She carved one large crucifix, and a fair statue of our Lady at its foot, and these were her books all those years. She heard Mass and performed her devotions, now at one convent chapel, now at another, so that she was not often seen in the same place. Well, she lived a long time in this wise, and still her prayer was, that the sufferings and the mortification of this austere life should help Messire Gilles, whether he was alive or dead, for naught did she hear of him; and this was the hardest penance she endured for the love of the poor prince. But one day, when the light was declining, she walked past the Castle of Hardouinaie, and lo, as she went by the moat, she heard the voice of one singing a carol, which she knew very well. She asked a little shepherd if any folks lived in that castle. The child answered that some days ago five or six men came there and had gone away; and no one dwelt there now. When the night was come and the moon was shining, she lay down on the moss when she had said her prayers, and tried to sleep; but the words of that carol were yet in her ears and kept her waking. The next day she returned and walked near the moat, and a very faint sound, like of one essaying to sing, reached her ear. She went to the gate of the castle and rang the bell, not knowing what she did; but no one came, and she went away. Then she prayed that night longer than usual, almost till the day dawned, and asked the Lord Jesus by His Five Wounds that she might do some good to Messire Gilles. The day which followed she went again to the side of the moat, but could hear no singing, only a cry like of one sighing in great pain. She crossed herself, and then began to sing the same carol she had heard there, and fixed her eyes on the wall within the moat, where there was a little opening with some bars. It seemed to her that something moved behind those bars, and then she heard these words said in a feeble voice: 'Who is it singing? If you are a Christian, speak.'

"She leant over the wall, and cried: 'I am the bedeswoman of a poor prince.'

"'Then save me; I am Gilles de Bretagne,' was answered.

"She could not tell me how she descended the wall, belike it was through the aid of shrubs which grew against it; but she reached the opening,—for there was not much water in the moat,—and looked through the bars at that prisoner, whose face was more like that of a painting of our Lord on the Cross, she said, than any she had ever seen. This dialogue passed betwixt them: 'Monseigneur, I am Jeanne.'

"'Sweet Jeanne, give me to eat.'

"'Alas, monseigneur, I have naught but a piece of mouldy bread.'

"'God be thanked!' Then he reached his thin pale hand through the bars, and took the piece of bread.

"She stood looking at him whilst he ate, and wot not what to say, her heart was so riven. When he had finished, he said, 'Give me to drink; I have no water.'

"She had no bowl; but she dipped her kerchief in the water of the moat, and passed it to him all dripping. When he had slaked his thirst in this wise, he said, 'Jeanne, death is cheated this time. They have left me already three days and three nights without sustenance. One came this morn and oped the door of this dungeon; but when he saw I was not dead, he shut it again and went away, albeit I prayed him to stay and kill me.'

"'My prince, think not to die but as God willeth and when He ordains. You shall not perish with hunger whilst I live. For this have I prayed and suffered for four years; and now the time hath come, my prayers are heard.'

"Many nights she brought him bread, which she begged, and walked all the day to fetch it. Then one night he said to her, 'Jeanne, Olivier de Meêl hath been here one hour ago, and is gone, but I read my doom in his visage. He was angered to find me yet alive, and I shall soon die by his hand; but my *brother* is my murtherer. O God, O God! we once sat together on our mother's knee, and she kissed us both in turns. Jeanne, dost thou remember that day at Gualdo, when my little wife kissed me, and said, O my poor prince! But it is little to die. God knoweth I have suffered long enough to be content to be released by means of death; but to deny me shrift is more than human malice.'

"'Have they done this?' she asked.

"'Yea,' he replied; 'and answered with mockings, jeers, and revilings, my supplications to see a priest.'

"'Never fear, my prince,' she resolutely said; 'you shall not die unshriven; you shall live till I return with a priest. For four years I have wept and prayed to win this from God, to do you some good once in my life; and now, behold, the time is come.'

"It was that day she came to Montcontour; and when I heard her tale I went with her. We walked for three hours through the forest: she seeming to fly rather than to walk. I could hardly follow her she went so fast, with her beads clasped in her hand. Once she stopped to wait for me, and then prayed aloud to God to carry us faster. Afterwards it seemed to me as if angels bore us in their arms. When we arrived, she showed me the place in the wall whereby she descended into the moat. It was almost perpendicular, and feeble shrubs the sole support; but I invoked St. Francis, and reached the bottom; then running on, came to the barred window, near which the ghostly shade—for such he looked—of that poor prince stood, which had once been the darling of his mother and the pride of Brittany. It was night, but the moon was shining, and I could plainly see his deathly visage and shrunk form. When he perceived me, and by my habit and cowl saw I was a priest, he fell on his knees, with his lean hands upraised together, and wept. O God, what a good confession he then made! How many tears he shed for his sins! how freely he pardoned his enemies! how saintly was that soul! what perfection suffering had wrought in it! what graces it had obtained! Verily, whilst the body had decayed, true life had begun. When the words of shrift had been uttered, a heavenly brightness illumined his countenance, which had been so pale before. It became as if inflamed with fire. His eyes were fixed on the sky with an ecstatic expression, but suddenly he shuddered, and then with a loud voice cried, 'Brother, brother! within forty days thou must meet me at God Almighty's judgment-seat to answer for my unjust death.' Then turning towards me, with the same singular light on his visage, he said, 'Father, I charge thee, as thou wouldst be saved, when thou shalt hear of my death, to go to the Duke Francis, wherever he is, and deliver this message to him; so that he may be warned, and his soul not perish everlastingly.' So I promised, and gave him my benison; and as the day had then begun to dawn, I returned to the convent, and his bedeswoman went to beg bread for him. But he was no more to eat bread on earth.

"After brief rest, with the Prior's permission I travelled to Avranches, which it was reported had then been surrendered by the English. The Duke of Brittany was there, in the midst of great rejoicings and triumph at this victory. As I walked through the city amidst the crowd, and saw the gay banners flaunt in the wind, and the upturned faces full of glee, the coloured tapestry garnishing the walls, the flowers scattered about the streets, loud strains of music filling the air, and the shouts of a people almost mad with joy mingling with it; as I beheld the duke riding with his knights, and smiling with such good cheer, as if himself and the whole world were in good fellowship, —it seemed as if that night in the moat beside the barred window had been a dismal horrible dream, which daylight had dispelled. But when the contentment of the people was at its height, a report spread through the crowd which froze the blood in their veins, killing joy like the news of the plague in a doomed city. It flew like lightning from mouth to mouth. Men and women stood aghast, striking their breasts. Confused sentences were heard. 'The holy prince is dead!' 'Monseigneur Gilles is murdered—strangled!' 'He is dead at La Hardouinaie!' 'Arthur de Montauban is the murtherer!' Then cries of hissing mixed with curses rose. Some cried, 'Slay him, slay him!' others rushed to the churches, the bells of which began to toll, and at once prayers were said for Monseigneur Gilles, and there was no end of persons kneeling at the several altars to pray for him.

"On the morrow Mass was said in the cathedral at the break of day for the repose of his soul, and the duke assisted thereat; but none could see his face. Then at the church-door he mounted his horse, and rode pensive and slow on the sands, looking towards

St. Michael's Mount. Step by step I followed him, watching his movements for I had his dead brother's message to deliver, and had to do it then or never. I passed swiftly by that troop of riding men, and then suddenly turned back and stood by the side of his horse. 'Monseigneur,' I said, 'bow down your head, for I have a message for you of the most consequence in the world.' He bent his head down to the saddle-bow, and I whispered to him these words: 'Monseigneur, I heard in confession Monseigneur Gilles your brother before he died, and he hath charged me to summon you to appear before forty days have passed, before God the Creator, to answer in person for his most cruel and unjust death. Therefore I deliver you this warning, with which the defunct prince charged my conscience; and I advise you to think thereon, and to pray God very urgently to have mercy on you.'

"Then I turned away, and neither the duke nor any one else said anything to me. I walked to the port, and there looking back I saw the duke riding along the sands as before. Our Prior had charged me to take ship and escape to England; for he said I should suffer, and all the friars in our house, if so be I was discovered, and the convent haply destroyed. For some said the Duke Francis had sold himself to the devil, and feared no more God nor man. So I took ship at Avranches, thinking to land on the south coast of this country; but the Lord God ordained otherwise, the contrary winds driving me here, where with great charity my brethren have harboured me, for the which I pray you, in your courtesy, to make them in your language my poor thanks, gentle lady, and rehearse to them this history, which has, I perceive, moved you to tears; and verily it is as pitiful a one as can be imagined."

As well as I could, I complied with his desire, and then returned home with Elisabeth. All that night I lay mostly awake; or if I slept, my dreams were dreadful. I saw a death-like face through bars, and struggled to break them in vain; or I was fetching a priest to shrive the Queen, and he would not come; or I was beset by ruffianly men in a wood; or methought I was summoned to the judgment-seat, and one said I was there to answer for the Duke of Gloucester's death. Each time I awoke trembling and covered with a cold sweat. O Jeanne, where art thou now? My brave companion, I pity not, nay I envy thee. Thy warfare is over; thy victory won. One thing thou didst ask of God, and hast obtained it. Yea, I can picture thee in some lone solitude lifting up thy thankful soul to bless the day and the hour when that resolve was taken, when that offering was made. Thou hadst thy meed; a smile on a dying face, an enduring hope, a comfort which none can rob thee of. O, more than sister, more than mother to that loved soul! now thou canst depart in peace whensoever God calls thee.—O Monseigneur Gilles, canst thou be of the dead, and could any one be found cruel enough to kill thee? I had no comfort for a long time but in procuring Masses to be said, and praying mine own self, for you, chiefly at night when others could not observe me.

CHAPTER XXIII.

The Queen at Norwich.

SOME time went by, and then the Queen came to Norwich, and sent for me to meet her there. Her visit caused a great stir amongst the folks of that city and the neighbouring country, for all desired to pay her honour. The ladies asked me all manner of questions touching the dresses they should wear, and what ornaments to put on. Mistress Paston was almost beside herself because her husband was in London, and had sent her nothing for her neck, as he had promised. She came to borrow Elisabeth Clere's device, who thought not herself to see the Queen (yet I was secretly resolved she should); for, quoth Mistress Paston, " I durst not for shame go only with my beads amongst so many fresh ladies about the Queen." Ellen wore those despised beads, and methought their red colour on her white neck became her well. It made me sad to listen to so much vain talk then. My most comfort was to speak with the French friar; and whilst the others were buying gear in the town, Dame Lizzy and I went to the convent. We could not often see him, for he was a devout man, and liked the chapel more than the parlour. But when we could procure to converse with him, our discourse was always of Monseigneur Gilles, and his pious life and end. I already canonised him in my heart; as did also, I afterwards heard, the peasants in Brittany, for he was called by them "the holy prince," and by no other name would they title him.

Well, the Queen came, and expressed much sorrow at his death, and would see the French friar. When she had heard his tale, she said, "And have you not heard, good father, that the Duke of Brittany is dead?"

"I never doubted he would die within the forty days," he answered. "God is just, and also merciful, giving him time to repent.

"Which report saith he did truly," the Queen replied; and then she gave us both to read this letter from my father to the King:

"SIRE,—The Duke of Brittany hath died last week, and this is the report which I have heard of his end, and I think it is true. The day after the tidings had reached him at Avranches that his brother had expired in prison, as he was riding on the sands opposite Mount St. Michael, a friar suddenly stopped him and delivered a message to him from the said Monseigneur Gilles, arraigning him to appear within forty days at the judgment-seat of God, and bidding him take heed of the warning, and pray for mercy. Many are of opinion that this friar was no live man, but a ghostly apparition, which vanished as speedily as it had appeared. And the duke, like one struck with a spell, rode on for two hours, and never spoke so much as a word to any one; at the end of that time he slackened his already slow pace, and at last stopped and looked about him. Seeing Arthur de Montauban, he beckoned to him. When the said Arthur approached him, he perceived that his face had changed to a death-like paleness, with two burning red spots in the centre of each cheek, which glowed like live coal. 'Arthur,' he said, 'I am arraigned, and have to appear at God's judgment-seat within forty days. The friar which spoke to me at the gate of Avranches hath brought me this summons.' Then the Maréchal de Montauban laughed, and his laugh made the duke shiver from head to foot. The maréchal said the friar was a deceitful knave, and he should be caught and hung. The duke replied, 'You shall never find him.' Messengers were sent to Mount St. Michael and Moncontour, far and wide they were sent; but no tidings of this friar could be heard. Then Arthur de Montauban cried, 'Forget this impostor, monseigneur, and enter Rennes as a conqueror.' But the duke turned his horse's head towards Vannes, and sadly, silently, and heavily went to his manor of plaisance nigh to that city. Then there came there in haste to him the holy Lady Françoise d'Amboise, and never more left the duke as long as he lived, which was till the morning of the fortieth day since his brother's death. And the last six days he was in great suffering and anguish; but that said lady and his confessor, the Bishop of Landes, ministered comfort to his poor soul, which was heavy burthened and much afflicted by reason of the great sins he had committed. He received the Sacraments, and besought all to pardon him and pray for him to God. And he lost not patience, 'tis said, though his pains were most terrible; and when his eyes were shut, yet his cold lips moved and uttered the Name of Jesus with so much resentment of His mercy, that no one which heard him could refrain from tears. And so he died; and may God assoilsie him!

"Now the Duke Pierre and the Lady Françoise, his wife, are the sovereigns of this duchy, which causeth no small joy to the Bretons. I write in haste to inform your majesty of this extraordinary event; and I pray your majesty to pardon this ill-constructed letter, and the abrupt conclusion thereof, which is owing to the lack of time and the hurry of the messenger. — Your liege's humble loving subject and servant.

"*Writ by the* LORD DE ROOS *at Guisnes.*

"P.S.—In the last ordering of the duke's will, provision is made for Mass to be said for ever at the Abbey of Boqueu for the repose of the soul of Monseigneur Gilles de Bretagne."

The Queen showed much kindness to the French friar, and furnished him with money to go into the Low Countries to a a convent of his order, where he died some years afterwards in repute of sanctity. She was concerned at the dreadful death of the prince; but at that time her joy was so great that her prayers had been heard, and that soon she looked to be a mother, that grief could not take much hold of her. She was the most happy person in the world, she then said, and showed her good cheer in many artless ways. When the ladies went to see her during the two days she stayed at Norwich, nothing would serve her Majesty, if they had children, but she must send for them, and chiefly if they were young. And whereas she had been wont to despise Englishwomen because their talk is mostly of their homes and nurseries, and seldom of the fine arts, or books and music, or state affairs, now she was well pleased to discourse with any one touching the nurture and good breeding of children, and even the gear they should have whilst infants. The second day of her stay I persuaded her Majesty to command the attendance of Dame Elisabeth Clere, who was very reluctant to come into her presence, but durst not disobey her order. The Queen made much of our Lizzy, and desired her to have a husband; for to be single and not a religious person was an ill state, she said laughing, and not what was to be thought of for a gentlewoman of beauty, fortune, and parts. Then this Mistress Lizzy took courage, and replied that she had a cousin with a heart as much set on marriage as hers was inclined against it; and that if her Majesty would speak a word in her favour to her mother when she came to wait on her the next morning, it should be a right good and royal action, for that sorrow was often dangerous to young women. and caused them to behave otherwise than they should do. The Queen inquired if this Ellen Paston was the gentlewoman which was brought up in the house of the Lady Pole, a kinswoman of Lord Suffolk's; and when she heard it was so, she said she would be a good lady to her, and obtain from her parents their consent to her marriage with Mr. Scrope. If naught else would do it, why then she would make her a maid-of-honour, and bestow on her a portion. Then she asked Elisabeth what favour she should confer on her; upon which that damsel smilingly answered,

"Well, I beseech your Majesty to suffer me, without risk of your displeasure, to live single and yet not be a nun, for such is my humour. Neither the authority of right worshipful husbands nor the rule of a convent accord with my liking."

Her Majesty smiled, and said she hoped Dame Elisabeth was a good subject, and obeyed the King, at least, if no one else.

"Yea, your Majesty," quoth the lady; "for the King lives in London and I in Norwich, which makes obedience easy. By the same rule, I am very obedient to the Pope, because he bides at Rome, and not so docile towards Friar Newton, my confessor in this town."

The Queen was right well pleased with her merry answers, and reported of her in the best wise to others she saw afterwards. She told me that, by her troth, she had seen no gentlewoman in Norfolk she liked better than she does her. I observe that royal persons, when they meet with simple folk who speak their thoughts bluntly, are often greatly pleased with their speeches; whereas if any one attempt the same thing out of design, they are then soon angered. The Queen fulfilled her word, and dealt so cunningly with Mistress Paston that Ellen will soon be married. Methinks, since her new hope, the Queen striveth more than ever to content every one, and is more affable in her manner than ever she was before. To have a son is now her sole prayer. She said to me to-day, when the crowd had been cheering her: "Meg, when I can show them a Prince of Wales, then methinks I shall be loved in England as once I was in France."

CHAPTER XXIV.

A new Joy and a new Anguish.

THIS is a letter the Queen wrote to her sister, the Countess of Vaudémont, when she had learnt the decease of their mother the Queen of the two Sicilies, who died when she was but forty-three years of age :

"RIGHT WELL-BELOVED SISTER, — Our mother is, then, no more. The heart which throbbed so nobly is now at length at rest ; cold and still is that warm ardent heart which loved so passionately. The brave spirit fled which animated the fairest form on earth. Alas, alas ! she hath died, than which a more virtuous woman, a more loving spouse and tender mother, did not exist. Methinks I am reft of a part of mine own being in the losing of that good parent, whose sorrows I shared from my most young years. For it is not possible to describe with how great a passion I affectioned that mother, which is now departed from this world, or how heavy my heart is at this moment. Lord Talbot, my very good friend, hath also died in Guienne. He was eighty years old, and expired with the sword in his hand. I wish he had lived to see my child born, for he loved me very much, and would have suffered any thing in my quarrel. But now that God is about to give me a son, I would fain have no quarrels, but be at peace with all the world. And methinks all that have English hearts will rally round us when we have a prince, which in two months I hope will happen; and then I shall be as happy as your Highness, or any other woman on this earth, which heretofore I have envied. And so, with great sisterly love I embrace you, and pray the good Jesus to have you and your husband and your children in His holy keeping.

"*Written at the Palace of Westminster
by* MARGARET THE QUEEN."

A short while after this letter was sent the King became suddenly very ill at Clarendon, with a kind of numbness which deprived him of the usage of his limbs, and his absence of mind then grew to be so absolute that now it could not be concealed, and not only the Duke of Somerset, who was the Prime Minister, but all the officers of state and chief persons of the court, and then the nation at large, were informed of it, and great sorrow fell on many; but those which were the most well-wishers to their majesties were the least surprised, for those nearest to them had long feared that which now had happened. The Queen then showed a singular courage; she was sick and very weary in mind as well as in body, yet lost not heart; for, quoth she, "God hath given into my care and heeping two beings which are now as helpless the one as the other, and nothing shall overcome my will to defend them till I die." So, she with speed assembled a council of nobles and gentlemen and right reverend prelates, and with great judgment and prudence took in hand the government of the realm. She removed the King as soon as he could travel—his body somewhat amended, yet his consciousness not returning—to Westminster, where in two months she expected to lie in. O God, how virtuous was her conduct and wise her haviour at that time! She often said the lack of money was the cause of much evil and embarrassment to sovereigns, and therefore she denied herself in all things save such as are needful for the glory of the crown, or else in the giving of alms, in which she was always very bountiful, and now more than heretofore; for she desired greatly the prayers of the poor, and that many should make suit to God for the King and the unborn prince, for she would not so much as think it possible that her child should be a daughter. On one day she gave to a gentleman of her household, who had been visited by heavy misfortunes, 6*l*. 6*s*. 8*d*.; and to two men, whose stables, which were all their living, had been burnt down, she sent no less than 13*l*. 6*s*. 8*d*. to rebuild them. And the while for the feeding and maintaining of herself and all her household, she did only spend 7*l*. each day. Howsoever she procured fine gear for the coming prince, and notably a christening mantle, which cost 554*l*., and twenty yards of russet cloth of gold to array the font in which he should be baptised, and five hundred and fifty brown sable backs for the trimming of the robe for her churching. The Bishop of Winchester said to her, a few days before the prince was born, " Madame, if God sends you a fair son—" Upon which she interrupted him, and cried, " I like not your *if*, my lord ; *when* should sound better in mine ears." " Ah, madame," his grace replied, " it shall be as God pleases." Then she turned away from him displeasured ; and I fear me it was in her thoughts, if not on her tongue, that she would not have it as God pleased, except His pleasure should be hers also.

Well, on the 18th of November of that year, as every one knoweth, the Prince was born at Westminster, and a more comely infant was never seen. The fair visages of his parents were reflected in his face like in a miniature of beauteous workmanship; the tiny features and little limbs being all shaped in so great perfection that nothing in nature or art could exceed them. The noble ladies which attended the Queen's churching—the most notable of which were the Duchess of Bedford and the Duchess of York, the Duchess of Norfolk, the Duchess of Somerset, the Duchess of Suffolk, and the Countess of Warwick—marvelled at the Prince's beauty, and complimented the Queen thereon, who smiled with good cheer; albeit methinks a sharp thorn was joined to the new-blown rose of her happiness, in the thought that he who should have been most glad of that fair boy's birth and christening was, through that grievous malady, ignorant thereof. The Countess of Warwick said agreeably to the Queen that till then she had thought her wenches, Isabel and her lately born Anne, the most beautiful babes in the world; but that now she feared the Prince exceeded them in fairness as in all things else.

But no sooner was this gracious infant born than the Duke of York's friends of all degrees began to wag their tongues in a shameless manner, and to utter horrible falsehoods touching the Queen, so that the most quiet heart which loved her must needs have resented them with anger. I, who was most often with her majesty, and beheld her innocent joy and moving grief in those early days of her first motherhood, when she would clasp her child to her breast and smile in its sweet face, the while tears dropped from her eyes upon his cheeks, which she would straightway wipe away, and declare they should not lie there, for that should be an ill omen; and who heard her, with the

eloquent tongue God had given to her, address him
with passionate fondness, and promise the fair babe
his father should soon welcome him; I, who listened
to the vehement prayers she put up for her son that he
should be prosperous—I, who witnessed these emotions,
took heed of all her actions, and knew her secret mind;
how should I, then, feel when these reports reached
me, which said this child was not her own, but a
common infant pretended to be the Prince, which
some declared had never been born, and others to have
died after its birth; or, if possible, yet more dishonourable falsehoods injurious to her good fame!—how
should I feel towards the framers of these vile calumnies!
O God, forgive me if I have hated them too bitterly,
then and since! All my fear then was that their
slanders, which were overspreading the land like a
poisonous vapour, blasting her noble repute, should at
the last reach her majesty's ears. As long as they
were privately uttered by her enemies, or buzzed about
among common persons, it was yet possible to hide
them from her; but one day when I was speaking in
the waiting-chamber with my Lord Clifford touching
this point, he told me with bursting rage that my Lord
Warwick went open-mouthed into the assemblies of
the nobility, and in the streets, and on the Mall, and
every public place in London, asserting in a shameless
manner that the infant which was called the Prince,
and Edward of Lancaster, was a base-born child of
vile parentage, which the King had never acknowledged
for his son, and never would. And yester-eve, by his
orders, as was believed, a herald appeared at St. Paul's
Cross, and proclaimed the same in the hearing of the
people. It so happened on the same day that I went
in the afternoon to see a poor person in Cheapside,
and I heard there three or four gossips of the common

sort, whose tongues wagged on this theme; and one of them declared the King would have taken note of the birth of the Prince if he had surely been his son; for it was well known he was a saint, and, even in a trance, could discern truth from falsehood; "but," quoth this beldam, "it is will not, not cannot, with his majesty. I warrant you he is inspired therein; and St. John, his good patron, letteth him from taking this false prince into his arms and blessing him, as every king doth his heir, and then all the great lords kneel and salute their future king. But, I pray you, has this been as much as thought of now? I promise you nay; but the Frenchwoman hath tried to cheat her husband and his rightful heir, the good Duke of York; but for all they pretend the King is mad, he hath too great a wit to be deceived."

I returned to the palace very sick at heart, and found my Lord Somerset with the Queen. One look at her face showed me she was informed of these vile slanders. The Duke had told her of the proclamation at St. Paul's Cross, and that the herald thereof had escaped, but he was thought to be a retainer of the Nevilles. O, her visage was greatly altered then! It was beautiful, but with the beauty of a storm at night — dark, fiery, charged with lightning. She was speaking rapidly in a tremulous voice. At first I could not catch what she was saying, but soon I understood that she had learnt the popular credence that the King, through a Divine inspiration, refused to notice his child. This thought seemed to work like fire in her brain. "It shall be proved!" she cried. "It shall be tried, it shall be seen!" and she walked to and fro convulsed with passion. Then suddenly standing still, she commanded the Duke of Somerset instantly to summon the lords

of the council straightway to his majesty's chamber,
for that she would there before them bring the Prince
to his father, "and if there is a God in heaven," she
cried, with a wild flash in her eye, "the King will
acknowledge him." I shuddered to hear her dare
Almighty God by this rash speech, as if she should
deny Him if He granted not her suit. But I could
not venture to approach, much less to speak to her
then. The Duke laboured in vain, beseeching her to
forbear this trial. She would not so much as listen to
him, but with her eyes upraised to heaven, less in a
prayerful than a defiant tone, she exclaimed, "I will
have justice from God and from man! O God, O
God! avenge me! Avenge me of these men!"

So she would be obeyed; and my Lords of Canterbury and York, of Bath and of Chichester, and all the
chief officers of the state and great lords of the court,
were called to the palace in haste, for she would brook
no delay. I trembled to see her so confident, and her
prayers affrighted me; for she called not on God like
a humble creature, but as one having a right to be
heard.

When the King's chamber was filled with persons
variously disposed, I can remember well that the stillness was awful, for his majesty took cognisance of no
one, and his face, as was its wont in that strange malady, was like that of a carved image, or of one who
had died in the act of prayer. The Queen went to the
nursery chamber with the Duke of the Buckingham,
whom she bade take the Prince in his arms and carry
him to the King. You would have heard a pin drop in
that full chamber, when, as she had commanded him,
the Duke presented the Prince to him in a goodly wise,
beseeching him to bless him. But his majesty gave
no manner of answer. Then the Queen came in and

took herself the Prince in her arms and presented him in the like form that the Duke had done. Till the day I die I cannot forget the too keen look of her face as she held the sleeping infant before the fixed unheeding eyes of the King, or the sound of her voice as she desired him to bless it, so piercing in its whispered tones that it should have almost awakened the dead, if that had been possible. But all that labour was in vain, for there was no answer or countenance on the King's part, save that once, which seemed to make the Queen start with an agonised hope, he looked on the Prince, but then cast his eyes down again without any more notice; and then the Queen went away. When she reached the door, she stood still for one instant with her gaze full fixed on those men who were most her enemies, and seeming amazed she held out the Prince towards them, I wit almost unconsciously; and this moved some of them to approach and make some cheer to her; but then she started and withdrew, and all those present went away in silence.

For some months after this the Queen took no heed of any thing but the King's health and the care of the Prince; and except that she always waxed pale when the Earl of Warwick was named, in other matters she seemed more careless than had been her wont of late. When the Archbishop of Canterbury died, and the Duke of York and his party would not suffer her to choose her successor, and then soon afterwards the Duke of Somerset was arrested, and the Duke of York was made Protector by the Parliament, she kept much silence, but day by day watched the King's countenance, as a mariner in a drifting bark watcheth the sky. All November she said he was amending; but methought her desire begat that thought. Howsoever, on St. John's day, when she had been some time gaz-

ing on him with much affection,—for she thought how
this great saint had been his patron and his teacher in
the love of God, and how often his name had been on
those now silent lips,—suddenly he spoke and asked
for his almoner; and she, fearing by word or look to
change the current of returning reason, rose as if this
had been a common hap and sent for the good priest.
When he came in, the King, who was like one
awakened from a long dream, bade him hie to Canterbury and make there his offering to the shrine of
St. Thomas, and he also sent an oblation to the tomb
of St. Edward. O, how the Queen wept and misdoubted if she should speak to him herself until he
called for her; and when he did, with what restrained
passion she showed her fearful joy, trembling like one
in the presence of a flickering light which is all his
stay, and which a breath may extinguish! But it went
not out that time; and on the Monday at noon she
came to him and brought my lord the Prince with her,
who was then fifteen months old. The King asked
what his name was, and then the Queen told him
Edward; and he held up his hands and thanked God
thereof; and he said he never knew him till that time,
nor wist what was said to him, and where he had been
whilst he was sick, till now. And he asked who were
the godfathers; and the Queen told him and he was
well content. Then he asked for the Cardinal, and
she told him that he was dead; and he said he had
never heard it till this time, and added, "One of the
wisest lords in this land is dead." And my Lord of
Winchester and my Lord of St. John of Jerusalem
were with him the morrow after Twelfth-day; and he
spake to them as well as ever he did, and when they
came out they wept for joy. And he said he was in
charity with all men, and so he would the lords were.

And now he says the matins of our Lady and evensong, and heareth his Mass devoutly.

The Queen hath taken the King to the House of Lords, where he dissolved the Parliament; and the Duke of Somerset hath come out of prison, and is in his old post again. The Duke of York resigned the protectorship with an ill grace, and hath gone to the Marches of Wales. There are rumours that he is raising an army with Salisbury and Warwick, and is marching on London. God defend this should be true! for the Queen hath only yet raised two thousand men.

Here at Greenwich, where the Queen retired with the Prince when the Duke of York advanced, we wait for tidings. She said to me yestereve, " Thus sat my mother twenty-three years ago, when the battle of Bulgneville was fought, and I was not older than this boy."

The King hath written to her Majesty that he sent a message to the Duke of York to ask wherefore he came in hostile array against him, and that the Duke had made answer that he would not lay down his arms unless the Duke of Somerset was dismissed from the King's council, and delivered up to justice. "This angered me," the King wrote, " and God forgive me that for the first, and as I pray and hope the last time in my life, I uttered an oath, and declared to this bold subject that I would as soon deliver up my crown as I would the Duke of Somerset or the least soldier in my army; and that I would treat as a traitor every man who should presume to fight against me in the field." This letter cheered the Queen a little, and she was right glad, she said, the King spake out so roundly;

but on the morrow we heard a battle of one hour only had been fought in the town of St. Albans, and a fearful slaughter made of the King's friends; his majesty himself being wounded in the neck by an arrow. York had bent the knee to his forlorn King, and bade him rejoice that his friend was slain. "For God's sake, stay the slaughter of my subjects!" was his answer; and then he was forced to London by these malignant rebels. The Queen hath been for many hours in a stupor of despair.

Here at Hertford Castle, whither the Lord Protector hath banished their majesties, the King being again unconscious, the Queen hath said these words to me: "My friends are killed; my lord the King is insane for a time; Sir John Wenlock, whom I loaded with benefits, hath betrayed and forsaken me; the Duke of York triumphs; the Parliament hath dared to censure my acts. But I am Margaret of Anjou, and my lord is King of England; and none shall crush me,—neither men, devils, or gods!"

"Hush, hush, madame!" I cried, venturing her anger; "for mercy's sake, defy not God."

"I spake not of the good God," she cried; "but of heathen gods, demons, fiends, if you will, which from my birth have made me their sport. If I had been foul, wicked, leprous, they had relented; but being what I am they shall not conquer me, and not one of mine enemies but shall one day confess it had been better for him to have died, than in an evil hour to dare the vengeance of Margaret of Anjou!"

CHAPTER XXV.

Harlech Castle.

I HAVE set down in this book the Queen's conversations with her poor servant at Harlech Castle in Wales, whither we retired in the month of July 1460, after a perilous flight from the field of battle at Northampton. The Duke of Exeter, the Earl of Richmond, the Earl of Pembroke, Lord Gray, and the Lady Isabella his wife,—who hath been since her marriage one of the bedchamber ladies to her majesty,—and some other noblemen and esquires of less note, have followed her grace to this fortress, whereunto it should appear Providence hath conducted her steps; for nature has furnished it with almost impregnable ramparts, and, like unto an eagle's eyrie, it defies the approach of invaders. The lord thereof is a Welsh chieftain, David ap Jeuan ap Einion, a very giant in height and size, and a most brave and loyal friend to the Queen. The little Prince, when he heard his name, said it should not be David but Goliath; and then the play betwixt them was for his highness to throw pebbles at the giant, who fell down and feigned to be slain. And then the Prince ran to cut off his head with his wooden sword; but kneeling down by his side, would kiss his huge cheeks, and pray him to stand up, for that he loved him very much. This made the Queen smile, which she had not done since that dreadful defeat and slaughter, and the taking of the King, news of which

had reached her since she came into Wales. The
pure air which bloweth from these high mountains
hath strengthened her frame, and revived hopes dawn
in her soul. Sometimes when the bards play on their
harps warlike strains, she listens to them, at first with
a wistful abstracted look, but soon the cloud of heavy
care rolls away from her brow, and a light beams in
her eyes like unto the gleams of sunshine which il-
lumine the stormy skies of these frowning regions.
The good people of this land would die for her and the
Prince, and the holy King, now a captive; and this
affection shows itself in an artless and fervent fashion,
which cheers her, she says, even as a ray of the sun of
Provence falling by some miracle on a northern land-
scape. I notice that the poesy of the Welsh bards
and their music awaken in her remembrances of her
childhood in other lands, and of the gay *savoir*, in the
which she was no mean proficient before weighty troubles engrossed her thoughts. Sometimes when the sun
is setting, and rosy tints adorn the peak of Snowdon,
she sits on the battlements with my lord the Prince on
her knee; and she tells him little tales she learnt in
France and Italy, or sings to please him the lays of
King René. Then gather round this rare mother and
child, one by one, ravished listeners. The old bard
brings his harp, and ever and anon sounds a chord in
unison with her wondrous melodious voice. The two
young Earls, Richmond and Pembroke, who well-nigh
worship their noble Queen and sister, sit at her feet
with clasped hands and upraised faces. I could not
refrain from smiling when Mary Beaumont, who is
also here, said in the hearing of Lord Pembroke that
Isabella Gray (Bessy Woodville she was before her
marriage) was the fairest woman she had ever seen.

"Marry, Mistress Beaumont," cried the young lord,

"and if you had said the fairest image or doll, I should be of your thinking; but for a woman, show me other eyes and another mouth than those blue beads and coral lips."

Lord Gray is the most loved and loving husband in the world, and a tender father to his two fair babes. When love is the theme of a lay, his eyes turn on his wife, and then she responds with a sweet smile; but she hath no soul for verses or music, and is more occupied methinks with her dress than aught else on these occasions. She repairs it in so ingenious a manner, and disposes it so becomingly, that one should think her gowns were new from Margaret Chamberlayne's tire-rooms in the Strand. Verily there are persons which have no faults, and yet one cannot affection them. The placid virtues of Isabella Gray cause me more sins of uncharitableness than any other person's offences. *Mea culpa* this is—*mea maxima culpa*. But I would fain like this gentle lady more, or have a better reason to mislike her. As to David ap Einion, he cannot contain his displeasure when a legend tells of cruel tyrants and ladies unjustly used. On one occasion he rose and brandished his weapon fiercely against a recreant knight in a tale. The Queen said to him, smiling, "Sir David, you mind me of the first Christian French king, Clovis, who, when St. Remigius related unto him the passion of our Lord, stamped his foot, and cried: 'O that I only had been there with my brave soldiers!'"

The Prince threw his arm round his mother's neck, and said, "Sweet mother, I love that king which would have fought for Christ our Lord; and I love Sir David, who would fight for us; and I love—"

Here he stopped, and the Queen, fondly caressing him, asked, "And who else lovest thou?"

"Thee, sweet mother, and my father the King," he answered.

"And who besides?" she said, yet more fondly.

And he replied: "O, I love also sweet little Anne Neville, who played with me last year in London on the love-day, when thou, sweet mother, didst walk to St. Paul's Church hand-in-hand with the Duke of York."

Then the Queen's face became dark as a thunder-cloud, and she said sternly, "Thy father's son, Edward, may not love any of the Nevilles."

The Prince thought for a moment, and then answered: "My father told me when we were at Coventry that I should love all men: he did not say all little damsels; so maybe I must hate them. But Anne Neville was very winsome."

The Queen's eyes filled with tears; methinks the words of her child had recalled to her mind the King's Christian spirit.

Night after night at that time her majesty lay awake, and often till a late hour she kept me with her to converse or to read aloud to her. That evening she said: "O Meg, my good Meg, there are two Margarets within my soul; one exceeding loving, and one fierce. Love in me begets hatred. If it were less passionate my hates would be less excessive."

I had not the courage to say it, but I thought if she loved God more, *that* love would quench hatred. She bade me bring her journal-book to her, and inquired when she had last written in it.

"Never in England," I replied.

"And have you," she said, "kept no record of the many years since I landed in this country?"

"Yea, madame," I replied "I wrote somewhat touching those years till the time when I was with your grace at Hertford Castle."

"That is well-nigh five years ago," she said. "Whither went we afterwards?"

"To Greenwich," I said.

"Yea, to Greenwich," she rejoined; "and there I abided the time of the King's second recovery with that patience which consumes the heart but gains its end. Well, take my pen and write that when there I called to my side the Tudors, which had been true young brothers to me since. Once I cried shame on my aunt Katharine for her unroyal marriage, but now I would fain canonise her for that deed, for from that union have sprung those gallant boys, the most loyal hearts in all England to the King and me. And I now perceive that a Welsh squire is worth an English nobleman, if I judge by Owen Tudor and his sons, and our good Sir David here."

"Am I to set that down, madame?" I asked.

"No, no," she answered, smiling. "'All truths are not good to be uttered,' saith a French Proverb; much less, I ween, to be written. But write, that secretly at Greenwich I gathered round me the flower of the English chivalry—the ardent sons of the brave fathers slain at St. Alban's—and bided my time. Then one blessed day my lord was himself again, and went to Westminster, to the House of Parliament, where he demanded to be restored to his rights and to reign again, which by acclamation was assented to, and the wicked three—York, Salisbury, and Warwick—retired once more from London. The King then was, as he hath been and ever will be, too good, too *débonnaire*. Forgive, forgive, is always on his lips and in his heart. In that he too much resembles my father; but I have now discerned the truth of the saying of a heathen philosopher, that a merciful disposition is a weakness."

"O madame, say not so," I exclaimed.

"I tell thee, Meg, this is true in this manner: that to pardon traitors is a cruelty to loyal men ; and to spare rebels an injustice to good subjects. The King's mild spirit, which will not suffer him to take revenge or to shed blood, leads to the wreck of his kingdom and the ruin of his son. If goodness and virtue, if justice and holiness could have procured peace and quiet in this land, surely it would have done so when the King was at that time restored, and Waynfleet was Chancellor, and the good Lord Fortescue Lord High Treasurer and Lord Worcester and Lord Cromwell, and so many wise and honourable men about his person and in state offices. My God, how he laboured in those years for the weal of his people! Either he was planning new colleges and schools for the diffusion of religion and learning, or hospitals and almshouses for the poor, and moving his friends amongst the nobles to found the same in their counties, which now exist. He had a passion for increasing the grammar-schools; and in London ordained that such should be established in St. Martin's-le-grand, St. Mary-le-bow, in Cheap, St. Dunstan in the West, and St. Anthony, as well as at St. Paul's. King's College and Eton he wearied not in improving, but had most at heart the teaching of poor men's children, by that same token that he often recalled the words of a holy Pope in the twelfth century, who said that the Church, as a pious mother, is bound to provide teaching for the poor, lest the opportunity of reading and improving themselves be taken away from them. And he commended that ecclesiastical institute, which ordained that all Mass-priests should have in their house a school of disciples, and that if any good man should desire to have his children taught by them, they ought gladly to receive and kindly to teach them, and require naught from their parents than what they were willing to give. I remember when my Lord of Winchester would found a college at Oxford in honour of the glorious apostoless St. Magdalen, the King was well pleased thereat, but would have moved him to build it at Cambridge. The Bishop would by no means consent thereunto; and my lord, with his accustomed mildness, said, 'Well, Master William, sith it be so, we think well of your piety, and will forward it to the most of our power.' The King was well contented also that I strove with my poor ability to set on foot new skilful trades, and sent for artificers from France and the Low Countries to instruct this people in many useful arts. All the while we held court at Coventry, my Lord of Winchester, my Lord of Wells, the good Duke of Norfolk, and many other learned and virtuous prelates and noblemen, held daily counsel with the King for the good government of the realm, and the advancement of commerce, and the arts of limning and music, and the writing of books. His gentle wisdom in all peaceful matters inspired so great a love and admiration in all who approached him, that nothing would serve some of his friends but to obtain license to make pilgrimages in his behalf to distant shrines. The noble Mowbray went to the holy city of Jerusalem, to pray at Christ's sepulchre for the complete recovery of his strength: and others to Rome and to Loreto. Then think again, and record it also, what labour was spent in the efforts to procure a reconciliation which should be lasting betwixt the inimical noblemen. I promise thee I was then almost as desirous of peace as the King, for the French and the Scotch were threatening our coasts; and albeit the abominable Yorkists slander me as being French at heart, there is not a greater falsehood in this world. I would fight for every inch of English ground, and shed my blood for this land. Often I knelt by the King's side, and prayed ardently that these strifes might be healed; but I could not, like him, end those prayers with the words, ' And if it please Thee, O Lord, to take the kingdom from me, Thy will be done.' I could not utter with my lips a prayer from which my heart revolted. When he was made arbiter between his friends and foes, how he strove to adjust differences and to hold an equal balance between them, so as to soften resentments and to win them over to make peace! How he would charge the Mayor of London with 5,000 armed citizens to watch during the conferences that no evil befell peaceable persons! When my Lord of Winchester went to Blackfriars to parley with the White Rose lords, how he would pray God to mend their hearts! And when he was to meet at Whitefriars the noble partisans of the Red Rose, with yet more fervent orisons besought the Lord Jesus to allay their anger. But sometimes he was sick at heart at the perverseness of some, the malice of others, and the profane lying and breaking of oaths he then witnessed. To see God so offended, verily smote him to the heart. One day, when he had striven in vain with a fruitless patience to obtain an honest compromise betwixt the rival lords, a great paleness overspread his cheek, and he said to the other councillors, ' My lords, do you go and consider these matters; I and my good chancellor will meanwhile offer our prayers together for the common weal.' And so he did, beseeching God to take mercy on his people."

"Ah, madame,"—I could not forbear to say this as I wrote those last sentences,—" this noble picture of a Christian king, doth it not cause one to worship so great virtue?"

"Yea, if virtue, which I grant you is as perfect as any one on the earth, could prevail over malice and force, then indeed naught else could be desired, and we might well worship it. But, I pray you, when these pious souls had thus laboured for well-nigh three years; when at the last peace was signed and oaths of allegiance were renewed, even under the seal of the Blessed Sacrament solemnly received; and when to St. Paul's Church behind the King walked the Duke of York with me, Lord Salisbury with Somerset, Warwick with Exeter, hand-in-hand, whilst the people shouted in lame verse,

'Our sovereign lord God keep alway,
And the Queen and the Archbishop of Canterbury,
And others that have laboured to make this love-day.'—

think you that, save in a small number of noble breasts; hatred was allayed? Think you that whilst tears of joy ran down the King's cheeks, and Bourchier and Waynfleet carried the cross with God-thanking hearts, the dissimulating Yorkist traitors verily renounced their rebellious thoughts?"

"How did your Majesty endure the touch of the Duke of York's hand?" I said, evading to answer her question.

She replied, "From my head to my feet there ran a shiver when he approached me, and I felt like to faint; but, as God hears me, I resolved to forgive him, and prayed for strength to do so. I dare not say the same of Warwick; I could not trust myself so much as to look on him. He hath done what, I ween, no woman can pardon, — blackened my fame, slandered mine honour. I never spoke to him at all that day. And now, Meg, set down, I pray thee, how, when a few brief days had passed, he accused me of falsehood, and thereupon raised a tumult in the city; and when some of the King's servants attacked his riotous retainers, pretended that was a plot for to kill him, and so lighted a flame which, I warrant you, shall not be extinguished till the last Yorkist is dead. The King fell ill with sorrow, and went to the Abbey of St. Albans. When he was somewhat recovered, we made a progress through the midland counties, and there one of those brief joys which have sometimes flashed on my dark days shone on us for a while. The noblemen of Worcestershire, Lancashire, and Cheshire, the gallant esquires and brave yeomen of those provinces, flocked around us with a love which reminded me of the worship of the Provençals in olden days. When I had Edward by my side, they fell at my feet. The King's piety they revered. They are not mean Lollards like many of the Londoners. They hung on my poor lips and wore Edward's badge; his little silver swans were on the breast and a red rose in the bonnet of every knight and every peasant. The women blest my boy, and the men cried, 'Long live the Prince!' I pray thee write, that with a sense and wit beyond his years, he said agreeable words to everyone, and kissed his little hand, and smilingly held out his badge to those brave men, ten thousand of which wore his livery. O God, that thou shouldst have to chronicle that of these ten thousand gallant men three thousand were doomed to die on fatal Bloreheath! When I had ordered Lord Audley to intercept the hoary traitor Salisbury, and to bring him to me dead or alive, I would see the fight, and went to the tower of Muccleston Church to watch its course. This was the first time I had with mine own eyes beheld a battle. I had a fierce lesson, a fiery teaching in those terrible brief hours. I saw the wild charge, the rushing encounter of the two armies, the fatal shock when they met. Like unto a map the heath was spread before me. I traced every false move of our friends; I marked the overreaching skill of the veteran rebel; I saw our brave troops borne down, and Audley's vain labour to rally them. Mine eyes followed his banner, for well I knew that as long as he lived I should see it. Like one watching a vessel on a billowy ocean, I gazed on its rise and fall with an eager sick heart. As if bowing before the blast, it swayed to and fro; yet I kept it in sight. At last it sank and rose no more. Then I was sure Audley was dead and the fight lost, and I fled to Eccleston Castle. Yea, I fled with an aching heart and passionate grief for the fallen, but with a new spirit within me. The blood of Charlemagne and a whole race of heroes was stirred in my veins that day, and through my brain there darted a quick sudden sense of warlike genius which could yet save a kingdom. All night, whilst tossing on my sleepless couch, I thought, 'If Joan of Arc rescued France from the lowest slough of despond by her inspired valliancy, shall not a wife, a mother, and a queen overcome in God's name a host of traitors?' The King was then so ill at Coleshill that, when his people were hastily removing him, he could only whisper in a low voice, 'Who hath got the day?' Salisbury had joined York, and no one spoke a word of hope to me. But in my heart its voice was loud and strong; and when once at Coventry I roused the courage of the loyal and shamed the cowardice of the weak. The King improved in health when restored to my care, and the love he always inspires rallied thousands again around us. It was then the impious Duke of York sought to rob me of that sacred shield. To his discomfiture

he had discovered his own vassals to be more loyal to
his master than he desired; and with devilish cunning
in his camp at Ludgate he spread the report that
King Henry was dead, and had a Mass performed—
the sacrilegious wretch!—for the repose of his soul
who was yet alive. O, this greatly moved my lord's
anger. He exclaimed when it was told him, 'Forsooth,
this is a wicked action, a grievous sin, thus to use
God's great instrument of mercy to cloak malicious
deceit!' and this audacious impiety was more displeas-
ing to him than any of the Duke's treasons. Being
then privy to the loyal leanings in his army, I caused
the King's pardon to be proclaimed to all insurgents,
and advanced with him nigh to the very gates of
Ludlow, the head-quarters of the arch traitor. The
rebel chiefs, thinking he would as lief give away his
kingdom as risk the slaughter of his subjects, essayed
to play the same game as heretofore, and sent messages
of submission to the King. But by prayers, remonstrances, and impetuous urgency, I that time obtained
that he should be firm and refuse to treat with the
leaders, the while he renewed offers of pardon to their
followers. Then the rebel army melted away like snow
in a sudden thaw; then rightful submissions ensued
without number. York fled to Ireland; Salisbury,
Warwick, and March to Calais. The Duchess of York
and her young children alone remained in Ludlow,
which surrendered and was raised to the ground by
my commands. I said to Dame Cicely, 'Your grace's
husband hath abandoned you to the King's tender
mercies.' With tears in her eyes, she replied, 'If
they be the King's mercies, then I know they shall be
tender.' 'Yea,' I cried, 'you will find him a better
lord to you, Dame Cicely, than some of your own kith.'
When Edward heard that these young Mortimers were

prisoners, he gathered all his playthings in a heap, and nothing would serve him but to send them to these childish traitors. And he said to his tutor, 'I pray you good Sir John, is Anne Neville a prisoner also?' When he heard she was at Calais, then quoth he, 'I will send her one of my swans, and it shall sail over the sea and carry our love-tokens to and fro.'"

"O madame," I cried, "the Prince hath a most loving, sweet disposition. Methinks I would fain write his history from his early years when yours is finished."

"When I am dead, Meg?" she asked, smiling.

"Nay, madame, but when you are peacefully seated on the throne."

"Yea, yea," she said; "and then thou shalt chronicle that he reaped in joy what his mother sowed in tears."

CHAPTER XXVI.

Evil Tidings.

WHEN the Queen sent for me on the morrow she thus addressed me:

"Of the reverses which ensued in that year wherein the great triumph was achieved, touching which we wrote yestereve, I am not willing to speak at length. Thou rememberest as well as I do what took place when Warwick returned from Calais with fresh-raised troops, and York's son marched against our army at Northampton. Would I had been on the field that day! That bold March would, peradventure, then have found his match in the Queen which held him on her knees at Mantes when his false father professed so great loyalty to the King. But a weakness came over my heart on the battle's eve—a woman's terror. I could not part with my son. O, God only knoweth the daily anguish of fear with which I watch over that life,—the hope, the joy, the worship of mine own. Thou canst describe—for thine eyes saw it—the spot where we stood near the field, and how messages went to and fro betwixt me and Buckingham and good loyal John Talbot, who were soon to die fighting for us. It should not thus have been; it would not thus have been but for that hellish traitor Grey de Ruthyn! May his name be by all men in all times abhorred, and his death be as miserable as his life!"

I dared not to write this imprecation. Her majesty noticed the staying of my pen, and, snatching it from me, wrote herself these words:

"I Margaret the Queen, do declare that man to be accursed and hateful to God and to men, who by a deceitful treachery caused ten thousand loyal Englishmen to be slain or drowned, and his king to be left all lonely and disconsolate on the bloody field, and then taken captive. If there is justice on earth or in heaven, that traitor shall perish miserably, and hardly save his soul."

Then she pushed back the book towards me, and her bosom heaved like a stormy sea. After a pause, I timidly said, "And you fled with the Prince, madame, from that fatal spot?"

"Ah, when I snatched him up in my arms and mounted with him the horse Jasper brought unto us, all was swallowed up in the fear of losing him. God forgive me that I thought less of my lord the King than of my son. What a flight that was! How full of hairbreadth scapes! One of the worse moments I have yet known was when, between Eggleshall and Chester, we were surprised by those ruffianly servants of Sir William Stanley's; they were very near killing us."

"Methinks," I said, "they would have done so, if your majesty, after they had taken all your clothes and jewels had not bethought yourself to present that sole diamond ring they had not seen to John Cleger,—for so I have heard the villain is named,—and thus thrown a discord into that vile company which favoured our escape."

"Yea, God sent that thought into my mind after a brief desperate prayer for help. But was it not like unto a horrible nightmare when we ran into that close wood, and the sound of those disputing voices still reached our ears? God bless thee for the bravery thou didst then evince, good Meg! Mine forsook me when Edward began to cry. Then it seemed to me as if I must despair. I said this aloud in my anguish, and then he put his lips to mine ear and whispered: 'I will not cry nor make a noise, sweet mother. If those fierce men kill us, we shall go to the good God in heaven, and be happy.' I was in no mood to think of heaven then, and his words affrighted me; for if Edward died, he would go straight to Paradise, and I ——O, worse than one of Dante's invented torments is the thought of life in this world or the next without him! Sometimes a horrible feeling comes over me that I shall be lost, and I see at night, as in a vision, the heavenly visage of my King and the angel face of Edward gazing on me in a sorrowful manner, and I wake in terror."

I knew that the Queen of late, by reason of her unsettled life and other causes also, had seldom sought the benefits of shrift; and I had the boldness to say, "Your majesty, peradventure, would find ghostly comfort in more frequent confession. Shrift drives away thoughts of despair."

"Shrift!" she impatiently exclaimed; "let those seek it who are angels or saints."

"Nay, madame, it is the Sacrament for sinners," I answered with simplicity.

"If to pardon traitors and renounce just revenge is the condition without which shrift cannot be obtained, how can I seek it?"

"Madame, lawful justice may be pursued, and punishment inflicted on rebels without sin or offence, if only hatred is not cherished."

"I can in no wise forgive them," she said gloomily; and then dismissed me.

"God help him, poor King!" were the words which passed the white lips of the Queen when, some time afterwards, she received tidings which at first she would not credit, but in the end proved to be true, that his majesty had surrendered the rights of his son, and yielded that the Duke of York should be named his successor. She was commanded in his name to return to London with the Prince, on pain of high treason. First a fearful smile curled her lip, then tears moistened her eyes and slowly rolled down her cheeks. She was never so beautiful or so majestic as when by a mighty effort she reined in vehement emotion. One look she cast on the Prince at play, and one to Heaven, as if mutely appealing to God, but not one other angry word did she utter. But in the evening she called together the small band of her friends at Harlech, and thus addressed them: "My lords, and you all which are my good friends, list to me, a very afflicted woman and queen. The King, my entirely loved husband, hath disinherited his son and mine,—this boy, whom you do all look on as your future sovereign,—and yielded his rights to the Duke of York."

A murmur rose amongst those present, which, in the noblest manner imaginable, she hushed by the motion of her hand and the glance of her eye.

"Believe me, my lords and sirs, he loveth his son not the less that he hath by this act deprived him of the crown. He deems that little circlet a heavy curse and snare for the wearer, and, for one not yet anointed king by a divine consecration, the loss of it a good. So, working craftily for their own ends on his religious mind, these cunning men have drawn him into their nets and forced his acquiescence. But God hath given me other things and another heart in this regard; and, albeit poor, unaided, and unarmed, a woman not wholly friendless, I thank God, whilst you live, who now stand round me, I will yet place this boy on the throne, where he shall reign a fourth Edward, and a more noble one than hath yet ruled this land."

Then, deep from the hearts of all those men, there rose a shout which reëchoed through the rocky glen of Harlech, and in the breasts of a brave people. This patience of the Queen towards the King in passages of their lives wherein she endured much suffering at his innocent unwitting hands had something almost beyond nature in one so vehement. Methinks his constant virtue, which never forsook him in any straits, filled her with a spiritual reverence which subdued all resentments. She looked on him as on one above humanity, and not to be judged by common rules; and this infuriated her the more against her enemies. On the evening of that day she led me to the side of the Prince's bed, where he was asleep, and whispered in mine ear: "This hath been the keenest stab my heart hath yet received. Those detested wretches with a wise malice made use of a loved hand to pierce me. But they shall not long triumph. To London verily! Into their hands! into their net! Nay, nay, they count without their host. Little do they know yet of Margaret of Anjou! The Duke of York shall yet madly curse the day he broke a mother's heart. Farewell, Wales! farewell, inaction! Mary of Gueldres is my kinswoman; and Scotland's hills shall be those, in the words of the Psalms, whence shall come my help!"

On the next day she embarked on the Menai, amidst the tears of women, the speeding songs of the bards, and the deep-hearted blessings of the noble Welsh.

CHAPTER XXVII.

Pages from the Queen's Journal.

I AM alone to-night. I would not keep with me even Margaret de Roos; and mine own hand shall record the glorious, horrorful, triumphant haps of this day. O my husband! my sweet, injured, patient, long-suffering king! thou art at last avenged! The scale hath turned—the pined-for hour arrived. I have been for many days in a fever of mind and body which forbade rest. Each hour of the march from Scotland seemed an age, but each of those hours brought me fresh strength, for the nobles of the north gathered round my standard, and my brave army swelled like a mountain torrent. The fire in my breast inflamed all who approached me. The resistless justice of my cause, my boy's noble beauty, the words which fell from my lips like sparks on inflammable hearts, kindled a flame which, when once it is lighted, nothing can tame. Providence must needs have had profound designs when it made me the wife of holy Henry. O most sweet saint! God who gifted thee with heavenly virtues, and ordained that thou shouldst live on earth a disguised angel, banished from thy true home, has called me to be the human, passionate, revenging champion of thy righteous cause, and nerved my woman's heart to do deeds and to see sights which now in the dark and lonely nights affright me. Yet I will relate them; for if I am to conquer others, I must needs conquer myself, nor falter one instant in the onward path. I once heard of a boatman at sea whose bark caught fire. He left not the helm though the flames were scorching him, and steered the vessel into port. This I think to be the type of my course. Only, God send the haven may soon be reached!

The time which hath passed since we came to York is like a dream, marvellous, incredible, and brief. Ah, the fugitive Queen took her foes by surprise! The while they were framing bills of attainder, forsooth, against her, and were ignorant she had yet crossed the Border, behold she was at the gates of York, of the old city,—too good a one to give its name to a traitor,—and calling on her followers to advance to London and rescue the King. But on Christmas-eve Lady Gray, who was then at Groby, sent me a messenger to say that the Protector—God save the mark!—was at his castle of Sandal, and would there wait the coming of his son with the Border forces. I received her letter as I was going into the chapel at Wakefield for midnight Mass. The beating of my heart was so violent, I could hear its pulsations as I leant against my *prié-dieu*. The singing of the *Gloria in excelsis* made my bosom swell with a good presentiment, for the glory of God is the triumph of His justice; and if there be on earth one man of perfect goodwill towards all others, it is my lord for whom I fight.

On the morrow I rode full nigh to the gates of Sandal Castle to provoke false York to issue forth and give me battle; for delay to us was fatal. Day after day I sent heralds to beard and defy the traitor, each time with more galling words than the last. Lady Gray paid him a visit, for she had always been much esteemed by him; and she reported that he was almost beside himself at these taunts, and would not long withstand being braved by a woman. This Isabel Gray hath a most rare talent—the only one I can see in her—of concealing her thinking without the utterance of an untrue speech. She is, I am assured, as well as her mother the duchess, very heartily devoted to my person, and as loyal as any one in this England to the King; but she can see the most inimical persons of all sorts, and is considered by them is an incredible manner, which is procured, I think, by her trick of silence and the beauty of her face, which charms beholders, and yet never by so much as a change of colour or the wink of a eye betrays her thoughts, or the least inward emotion. Be that as it may, she related to me what a friend of that arch traitor's had told her: how his old servant, Sir Davy Hall, had prayed him to abstain from coming forth to give me battle, but rather to keep within the castle and defend it till the arrival of his son; and that he had replied, "Ah, Davy, Davy! hast thou loved me so long, and wouldst thou have me dishonoured? Thou never sawest me keep fortress when I was Regent in Normandy, where the Dauphin himself with his puissance came to besiege me; but like a man and not like a bird cooped in a cage, I issued and fought with mine enemies—to their loss ever, I thank God; and if I have not kept myself within walls for fear of a great strong prince, nor hid my face from any man living, wouldst thou that I for dread of a scolding woman, whose weapons are only her tongue and nails, should incarcerate myself and shut my gates?

Then all men might of me wonder and report that a woman hath made me a dastard whom no man could ever prove to be a coward."

O York, York! where are the boasting lips which uttered these proud words? A woman hath made thee a mock, a derision, a thing for the finger of scorn to point at, and the very birds of the air to flout as they fly by. O doomed man, graceless rebel, unnatural kinsman, thine hour was come; the cup of thine iniquities full to the brim! And when thou didst dare with impious pride to advance thy shameful banner in the most holy name of God and St. George, then thy guardian angel fled affrighted, and the Holy Trinity forsook thee.

This morn I thus marshalled my forces: with Somerset I commanded the centre — Lord Clifford being ambushed in a wood on the right side, and Lord Wiltshire on the left. Ah, the joy, the wild expectancy, the tumult of the heart, veiled under a motionless attitude, with which I beheld the Yorkists issue from the castle-gate of Sandal and descend towards us! It was but a short time before they reached the plain, but it seemed like an age. I discerned York riding in front; an instant after, the fighting began. I would fain have dashed into the *mêlée*, but was restrained. Our ambushed troops, like cataracts falling into a torrent, joined the vanguard, and as fishes in a net or deer in a buckstall, the enemies were surrounded, closed, hemmed in. All was noise, shrieking, confusion; and in one half-hour louder than all other sounds rose the cry of victory—" A Lancaster! a Lancaster! Long live the Red Rose!"

I stood in the field of battle, trembling, burning, exulting with a feverish joy; the cry of those around me resounding like clarions in mine ears: " They are flying! They are slain by thousands! The day is won! The kingdom saved! Long live the King! Long live the Queen! Long live the Prince!" I know not how long these deafening shouts, this frantic rejoicing lasted. I held no count of time. I had dismounted, and was leaning on the arm of Isabel Butler, when I saw one riding towards me at full speed with something in his hand. In another moment Lord Clifford was kneeling at my feet; and as he said, "Madame, your war is done; here is your King's ransom," mine eyes fell on the thing in his hand, and I saw, O God, that once familiar face, those well-known features, fixed in death, and the blood-stained hair by which the head was held. A deadly sickness seized me; I felt the blood forsaking my cheeks, my limbs giving way, and I covered my eyes with my hand. Many voices shouted: "Look, madame, look!" and one added, "At this king without a kingdom;" and another, "At this rival of our noble sovereign;" and then I heard them say, "O, he shall have a crown;" and "Crown him, Clifford, crown him;" which were followed by bursts of laughter. I glanced at the gory head, and saw it surmounted with a paper coronet, and a horrible contagious uncontrollable fit of convulsive laughter shook me from head to foot.

"What shall be done, madame, with the traitor's head?" Somerset asked.

"Fix it on the gates of York," I cried, willing to be relieved from the ghastly sight.

"Lord Clifford hath made sharp work of it to-day!" Isabel Butler exclaimed. "He says he has slain young Rutland on Wakefield-bridge as he was escaping with his tutor."

"Not the boy?" I cried. "O Lord Clifford, you

did not kill the boy?" Then I saw on his grim visage a look which affrighted me.

"Madame," he cried, "when my aged father was slain in cold blood by the Yorkists at St. Albans, I swore never to spare one of their accursed race. I looked for praise from your Majesty this day rather than for those reproachful glances. If you play the woman, not the Queen, we may as lief disband our forces and sue for pardon to the Earl of March."

A murmur rose among the lords, and the fear seized me that I had angered my friends; and when the Duke of Somerset and the other peers came to ask what I commanded to be done with Lord Salisbury, who was taken prisoner, and I saw they would not be denied his head, I straightway ordered him to be executed, and his head placed by the side of that of York; and to please them, I cried that space should be left betwixt these two for those of the Earl of Warwick and the Earl of March, which I intended should soon be added to them. Loud applauding shouts followed this speech, and then I felt almost mad for awhile and as if my brain was on fire. I longed to be alone, to kneel down, to weep, to pray. O my God, Thou knowest I would not willingly do a false or unjust action; Thou knowest I would lay mine own head on the block sooner than shed the blood of an innocent person. Lay not to my charge, O Lord, that which has flowed to-day in the just quarrel of the King by Thee ordained. O, I would fain Clifford had not slain young Rutland! If ever a man was justly sentenced to death on this earth, Salisbury is that man, and I fear not to meet him at the day of judgment, if a thousand times I had doomed him to death. But that fair boy, Dame Cicely's young son! To-morrow, I ween, she will hear of his death. God help her! how could Clifford do it! How is it possible a man can kill a boy of twelve years of age! When I went into Edward's chamber and knelt by his bedside, a dreadful thought came to me that the Duchess of York would curse her son's murtherers, and that this curse would cleave to me, albeit Thou knowest, O Lord, I am not guilty of this hap. I wondered where Clifford had stabbed him; and if he had died at once, or cast a piteous look on his destroyer. And then mine eyes became dim with tears, and I thought I saw blood streaming from Edward's bosom on to the white sheet, and screamed in an agony. He opened his sleepy eyes on me, and smiled. O Dame Cicely! Dame Cicely! you will never more see *your* boy smile! But curse your treacherous husband; curse the day he became a rebel and a traitor; curse Clifford, if you will. O, how I should curse him in your place! But curse not me; curse Warwick who slew Clifford's aged father; curse all those who began these dreadful wars. Good heavens, under what star was I born that strife and bloodshed dog my footsteps?

St. Alban's Abbey, February 1461.

God knoweth I have suffered more than most women; but hath any woman or queen in ancient or in modern times been more blest than I to-day? Can a more rapturous hour be thought of than that in which I fell first in the arms of my husband, and then at his feet to beseech him to knight our gallant little son, who through all the fierce conflict in St. Peter's Lane never left my side, and while a shower of blinding arrows assailed us, cried aloud in his childish clear voice, "Forward, sweet mother, forward!" and brandished his little sword with as great an unconcern of danger as if he had been at play with his companions. Heavens, in how desperate a manner both sides fought! But Warwick's Londoners could not withstand our northern troops which poured in upon them like an avalanche, while Lovelace with his city bands attacked them in the rear. When the light declined, the Yorkists fled on every side, and I cried "To London! to London!" for there I thought to find the King, and the while he was at hand in his lone unguarded tent, abandoned by the disbanded traitors. His good servant Howe ran to tell Lord Clifford, who fetched me to him. Wild with joy, I flew to my husband. O God, there are instants which repay whole years of suffering! When my head sank on his breast, and I heard his low gentle voice utter my name in grateful amazement, I could have wished to die before I raised it again. O, what noble thanks he gave me! and how fervently he blessed the child which had so royally won his spurs, and knighted him on the spot, with Lord Shrewsbury, Lord John de Roos, and thirty more of my brave followers! Then we went to the Abbey to praise God; and the Prior and the monks met us, chanting thanksgiving hymns for the King's deliverance. I would not have dispensed with one of the pangs of this last year, since they have wrought this glorious ending.

The King hath been kept in so great ignorance of state affairs in his captivity, that he cannot conceive the stern necessities of justice. He made a rash promise that the lives of Lord Bonville and Sir Thomas Kyriel should be spared, because they protected him in the rout; but they are nevertheless very malicious rebels, and the lords on our side, whose brothers and sons were villanously murthered at Mortimer's Cross by the new Duke of York, will revolt, if mercy is extended to these men. His own brothers, Edmund and Jasper Tudor, are wild to be revenged on the

Yorkists for the beheading of their brave father. Rebellion must be crushed, or else victories are vain. The Duke of Somerset hath my orders to act with vigour, and I have despatched Lord Scales to London to command the citizens forthwith to send provisions for my army. The Lord Mayor is my very good friend, and I have charged him to execute this order without delay.

Heavens! are these Londoners weary of their lives, that they audaciously brave me in this wise? But if they reck not of their mean existences, they can be touched in their possessions, which are like to be yet dearer to them. The Commons have dared to seize on the cartloads of Lenten fare which the Mayor had procured for my troops, because forsooth there was a rumour that Warwick had joined York, and was marching towards the City. We shall see which of the White or the Red Rose shall reach it first! I have licensed my loyal northerners to plunder as they list this rebellious county, and to sack London when they come there.

This morn nothing will serve the Duchess of Bedford and Lady Scales and Lady Gray but that I should admit to a private audience the Mayor of London, who hath come to sue for a withdrawal of the license to my troops to plunder London and its neighbourhood. I would not listen to the duchess or Isminia Scales; but when Isabel Gray brought a message to the same effect from her brave lord, who is, I fear, in a dying condition,—albeit I hope in God he may yet amend of his wounds,—I was forced to yield.

I, Margaret de Roos, by the Queen's commands, take up the pen she is loth to use any more to-night;

for her grace is most discomposed and quite overwhelmed with trouble. The Mayor of London saw her at noon, and, with tears in her eyes, assured her majesty all was lost if she withdrew not the said license.

"On one condition only will I recall it," she cried: 'Let the gates of London be thrown open to me and to mine army.'"

"Alas, madame," he replied, "fain would I on my knees receive your majesty into the City; but—O, pardon me that I must needs utter an unpalatable truth—save your grace's poor servant, there is not one man of note amongst the citizens that will consent to it. They are all Yorkists in their hearts."

"Then," she passionately exclaimed, "they merit the worst fate a lawless soldiery can inflict upon them; and I vow they shall suffer it."

He urged and reasoned, but she would not hear; and when the argument was most hot, the door of her chamber slowly opened.

"Who dareth to come unbidden into my presence?" she cried; but turning, saw it was the King, who looked very pale, and walked feebly, as one in pain.

"Madame, for Jesus' sake," he said, "stay the fury of your soldiers. Forsooth and forsooth you do not well to let loose the rage of covetous men on my people. They have now fallen also on God's house; the fair abbey is in their ruthless hands. God send you may be able to lay the storm you have raised!"

Then he fainted away. The Queen clasped him in her arms with an imploring countenance, and summoned his attendants.

She hath been riding all day, from one place to another, to stay the pillage. The abbey is sacked; the mischief, if checked in one place, bursts out in another, as when men seek to extinguish fire in a building —here it subsides, there it breaks forth anew. And ill news are pouring in. The Lord Gray is dead. Most of the towns and villages betwixt this and London have raised the standard of York. The Earl of March is drawing nigh to the city-gates. Provisions are lacking. The troops murmur. There is a report that their majesties will depart this night for the north, and the army retreat thitherward also. God send this may not be true. I have seen Lady Gray for one moment—a most disconsolate mourner. She is gone to her mother's house at Grafton with her two babes.

In an hour I go with the King and Queen and the Prince from hence to York. Nothing is lost, the Queen says. Somerset and Clifford will follow them there with sixty thousand men at the least.

CHAPTER XXVIII.

Meeting with Old Friends.

A LETTER from the Lady Margaret de Roos to Mistress Elisabeth Clere:

"Nantes, the 7th of May 1462.

"MY WELL-BELOVED DAME ELISABETH,—I little thought to have seen Brittany, this land whither in past years my fancy so often travelled, and which never-dying memories hallowed to my poor heart. When the Queen asked me in Scotland if I would cross the seas with her, I answered 'Yea, I would;' for I would follow her whithersoever she went—to the ends of the earth if need be. She had not then one groat in her purse, but Monsieur Duluc, to whom in her young days she had rendered an important service at Nancy, and who is now a rich trader betwixt Scotland and the Low Countries, procured her a well-fitted ship, and lent her money for the voyage. She could not stay at Kircudbright, for the envoy of the usurper was expected at Dumfries, report said, to propose a marriage between his so-called king and the Scottish queen, which is an almost incredible thing, seeing she hath so lately betrothed her young daughter to the Prince of Wales, and did excellently well entertain their majesties since they came into her son's kingdom from Alnwick, after the fatal battle of Towton and the crowning in London of the Earl of March. I ween the Duke of Somerset's ill conduct to that queen, in that he boasted to the King of France of the favour she had showed him, which was reported to her and incensed her not a little, wrought this change. Ah me! those Beauforts have, and I fear ever will ruin the royal cause. The King hath gone into Westmoreland, into a friendly place of concealment; and the Queen is resolved to see her cousin-german, the King Lewis; for she has had letters from Dieppe, which to her no small grief have advertised her of the death of her uncle, King Charles, and that his son, the present king, is not so well disposed towards her majesty by a great deal as was his father; by the same token that he caused Lord Somerset to be arrested in that city, where he landed in the disguise of a merchant, and confined in the castle of Arques, whence he has been only released at the instance of the young Count of Charolais, to whom she wrote. But if she can have speech of King Lewis, then, she says, all will be well, and for that end we are on the way to his court. And now, having related to thee, well-beloved friend, the events which led to my coming hither, I will now speak of our arrival at this town of Nantes, the capital of Brittany, and of the good cheer which the young duke hath made to our sovereign lady the Queen in this her forlorn estate. He was the Count d'Etampes till his uncles all died without children, and as gay and gallant a young prince as can be met with. He is married to the Lady Margaret of Foix, a princess in great renown of virtue, and almost as charitable towards the poor as her kinswoman Madame Françoise d'Amboise, the widow of the Duke Pierre. When the common people see these two royal ladies, who are close friends and companions, issue together from the palace with their hands laden with provisions which they carry to the lepers' house, and to the sick persons in the town, it is

s

their wont to smile and say, 'There go our duchesses a-pleasuring.' And now whom thinkest thou I have seen in this city at the convent of the Poor Clares, whither the ladies of the court directed me? Who but Jeanne de Kersabiec, mine own old loved friend of bygone days! O, with what joy we met, and how great a contentment we found in conversing together after so long a separation and such great and various haps! After many mutual questionings about the past, before parting we exchanged a pledge which, I pray God, I may observe as religiously as Jeanne will surely do. As life had in its outset only one aim for us both, and hath left us one common tender memory daily remembered in our prayers, so we have now resolved to leave no virtue unattempted, no perfection unsought, which we have heard or read of in the lives of holy persons —she in the cloister, and I in the world; she like Anna in the Temple, in long fastings and prayers, I on the stormy sea of a most tempest-tossed existence; she serving God by a direct consecration, I my sovereign lady the Queen, not with a vain human worship, but as ordained by Him to be my mistress. When we had made this promise to each other we parted; not embracing, for that the grate betwixt us forbade, but with hearts close meeting in that resolve, and so great a comfort in our souls, if I judge of hers by mine own, that nothing can exceed it. No, nothing more sweet could have befallen me in the midst of my trials than this brief sight of Jeanne, the Poor Clare. When I waited on the Queen at my return, she told me she had seen the Duke of Brittany, and that he had been a very good kinsman to her, and made her a gift of twelve thousand crowns. I almost leapt for joy at this news, for our necessities were great indeed. Straightway her majesty commanded me to despatch sums out

of this money to the most needy of her friends.
Little, indeed, did she retain for her own use.
'Madame,' I said, 'if you hope to receive a like bounty
from your cousin-german King Lewis, if I am to credit
what I hear, you are greatly deceived.' She said she
would not forecast the future, but that when she heard
of a nobleman like the Duke of Exeter, compelled by
hunger in the Low Countries to beg for bread, running
after the Comte de Charolais's coach, who to his
sorrowful amazement discovered him, she could not
choose but share with her brave suffering followers
what God's Providence had sent her. As she was
thus discoursing, one of her suite came to tell her that
the Sieur Guy de Laval, her stepmother's brother, and
Madame de Dinant, his wife, desired to visit her.
'Ah, let them come,' she exclaimed; 'they are thrice
welcome;' and when they came in she tenderly embraced them. I could not take my eyes off this young
princess, for she had been Monseigneur Gilles' little
wife; and whilst she and her husband conversed with
the Queen, I sat with her lady, Madame Anne de
Coetlogon, who is cousin to Jeanne and like her in face
and in voice. She told me Madame Françoise de
Dinant had been married for some time to the Sieur
de Laval. When she heard Monseigneur Gilles was
dead, she cried very much, and said she should live
and die a widow. But as she was then only eleven
years of age, it was not to be thought of. And the
Duke Pierre and his wife Madame Françoise, for the
great fear they had that Arthur de Montauban should
renew his suit with the aid of powerful friends, made
her sign a promise to wed in two years the Sieur de
Gavres, Monseigneur Guy de Laval's son, who would
then be fifteen. 'And wherefore,' I asked, 'did not
that marriage come to pass?' Madame de Coetlogon

smiled and replied: 'When the time for this union arrived, monseigneur brought his son one day to see madame. The Sieur de Gavres never spake so much as one word to her, but watched a bird in a cage on the window-sill. Monseigneur his father conversed with madame all the time they stayed; and she answered him with so great wit and modesty, that he seemed amazed to find in so young a princess so much excellence and good parts beyond her years. When he rose to retire, he took her hand and said, looking at his son, 'Madame, I am of opinion that my son will be the happiest person in the world when he is your husband.' 'Nay, monseigneur,' madame answered agreeably, the colour rising to her cheeks, 'methinks I will send that bird to the Sieur de Gavres, for it will, I ween, give him more pleasure than anything else in the world.' 'Madame, pardon his silence,' the count replied; 'he is young, and youth is not always allied with maturity of mind like in yourself.' The second time the little bridegroom came to see madame, he had his governor with him, and then he talked to her a great deal. But it was all touching his dogs, and his new horse, and the feeding of his hawks; and when he went away, 'My father,' quoth he, 'charged me to converse with you, madame: methinks I have fulfilled his behest, and can now go play at barre with my friends.' That evening madame lay abed a little indisposed. She had been sad all day; and when the Duchess Françoise came to see her, she threw her arms about her neck and said, 'I am not of good cheer, sweet godmother.' 'What aileth you, my child?' quoth the duchess. 'I would fain not marry the Sieur de Gavres,' she replied; 'for I had once a husband who, albeit I was so little, loved me, and I did all he told me; but this one is a child, and careth only for dogs, horses, and birds, and not at all for me.' Then the duchess sighed, for a promise had been given, and the Sieur de Laval was a lord of so great puissance that to break troth with him was not to be thought of. So she sat silently awhile by madame's side praying, I think; for this was her wont when in any trouble. Madame de Dinant soon sat up in her bed, and said, 'I would the Sieur de Gavres was as old as his father, and like him too. Then I should be happy; for he is a very good lord to me, and he would call me his little wife, like the good prince my husband used to do.' 'But he is forty years of age, and you only thirteen,' the duchess said. 'Yea, and if he was sixty, I should be glad to be his wife if he would have me,' madame answered. The duchess bade her lie still and say her prayers, and she would see her again on the morrow. When she did, 'I pray you,' quoth she, 'madame, my little sister, are you of the same mind as yestereve, and will you be the wife of Monseigneur Guy de Laval, who should be a better shield for your youth and a more safe protector than a young man of his son's years?' Madame well-nigh jumped for joy at this exchange, and then thanked God with all her heart. Nothing would satisfy her but to send her bird to the Sieur de Gavres; for, quoth she, 'I am now to be his mother, and I will be a very good one to him.' And so she has been, Madame de Roos; and the most loving, obedient wife imaginable to monseigneur his father. But she has told me that the first time after she was married, when he tenderly called her his little wife, she could not restrain her tears; for she thought of her first husband, for whom, with a singular constancy of affection in a child, she always retained a fond remembrance.'

"I thanked Madame de Coetlogon for this little

history, which moved me to a yet greater interest in this noble lady, and I was right glad to kiss her hand when she departed. She little thought, as I pressed my lips upon her glove, how tender a heart I bore towards her.

"When the Queen was alone with me, she said: 'What strange vicissitudes life presents, and mostly for royal persons! These kinsfolk of mine have related to me to-day the adventures which have lately befallen the holy widow of the Duke Pierre, here in this very city but a short time ago. She is reputed a saint. I remember when I was a little child, the good Théophanie, my nurse, was wont to set her before me as a model. Hast heard much about her, Meg?' I answered that from Jeanne and others, I had heard much of her virtues, which exceeded all praise, and mostly of her singular patience, when for a time her husband, who by nature was violent and fierce, conceived a most groundless and abominable jealousy, which led him to ill-use and maltreat her in a most cruel manner, so that she nearly died of his ill-usage. And never, as long as this persecution lasted, did she open her lips, save to pray for this hard lord and to bless God for her many sufferings. At the last, the duke came to his senses when he was like to lose her ; and then his eyes being opened, he hated himself, and falling on his knees by her bedside besought her pardon. This was her answer, which drew tears from all who heard it : ' My lord, my good friend, I forgive you with all my heart. Do not weep ; for this ill-thinking came not from yourself but from the devil, who is envious and not ashamed to sow discord and evils, for this is his office to prevent good and work us harm. I assure you, my lord, my friend, that I, your little servant, have never with so much as a thought transgressed my duty to you. So I beseech you think no more ill of me, for verily you have no cause.' Then she recovered; and Jeanne says they both served God together for many years in exceeding great peace and piety, and that the years they reigned were the most happy this people have known. But that good prince wore a hair-shirt all his days, and performed many penances till he died, because of his bad usage of this virtuous lady. Then the Queen said: 'Her patience is the more admirable that she hath shown herself one of the most wilful princesses in the world since her husband's death.' 'Truly,' I answered, 'this amazes me; for Jeanne told me that in the convent where she is now a novice, she is so obedient, that to the least order given her she submits, and if she thinks in the least point to have offended, kneels down like a little child to ask forgiveness.' 'Ah,' quoth the Queen, with one of her old bright smiles, 'but she hath for all that fought and won a battle most arduous, and defeated the King of France himself.' 'What, King Lewis?' I exclaimed. 'Yea, King Lewis and the Duke of Brittany and the Comte de Thouars, her father, and the Maréchal de Montauban, Arthur's brother, and as many more puissant princes and lords. This is the story which Guy de Laval and his wife related to me. The day her husband died, this princess made a vow that she would never marry again, but live and die a perfect widow, and serve God in some austere religion when she had opportunity. This vow greatly displeased her father, M. de Thouars, who would have her marry again for his convenience; and the Duke of Brittany was loth she should go into religion; for albeit a gay prince himself, he wished her to continue in his court, for he and his wife did very much esteem and love her, and were displeasured she should think of leaving them; so he bade her think no more on it, for he would never give his consent. But nothing moved this widow. She bided her time; and one day in the parish church of Pleherlin, in a loud voice, in presence of all the people, she renewed her vow before she received the Body of our Lord, to the no small affright of her ladies, and even her confessor. For now the king of the French people, moved by the Vicomte de Thouars, desired that she should wed his own brother-in-law, the Count Lewis of Savoy, and then M. de Thouars would disinherit his eldest daughter, and bequeath all his havings and lands to the Duchess Françoise. So the Sieur de Montauban, her uncle, came with this message to the lady; but none other answer had he than this: 'Mine uncle, God save the King, and my lord my father and all my friends! I was glad when you came, but now I am not rejoiced thereat, for what you have told me breaks my heart. Howsoever, to cut long speeches short, know that I will not marry, and nothing shall shake this my resolve.' There was a round speech, Meg! This princess had not lived so long in Brittany for nothing.' 'Madame,' I said, 'had your Majesty been in her case, methinks you would have spoken with equal resolution.' 'Well, they said the Sieur was taken aback with this straight reply, and left the Duchess's chamber without uttering one word, or so much as a leave-taking or obeisance. But he went to seek her confessor, and threatened to cast him into the Loire, if he did not straightway reduce the lady to the king's obedience and her father's in the matter. But he got no satisfaction from the reverend man; for albeit he denied having moved the duchess to make this vow, 'now,' quoth he, 'she has made it, I will in no wise forsake her highness or deny her spiritual consolation; and as to your threats, Monsieur le Maréchal, be assured I am ready to die for this cause.' Then the baffled ambassador was forced to vent his anger on the ladies of the duchess, and menaced to have them all beheaded and thrown into a ditch, if they dissuaded her not from her resolve. Loud were the tears and sobs of these poor damsels; but their mistress bade them be of good cheer, for that no harm should befall them, and yet she should never break her vow nor marry any man, if the whole world were to exhort her to it. Her father, M. de Thouars, when he and his brothers had vainly sought to move this stubborn lady, then sued to King Lewis to reduce her to a prompt obedience. His majesty was coming on a pilgrimage to Redon, in Brittany. He is always very pious when he has some treachery in view; — God defend when I see him, I should find him on his knees! He had a quarrel then with the Duke of Brittany, but not an open one, and came into this country to stir up against him some of his nobles; so at least Guy de Laval says. He sent an order to the Duchess Françoise to meet him at Redon, there to do homage for her lands in Poitou. She at first refused; for it is not the custom for widows, she said, to be thus summoned; but being secretly warned that her castle would be invested and her person seized, she resolved to go to the king at once and bring the matter to an issue. She followed him from Redon to Nantes; and her servants having been bribed she was carried unawares to a house outside the town, and locked up by them in her chamber. The fear she was in of being forced away to France made her so ill that they thought she would die, and in their affright they suffered her to escape from their hands. She walked straight to the gate of the town, for to go to our Lady's church to hear Mass; but one of her uncles met her, and cried in a rough voice, 'Halte là, madame! whither are you going?' 'To church,' she said, 'to pray God to have mercy on me, since men have no pity.' 'No, forsooth, you shall not do so,' quoth the uncle; 'for the king is coming to see you.' 'Nay,' she replied 'I know full well the king is not coming so soon but that I may first hear Mass, and pray at my husband's tomb.' And she would have passed on, but the enraged gentleman seized hold of her, and cried, 'Nay, you shall not go to the church; I arrest you in the king's name.' Then she, with a royal and womanly dignity, exclaimed, 'What! are you so bold as to lay hands on me, and in the city of Nantes? In whose name you do it, I shall soon learn;' and she bade one of her esquires go to the duke. But the while some of the common people had gathered together and seen M. de Beaubois insult his niece, whose name fled from mouth to mouth. Then, like one man, the inhabitants of Nantes arose to defend the holy duchess. The workmen, the shopmen, the artificers, the women, even the children, flocked around her, and the whole city rose in an uproar. Four thousand armed men in an instant formed her bodyguard, and with this escort she walked to the church with her eyes bent on the ground, the women kissing her black weeds and her long veil. She knelt at her husband's tomb and made her prayer, the populace on their knees outside the church in hushed silence guarding the door; and when she rose, with loud blessings hailing her, they would see her to her house, and only dispersed at her prayer, when the Duke appeared at the window by her side. Then there came to her that day the King Lewis, and with many artful words invited her to his court, and right piously discoursed on the duty children owe to their parents, which methinks, Meg, in lou Daouphin's mouth, as they called him in Provence, must needs have been a very touching homily. Not one voice but that of the people was raised in her behalf. Not one kinsman took her part. Either through fear or interest or policy, they were all adverse or silent. I admire the baseness of men which would not fly in a battle, but have less courage than a woman to face the frowns of their superiors. Yet she stood her ground, and no otherwise would she say but that her vow she should keep, and die sooner than break it. At the last the Duke quarrelled with the King, and his Majesty departed ill-pleased from Nantes. Her father and her uncles would have carried her off by force to France, but the night when the boats they had hired were in the river, it suddenly froze so hard that their purpose was defeated. The duke, when he heard of this plot, was at the last aroused to anger, and drove these lords from Brittany. And now this brave and faithful woman, which I would to God I could have seen, hath fulfilled her vow, and serves God in the religion of Mount Carmel. Meg, there be many sorts of valiant women in the world: there needeth force of heart to be a saint as well as a queen.' 'Only in the one case,' I answered, 'force is shown within as well as without. There are internal as well as external triumphs.' 'But I need all the force I have for action,' she cried. 'Should you have less of it, madame, if you conquered yourself first and others afterwards?' (I had become more bold since my pledge to Jeanne.) 'Yea, far less,' she replied; 'for to conquer self would be to forgive my foes; and if I detested them less, I should not go through fire and water to be avenged on them.' 'Would not love achieve greater triumphs than hatred?' 'No, no,' she passionately exclaimed; 'love would break my heart, not nerve it like hate. Love would drive me into a desert with my child, like another Hagar; but the thought of revenge is the spur which will regain a throne.' 'A throne, madame—a throne! Have you yet so great an esteem for that slippery seat?' 'Not now for my own sake, Meg; God knoweth I care little now to be a Queen; but He hath given me a son, the most royal in nature as in birth a mother has ever looked on, and I will have him a king or perish in the quarrel. Hast heard the Prince's last piece of wit?' 'Nay, madame; by your smile I see it hath pleased you.' 'Nay, it made me laugh at the time. Some one said "Arthur de Montauban is resolved to become a monk." "What, that devil!" I cried; and then Edward said, "Is he sick?" "No," I replied. "O," quoth he, "I thought devils would be monks only when they were ill; for so saith the rhyme I learnt from the King of Scotland at Dumfries." After a pause her Majesty said: 'I wonder if the good matrons of Dumfermline persevere in the use of the needles I taught them to handle. There was not one woman in that town that could sew. They all had distaffs, but no needles; i'faith, Meg, some of the most peaceful hours I have spent were with those simple souls, teaching them this new cunning.' 'The children,' I said, 'laud your Majesty in an uncouth rhyme. I hear they sing about the streets:

> May God bless Margaret of Anjou;
> For she taught our Dumfermline women to sew.'

'Talking of rhymes,' she replied, 'how truly doth the spirit of a people show itself in those artless ways! There is not a village in that England which for the nonce dares not wag a finger in our behalf, where the praises of my saintly King are not sung by pious souls in all sorts of rude verses. Before I left Scotland, at a time when for many long days a dead hardness had come over me, and not one tear had softened the arid soil of my heart, some one showed me a little distich of this sort, written by a poor blind poet. I promise you I wept when I read it more than at the most pathetic speeches of great persons. This was it:

> I pray you, sirs, of your gentry
> Sing this carol reverently,
> For it is made of King Henry;
> Great need have we for him to pray.
> If he fare well, well shall we be,
> Or else we may lament full surely.
> For him shall weep full many an eye:
> Thus prophesies the blind Audlay.

God bless the blind poet,' added the Queen, ' and all who love my holy King and pray for him!' O, I would fain her majesty could see the Duchess Françoise; for her soul is more inclined to godly thoughts and womanly tenderness than it hath been for a long time, and in that pious princess there is a virtuous boldness not dissimilar in its origin to her own courageous disposition, albeit otherwise schooled and directed. She might be turned by her gentle guidance from desperate courses of adventure, and more resigned to God's will in untoward events. But to-morrow we travel towards Chinon, and God knoweth what the upshot of that enterprise shall be. So fare thee, well, sweet Elisabeth. Pray for the weal and worship of this noble Queen and her poor servant, thy loving friend,

"Margaret de Roos."

CHAPTER XXIX.

Sir Pierce de Bracy.

THE Queen and the Prince and we her majesty's servants have made a long voyage through France, and tracked King Lewis from city to city, who still appointeth meeting-places with the Queen, and then cheats her of her hope, and departs often the day before she can arrive, alleging mostly some devout cause or other to give a colour to these deceptions. We have followed this royal will-o'-the-wisp to Poitiers, then to Bordeaux, to Tours, and now to Amboise. Like persons in a dream oppressed with nightmare we seem to approach the end of this long pilgrimage; but ever as we appear able to seize what we pursue, it eludes our grasp. God send he does not intend wholly to deceive her majesty and to drive her to despair! Long journeys prove wearisome after a time even to happy folk; but to those who suffer from a cruel suspense and the sickness of hope deferred, God only knoweth what a torment lieth in them. When the country we traverse is fair and smiling, then the sense of contrast chafes a vexed heart; when gloom and savageness disfigure the scene, a sorrowful mind is yet more saddened by nature's untoward aspect. A royal traveller with a scanty purse endures a thousand discomforts and humiliations. Battles are less terrible than the terrors we have often suffered. The sight of France embitters the Queen's grief. There is no worse loneliness than that of one returning to old familiar scenes whence friends have departed. Her father and her brother are engaged in war with the King of Aragon; her mother dead, and her uncle and aunt, the King Charles and his virtuous wife, also. There is none in this Touraine, where she was once the idol of kings and princes, to give her a welcome; and she is not of good cheer at the news from England. As we travelled alongside the banks of the Loire her eyes sometimes fixed themselves on the pleasant castles and gardens which adorn them. We saw ladies gaily riding on their palfreys, and children with happy faces at play on the terraces; and I heard her say to herself, "There is happiness on earth for all but me." Another time, when at the end of a long day the Prince had fallen asleep with his head against her shoulder, a tear fell from her eyes on his brow, and she murmured, "O, but for thee I would that that deep stream could receive me into its tranquil bosom, for I have a thirst which kills me!" One hath sent her here a letter written by this eluding king to one of his ministers, and which by a singular hap fell into the hands of that friendly person. This is a copy of it:

"As soon as you receive my letter, come to Amboise. You will find me there preparing for the good cheer I shall have to recompense me for all the trouble of this winter. The Queen of England hath arrived. I pray you to hasten hither, that we may consult on what I have to do. I shall commence on Tuesday, and I expect to play my game to some purpose; if so you have nothing very good to suggest, I shall work it out mine own way, and I assure you I foresee good winnings."

This despatch her majesty cons over with a fevered curiosity, and augurs no good from it. Yet she says it proves at least that he intends at last to see her, and she builds hopes on this interview. It is the property of the Queen's mind to attach itself to one means towards her end, and on the success thereof to repose all her confidence. For my part I fear this meeting as if an impetuous noble bird should fly into the meshes of a cruel fowler.

On the Tuesday, as announced, this long-looked-for interview took place. When I saw the king's visage as he came into the Qneen's chamber every hope I had—and that was little enough—deserted me. The outward form of this monarch should be a meet clothing for a treacherous soul. The humility of his carriage, his downcast eyes and stealthy step, accord with his renown of hypocrisy. When he went away she looked very pale, but said nothing to me of his visit; but I heard from the Prince, who had been present at the interview, that as soon as he entered she fell down on her knees at his feet, and shed many tears, while she adjured him as her kinsman, and for the love of God and the Blessed Virgin, to aid her with men and money to recover her husband's kingdom.

"And what did his Majesty reply, my lord prince?" I said.

"Well, he looked down like this, as if he was counting the squares on the floor, and rolled his beads in his hand all the time. He told the Queen that she should go and pray to Monsieur St. Sauveur at Redon, or to our Lady at Embrun, and that he should himself say a chaplet for her. The Queen answered that she had prayed very hard night and day that his Majesty's heart should be touched by her misfortunes, and that he might espouse her quarrel, who was the niece of his own mother, and the most cruelly treated princess in the whole world. O, Lady Margaret, my mother's eyes looked all glowing with fire, and big tears rolled down her cheeks; but the King's eyes are like stones, or little pieces of glass, albeit not windows that you can see through. He begged the Queen to sit down, and then they had a long discourse together, which I did not well understand; but once he said something—"

"Stop, my lord Prince," I quickly said, interrupting his Highness; "you do not well to relate nor I to listen to the secrets of their Majesties."

"The Queen," he replied, "keeps no secrets from you, Lady Margaret; I heard her say so at Bordeaux when the envoy from the King of Sicily craved a private audience."

This was very true, for I thank God her Grace doth greatly confide in her poor servant. Nevertheless I would have the Prince practise even in my regard a discretion so needful to all of his birth and condition, and all the more to such as have to contend with so many enemies. But before long the Queen herself revealed to me the deep game which that royal fox, as he had himself announced, was playing and like to play to the end. Forewarned was not, alas, forearmed in her Majesty's case; for poverty and extreme needs of all kinds threw her on his mercy, to whom mercy is, I ween, a word without any sense. He hath an aim, which day by day he pursues, like a cunning angler, baiting his hook, with the passionately desired assistance which he holds in sight and yet continues to withhold, alluring with hopes, checking by delays, enticing by evasive words, despairing by sudden refusals. And the while the Queen's money is well-nigh expended, and actual want, like a grim phantom, rises before her. Here she is in the heart of France, whither he has deluded her from place to place, with

T

the Prince and her suite, and must needs turn a common beggar, except she makes terms with this cruel cousin. This has lasted a long time; God only knoweth how it will end.

This morn, several days after I wrote that last page, the Queen asked me with a constrained indifferency what money she yet possessed. She read in my face I dared not answer, and hers turned very white. She was to have an audience with the King at noon. "Get paper and ink," she said to me in a resolved tone, "and straightway write what I shall dictate." I obeyed, and this is what she bade me write:

"Margaret, Queen of England, being empowered by the King of England, Henry the Sixth, her husband, acknowledges the sum of twenty thousand livres lent to her by the King Lewis XI., to the restitution of which she obliges the town and citadel of Calais, promising that as soon as the King her husband shall recover it, he will appoint there as captain his brother, Jasper, Earl of Pembroke, or her cousin, Jean de Foix, Comte de Candale, who will engage to surrender the said town to King Louis XI. within one year as his own, or pay the said king forty thousand livres."

The pen fell from my fingers, and I hid my face in my hands.

"Go to, go to!" she exclaimed impatiently, yet not unkindly; "I know thou lovest me well, but displease me not by comments on my actions."

"O, madame, madame!" I cried; "pardon me; but Berwick yielded to the Scots has robbed you of thousands of English hearts. What shall the loss of Calais do?"

"Heavens! art thou mad?" she rejoined. "Calais

is hereby pawned to this royal usurer, not sold to him. His loan repaid twice over shall redeem it."

"They will not report thus of it in England," I said despondingly; "the old lies of your Grace's French partialities will revive."

"I tell thee," she cried, "I am like an animal at bay, which wounds itself in its struggles to get free. Wouldst thou have me, Margaret of Anjou, King René's daughter, King Henry's queen, run begging in the streets like the Duke of Exeter, carrying my son with me, and like the famishing women of Naples, throw him at the feet of this king, crying '*La creatura si muore di fame*'? Give me that piece of parchment."

She signed her name to what I had written, and then slowly uttered as she penned these words: "Sealed at Chinon, June, 1462."

For several hours after she had seen the King, and given this document into his hands, she sat at the window of her chamber silently gazing on the Loire, chewing, I ween, the cud of memories, the sweetness of which made the present seem more bitter. Even the Prince's caresses and his innocent prattle failed to win any notice from her, at the which he pouted a little, and went to play in the antechamber with the gentlemen-in-waiting. When the sun declined, and rosy clouds chequered the blue azure of the sky, when a long line of light shone on the glittering water, and a fresh breeze, after a burning day, rippled its surface and fanned her cheek, which was burning also, I heard her speaking to herself in this wise:

"O, for an hour's refreshment to my soul like unto this cooling breeze to my hot brow! Youth, joy, hope of departed days, whither have you fled? Fair Loire, pleasant sky of France, sunset hues, gazed on of yore with unthinking glee—for the morrow's promise was yet brighter than the day's delight—now you pain me with your sweetness. This new sadness is insupportable. What is life without hope? and whence shall hope arise? Esau sold his birthright for a mess of pottage, and Esau-like, I have pledged Calais for a few pieces of gold! What is gold without men? What are men without chivalry? O, for an hour of my father's and my brother's aid! O, for a heart and an arm like Pierre d'Aubusson's! Ah, gallant soldier of the cross, scourge of the infidels, do you sometimes think of the night when for the last time we met at Nancy? You verily then chose the good part. Better for a man never to have been born than to love me, or for a woman too," she added, casting her arms about my neck, for I had fallen on my knees before her, gazing on her beloved visage with all the affection of my soul.

"Nay, nay, my sovereign lady!" I exclaimed; "Love has its own reward. Would to God you loved Him, if only as much as I dare to love you!"

"Love Him!" she murmured. "O, awful, terrible God, severe to me only, and merciful to my foes, how can I love Him! If He were just, would that lying hypocrite prosper, and my virtuous king be a fugitive in his own kingdom?"

"Hath He promised *this* world to the good, or rather hath He not said, madame, Blessed are those that mourn, blessed are those that are persecuted? The day of justice will dawn at last. God defend it be not too soon for us all!"

She leant her head despairingly on her hand, and made no reply. I did not dare to speak again; but in a few moments the Prince ran into the chamber, climbed on her Majesty's knees, and gently drawing her hand from her face, said,

"Mother Queen, there is one here outside the door which would fain see you. I think he loves you very much."

"Who is that, dear heart?" she said with less quickness than was her wont.

"One Sir Pierce de Bracy," his Highness said.

"I know not any knight of that name," the Queen replied. "Send Sir John Fortescue to me."

"He is abroad, and Mr. Booth also," the Prince answered, "I pray you let Lady Margaret speak to this gentleman. He is a monsieur, not an Englishman."

"Go, Meg," said her Majesty, "see who this stranger may be."

I found in the antechamber a person of very noble mien and figure, who straightway addressed me in French, and in a voice which sounded as if some strong emotion made it falter. "Madame, will the Queen of England dispense with ceremony and grant an audience to one well-known to her in by-gone days; one who once broke many lances in her honour, and at any time these eighteen years would have given one half of his life to be allowed to spend the other half in her quarrel?"

He paused an instant, and then added,

"Tell her Majesty, I pray you, that Pierre de Brézé, the Sénéchal of Normandy, craves to be admitted to her presence."

"O God!" I exclaimed, transported with surprise and joy; for the sighing prayer she had made for one sight of a once familiar friendly face seemed now to be granted,—" O God! Monsieur le Sénéchal, I ween our Lady hath sent you. Wait till I have told the Queen of your coming."

"Madame," I cried, trembling with eagerness, "this

is a friend indeed who solicits admission; no other than the Sénéchal of Normandy—the Sieur Pierre de Brézé."

"Heavens!" she exclaimed. "Then I am not wholly forgotten by the brave knights of France."

"I said it was Sir Pierce de Bracy," the Prince resentfully exclaimed.

"Bring him to me," the Queen cried; and straightway she composed her visage, commanded her voice, and when the Sieur entered and knelt to her, gave him her hand to kiss with as great royalty as if she had been seated on her throne at Westminster. "Welcome Messire Pierre," she said; and then, "This is my son, the Prince of Wales;" but in the utterance of those words her courage broke down, a violent fit of weeping shook her frame, and she vainly essayed to speak.

"Weep on, Madame, weep on," Monsieur de Brézé cried; "every tear which you shed inflames in my heart a fire which nothing can quench but the blood of those who have drawn these tears from Marguerite d'Anjou's eyes. I have waited for this hour with a long patience. When you had other friends, when English lords and knights surrounded your throne, Pierre de Brézé kept aloof. He was your bedesman and your servant; he consumed his life in empty desires to avenge your wrongs. But at last you are alone; at last you have no court, no army, men say no hope; but, by God, they say not well; for when a quarrel is just, and there are two to fight for it, a queen with a great heart and a soldier with a strong arm, by our Lady of Liesse there is much hope!"

Then her eyes flashed through their troubled shroud: then she raised her head like a war-horse at the sound of the trumpet; then she fixed on Messire Pierre that

bright gaze which in early youth had made him madly
in love with her, and in a voice which no agitation or
passion could rob of its melodiousness, exclaimed,

"Will you indeed help me? Will you fight with
me, and for me? Will you espouse my quarrel, deliver my king from his enemies, and be this boy's
saviour?"

She looked into her champion's face, and the impassioned fervour of his glance seemed to startle her
as, in an almost inarticulate voice, he murmured,

"For love of Marguerite d'Anjou I will serve the
English king."

"Messire Pierre," she rejoined, "mistake me not,
and let me not mistake you. Will you give me the
might of your arm, the ardour of your soul, the blood
of your veins, the sweat of your brow, and the risk of
your life? Will you follow me in perils, cleave to me
in adversity, cross the seas and wander in desert places,
suffer and perhaps die by my side, and never seek any
other guerdon, never so much as dream of any reward
but fame, honour, and the leal gratitude of Margaret
the queen, the mother, and the wife?"

"Madame, behold your servant," the Sénéchal replied; "behold your knight! If by the feeble aid of
my poor arm you recover your kingdom and conquer
your foes, I shall have obtained the boon I have asked
of God for many a day on my bended knees; and when
a Christian soldier thus prays, he mingles no base
human thoughts with his high vows."

"God hears you," she replied; "and my trust in
you, Messire Pierre, is henceforward without bounds.
You say well that there is always hope where justice
exists. One hour ago despair had invaded me, but its
dark shadow now disappears. In sooth, I have no
army—"

"I have five hundred men, madame, ready to take the field for you."

"Five hundred and one, Sir Pierce!" cried the little Prince; "for I will be one of your brave soldiers."

"He is no new soldier, Monsieur le Sénéchal," said the Queen with a proud smile. "He won his spurs at the *journée* of St. Alban, and was knighted on the field of battle by the King his father. You may safely enrol him in your gallant band."

"I will serve under his highness," Monsieur de Brézé said, kissing the Prince's hand. "He will deign himself, I hope, to present a flag to our little army."

The Queen's cheek flushed, and she said with an effort,

"Messire Pierre, men without money are of small avail; I have only twenty thousand livres from King Lewis."

"But I have estates," the Sieur replied, "the sale of which shall furnish the cost of our campaign."

"Nay, nay," the Queen exclaimed, "God forbid I should be the ruin of your fortunes. Alas, I have been rash and cruel; but I retract my hasty words. Leave me, leave me, Monsieur de Brézé. God knoweth I am much indebted to you for this hour of revived courage. Dreams sometimes give comfort to the desolate heart. But I will not, O no, I will not drag one who hath had a noble and persistent love for me into the abyss of my misfortune. I have never had a friend to whom his affection for me did not prove fatal. Leave me, Pierre de Brézé, leave me. Blood hath marked each of my years with a terrible impress. Sometimes I think I am accursed of God."

"Come, come, madame," the Sénéchal cried; "you have learnt in England to be superstitious. You need French enlivenment to charm away melancholy.

Mort de Dieu! the worst curse in the world is despondency, and to laugh the sovereign remedy in the ills of life. We will make this time a merry campaign; and if French valour and French gaiety fail to turn the tide of success in our favour, why, then, I will turn a monk for the rest of my days. But, madame, I promise you I shall not laugh if your majesty again insults me by any like speeches to your last. It is *à la vie et à la mort* that I am your servant; and at the point of my sword I will defend my right to that title."

The Queen's spirits from that hour revived, and at a higher pitch than at any previous time. A more bold and reckless spirit seemed to govern her actions. I think she sometimes drowned thought in merriment, or else the gaiety of Sir Pierce de Bracy, as the Prince always called him, proved contagious. He travelled with us to the northern coast of France; and albeit my perhaps too timid nature recoiled from his impetuous daring and adventurous spirit — which nevertheless well accorded with the Queen's dispositions — I yet rejoiced that she had found a partisan so generous and noble, who, albeit he worshipped her with incredible devotion, never for one instant and in the most singular haps transgressed the bounds of the most profound and reverent respect.

CHAPTER XXX.

A Chapter of Letters.

FOR the first time since his birth the Queen hath parted from the Prince. She would not expose his tender years to the severe hardships of a campaign in the midst of the winter. Nothing would content her majesty but that I should stay here at Berwick with his highness to watch over his health and his school, during Sir John's absence, and as often as should be possible let her know of his well-doing; which trust I hope to discharge to her contentment, and according to the rules she laid down for his manner of life. Such as, that he shall rise every morning at a convenient hour, and till he be ready none to enter his chamber but his attendant and a priest to sing Matins; that he hear every day divine service, and on principal feasts likewise a sermon; that he breakfast immediately after Mass, and be occupied an hour at his school before he goes to meat, and to be at his dinner at a convenient hour; and there be read before him (which office I daily perform) noble stories, such as it behoves a prince to understand; and above all things to procure that all the communications in his presence be of virtue, honour, cunning, wisdom, and deeds of worship, and of nothing that shall move him to vice. After his meat, to eschew idleness he is to be occupied two hours at his school, and afterwards to be shown convenient disports and exercises. He is to go at a becoming hour to his even-song, and soon after to be at his supper; and then have such honest recreation as can be devised for his grace. I pray my heart doth not set itself with too great worship on this prince. As he increaseth in years, I notice in his disposition as well as in his visage the various excellences of both his parents. If he is at his prayers, or if talk is ministered of God and His saints, or of goodness to the poor, or of learning which shall make a man wise unto salvation, then the holy aspect of the King is to be seen in this small counterpart of his majesty. If chivalrous acts, or noble daring, or playful wit form the theme of discourse, straightway in his lustrous eyes and sudden smile a likeness to the Queen appears. He hath written down in a little book the names of all the princes he can read or hear of, which in their young years have been great and good, and studies to copy them; and he is very devout to kings which have been saints—foremost to his patron St. Edward, and then to St. Lewis. Some days ago he said to me, "Lady Margaret, when I was in France, I heard my father called an unfortunate King. Think you not that when St. Lewis was sick and a prisoner he was likewise called unfortunate? and yet we think him now most fortunate in his godliness. It might so be that my father should be one day canonised, and then every one will call him blessed. Think you he will be titled St. Henry in after times, when we shall all be dead?"

"God only knoweth, my lord prince," I answered. "Of this I am assured, that he will be called the holy king."

Then he thought a little, and said,

"Great soldiers have been saints — there were St. Sebastian and St. Maurice; and my ancestor Charlemagne and the good King Alfred fought battles and conquered their enemies." A beautiful smile illumined his face, and he added, "I pray God to make me holy like my father, and as brave a soldier as my mother; for albeit she fights not with a sword in her hand, methinks she hath a heart the most valiant God ever made. And the King likewise is very brave. He would fight too if he was not stricken with sickness; my mother told me so. Yet he said to me once that war is naught else than fury and madness; that therein is rashness, not advice, and in it rage, not right, ruleth and reigneth."

"I ween his majesty spoke of civil broils," I replied.

"Ay; he said it tortured his heart to see his subjects slaughtered, and that he would the Christian lords and nobles turned their arms against the Turks; and I would so too; but I would fight also to recover his kingdom, and it sorely displeases me that the Queen leaves me shut up here, when two years ago I fought by her side at St. Alban's. It ill becometh a knight to be at his school like a clerk when war is going on. It chafes me, Lady Margaret, to be so used."

"Patience, my lord prince," I said; "many a bloody field you may yet see; and obedience is a soldier-like virtue."

"I wot not," he answered, smiling, "if it be a virtue when one is compelled to it." Then after a pause he said, "I think neither St. Lewis, nor St. Edward, nor my father the King, would have said what I did when Mr. Booth told me those cowardly French hired troops, which abandoned us on the coast where we landed, because they heard that Lord Warwick was nigh with forty thousand men, were all cut in pieces in Holy Island by Sir Robert Ogle."

"What did you say, my lord prince?" I asked.

Then, colouring a little he answered: "I said I was glad, for that they merited to be killed."

"But they had sought sanctuary," I said, "and their lives should have been spared."

"But it was so base of them to fly to their ships and leave the Queen, and me, and you, and Mr. Booth, and Sir Pierce de Bracy on the shore alone."

"But God showed favour to those whom men thus forsook," I said; "for whereas their tall goodly ships were dashed to pieces on the rocks near Bamborough, the little fishing-boat which we sailed in bore us safely through that great storm to this place."

"Did the great waves affright you very much, Lady Margaret?" the Prince asked me.

"Not a little," I replied; "but I said Hail Marys all the time, and that gave me courage."

"I liked," he said, "to feel the spray in my face, and to be tossed up and down by the big waves. Sometimes I thought we should be drowned; but Sir Pierce laughed with such good cheer at those green monsters, as he called them, and made wry faces when the boat lay on one side, that I laughed too. I am sorry I said I was glad that those Frenchmen were killed. But if the usurper was slain, I must needs rejoice, Lady Margaret, or if Lord Warwick's head was cut off."

"Yea, because their deaths would end the war," I replied, "and thus save the lives of many good men. But methinks, my lord prince, if you should see that wicked earl's children weeping because their father was dead, you would be a little sad thereat."

"O, poor little sweet Anne Neville!" he cried. "I will pray the King to forgive her father when he is vanquished. I hope the Queen will not order his head to be cut off before I see her, Lady Margaret. I like not the Princess of Scotland one half so well as Anne

Neville. She is not pretty and winsome like her. Cannot a prince marry an earl's daughter? My aunt Yolande married the Comte de Vaudémont, and a count in French signifies an earl."

" But the Earl of Warwick," I answered, "is a traitor; and the Queen would as lief your highness married any wench of low degree as his daughter."

The Prince looked grave, and said : " I would there were no traitors. Is it true that the usurper calls us traitors ? "

" Yea, and verily holds you to be such," I answered,

" But then if he thinketh he hath a right to the throne, he is not so wicked."

" He is most wicked," I replied; and to end this talk I told his highness it was time to learn his lessons.

Whilst I was at Berwick I received letters of notable curiosity, which I shall now transcribe. The first was from the Lady Isminia Bouchier, which had been one of the Queen's maids before she married :

" RIGHT WELL-BELOVED FRIEND,—A trusty man from this neighbourhood will ride within three days to Berwick, and will do me the good to carry this letter to you; for report saith you have landed there with the Queen. I would have you to know that I was staying at Grafton Castle with my husband in the month of September, and I should be glad if what I had seen and heard there had been other than what it was. The Duchess of Bedford and Lord Rivers profess a marvellous great worship towards the King and our sovereign lady the Queen when any of their lovers and adherents are present. But methinks I shall do well by your means to advertise her majesty to be on her guard touching these warm friends. I had been told in London that no small wonder was created amongst the Yorkists when their so-called king continued to pay to the Duchess Jaquetta and her husband the stipend of the dower she holds of the crown, and moreover, as is said in the entry of the rolls, that, affectionately considering the benefit of her grace and her husband, he had disbursed one hundred pounds thereof in advance. There was a revived talk in consequence of the duchess's dealings with one I will not name, so incredible did this favour appear, towards a family the most devoted to the King and the Queen of any in the realm. I promise you, the bare thought of these surmises made me adverse to sleep under the same roof as her grace. Her affability disarms the most inimical persons. I pray God it be a lawful effect, and not diabolical influence. Her smile hath in it a baleful sweetness, like unto that of honey when the bees have fed on poison. My husband refused to credit any of the reports which went to prove her grace disloyal to the King. Our Lady defend she did not cast a spell upon him! He was angered when I said she was commonly impugned for witchcraft, and said many a virtuous woman, which no accusation could touch, had been attacked falsely of this crime; and that there is not a more cruel thing in the world than to give ear to these reports,—how so much the more to spread them! But, spell or no spell, witchcraft or no witchcraft, my lord hath been forced to suspect the loyalty of this lady and her kindred.

"Lady Gray and her children were likewise at that time at Grafton, after the battle of St. Albans and Lord Gray's death, who was most detested by the Yorkists. They were deprived of their inheritance of Bradgate, and she depends on her mother for their support, and even the clothes they wear. She is more fair than ever she was. Her weeds heighten her natural fairness, and sorrow lends a charm to her beauty. She is sometimes chidden by her parents for her persistent grief, and then tears fall on her delicate cheeks like dewdrops on a rose. Talking of a rose, the proverb saith, '*In vino veritas;*' but I say, give me a child's prattle, and then the truth shall transpire. One day I was playing at closheys on the bowling-green with little John Gray, who is four years old—a winsome urchin, full of frolic and merriment. As he was running to and fro to pick up the fallen pins, he began to sing this lay—I leave you to judge how well it sounded in mine ears :

> " Now is the rose of Rouen grown to great honour ;
> Therefore sing we every one, aye blessed be that flower !
> I warn ye every one, that ye shall understand
> There sprung a rose in Rouen that spread to England.
> Had not the rose of Rouen been, all England had been dour.
> Aye blessed be the time God ever spread that flower !
>
> The rose he came to London, full royally riding ;
> Two archbishops of England they crowned the rose king.
> Almighty Lord, save the rose, and give him Thy blessing,
> And all the realm of England joy for his crowning !
> Had not the rose of Rouen been, all England had been dour.
> Aye we may bless the time God ever spread that flower !"

'Prithee, Johnny,' I said, disguising my trouble, 'who learnt thee that song?' 'My grandam,' he replied, 'when she was playing on the gittern.' This so confirmed my suspicions, that I had no patience afterwards to listen to that fair-spoken duchess when she bemoaned the misfortunes of 'our holy sovereign, and of her entirely beloved cousin the Queen.' On the morrow I was sick with vexation and secret wrath, and, as is my wont when in this case, I went early abroad to walk in the cool air under the trees of the park. All outward things were sweet and fair that day, as if there had been no pain and trouble in the world. It was warm for the time of the year; the bees busily plied their trade amidst the wild honeysuckles and the patches of thyme; the squirrels ran up the trunks of the trees; and nature's sweet carpenter the woodpecker was hard at its work. I forgot a little while my uneasiness in thinking of the goodness of God, who hath scattered over the earth so many beauties, like fragments of the once perfect whole which was paradise. As I was thus musing, a herd of red deer came sweeping across the glen where I was, and my terror of these animals awoke me as from a dream. I ran as fast as I could in the contrary direction whence they came, and so into the Forest of Whittlebury; and when I stopped to take breath and look about me, I mistook one green alley for another, and became bewildered in the intricacies of the chase. After wandering about some time unable to find my way, I sat down to rest on the trunk of a tree. When I had sat there a few moments, lo and behold, at a short distance from me I saw Lady Gray dismounting from her palfrey, and her two children with her; she took one in her arms and the other in her hand, and advanced with them towards a fine oak, beneath which she seated herself on the grass. My first thought was to rise and approach her; but a sudden diffidence restrained me, and I remained concealed from her sight by the boughs of the underwood. Her attendants withdrew, and she stayed there under the spreading branches, through which the sun shone on the grass, chequering it with quaint patterns. Little John Gray kept darting to and fro in chase of butterflies, but she quickly recalled him; and I thought she seemed ill at ease, ever and anon walking a few paces forward and looking up and down the vistas of the forest, and then returning to the same place where she was before. The children gathered flowerets and gave them to her; she took them from their hands, but soon let them fall again. When a little time had elapsed I was startled by the sound of a horn, which was twice again repeated; and then I saw a horseman appear at the end of one of the green alleys of the chase. Lady Gray rose, and with a child in each hand, advanced a few steps towards the approaching rider. As he came near I felt the blood rush into my face; for I perceived, to my no small amaze, but so evidently that I could not doubt of it, that this was no other than the Earl of March, the so-called king. I could hardly draw my breath, I was so keen to watch what should happen. When he was quite nigh to her, she fell on her knees, clasping her children to her bosom. He reined in his horse, glanced at her face, and straightway his own became suffused with a deep flush. He hastily dismounted, and she fell at his feet. He tried to raise her; and then she lifted up towards him her lovely visage, which I had never seen so beautiful. Tears adorn this lady as much as they disfigure others. They roll down her cheeks like a stream of live pearls, and the composure and restraint of her grief lends to it a womanhood and sweetness which I could not choose but admire, though I was so angry. I could perceive that the usurper was enraptured with that beseeching countenance. He looked as if he could have remained there an age gazing on it. Some talk passed betwixt them, and then Lady Gray made a very low obeisance and retired a step or two, taking her children by the hand. The so-called king bowed in return, and remounted his horse; she remained standing with her eyes fixed on the ground till he was out of sight, then summoned her attendants and prepared to depart. I stepped forward; and when she saw me she gave a start of surprise, and inquired how I came to be so early abroad. I said I had strayed and lost my way, but indignantly added, 'I wish you joy, Lady Gray, of your audience. I had not thought to have seen the widow of Lord Gray at the feet of Edward Plantagenet.' She replied with great gentleness: 'Sweet Lady Bouchier, the widow of Lord Gray must stifle the dearest feelings of her heart to save from ruin his innocent children.' She makes no secret of this interview; and if anyone charges her with it in a reproachful wise, she says: 'A mother will go into a lion's den for her child's sake; I made my suit to him who alone can restore to my babes their natural inheritance.' But I ween, Lady Margaret, this plain narrative, and the song of the rose of Rouen, which I told you of, will open your eyes, as it hath done mine, touching the loyalty of Grafton Castle. Your wisdom will, I doubt not, find means to warn the Queen of this lamentable defection, though it cuts me to the heart that she should learn how lukewarm is the affection, not to say false, of persons whom she has loaded with benefits. Our Lord be with you!

"ISMINIA BOUCHIER."

Written hastily on the 3rd of November, 1462."

This letter did not come to hand until some time after it was despatched. Since then I have heard that the usurper hath made more visits than one to Grafton Castle, and report saith he is enamoured of Lady Gray. O God! who can marvel if women, like weak saplings, yield to the pressure of triumphant treason, when those we had deemed oaks for strength and firmness—men of tried fidelity, such as the Dukes of Exeter, Somerset, and Suffolk—have faltered in their allegiance, and negotiated their peace with the usurper? albeit now they give tokens of repentance and return to duty, which I pray may prove sincere. God forgive me! but in matters of faith and honour and dutiful allegiance, when a man hath once offended, I can never trust him more. God only, and those which are like Him, have patience with such. I am yet far from the perfection which I promised Jeanne to aim at; but verily there is more difficulty in bearing with the world's cruel malice and its base treachery than those wot of which are removed from its daily effects.

A messenger brought the letter I will now copy from the Queen to the lord Prince at Berwick, in January 1463. It was written in French, but I have done it into English:

"MY ENTIRELY-BELOVED AND MOST DEAR SON,—I wot you would fain be with me at this time; and if I listened only to the great desire I have of your sight and sweet company, it would not be long before that came to pass which we have both so great reason to desire. But your young years, and the exceeding great importance which exists that by a regular and convenient manner of life your body should be strengthened and your mind furnished with good learning and nurture, constrain me most reluctantly to endure a separation otherwise most grievous. The Lady Margaret de Roos or your tutor will have, I doubt not, informed you of what I let them know, that is, of the success of our arms since I left Berwick. The King hath now joined me, and is, I thank God, in very good health at the present time, and sends you his paternal blessing. The Queen of Scotland hath furnished me with a power of men; and under the leadership of Monsieur de Brézé, they took the fortresses of Bamborough, Dunstanburgh, and Alnwick. This last place was garrisoned by Messire Pierre and the five hundred French knights which have volunteered in my quarrel. I leave you to judge, gentle son, of my despair when I learnt that my Lord Warwick, my evil genius, had with twenty thousand men invested that castle, and there seemed not so much as a hope of escape for this noble band. I could neither eat nor sleep for thinking of their sore plight; and nothing until then, I think, hath caused me so much disquietude as the danger of these brave men. Then in this urgent distress I bethought myself of Lord Angus, the most in renown in his own country and beyond it for valour, of a family where to be valiant is a never-failing heritage. Who says 'a Douglas,' says 'a *chevalier sans peur et sans reproche;*' as in France when one names a Bayard. I made suit to him that he should rescue by some means this flower of French chivalry encompassed, like a lion in a net, by the forces of these Saxon miscreants. He listened to my tale, and replied in six words—the briefest and most welcome answer I ever in my life received. 'Madame,' quoth he, 'I will do my best.' And presently, with one thousand riders leading five hundred horses saddled and bridled, he rides straight to Alnwick Castle, and spreads his followers, by favour of the night, in one long line in view of Warwick's army, which amuses the rebels, and sets them wondering what puissance he hath behind him lying in ambush; the while he sends the five hundred horses, under cover of his front, to the postern gate of the fortress; and before the enemy hath time to think or move the garrison is mounted, and with, I promise you, no small speed gallop with their saviours to the

Border. Lord Angus's words at his return were almost as brief as at his *congé*. 'Madame, here is a present for you—your five hundred French knights.' And now methinks this story, sweet son, will please you likewise more than twenty presents. I pray God we had more friends like Lord Angus and the Sieur de Brézé; then we should soon see an end of rebellion and treason. When the year is a little advanced there must needs be a great battle, which will decide this campaign. We suffer at present incredible hardships, which the King endures with godly patience, never so much as once complaining of his scanty fare, or rude couch, or great fatigue; wherein, gentle son, thou shouldst study to copy his example, and to be content to lack many things which other young princes enjoy. Thine is a rough training; but when this long struggle is ended thou wilt be more fitted to wear a crown than royal striplings nurtured only in pomp and pleasure. If in my young years I had not shared the many vicissitudes of my parents' fortunes, I misdoubt if I should now so well endure long warfare and privations. And now, sweet son, my gentle boy, more beloved than any son by any mother in the whole world, I commend thee to the blessing of the Holy Trinity and our Lady, and all the saints. Be not forgetful to pray each day that God may avenge us of our enemies, and prosper our arms.—Thy tender loving mother,

"MARGARET THE QUEEN."

At the end of March my own father, the Lord de Roos, who had returned to England with the Queen's French volunteers, wrote to me as followeth:

"MY MOST DEAR DAUGHTER,—I am now with their Majesties nigh unto Hexham, whither they have

advanced to give battle to the rebel forces. Somerset
and many others have returned to their allegiance.
God send us victory, for a decisive blow is to be
struck. If I live and we win the day, I look to
seeing thee, my dear child, in great triumph and joy;
and happy days may follow. If I die, be my bedeswoman, and pray for my poor soul. I was, I thank
God, shriven yestereve; and so God will be pitiful
to me, I hope, if I fall in the fight. Thou wilt not
be far off, I ween, from the field of battle; for the
Queen, who is confident of success, hath sent for the
Lord Prince; as she herself will not be in the *mêlée*,
but nigh at hand, she chooses to have him with her,
come what may. And her Majesty looks that her
good Meg, as she styles thee, will conduct my lord the
Prince to her. Fare thee well. We have spent but
few days together on earth, sweet daughter, and have
unknown visages to each other. But in Paradise we
shall not be strangers, I ween; and sith we meet not
again in a less good place, receive now the blessing
of thy loving father,
"The Lord de Roos."

I conducted the lord Prince to his mother; and on
the next day the battle was fought. This was the
Queen's writing in her book in the night before the
battle:

"I cannot sleep so I will write, to make the time
pass more quickly than by watching the dying embers
of this poor fire. Somerset, Hungerford, de Brézé,
and the lately-arrived Lord de Roos have retired, after
holding a council of war; and I was alone then with the
King and Edward, who sat on his father's knees; and
I listened to the talk they held together, as if they had
been two angels discoursing, and this earth we live

in exchanged for an unreal world, where goodness and truth and love prevailed. All the past and coming turmoil seemed to subside for one brief hour into a vision of peace. It was pretty to see the boy lay his blooming cheek against his father's pale visage and fondly stroke his cheeks. The King questioned him of his school, and would see how he had advanced in learning; for, quoth he, 'Virtue and knowledge are the only treasures any man can call his own: for the rest this verse showeth, sweet son, what I have learnt in these changeful years; and thou shouldst commit the lines to memory, and call them King Henry's lay:[1]

> 'Kingdoms are but cares,
>   State is devoid of stay,
> Riches are ready snares,
>   And hasten to decay;
> Pleasure a secret pride,
>   Which vice doth still provoke;
> Pomp vain, and fame a flame;
>   Pow'r a smouldering smoke.
> Who meaneth to remove the rock
>   Out of the slimy mud
> Shall mire himself, and hardly 'scape
>   The swelling of the flood.'

Alas! sweet King, not thine but my soul hath mired itself, and I have too often lost my footing in the swelling flood! 'Ah, gentle son!' then he exclaimed, 'I would Eton and Cambridge and my good friend Bishop Waynfleet's beloved Oxford had the care I once gave them, and will again, if God restores me to the throne!' 'Sire,' I said, 'the Bishop of Winchester doeth homage to the usurper, and is therefore no friend to your Majesty.' 'Fie, fie; say not so, sweet Margaret,' the King replied; 'a Bishop must

---

[1] Sir John Harrington gives these lines as King Henry the Sixth's own composition.

yield the dearest allegiance he doth hold for the sake
of his flock; and when an unlawful king reigns un-
opposed, the ministers of God submit, albeit with a
painful submission.' 'This is a new doctrine,' I cried,
'and an easy one for cowards.' 'Nay, nay,' he said;
'the shepherd must not forsake his flock because the
owner thereof is banished. I warrant you, sweet wife,
that that holy man loves his king more than many which
wag their tongues at him for his needful conformity.'
'I would God made bad persons to die,' Edward cried,
'and then we should see He misliked them.' 'Come
hither, gentle son,' the King said, 'and listen to these
words of Holy Writ: "The just that is dead condemns the wicked that are living, and youth soon
ended the long life of the unjust."' 'Is it good, then,
to die young?' quoth the boy. 'Yea, for if one hath
been made perfect in a short space he hath fulfilled a
long time, and then if God removes him hence he is
blest.' 'Sweet King,' I said, 'Edward will continue
the noble foundations and pious works you have raised
in this land, if your life hath not sufficient length of
years for the great ends you would achieve.' He laid
his hand on his son's head, and said, 'God bless thee,
Ned; be a good lad;' and so dismissed him to his bed.
Some say—and it is much credited by the poorer sort
—that the King hath the gift of prophecy. God defend this should be true, for from his lips no word of
hope hath cheered me this night. When Edward was
gone I knelt by his side, and said, 'Bless me also, sire.
Have you no word of comfort for your poor wife and
servant?' He took my hand, and answered, 'God
knoweth I bless thee, sweet Margaret; but ill can I
give the only comfort I know thou dost seek. I am
not like the Earl of Warwick, who crowns and dis-
crowns kings at his pleasure. My arm hath no

strength; God's sweet will hath paralysed me. And on my mind, if I strive to compass worldly ends, dark shadows fall, making deep nights in the midst of my days. In an evil hour for thee, poor Margaret, thou didst link thy fate with his on whom are visited the sins of others as well as, God knoweth, many of his own, albeit not wilfully committed.' 'Nay, sire,' I cried, kissing his hand, 'call it not an evil hour. When I wedded the sweet rose of Lancaster I embraced with it all its thorns, and God forbid I should lament my destiny. If we suffer, Edward shall be great. His father's virtues shall warrant him prosperity.' 'St. John! speak not so rashly. Who knoweth his secret offences, and shall dare to think himself good? And O, sweet wife, gentle wife, is there no stain of blood on our hands? Are there no evil passions in our hearts to call down God's judgments?' 'Not in your heart, sire. They rage in mine; but had I been meek like you, poor should be Edward's hope of a throne.' 'On earth or in heaven?' the King asked, which angered me; and I said, 'Let heaven alone for awhile, sire; there are royal duties to be performed in this world.' 'Yea,' he replied, 'I know it; and therefore I am here in the midst of these civic broils, wherein I suffer so great anguish that to die would be better. I know it; the throne of a great kingdom is a trust from God, and none may forsake his assigned post.' 'There spoke my noble king!' I cried; and then I saw his face turn pale and drops of sweat on his brow, as he exclaimed, 'They come before me even now the ghosts of those which shall die to-morrow. I see them—the wounded, the dying, the dead—the mangled bodies lying in blood on the cold ground, and a long troop of unshriven, sin-burdened souls dropping into hell like autumn leaves in a hurricane. O God, save them! O God, have pity! O, spare my people! Let every earthly hope perish. Let my life be one long suffering, and my death a terrible one for the body, and what I love most take it from me before I die; but let not immortal souls for which the good Jesus died perish in my quarrel. O God, have mercy!' Then he sank back exhausted. Now he is asleep; but ever and anon I hear him cry in his dreams, 'Stop the carnage; save my people; deliver me from blood-guiltiness, O Lord!' Alas! if I am to struggle on in the sacred cause I have in hand; if my heart is to be strong and my soul brave, I must part for a while from the King. I must live not with saints, but with men of fiery spirit and desperate resolve. Woman's softness gains upon me. If once I yield to it, if I cease to be fierce, I shall be weak. Clifford's wild hate, De Brézé's reckless merriment, are the medicines I need. Ah, the day is dawning! My God! give us victory!"

CHAPTER XXXI.

A Wilful Woman Maun have her Way.

ON the evening when we landed at the Ecluse, on the last day of July 1463, the Queen, who since my father perished on the scaffold after the battle of Hexham, has been more tender than ever she was before to her afflicted servant, said to me as we sat in the melancholy parlour of the Golden Eagle, "Dear heart, I pray thee go and make a thank-offering for me at the church for our deliverance from the storm."

I dared not tell her majesty that there was not so much as one groat in her purse wherewith to make an offering, or even so much as to buy a piece of bread. The poor supper we had on landing was yet unpaid for; and I was affrighted, if the host guessed we had no money, that his civility, which was not over great, should be altogether lacking. But I went, as her majesty desired, into the church; and having naught else to give, made there an offering of my tears and of the sufferings I endured both from the remembrance of my father's death—of which time effaces not the keen resentment—and the present desperate plight of my sovereign lady and mistress. For there we were in Burgundy, whose duke is one of her greatest enemies, leastways she has always accounted him to be such. Lately he sent the Lord de Granthuse, an especial friend of the usurper's to Scotland, to signify to his niece the Queen Regent that she should forthwith dissolve the contract of marriage betwixt her daughter and my lord the Prince, for that he would by no means consent to that alliance. When this was reported to the Queen, she fell into a passion of anger and indignation, and exclaimed, that if that duke should ever come into her hands, she would make the axe pass betwixt his head and his shoulders. Alas, such words as these, since our bloody wars, have become familiar to her lips, to whom all kind of cruelty was once strange! God knoweth I prayed very hard that eve in the church at Ecluse, for we were indeed in dismal straits. Seven or eight persons with her Majesty, including Sir John Fortescue the prince's governor, Dr. Morton the chaplain, Sir John Carbonnel, and one or two more gentlemen and servants, besides three chamberers and myself, in a foreign and inimical country, where the fury of the elements had obliged us to land without a safe-conduct, and where we were met by no kindly welcomes, but rather sour glances and cutting speeches. As we walked through the streets to the inn, scornful taunts were addressed to us by persons who marvelled that Queen Margaret should show her face in the Duke of Burgundy's dominions; and I thought, when our penniless condition became known matters would be yet worse. But as I left the church, whom should I see coming towards me along the narrow passage but the Sieur de Brézé, who we feared had been driven by the storm in another direction! I could hardly restrain a scream of joy. The light of his merry smile gladdened me like a sunbeam.

"Ah, Monsieur de Brézé!" I exclaimed; "I see God has not forsaken us, since you are here."

"Where should I be?" he answered with good cheer. "At the bottom of the sea? O, I promise you, miladi, then you should have seen my ghost. I would not be so discourteous as to die and give you no notice thereof."

Then for the Queen's sake, albeit ashamed, I said, "Messire, have you money? we have not one sou."

"Yea, yea," he answered; "one hour ago I had none; but I have made the rencontre here of an old friend, George Chastellain, herald of the Golden Fleece, and he hath lent me a sum, for which I pawned to him the diamond ring I won eighteeen years ago in Place de Carrière at Nancy, when I combated more merrily, but not less heartily, for the honour of the Queen's beauty than I do now for her throne."

"O most true friend!" I exclaimed, "what boundless sums you have expended on her quarrel!"

"Fifty thousand gold crowns," he answered, laughing. "That is a trifle. My last estate and the last drop of my blood shall be spent for Marguerite d'Anjou; not for the Queen of your bloody, dismal country. By our Lady of Liesse, I am glad to breathe another air. I thank God we are here."

"Do you, indeed, thank God for it?" I said: "we must I know, bless His Divine Majesty for all that doth befall us; but methought the prospects of the Queen had never been less hopeful than, now."

"Miladi, I am persuaded," he replied, "that, after all she hath endured since the *journée* of Hexham, her Majesty should have lost her wits if she had remained concealed and inactive in English or Scotch hiding-holes."

"But here," I urged, "she is in an enemy's land."

"But an enemy which may be turned into a friend, if she can see him; for who is there that she cannot win to her cause, save those rude English nobles, which are more heavy than lead, and harder than millstones? This evening I will present to her grace the Sieur

George Chastellain, and advise with him how she can get speech with his master the Duke."

"You are the most true friend a queen ever possessed," I said, with tears in mine eyes.

He kissed my hand, and replied, "Madame, I worshipped this princess with a distant, hopeless, bootless love in the dawn of her incomparably beauteous youth; and now in the full radiance of her matchless perfections I no less passionately affection her service. She was the lady of my thoughts from the day I broke a lance under the the tuition of her sire, the good King René; and through all the perils and sufferings of the last months I have never ceased to thank God for making me her servant, who could aspire to no higher title."

"There is," I answered, "a tie therein betwixt us, Monsieur le Sénéchal. Verily I think no sovereign on a secure throne reigns more absolutely over devoted hearts than this fugitive queen."

In the parlour of the Golden Eagle that night a council was held, composed of her majesty's household, the Sieur de Brézé, and his friend Monsieur Chastellain. This gentleman is a scholar of renown, attached to the Court of Burgundy; a man of excellent wit and parts, and, as I afterwards learnt, desirous above all things to see and converse with the Queen. In France she hath always been so celebrated, that many unknown persons have conceived a kind of passion for her, founded on the report of her manifold excellences, which would not be credited in our country, where men have not the same esteem for women superior to their sex. How noble is majesty when it shineth through mean habiliments, and most admirable when it can least exact reverence! This lady, the greatest queen then in Europe, had no other dress but the poor robette she wore daily, with no clasped sash or hanging crape, or one attribute of pomp and regal attire; her head covered with a common black veil, enclosing her marble pale cheeks as if with a funereal shroud; but when she greeted the Burgundine poet and gave him her hand to kiss, she seemed not the monarch of one kingdom, but a meet one for the whole universe. This was her speech to him:

"Messire Chastellain, you see before you a person who was erewhile a mighty princess, and now by a dire vicissitude, after a narrow escape from most extreme peril, is constrained to give herself up to a prince who is of all the world most exasperated against her. Yet, messire, I am not without hope that if I can obtain so much grace as to be admitted into your sovereign's presence, my sufferings, my confidence in his loyalty, my courage in adversity, and sole recourse to his protection, may move a generous prince to pity, and perhaps to aid me."

I could see the French gentleman's eyes fixed on her beautiful face with so irrepressible an admiration, that they seemed to twinkle like two stars under his bushy eyebrows.

"Madame," he replied, "if my sovereign's heart doth resemble mine—and in this I desire it may do so, albeit in all other points I should not dare express this wish, his soul exceeding mine in greatness as much as his royalty my poor nobility—he will be ready, as soon as he has seen your Majesty, to do you all the service in his power, if at least he is convinced you are not his enemy; for otherwise, madame, his only politic course would be to debar you from the sight of men, and confine you in a desert, who if you willed to overthrow him, could raise as many partisans by the noble witchery you exercise as should serve to hurl him from his throne. Ah, madame, who could look on your majesty and not desire to do you worship with all his heart?"

"Madame," said the Sieur de Brézé, "see, you have already vanquished this gentleman, who, although a poet, is the most truthful person in the world, and would in no wise deceive you."

"Pardon me M. de Brézé," the Queen agreeably replied, "this is not a victory I have gained; for I think no poet in France would be an enemy to the daughter of King René. The *gai savoir*, Messire Chastellain, maketh kinsfolks of all who cultivate its sweet lore."

Then they spoke together of the King of Sicily and his fair delicate wife the Queen Jeanne, and of the deceased Duchesse de Calabre, and her mother Madame de Bourbon. I could see a faint colour revive in the Queen's cheeks as these familiar names recalled dear images to her memory; and when Messire George said that my lord Prince was very like her majesty's brother the Duc Louis de Barr, which had died in his youth, she exclaimed, "Yea, and he likewise resembles him in the noble ardour of his spirit, tempered with a mildness he doth inherit from the King his father. The darkness of our Southern eyes hath in him likewise changed into a deep violet hue, only umbraged with black lashes. But God knoweth he hath the most courage for a child in his tenth year which ever was beheld. My brothers fought bravely in the field at his age; but this boy hath had the assassin's dagger pointed at his breast, and never winced or screamed, but cried, 'Mother, prithee save thyself; let them kill me.'"

"Ah, madame," cried Messire George, "what fearful events have marked your life! Would I might hear

v

from your own lips these terrible but heroic adventures, so as to recount them to posterity!"

The Queen raised her eyes quickly, and answered: " I have not strength at this time to grant your request; but if, as I hope, we shall soon meet at the duke's court, whither I desire to travel, no greater good fortune could happen to me than to relate the strange vicissitudes of my life to one who, like you, sir, hath the pen of a ready writer, and is a lover of truth. For the English disfigure my actions, disguise my aims, publish false slanders tóuching my fame; and I would not that posterity should think of me as they do paint me. My enemies have called me 'the she-wolf of France.' Is there not a fable, Messire Chastellain, wherein the wolf charges the lamb with sundry offences invented by himself, and then ends by throwing himself on the innocent beast and devouring him!"

"Yea, madame," the gentleman replied; "and I doubt not that England is the wolf, and your sweet majesty that innocent lamb."

A faint smile passed over the Queen's face, and she said: "Nay, in sooth, not quite a lamb. Yet even a lamb will, I ween, seek to rend the murtherous beasts which assail it; for the very worms will turn on those who crush them. But my lord and husband is verily the true semblance of that fabled lamb, and the close imitator of the great Lamb of God, our Saviour."

Before this parlance came to an end, it was resolved that Sir John Carbonnel should proceed on the morrow to the Duke of Burgundy, to apprise him of the Queen's arrival, and pray that he would appoint some place where she might come and speak to him and explain the circumstances which had obliged her to land in his dominions. For she had a long time before asked a safe-conduct to pass through his territories; in which, however, she had been circumvented. But she came now strong in her weakness, made bold by her misfortunes, in poverty and humility, to seek of his greatness a refuge for herself and her child in her extreme distress, which she trusted he was too proud to deny her.

When the French poet heard these last words, he smiled and said, "Therein, madame, you show your great and excellent wit; that thrust is worthy of your majesty to give, and of my master to receive."

Weary were the days which followed Sir John Carbonnel's departure; for albeit we lived in the poorest manner imaginable, each day exhausted some portion of the sum M. de Brézé had procured. From the hostelry we removed to a mean lodging, where the Queen tasted all the bitterness of weary suspense. At last her envoy returned with the tidings that the duke was on his way to the shrine of our Lady of Boulogne, whither he and his sister the Duchesse de Bourbon were making a pilgrimage, and that he was arrested by sickness on the road.

"I will straight go to him, wherever he is," the Queen impetuously exclaimed.

"Nay, madame," rejoined Sir John, "this was the answer which the duke charged me to deliver to your majesty: 'Tell your Queen,' he said with great gravity and courtesy, 'that my lodgings here are too small to receive a princess of her quality, and that I can by no means suffer her to undertake the fatigue of a journey to come to me, whose duty it should be to go to her; and assuredly I should have done so but for my sickness. Howsoever, I will soon despatch one of my knights to welcome her majesty to my dominions in a dutiful and honourable form.' Before I departed," added Sir John, "I heard that the Baron de la Roche, a very excellent nobleman, was appointed to that office, who will incontinently arrive at Bruges."

This civility of the duke cheered her majesty not a little; and nothing would serve her but that M. de Brézé should go to Bruges to meet the baron, and conduct him to her.

On the day he arrived at Ecluse I was present at the audience the Queen gave him. Methinks this nobleman was the most proper person in the world to pay a reluctant prince's devoirs to a distressed royal lady with all becoming respect and homage, yet with not so much as one grain of warmth of heart or natural pity. La Roche was a becoming name for this stony-visaged gentleman, who, after many bendings of the knee and long-winded compliments, addressed her majesty as follows: "Madame, his highness my master, to his exceeding great regret, cannot wait on your majesty by reason of his absence on a pilgrimage; and moreover he is engaged in most weighty matters touching peace betwixt France and England."

At these words the Queen's cheeks were suffused with a deep red, and her lip curled with ill-repressed scorn; but she might have darted lightning from her eyes which should have blasted common mortals, and yet not have disturbed in the least this baron's composure, who continued his harangue in this wise: "And touching your grace's desire that his highness would appoint a place where your majesty should meet his grace, he entreats your highness not to think of it; for that your majesty and his highness are now a long way apart, and the neighbourhood of Calais would make it very dangerous for your majesty to travel on that road."

The Queen, with her wonted suavity of language and demeanour, thanked this envoy for his fair words and the affectionate expressions he had used, and then addressed him as followeth : " Lord de la Roche, in departing from the place where I had the grief to leave my lord and husband, he charged me not to allow any consideration on this earth, either of good or ill, to prevent me from coming to his fair cousin of Burgundy, to explain to him the malicious falsehood of certain reports which have been made to him of us by our enemies. To obey my lord, and with no other aid but that of God, I will go in quest of him, whether it imperils my life or not; for what is life compared with duty? Sir, you are a knight of the Golden Fleece; and so I adjure you by your chivalry, which doth bind you to succour all distressed ladies to the furthest extremity of your power, to benefit me in this matter with your counsel, and direct me how to act."

Not one muscle of this adjured knight's visage moved, albeit this passionate appeal thrilled through the hearts of all others present at that time. In the same cold, measured tone he replied: " Madame, I have told you all I was charged to do, and wherefore my lord the Duke sent me to you. As to advise your Grace in any way, that is beyond my charge; and as my lord hath not directed me how to answer you, I dare not do it. Truly am I a knight of that Order you speak of, though unworthy, and would willingly acquit myself of my duty to your Majesty, and others in a like plight, if so be I was acting for myself in this matter; but having received a commission from my master, I have no license to exceed it."

" Sieur de la Roche," exclaimed the Queen with impetuosity, " you have well executed your charge, and no one in the world can blame you; but I have also to answer touching the charge I have received from my lord and husband. Will you, then, shun replying one word of counsel in this strait I am in, for fear of overpassing your commission, when I, in the performance of a duty I have taken on myself, may meet death? For be assured of this, my lord, if my fair cousin of Burgundy were to go to the very end of the world, I would thither follow him—yea, and begging my bread till I found him. Now then, since this resolution is immovable in me, and your master is ignorant of it, what law should hinder you from advising me how to effect this my resolve?"

Then the knight sighed, as if he would say, "When one meets with a wilful woman, what help is there for him!" and then replied: "Alas, madame, since you have so entirely made up your mind, that nothing can move you to alter it, methinks the best way will be to let me return to the Duke and tell his Highness that your Majesty is coming to him, and then it may be he shall take it so much to heart that he will come to you."

With this the Queen was satisfied, and she entertained the Baron with such scanty fare as she was able to command, seasoning the poor food with her agreeable conversation. The next day he went towards Boulogne and we travelled to Bruges. There, after a few days, M. de Brézé received a letter from M. de la Roche, informing him that he had reported to the Duke of Burgundy that nothing could dissuade the Queen of England from setting out in quest of him; upon which he had said, "If she *will* see me, I must e'en see her—for the proverb saith, 'What a woman willeth, that God willeth;' and if she takes so much trouble to come to me, I must needs receive her with such measure of courtesy as befits her and me. But verily the journey is too perilous for her to take. The English at Calais will of a surety intercept her on the road to Hesdin."

His Highness then commanded the Baron to write by a messenger that he did entreat the Queen to advance no farther than St. Pol, where he would strive to meet her before the end of August.

Her Majesty debated with many conflicting doubts if she should carry my lord Prince with her to St. Pol, or leave him at Bruges with Sir John Fortescue and Dr. Morton; and finally, though not without tears, resolved on the last issue, partly by reason of the dangers on the road, and partly that his Grace had no befitting clothes to appear in before the Duke, and she had no money to purchase any. So at the time appointed, in a common stage-cart with a canvas covering, like a poor housewife travelling for the despatch of business, with only me and two chamberers, she set out for Bruges; Sir Pierre de Brézé, and four other gentlemen following privately in another cart, for to defend her if attacked. Ah me, what a worse journey was that than even a flight across a desert or a passage through a dark wood! The staring people ran out of their houses to look on this May game of fortune, this rich piece of shipwreck, whose resolved and noble countenance flinched not under their rude gaze, but preserved a majesty most truly royal in this her hour of humiliation. My terrors painted to me English soldiers in every distant group of men on the highway; and at night, when we rested in poor hostelries, I could not sleep, for only the noise of horses' feet in the street set my heart beating with terrible fear.

Courage is a word with various meanings. The most brave person imaginable in some dangers is sometimes the most timid one on other occasions. In an inevitable suffering, or even the presence of death itself, methinks I could be always courageous, if I had a good conscience. One of the chamberwomen in the storm at sea in our last voyage made so great a screaming when the ship seemed like to founder, that it disturbed the sailors; upon which Dr. Morton walks up to her and says, "I pray you, mistress, have you bethought yourself that nothing can happen to you if the ship goeth down worse than that you will die? and is that so dreadful for a good Christian?" She stayed her shrieks, and said she had been shriven the day before, and was not much afraid to die. "God save you, mistress," quoth her adviser; "then be of good cheer, for I warrant you death is the only evil you have to apprehend." The good soul fell to saying her beads, and wholly ceased to scream, after this comfort had been given her. But concerning myself, suspense makes a coward of me, and apprehension freezes my blood. The daily watching of the bleak road, the noises in the dismal nights when we slept in wayside inns, the fear of showing my terrors to my companions, caused me a veritable sickness, which I could only surmount by great efforts. One evening we were in a small hostelry at the foot of a hill, where we had been constrained to stop to rest the horses. It was raining very hard, and I had lighted a fagot, rather to cheer than to warm the mean room, in which the Queen had from fatigue fallen asleep on a chair, whilst a scanty meal was preparing. The chimney began to smoke, and I went to open the window. By the declining light I saw a troop of horsemen coming along the road at a gallop. A sudden affright seized me; for that was the side one would come from Calais. I hastened to the kitchen, where the esquires were standing, and with a face as white as a sheet, I ween—for he looked as if he had seen a ghost—I called M. de Brézé. *Mort de Dieu!* he exclaimed, as I pointed to the road, "if those are the English, we are lost. If it be so, these gentlemen and I will stand at the door, and they shall pass over our bodies before they enter. The while, if when they arrive I cry 'God and St. George!' fly with the Queen through the back way into the thicket. Take my cross of the Los Croissant; it is studded with gems. If she escapes, you can pawn it."

I went to the back room and roused the Queen. "There are strangers coming this way; we may have to fly," I said; and we stood listening to the advancing sound of the horses' feet. The minutes seemed hours; and the Queen's quick breathing seemed loud to my overstrained ears. There was a stoppage at the door, a rumour, and then the Sénéchal cried, "Vive Bourgogne!" The Queen seized my arm, "Is it the Duke?" "It is not the English," I answered; and burst into tears. Creeping to the front door I saw a horseman dismount, and heard the folks crying, "Vive Monseigneur! Vive le Comte de Charolais!" and then a clear cheerful voice said out loud, "You here! Pierre de Brézé! is it you or your ghost?" I returned to the Queen and said, "It is the Comte de Charolais, I think." Then she clasped her hands amazed. In a very few moments the Sénéchal opened the door, and the Prince of Burgundy was at the Queen's feet, crying, "Madame, O madame, forgive this abrupt intrusion; forgive Charles of Burgundy that he cannot restain his impetuous desire to do worship to the sister of Jean de Calabre, his brother-in-arms—his model and his friend. Is it you I see in this mean abode, heroic Queen, most valiant of women, worthy sister of the hero of Lorraine, of the *preux chevalier par excellence*, my brother and yours!"

The prince's tears fell fast; and the Queen, which

no dangers can subdue, was overwhelmed with this little sudden unlooked-for joy. She raised the count and silently embraced him. It was well known his father and he had been at variance of late, and that he was the closest friend in the world of the Duke of Lorraine. "O God!" he said when he was seated by the Queen, "is it thus you travel, madame, with no token of your rank, no state, no pomp to attend you? Your progress through these dominions should have been a triumphal march. Whither is your majesty bending your steps?"

"To St. Pol, monseigneur, to meet your royal father—the only person in the world which can now take my part. If he receives me with only one tenth of the goodwill his son shows me, I shall be the most thankful person in the world."

"Alas," the prince replied, "I would that my ability to serve you equalled my father's power, or that his inclination thereunto resembled mine. Is it true, madame, that your adversities have been so great that nothing can be compared to them, except the courage with which you have endured such unparalleled misfortunes?"

"My disasters have been indeed great," she replied; "but I must needs confess that God hath given me one of the greatest bounties He can bestow—the faithful friendship of a brave and disinterested heart. I thank God that if I should die to-morrow, I shall this night have expressed in the presence of the Comte de Charolais—a fitting judge of heroism—what I owe to Messire de Brézé. Look at that knight, my lord count; you see in him a man who hath exceeded in valour, generosity, devotedness, and self-forgetfulness all that the annals of chivalry have ever recorded."

"I should have expected no less of the noble Sénéchal of Normandy," the prince replied. And then a brief conversation ensued touching the exploits of the Duc de Lorraine in Italy and the objects of the Queen's journey to St. Pol. The count had short time to tarry, and as soon as his horses were rested he pushed on towards Bruges. But the Queen was more comforted by this hap of meeting the prince, and the good cheer he made to her, than can be imagined. And before he departed nothing would satisfy him but to leave one hundred pieces of gold he had with him in the Sieur de Brézé's hands for her use. This was the most timely aid that could be thought of; and with revived hopes and better courage we travelled onward on the morrow through the bleak country, which the sunshine enlivened a little. The red and blue flowers in the great wide-spreading cornfields, which were white for the harvest, refreshed the eye fatigued by the long dusty road. The Queen explained to me as we rode that day the statutes of the order of Los Croissant instituted by the king her father, and which bound its knights to most religious, brotherly, and humane observances, softened the bitterness of war, and exalted virtue to an ever-increasing height, as its name signifies.

As we approached Bethune, where we were to have slept that night, a horseman rode up to our cart and bade the driver stop. We thought he was a robber, and a violent trembling shook me; for I had concealed in my bosom the count's gold pieces. But he only thrust his head under the canvas cover, and said, "Mesdames, if the Queen of England is amongst you, tarry not at Bethune to-night; for two hundred English soldiers are lying there in wait to seize her. Good-night, mesdames." Then he galloped off at full speed. We waited for the other cart to overtake us, and then held a council what to do. M. de Brézé made the Queen exchange outer garments with him, and took her place in our vehicle, she going with the esquires. He bribed the driver to push on with full speed, so as to cross the town sooner than should be expected, and stopping nowhere, reach an inn he knew of beyond it in a village aside from the highway. We were spoken to at the gate; but the warders taking us to be country folks, took small heed of our passage, and a thick fog, which by the mercy of God then suddenly increased, in a great measure shielded us from sight. All the night, in that poor quiet house we sat shuddering at every sound, and before daybreak departed in fear and trembling. This was one of the closest dangers the Queen ran; for if that stranger — whom God reward — had not warned us, she must of a certainty have been captured. We afterwards heard the English soldiers had scoured the roads half the night, swearing at her escape.

When the walls of the little city whither we were bound appeared in sight, the Queen said to me: "Now for the wisdom of the serpent and the gentleness of the dove, good Meg! In sooth, I am less endowed with these qualities than should be needful in these rencontres; but I will school my pride, tame my spirit, rule my discourse, and who knoweth that my fortunes are not now about to change? You say in England, It is a long lane which hath no turning. Then Picardy roads are like unto these long lanes, I trow, and my ill-fortune also. But to both, I ween, an end must come at last."

CHAPTER XXXII.

A Week at St. Pol.

AT the entrance of the town a deputation from the Duke of Burgundy met the Queen and complimented her in his highness's name, who was himself expected to arrive on the morrow, and then conducted her to the quarter where lodgings were prepared for her. She smiled when she saw the splendour with which these chambers, which would otherwise have been mean, had been adorned for her use. Each of them was furnished with rich pieces of damask silk and curious tapestry, and her bed hung with lace. The food set before her majesty was of the most delicate sort, and very good entertainment provided for her suite. But the most extraordinary and unlooked-for comfort to her grace's attendants and to me, if not to herself, was a fair gift from the Duchesse de Bourbon, which we found in the wardrobe of this apartment— two rare gowns of fine stuff, with head-gear to match, and other ornaments and linen. Methinks we often suffer more than is thought of from slight causes. Verily the distress I had endured from the foresight of the Queen's appearing before the duke and his courtiers in her faded tattered robette had deprived me almost as much of sleep as more mighty cares; and even since the Count of Charolais's munificence I yet misdoubted a tirewoman should be found at St. Pol cunning enough to make apparel for her grace.

Repose was sweet that night, and from excess of fatigue even the Queen closed her eyes in profound slumber.

On the morrow at an early hour a flourish of trumpets announced the duke's arrival. I saw the Queen rise and press to her lips a little cross which she always wore. M. de Brézé opened the door and said, "Madame, the duke hath reached his lodgings, and when he heard your majesty was already arrived, he said he should instantly repair to your grace's house to salute you; so presently he will be here."

"The duke is coming down the street," one of the esquires cried. Upon which the Queen descended the stairs and went into the street, almost to the centre thereof. What a meeting was this! Every one held his breath, watching to see how these inimical friends or friendly enemies should act. Both stopped at the same time; and I observed the duke fix his piercing eye on the Queen, who then twice made a lowly reverence, which he perceiving, then he likewise bowed so profoundly that it seemed almost as if he bent his knee to the ground. Advancing, he was about to repeat this homage, but she, with a graceful impetuous gesture, caught his arm, and said in a faltering voice: "Monseigneur, such honours are not due to me from you. I thank God I have been spared to meet him whom of all Christian princes I have most desired to see." Then they embraced, and the duke craved license to retire for a time.

The Queen was well pleased with this beginning, and augured favourably of the issue of her journey. About two hours afterwards there came to her Sir Philippe de Croye, a knight of noble birth, with compliments from the duke, and an urgent request that when he should visit her, she should on no account come out of her chamber, for that he should bring very few persons with him. And very soon his voice was heard on the stairs. Though she hastened to meet him, before she had advanced three steps he surprised her and entered the room. His manner was more kind than before. He took her by the hand and led her to a couch, whereon they both seated themselves—the Queen's suite standing on one side, and the duke's courtiers on the other. She lifted her eyes to his visage, which is one of the finest in the world,—as beautiful for a man as hers is for a woman, and on which age hath only stamped greater majesty, and no disfigurement,—and addressed him in this wise:

"Fair cousin, I know well that you have been informed against my lord and husband and me as if we had been your mortal foes, endeavouring to injure you by every means in our power: and although, fair cousin, if you imagined it to be so, you would have had reason to wish us no good, yet at all times my lord and husband the King and I, knowing our own innocence, and how falsely we have been accused in this matter, have been most desirous to meet the charge. It is for this cause that my lord the King commanded me never to cease from wandering in search of you till I had found you, even if I should have to travel on foot to the end of the world in quest of your highness. But now, thanks to God and you, we have met; and I am here in your realm entirely at your mercy, a poor outcast queen reduced to the condition of a servant, requiring nothing but that you will be pleased to hear me speak in the name of my lord and husband and mine own. If ever that poor King and I should be again, as we once were, on the ascent of the wheel of fortune, we should bear ourselves to you in the same manner as we do now. And if we had continued as we formerly were, my lord intended to have deputed a prince of his own blood to explain this matter to you. But as this cannot be, I pray you to hear our good cousin the Sénéchal, who will speak more fully on the subject, if you will deign to listen."

This was said in very well-expressed and pretty-sounding French, which I translate into plain English. The duke listened with a frozen countenance, ever and anon waving his hand, as if to signify that the less said on that subject the better. And when the Queen had ended, he replied: "Madame, it is a trifle, not worthy of another thought. I do not attend to all I hear, though people report many strange things to me; but words come and go, and for my part I let them run on as they like; for I know pretty well what they would have me to believe, and I am sure I have not given the King your husband and you cause to be mine enemies. But let that pass, and turn we now, I pray you, to some more agreeable subject; for when with ladies, one ought not to speak of anything but joy."

At that last word the Queen's visage changed, and her lips quivered. O, there is not a more cruel thing in the world than to address to a sore-bruised heart, passionately looking for a response, light words of common parlance touching a matter simply troublesome on the one side, but to the other of life and death. Alas, poor Queen! She made an effort to answer, or to smile; but failing therein, turned with an anguished look to the Sénéchal, as if beseeching him to speak. Whereupon he advanced, bent the knee before the duke, and began thus:

"My very redoubted lord, I am not used to the language of worldly speakers, but my friends know I always speak the truth; and if I presume to address you now, it is to set forth the truth. My redoubted

lord King Henry, and this his Queen, who has freely
come to you of her own high courage, have always
esteemed you to be the most illustrious prince in Christendom; and following the general voice, which sounds
the fame of your noble deeds, your virtues, and renown,
they have sounded your praises. You see, monseigneur, this queen here present, your near relation,
as every one knows, and one of the greatest and most
powerful princesses in the world, but now reduced by
oppression, by cruelty, by the disloyalty of men and
the fickleness of fortune, such as was never heard of
before, to a miserable poverty, driven from a throne,
degraded from her natural rank, deprived of every
hope, save that which she and I also repose in you,
that you will be persuaded to take part in her quarrel,
instead of supporting the cause of her foes, which are
nothing to you in blood, as she is. No wonder if, dur-
the course of this long and unnatural rebellion of their
subjects, this King and Queen have obtained occasional
succour from the French, who had good reason to give
it; for King Henry is the nephew of the late King
Charles, and the Queen Margaret is niece to the Queen
of France, who is yet alive; and in this seeking there
was no enmity to you; although even if it had not
been so, King Henry would not have been to blame,
since it is very well known to him and to the Queen
here that if you had been as favourable to them as
you have been to the Duke of York, they would not
have been brought to the pass in which they are at
present."

The duke heard the first part of this speech as one
who gives heed out of civility, but with a marked indifferency, until that last round piece of truth burst
from the natural tongue of Messire Pierre. He could
not restrain a smile, which he strove to conceal with

his hand. Quick as lightning the Queen perceived this change in his countenance, and with one of those enchanting glances which are her chief seduction, she exclaimed, "O, I pray you, fair cousin, hide not that smile, which like a ray of sunshine melts the ice in which you incase yourself!"

"Ah, madame," he cried, "what ice can resist the fire of your eyes? Even if the axe was about to sever his head from his shoulders at your command, a man if he looked at your face would forgive you."

This was said with an open smile, and the Queen smiled also, and answered: "Fair cousin, I confess and deny not that with a woman's anger, which vents itself in passionate unmeaning words, like a checked child who threatens revenge it never intends, I did use some curst speech touching your highness; but, my lord, if my poor face, as you deign to say, moves you to pardon me, much more, could you see my sad and grateful heart, would you pity the Queen and the kinswoman whose only hope lies in you now."

With an abrupt frank cordiality the duke said in answer to this natural and yet politic speech: "Whatever hath or hath not been in the past, madame, you are welcome now to Burgundy; and I am very sorry for your misfortunes."

Then he prayed her to suffer herself to be conducted to a banquet which was prepared for her entertainment; and a very fine one it was, with a greater variety of dishes and ornaments and curious devices on the table than one should have thought to see in any house which was only, as it were, for a time a palace. Agreeable music was provided, and every honour due to a crowned head paid to the Queen. Amongst the guests which sat at the royal table were Messire Adolphe of Cleves, Messire Jacques de Bourbon, the Baron de la Roche, Messire George Chastellain, and the Sieur de Brézé. The Queen and the duke sat side by side, and she appeared merry of cheer. They talked much together, and with as great freedom as if they had been brother and sister. With an innocent art she sought to please him by her witty discourse and a gentle reverential demeanour, as if she had been addressing the greatest person in the world. And this was no copy of her countenance, for indeed his favour was then of more importance to her than aught else on earth; not so much because her very life was in his hands, but because he was about to be umpire in the congress for a general peace at St. Omer.

Messire Chastellain, who was placed near me, said, "Madame, methinks we see before us the types of all that is majestic in man and beautiful in woman. Where shall one behold a more perfect semblance of a hero than in our duke, or a fairer lady, and one of a higher bearing, than your Queen?"

"Yea," I replied; "and albeit the poverty to which cruel fortune has reduced her might have crushed any other woman with humiliation, her manners are unchanged."

"Madame," he rejoined, "she has come here with only three women in a stage-cart, and she deports herself with no less dignity than if she yet swayed the sceptre in London, and exercised in her single person the whole of the regal authority there. She hath verily an admirable wit. Did you hear the ingenious compliment she paid to the duke touching his skill in hunting? Every great man hath a point in which he is sensible to praise. One might call our sovereign a Solomon or an Alexander, and the shaft of flattery would miss its aim; but speak of Nimrod, and you will see it hath sped to the mark. I was tempted to smile when your Queen said that ambition groweth with success; and that whereas her one great desire had been fulfilled, which was to see her fair cousin, now it was satisfied, another had taken its place, which was one day to hunt with him, and judge if what report said was true touching his incomparable skill in that disport."

"O, then, she hit the right nail on the head there," I said, translating this English proverb into French, which made the gentleman laugh. "Think you, monsieur," I said, "that your duke is won over to our Queen's cause?"

"Madame," he replied, "I can see in every lineament of the duke's visage, in his every gesture and the sound of his voice as he addresses her, that he admires her majesty's singular beauty, that he compassionates her sorrows, that he is ravished by her wit and delighted by her eloquence; but I predict to you, that the more he is touched and seduced by her incomparable merits, the sooner will he withdraw himself from their influence. He will aid her as far as aiding her will in noways be injurious to his interests as a sovereign; but to sacrifice his own designs, as our friend Pierre does his estates, for the fine eyes or witty tongue of any woman—be she the first in the universe—this is not the part the good Duke Philip will play."

These words made me of less good cheer than I had been at first, seeing the good entertainment given to the Queen and her joyful looks. The praise of Pierre de Brézé was in every mouth that day, and mostly in the duke's. The noble devoted champion of the red rose was extolled to the skies; but Messire George is right. Disinterested friendship, heroic sacrifices meet with applause, by some heartily expressed, by others tinctured with a secret pity; but few are found to rise up and say, " I will go and do likewise."

The Queen was full of hope that night; and when on the morrow the duke came to take leave of her, he spoke with exceeding great kindness and courtesy, and said if she would tarry a short while at St. Pol, he should send his sister the Duchess of Bourbon to visit her. Moreover, he promised not to do anything to her prejudice at St. Omer; but as the envoys of the King of France would be there, he would not pretend to take any charge upon him, lest he should mar their arrangements.

The Queen then said to him, " Fair cousin, I thank you for your generous behaviour and noble treatment. I bless the hour when I set forth in quest of you. It is the best exploit I have achieved since my reverse of fortune. Adieu, fair cousin!" She could say no more, but broke into a fit of weeping.

In the afternoon of that day, when the duke had ridden some leagues from the town, one of his knights returned, bearing gifts from his master, which with a noble bashfulness he would not present himself. He sent two thousand gold crowns to her majesty, and a very rich diamond, which he besought her to wear as a token of his friendship. On all who had shared the Queen's dangerous journey he bestowed one hundred gold pieces, and to Sieur Pierre de Brézé he gave two hundred. In a letter to the Queen he moreover enclosed an order on his treasury for twelve thousand gold crowns. When afterwards she was alone with me, she threw her arms round my neck, and said, " The Scotch say, ' A wilful man maun have his way '; a wilful woman has had hers, Meg, and hath done well. This prince's kindness hath poured balm into my heart's festering wounds." I could not forbear to say (as I wax older, methinks I grow more bold in speech), "And yet, madame, this is that duke between whose head and shoulders you would have passed the axe!"

"I will have thy tongue chopped off, Meg," she said, "if thou lettest it run on in this wise."

But there was no anger in her eyes or in her voice. Methinks no one can be truly angered with those which love them as I do this Queen. On the morrow of the duke's departure the Duchesse de Bourbon arrived at St. Pol. Tears, illumined by smiles, attended her meeting with her royal kinswoman. Very tender memories, I ween, were re-called to these noble ladies by the sight of one another. The duchess thought, in that hour, of her fair and virtuous daughter, the Duchesse de Calabre, who died in her springtime; for I heard her say "Marie" as she clasped my Queen in her arms, who answered that one eloquent word with a yet closer embrace. Then they walked together in the garden of the house where the Queen lodged; and that day and all the following ones great cheer was made by the duke's orders, and banquets prepared for his sister's guest. Very pleasant shows and entertainments were likewise provided to divert her from her sorrows. It was strange to be again hearing music and witnessing sports. The world itself seemed to me an unnatural phantasy, sometimes offering to the sight dreadful spectacles, and then an untimely gaiety. I listened like in a dream to the talk of the duchess's ladies, which ran much on the present fashions, and mostly on a head-gear which resembles in shape a church-steeple, and is crowned at the top with two large wings, whence some do call it "the great butterflies." One lady said that she had been told that some preachers anathematised this fashion, but for her part she should continue to wear it until the Church condemned the excessive length of the men's upturned boots; for she did not see why the one sex might extend their feet if the other should not raise their heads.

"But, madame," cried another, "I declare to you that the Church, so far from condemning the great butterflies, does rather defend them; for brother Thomas, the most bitter railer against this head-gear—"

"Ay," interrupted the first speaker; "I am credibly informed that he said all who did wear it should go to hell."

"Well, if he did, all I can say is," replied the other, "that he is now in the Inquisition on suspicion of heresy."

"Touching head-gears?" asked M. de Cleves, who had been maliciously eavesdropping during this discourse.

Then they fell upon him, and declared that men were more fanciful and extravagant in their dress by a great deal than women; not only adding unnatural-shaped toes to their feet, but widening their backs with artificial shoulders, and letting their hair fall on their faces so straight and thickly, that it deprived them almost of sight.

"In sooth," one lady said, "methinks to look like monkeys is now the aim of our marvellous gentlemen."

"O, but," cried another, "you have not seen the last fashion. The shoes, instead of being pointed, are now made in the shape of a goose's foot; and these gallants carry in their hands silver-gilt vultures, wherewith to pick their teeth."

"Ah," said M. de Cleves, "yon describe Jean de Ternant, whom the duke our lord knighted last month. His impertinent apparel misliked his highness; and when he dubbed him, it was in so lusty a fashion that the sound of the blow resounded through the hall."

They asked me of the fashions in England. I said they were mostly copied from those in France; but that now in my country the niceties of dress were less observed since so many wars had distracted men's minds.

"But the King of England," said a young lady, "is reported to be most magnificent in his apparel, as well as the handsomest man imaginable."

"Mademoiselle," I said, with an emotion I could not repress, "the King of England is now a homeless wanderer in his own realm, with no magnificence left him, and only so much beauty as sorrow and deep care hath failed to efface from his serene and well-favoured visage."

The damsel waxed very red at these words, and methinks was afterwards rebuked by the other ladies for her thoughtless speech.

The Duchess sought by all means in her power to detain the Queen at St. Pol; for she had conceived a marvellous liking for her Grace over and above the old affection which dated from past years. Nothing would content her but to hear from her own lips the narrative of her misfortunes; and she listened to those recitals with a passionate curiosity, as if they had been tales devised for her entertainment. I was often present on these occasions; and the gentlemen and ladies of the Queen's suite, and the Duchess's also, prayed to be permitted to hear the narrative wherewith she had promised to close these recitals the evening before her departure. For her heart was at Bruges, and albeit very loth to part with her friendly kinswoman, each day which she spent far from my lord the Prince was grievous to her. It was on the second of September that, in an arbour in the afternoon, by the side of Madame de Bourbon, their ladies on their right hand and on their left, and the gentlemen of this little court sitting at their feet, my Queen spoke as follows. I can set down the substance of what she said; but who could render the language of her speaking face, the music of her voice, the nobility of her gestures—the responsive emotion of those who heard this incredibly true tale? In Messire Chastellain's visage sympathetic genius beamed; in Madame de Bourbon's a very storm of compassion reigned; Francisco of Ferrara's eyes flashed with Italian fire; Messire de Renty and the Lord of Moreuil held their breath, as if afraid to lose one word; Pierre de Brézé gazed on her with idolatrous worship; Sir John Carbonnel hid his face with his hand. No sound was heard during an hour but this royal voice, and now and then a stifled sob from the Duchess and her ladies. This is what I wrote down from memory; but it is a picture without hue, a skeleton without life, a poor remembrance of an incomparable eloquence.

CHAPTER XXXIII.

The Dead Man's Ground.

"MADAME my cousin, hitherto you have listened with a very tender compassion to the narrative of my misfortunes and my wrongs, and not a few tears have fallen from your eyes at the thought of my sufferings. You have declared that it is a mystery to you how a Christian King and Queen, who had been lawfully inaugurated, and had never committed notorious crimes, such as provoke the wrath of God and forfeit the allegiance of subjects, should have been brought so low as not to possess a foot of land or a house to shelter them in their own realm, nor yet a penny of silver or copper, unless borrowed, to purchase the common necessaries of life, When I described to you the suffering we endured after the rout at Towton, the hunger, cold, and poverty, which endangered our lives as much as if we had fallen into the hands of our foes, it seemed to you like an incredible thing; and I almost feared you would question my veracity when I said that once for five days the King my husband, the Prince my little son, and I had but one herring to eat betwixt us all, and not more bread than would have sufficed for one day's nourishment. Your cheeks also burned with a painful flush when I told you that being one day at Mass on a solemn festival, I had not even a black penny to give at the offering; and when I prayed a Scotch archer by my side to lend me something, he at first refused, and then grudgingly handed me a half-farthing. You exclaimed that so sharp a humiliation had never befallen a great queen, and that the recital of my escape from the ribald knaves of Sir William Stanley had robbed you of your sleep, so terrible did that danger appear to you. Alas! sweet cousin, what I am now by your command about to relate doth as far exceed all you have yet heard of my perils as those already recited, or any you had imagined. I should hesitate to sadden your compassionate heart by so terrible a history, did I not know that you take a melancholy pleasure in the recital of these singular vicissitudes, to which no parallel can be found in books. Therefore, madame, imagine if you can the sight of a battle-field; not one on which victory waves its empurpled but triumphant flag, disguising the horrorful scene; not one on which the eye rests with a half shuddering, half exultant gaze, but one where, like in a dismal wreck, you behold the overthrow of every high and fair hope and presage without yet seeing it—the destruction of the loved, the honoured, and the faithful which have perished in your quarrel; one over which despair throws its dark shadow, like the raven extends its wing on the unburied corpse. Ah, even when success intoxicates the soul with its wild rapture, the battle-field is a terrific sight. When defeat lends its leaden hues to that spectacle, it is so ghastly that even the man that is reckless of life turns from it and flies. On the fatal day of Hexham news was brought me that the King had disappeared and been hotly pursued—then that he was taken; but this was false: one of the servants which wore his cap had been seized, and this had saved him. Somerset and Hungerford and Sir Ralph Percy were driven back; even you, Sieur de Brézé, were forced from the field, and parted from me. I too then fled with my son and three or four attendants: that lady was one." (This the Queen said pointing to me.) "We made for the Scotch border, and carried with us vases of gold and silver, and whatever of value I yet possessed—some of the crown-jewels and mine own. The hills of Scotland were in sight. A few more hours, and safety would be reached. But on a moor which lies between the forest of Hexham and the much-longed-for Scottish hills we were of a sudden environed by a party of ruffianly men, the most brutal and fierce I had yet beheld. They seized on Edward and me, separated us from our suite, and with an incredible violence tore from us even the most of our clothing, which pointed us out, they said with derisive laughter, to be no mean booty. 'Ah, ah,' said one, 'this is a queen; for no less a personage should dare to wear this rich velvet trimmed with fur.' And another, in whose hands I shuddering beheld my son, exclaimed, 'This is of a surety the lioness's cub, as daintily attired as herself.' 'A lioness!' screamed another; 'nay a wolf,—the she-wolf of France; and like a wolf we shall treat her;' and then they dragged me in a ferocious manner before their captain, and with furious menaces brandished a sword before mine eyes, threatening to kill Edward first, and then me; and the wretch added, they should mangle and disfigure our dead bodies and cast them unburied for the vultures to devour, so that no traces should be left of them. And one cried, 'Nay, pile up a fagot and burn them alive, as my Lollard father was burnt the year I was born.' And insults far more horrible yet were threatened; so that if my son had not been with me exposed to the same rage, the bare sword they approached to my throat should have been welcome. But despaired with the agony of fear for him, I sunk on my knees before those ruffians, with clasped hands and upraised eyes, adjuring them, alas! by all they recked not of,—God, royalty, pity, nobility, womanhood, the Cross of Christ, their mothers, wives and children, if so be they were men and not beasts, at least not to commit on our bodies the last outrage, so that Christian burial should never be ours. 'O, I have had the misfortune,' I cried, ' to fall into your hands; but I am the daughter and wife of a king. I was in past time recognised as your queen. If now you stain your hands with my blood and the blood of my innocent child, your cruelty will be held in abhorrence by all men throughout all ages.' Torrents of tears choked further utterance, and I turned from man, which had no ruth, to God, who alone could save us; and not in vain, for, as once before in my life, the greed of wicked men became His mercy's instrument. Those in whose hands we were saw others stealing our jewels and gear, and with a shout of fury rushed on their fellow-robbers. I sprang to where Edward was, folded him in my arms, and cast a despairing look around me. I saw one man clad like the others standing by the side of a horse, and taking no part in the fray. Running towards him, I fell on my knees, and conjured him by the Passion of our Lord Jesus Christ to have pity on me, and to do what he could to make us escape. He replied, 'Madame, mount behind me, and you, my lord Prince, before, and I will save you, or perish in the attempt.' With incredible velocity we clambered on to the horse's back. 'Whither?' the stranger asked. 'To Scotland,' I said. 'Nay, that is through the open plain,' he replied, dashing forward to the westward. 'The forest —the Dead Man's Ground—is the only shelter at hand.' 'Yea,' I whispered, 'the forest, the forest!' for I had lost all power to think; and that ride began of which none but God knoweth the horror, or those that can guess at it the length. For my brain was wildered, and every vein and nerve of my frame convulsed with the terror I had endured. One night of horror round me grew; or when I saw or felt, it was only when we plunged into the depths of the forest, and in the ghastly light of the moon I thought every tree was a man with a naked sword in his hand, who kept crying to me, as the wind rustled in the bare branches, '*A la mort! à la mort!*' Then ghastly terrors took possession of my soul. Methought it was a phantom horse and rider which was carrying us, and that this should be my hell, for ever to wander in a horrible darkness, and a barrier betwixt me and Edward, which, though I was nigh to him, forbade me to reach or touch him. This agony grew so insupportable, that ever and anon I lifted up my voice and cried, 'Edward! Edward!' and then the little voice answered, 'Sweet mother!' and the anguish abated. At last a fever seemed to burn in my veins, and incessantly I kept addressing our protector: 'O sir, it is not for myself I fear, but for my son; my death would be of little moment, but his would be too great a misfortune—utter ruin to everyone, the end of every hope. He is the true, the sole heir to the crown. All may go right again if his life can be preserved.' And terror seizing on me, I felt almost in despair, not thinking it possible we should escape without falling once more into the hands of those dreadful men. The name which the stranger had given to the place wherein deeper and deeper we were advancing gave me a shivering horror. 'Dead Man's Ground,' I repeated to myself—'Dead Man's Ground; who ever came out of it alive?' All of a sudden the horse stopped; the horseman dismounted, and made us descend also. Then he briefly said, 'You are safe

here, madam—farewell;' and before I could speak he
had mounted again and disappeared. To this day I
am ignorant of this man's name, person, or history.
Sometimes I think that, as an angel was sent to Hagar
in the desert, so to another despaired mother God sent
a disguised heavenly messenger under the figure of
that horseman. If he was a man, he lacked mercy in
abandoning us when he did; if an angel, God recalled
him when his task was performed. The trees closed
over our heads where we stood, the pale stars gleaming
through the branches, the receding sound of the horse's
feet the only sound in that profound solitude. I sank
on the ground, and held Edward clasped to my breast
to warm him. O, I thought of Hagar when he said to
me, ' Sweet mother, are there blackberries in this
wood? I am so hungry.' ' It is not the time of year,
gentle son,' I said, with a choking sensation in my
throat. ' Will it come to that pass,' I murmured, ' that
I see him perish with cold and hunger?' Then I took
him by the hand, and we wandered to and fro—wherefore I know not, for I dared not have approached a
human habitation if I had seen one, none but outlaws
and robbers lurking in those wilds. But to sit still
maddened me; and if I stopped, a rustling in the bushes
or the hooting of an owl made me fly on in terror.
The courage of my little son caused me a strange
anguish. ' I am very tired,' he once said; ' but I am
resolved not to shed tears, for a knight should bear all
hardships;' and another time, when we heard the cry
of an animal, he pressed my hand tightly, and whispered, ' Do not be affrighted, sweet mother; our Lady
will not let the wild-beasts hurt us.' ' O God!' I
thought, ' hast Thou made this child so fair, so wise,
and so brave, that he should pass through this world
unknown, and out of it without fame, whose soul is as

a noble jewel set in a peerless frame?' Again he said, 'Gentle mother, where thinkest thou is my poor father the King?' These words pierced me like with a dagger, for this was the misdoubt which doubled my torment. The gentle boy perceived it, and said, 'Be of good cheer, sweet mother; the good Saviour, whom he loves so well, will take care of the King; and methinks he would not be sorry to die and go to heaven; and I am so weary to-night, I should like to die too, but I would not leave thee alone in this dark wood, dear mother queen.'

"This innocent prattle lasted a little while, but soon it ceased; and by the light of the moon I saw the fair visage look white, and felt the little limbs slacken their pace. I was about to sit down again, to perish, I thought, when of a sudden a gaunt tall figure came through the trees towards us, swinging a battle-axe. At first I thought this was one of the ruffians we had fled from, but at the second glance I guessed it was a new robber, and in the extremity of fear, hopeless of all other aid, powerless to move, afraid to stir, I cried with a loud voice to this gigantic man to save us. He approached; it was too dark to see his countenance, but with the courage of despair I thus addressed him: 'O sir; if you are in quest of booty, we have, alas, nothing to yield you but our lives; for we have been rifled, my little son and I, of all we possess, and even of our upper garments. I suppose it is your custom to shed the blood of travellers; but I am sure you will take pity on us when I tell you who I am.' I raised my eyes, and a cloud passing away from the moon, I saw the visage of the man I was speaking to. I could augur nothing from it. He was gazing on me with an amazed, misdoubting expression, but not a savage one. I burst into tears, and cried, 'It is the unfortunate

Queen of England, thy princess, who hath fallen into thy hands in her desolation and distress. O man, if thou hast any knowledge of God, I beseech thee, for the sake of His Passion Who for our salvation took our nature on Him, to have compassion on my misery! But if you slay me, spare at least my little one; for he is the only son of thy king, and, if it please God, the true heir of this realm. Save him then, I pray thee, and make thy arms his sanctuary. He is thy future king, and it will be a glorious deed to preserve him—one that shall efface the memory of all thy crimes, and witness for thee when thou shalt stand hereafter before Almighty God. O man, win God's grace to-day by succouring an afflicted mother, and giving life to the dead!' When these last words passed my lips, the axe fell from the outlaw's hand, and he sank on his knees. I placed Edward in his arms, and said, 'I charge thee to preserve from the violence of others that innocent royal blood which I do consign to thy care. Take him and conceal him from those who seek his life. Give him a refuge in thy obscure hiding-place, and he will one day give thee access to his royal chamber and make thee one of his barons, if by thy means he is happily preserved to enjoy the splendour of the crown which doth of right pertain to him.' O ye who hear me, marvel at the change which a moment may work! The Holy Ghost softened the heart of this man, which had approached us with uplifted arm and ferocious gestures. He received the child in his arms; his tears flowed as fast as mine, and he cried in a loud voice, 'I will die, lady, a thousand deaths; I will endure all the tortures that can be inflicted on a man, rather than abandon, much less betray, this royal child. But before I rise from my knees' (for he had fallen at my feet), 'O madame, pardon my offences

x

against the law. Forgive the outlaw and the robber, and then he will dare to carry in his arms this noble burthen, his innocent prince.' 'God knoweth thou hast all the pardon I can grant,' I cried; 'and may He also for this deed forgive thee all thine offences!'

"Then with my son in his arms he led the way, and I followed him, walking as one in a dream, till he stopped at the entrance of a cave, surrounded by wild wood and tangled bushes, nigh to a swift little bourn. He whistled, and a door opened; a fire and a kind of rude lamp lighted this place, and I saw by its shine that it was a woman which had let us in. He whispered in her ear; on which she gave a little scream and knelt down before me, kissing my soiled garment. The warmth and light of this singular cave amazed me not a little, after the long wandering in the cold and the darkness. Edward had fallen fast asleep in the outlaw's arms, who laid him down on a coarse pallet nigh to the fire, covering him with a sheepskin. The woman threw on my chilled limbs an old mantle which had some richness in it, though soiled and tattered. 'God defend,' I said to myself, 'that this should be the spoil of some murthered traveller.' The man brought me a pillow, and I lay down by Edward's side, but not to sleep like him; for every nerve in my body was aching, and the least sound caused me to start as if an explosion had taken place. With eyes wide open, as if I could never close them again, I watched those two persons moving about the cave. Soon they brought me bread and hot sugared wine. With what a God-thanking heart I awoke Edward and saw him eat and drink, and then sink back into a deep slumber, with a less paleness in his cheeks. I also swallowed a little wine, but the bread seemed to choke me; for present terror being assuaged, the insupportable thought of that day's rout, and the misdoubt as to the fate of the King my husband and all my faithful soldiers and servants, returned with violence and wrung my heart; I closed my eyes, feigning to sleep. The outlaw went into the outward cave, for it was divided into two parts, and the woman removed the torch into a corner, where, before lying down on the floor, she knelt and crossed herself. 'God be praised,' I said to myself, 'she is not a Lollard;' and felt more secure.

"In one or two hours the gray morning began to dawn; and unable to endure to remain still, I went to the entrance of the cave and looked out. All was quiet, save the brawling rivulet, and a bird which hopped amongst the bushes. I returned to my rude couch, and lying down again, fatigue prevailed, and I fell asleep. When I awoke the sun was shining across the floor through the open door. I started up affrighted, not seeing Edward by my side, and calling him, went out into the thicket. The sound of his merry laughter reached my ears, and soon I perceived him on the back of the outlaw, who was wading across the bourn. When he perceived me, Edward cried, 'Sweet mother, gentle mother, this is the most pleasant disport I have known for a long time. We have been shooting with a bow and arrows, and killed birds for our dinner. I have had my breakfast; it was very good. Now we are playing at crossing the river. He is St. Christopher carrying the little Lord Jesus on his back; only I am too old to be carried. I have told him the story of St. Christopher, and it likes him so well that I have promised to tell him another tale to-night.'

"Then for the first time I saw plainly the visage of the man who had saved us; it was one of a doubtful aspect, heavy and lowering when not speaking; but I noticed that when Edward made that speech and patted him on the head, a softened expression came into his face. He hastened towards me, and setting him down by my side in a worshipful manner, he said, 'I am not worthy, madame, to carry an innocent child, much less my prince; but nothing would serve his grace but to cross the bourn, and I would not suffer him to wade through the water.' 'Gramercy for your careful kindness,' I replied. 'Alas, my son hath no clothes but these few he wears, and so we must needs preserve them from destruction.' 'Madame,' he said, 'there are garments in this cave which would, I ween, fit his grace, and likewise well conceal his rank; I would not any man's son in England but the King's should wear them.' He then called his wife and whispered something in her ear; she turned to a coffer and drew from it some boy's garments, which she spread out before us; and the while I perceived her tears fall apace. I misliked Edward should put on stolen gear; maybe she read my thoughts, for she said quickly, 'Madame, the lord Prince may put on these clothes without fear.' Upon which I thanked her, and dressed my son in this coarse apparel. 'And now, madame,' the generous outlaw said, 'command your poor servant; how can I aid your majesty to find a more secure shelter than the outlaw's cave?' 'My friend,' I replied, 'your abode is, alas, at this moment the only shelter, ay the safest refuge for us; for who would dream to seek the Queen'—I stopped, and in a half-bitter, half-sorrowful manner he finished the sentence, 'In a den of robbers, your majesty would have said. Ay, of a surety, none could conceive that the Lady Margaret of Anjou and the heir of Lancaster should be the guests of an outlaw.' 'God,' I replied, 'worketh His ends by strange means. But if,' I added, 'you durst adventure so far as the outskirts of the forest, it may happen that some of my leal friends, who are doubtless seeking me, shall encounter you, and thus learn where we lie conceal.' 'I will find your friends or perish,' he answered. 'Nay, nay,' I cried, 'for the sake of God, for mine, for Edward's, imperil not your life. Who shall protect us if you return not?' 'Is it come to this,' he said, with a melancholy smile, 'that anyone, much less my sovereign princess, should desire, and not detest my presence? Be contented, madame; I have not so long preserved a life abhorrent to God and man to cast it away when it is your hope of safety. I will explore the confines of the forest, and spy if any wanderers have fled to it.' 'Prithee, let me walk with my good St. Christopher,' Edward cried, and was not well pleased when I refused to let him go. He sat down in a corner of the cave, a little angered, and played with snails he had collected on the walls.

CHAPTER XXXIV.

A Robber's Cave.

"THE hours passed heavily by, and I mused in agonised suspense on our singular destiny, murmuring the names of absent friends, calling foolishly on those which could not hear me, terrified lest our strange protector should meet with any mishap. At last my brain became so weary that I feared to think on the past or the future—for what would befall my son if I should lose my senses? With shudder I rose and walked to and fro in that narrow space, like I remember to have seen caged wild-beasts do in their dens; and this simile misliked me. My eyes fell then on the outlaw's wife, which I had hardly yet noticed, though she had ministered to me in many silent ways. She was a woman not far advanced in years, but aged before the time, if the lines in her face were to be believed. She had a weary look, like one used to suffer, and that longed to be at rest, but too weak to compass any end. I said to her, 'God defend your husband should run into danger for our sakes.' 'Madame,' she replied with a quivering lip, 'he hath so often run into danger for unlawful purposes, that I hope now when he doth imperil himself for a good cause he shall not lose his life.' 'Have you been long married?' I asked, willing to divert myself by any kind of discourse from mine own thoughts. 'Ten years,' she answered with a mournful countenance.

'I am a gentlewoman by birth, and was bred at Alnwick, in the countess's household.' 'Holy Mary!' I exclaimed, 'and how have you come to be the wife of an outlaw?' 'Alas, madame, I ran away with my husband, who is the son of a poor esquire. The Countess would not suffer me to marry him, partly because he had no pelf or land wherewith to keep me, and also that he was reported to be unsad; and men said foul things of him more than he deserved. He had been wont when a boy to run into this forest when he was corrected at home, but only for a frolic; and then frighted his sisters with tales of the Dead Man's Ground, and that he had been consorting with robbers and the like folks; but this was done in sport, and he was a kind lad in those days when he wooed me. He heard his Mass on Sundays and holydays, and gave alms when he had wherewith to do so, which was not often. When we found we could not be otherwise married, we took one day the priest by surprise, and appearing suddenly before him, plighted our mutual troth, without his or anyone else's consent. But no blessing attends these stolen marriages. Every door was shut against us. I had no parents, and the Countess would not have so much as my name mentioned to her. His kinsfolk said he was born to be hanged, but that he had now hung a millstone round his neck, and might as lief drown. No one lent us a helping hand. He was of too gentle blood to labour for his bread; and no scholar, for he had not kept to his school. So we well-nigh starved; and then one day he brought me here, for he had known this cave in his young years; and as it was in the summer, we made shift to live on berries and roots, and the birds which he killed with his bow. Those were the most happy days I have known; but when the cold weather came then hardships began, and we could not live as we had done. I fell very sick, and he walked many miles to a cottage outside the forest and begged an alms for the love of God, which was denied him; and on his way back, for the first time—' Here the poor creature stopped and shed tears. I took her by the hand and said, 'You have no children?' 'One little son I had,' she replied. 'He would be now of the age of my lord the Prince. Those were his clothes which his Grace hath put on. He died two years back. When he was lying at the point of death, I prayed my husband to make a vow that if he recovered he should never again—' Then once more she broke off her speech. 'God knoweth,' she continued, 'how we then should have lived. Howsoever, my fair son died; and albeit I grieved sorely, there was comfort in the thought he would not live the godless life we have done. I had walked a whole day to carry him to a church to be christened, as soon as I could walk after his birth; so he is now in heaven, and I have asked him every day to pray to the Lord Jesus not to suffer us to die as we have lived. But my husband was enraged with Almighty God when his child was taken away; and since that day hope hath almost left me that he should change. Madame, you have pardoned him; pray God, I beseech you, He also may forgive him. It is ten years and more since I have been shriven. I should die of joy, methinks, the day I knelt to a priest again.' Then she went to prepare some food, and I looked to see what Edward should be doing, who had not stirred from the same place whilst I talked with the woman. He was standing before a kind of pilaster which supported the rough wall across the cave, his eyes intently fixed upon it. 'Hist, sweet mother!' he said when I approached; 'I am telling a fortune. Dost thou see those two snails? My St. Christopher told me this morn that in a part of the country whither he once went, if two men quarrel touching a piece of land, or a tree in a hedge, or any other doubtful thing, to whom it shall belong, they each set a snail to creep along in this manner, and then the one whose snail first doth reach the top is the winner. Methinks this should be a better way to settle a dispute, and resolve who shall be king, than to kill thousands of persons. I have set this snail to creep for the red rose, mother, and this one for the white rose. Now, sweet Queen, watch; methinks the red rose is the most swift. If it reaches the top first, methinks my father King shall regain his crown.' 'Foolish, witless child,' I said, angered; and then I remembered the tale I heard in Scotland of the spider which Robert Bruce, when his fortunes were at as low ebb as ours are now, had watched, to draw from it an omen of his fate; and I looked alternately at the slow progressing ascent of these slimy travellers, and at Edward's eager countenance, with an unwise breathless desire that the one he called the champion of Lancaster should win that leisurely race. Forgive my folly, sweet cousin, and all ye kind friends around me; misfortunes long continued unnerve the stoutest heart. I am ashamed to have been so weak; but at the last I became quite wild to have a good omen; and when I perceived that the adverse snail gained on the other, so that it must needs succeed, I swept them both down passionately on the ground, exclaiming, 'Fair son, this is folly, and what Dr. Morton would chide thee for.' 'Poor snails!' he said sadly; 'thou hast bruised their little houses;' and tears stood in his eyes.

"Hope deferred that night was my portion. The

outlaw returned, but with no tidings of my friends. My heart sank within me, and I sat with my face buried in my hands. One other night of sleepless misery ensued, and the next morning that patient man departed for the same search.

"Once that day, when the woman was outside picking up sticks, Edward sat on my knees; and after silently coaxing me some time, he said, 'Mother Queen, I heard yesterday what my St. Christopher's wife told thee. Prithee, are outlaws and robbers always evil persons? And is this our good friend one?' 'Yea,' I said, 'to be a robber is wicked, and those that rob become outlaws; for if the law should reach them they must die, and so they lurk in places such as these. But an evil man may repent, and do a good deed; and so I have pardoned this outlaw; and when we regain the kingdom, he shall come out hence unscathed, and with great honour, for this good he hath done us.' He thought a little, and then said, 'Hath God forgiven him?' 'I know not,' I replied, 'if he hath prayed to Him yet for pardon.' 'I shall ask him,' he said.

"Once more the night closed, and almost in despair I learnt that the outlaw had adventured himself beyond the forest and questioned some boors without obtaining any clue to fugitives in the neighbourhood. I lay down exhausted with misery, turned my face to the wall, and wept unseen. This was the first time I was reduced to so impotent a condition that the future seemed a blank. How to act, whither to go, what to essay, I knew not. From these despairing thoughts I was roused by the sound of Edward's voice conversing with our protector. Bear with me while I relate this discourse; for I would you all should know the good parts and early goodness of my little son, whose mother I am not worthy to be. This is the dialogue I heard:

"'Good friend, thou must needs be very weary, since thou hast been beyond the forest towards the moor whence we came, for it is a long way off.' 'I am not so much weary, my lord prince, as displeased that my quest for your friends hath been vain.' 'My gentle St. Christopher, I would fain I had here one of my little silver swans, which are my badge; but those wicked men took them all away.' 'What would you have done with it, my lord prince?' 'I would have fastened it here on thy breast, good friend, because I am affrighted that if our friends see thee coming to them in the forest they will think thou art a robber come to despoil and perhaps to kill them. But if they saw my badge they would be comforted.' 'You speak well, my lord prince; but I durst not wear your badge.' 'Wherefore durst you not put it on?' Then the outlaw not answering, he lowered his voice and said, 'Is it because you are a robber? But you are a good robber now; we love you very much, and the Lord Jesus will love you too if you ask Him.'

"Then he climbed on to the man's knee, and put his arm round his neck; and albeit I was not wholly pleased to see him so familiar with him, the thought of the night when I had placed him in his arms stayed me from checking him. 'I promised to tell thee a tale, good friend; wilt thou I should do so now?' 'Yea, my lord prince, I list to you.'

"'Once on a time the Blessed Lady Mary, with her Son and good St. Joseph, fled from Nazareth, where they lived, to a far country called Egypt; and it so happened that one night they took shelter in a cave where there were robbers. And one robber's wife had a little child which was a leper. The Blessed Lady

Mary told her to wash him in the water wherein her little Lord Jesus had been bathed, and straightway he was cured. When this little child which had been a leper became a man, he did many wicked actions, and was a famous robber. And one day he was caught and put into a prison, and then taken out to die on a cross, because he was a robber. When he was on the cross, the Lord Jesus was also crucified; and when he saw He was so good, and forgave those who tormented Him, he said to another robber which was on another cross, and who reviled the good Saviour, that they deserved to suffer but that the Lord Christ had done nothing amiss. And then he asked the Lord Jesus to remember him when He came into His kingdom; and O, what thinkest thou the good Lord answered? He said he should be that day with Him in Paradise! Was not that good news for this good robber?'

"I did not hear the man reply, but Edward came to my side and whispered in mine ear: 'Sweet mother, he has said nothing to me; but his wife fetched a little crucifix and put it into my hand. I held it to his lips, and he kissed it so many times. I think he hath asked God to forgive him.' I hoped so too, and I likewise thought that God would not suffer one like my son to be deprived of his inheritance, and banished from the throne by the vile and impious enemies of his race.

"On the morrow—the third on which we had opened our eyes in that secret cave—the outlaw, or, as Edward called him, St. Christopher, set out on the same errand as before. This man had acquainted me with his name; but I had promised not to divulge it until such time as he might be openly pardoned, and guerdoned for his services. About noon, Edward, who was very weary of his captivity within the cave, peered out of the narrow entrance at the squirrels frolicking amongst the trees. Suddenly he gave a joyful shout, and I heard him cry, 'Sir Pierce de Bracy!' Ah, Messire Pierre, neither you nor I shall, I ween, ever forget that meeting—its joy and its anguish! Alas, when I beheld you and Master Barville alongside of our outlaw, it seemed like an awakening from a dreadful dream; and the words which you first uttered, 'The King hath escaped!' lifted the heaviest burthen from my breast. But the tiding which followed! Ah me, with what torrents of tears I received them! O, with what grief, with what pain, with what resentment, they filled me! Yea, my good Margaret,—my true, valiant, patient friend, to thee and to me Hexham shall ever be a dire memory—a bleeding remembrance. That lady's noble father, the Lord de Roos, and Somerset and Hungerford, had paid on the scaffold the price of their devotion to my cause. I could do nothing for some hours but wail and weep. In the evening Master Barville went into the villages on the outskirts of the forest for to gather reports of the public haps for our guidance; and who should he there fall in with but Edmund Beaufort, hapless Somerset's brother, and the Duke of Exeter whom, in my despair, I had feared had also perished. When I beheld yet assembled around me this little band of friends, my spirits somewhat revived. I resolved to send those noblemen to solicit what I have now so happily obtained—an asylum in the dominions of their great kinsman, and my fair cousin of Burgundy, whilst I rejoined the King my husband in Scotland, whither I then thought he had escaped. But ere we left the robber's cave, Messire Pierre completed a work Edward had begun. The knights of Los Croissant serve both God and the ladies; and the same devotion which flies to the succour of a distressed queen moves a truly chivalrous heart to lend its aid to a repenting robber. The sénéchal turned priest, methinks, on this occasion: for he spent the night in hearing the confession of that man's crimes, and ministering counsel to his soul. Is this not the truth, Messire Pierre?"

"Madame," the sénéchal replied, "that man was twice my brother, insomuch as he was a Christian, and furthermore as your majesty's deliverer. And never did I perceive so notable an instance of what the Gospel saith, that many last shall be first in the spiritual race; for in this robber, this outlaw, this man guilty of many crimes, what sudden virtues had blossomed on the stalk of one good action! What contrition for past sins, what ardent desires of penance, what thirst for expiation, what readiness to atone for past guilt! No common life would satisfy his anger against himself; and nothing would content him, when he found that his wife was of the same mind as himself, than for each of them to retire into a religious house, and by prayers and tears to wash away past offences. When the Dukes of Somerset and Exeter from their scanty store of money offered to reward these virtuous penitents, they refused the gifts with tears. The Queen thanked them as she alone knoweth how to thank, and furnished them with tokens to the superiors of religious houses, such as they desired to enter. When near Carlisle, whither he guided us, the outlaw took leave of the Queen and her son. He knelt at the Prince's feet, and said: 'Sweet Prince, I will be thy bedesman all my life in guerdon for the tale of the robber which went to Paradise with Christ; and if it shall please God to admit your grace's poor servant into one of His houses, he shall be hight brother Christopher.'"

Then the Queen resumed her narrative as follows:

"Sweet cousin, and you gentle listeners all, I ween you deem this forest tale the worst of my adventures; but before you resolve yourselves thereupon, I pray you hearken to the haps which befell us soon afterwards. From Carlisle I came to Kirkcudbright, and there I heard the King had not reached Scotland, but was concealed in Yorkshire, at Bracewell Hall, from whence he would soon pass for greater safety into Lancashire or Westmoreland. On my arrival, private notice was sent to me strictly to conceal my presence in the Scottish king's dominions, by reason of a treaty which had been concluded betwixt the Queen Regent and Edward the usurper. So I retired to a small cabin in an obscure hamlet by the coast, where only fishermen and seafaring persons dwelt, which were too rude and ignorant to take heed of us. There my son and I lived concealed under the care of Messire Pierre and Barville my esquire. I procured a gown and hood such as the fish-wives wear; and the sénéchal, also disguised, travelled hither and thither to seek for news. By this means I learnt that the King had left Bracewell, and taken shelter in a cave for some days—but with a hermit, not a robber—and that the most of my household had reached the Castle of Bamborough, which yet bravely held out for us. The tidings I then had of the King, which are the last I received, reported him to be lodged at the house of one John Machell, at Crackenthorpe, a leal adherent of his cause. I pray God he is there now!

"One day the Sénéchal told me that one Cork, an Englishman, had been at Kirkcudbright, and questioned much the people thereof if I was yet residing there, and dropped words which imported he had a weighty message to deliver to me. This worked in me a fever of expectation, and I prayed Messire Pierre to be on the look-out for him. One evening he and Barville left us to fetch a box from a cottage where a messenger brought the provisions which friends at a distance sent us. They did not return for some hours; and as the evening advanced, I feared some evil hap had befallen them. About one hour before midnight the sound of footsteps was heard, but of a greater number of men than two, albeit treading cautiously. I looked through the chinks of the door and saw several persons, at the least five or six, carrying lamps and weapons in their hands. I woke Edward, and sprang with him to the back-door, thinking in the darkness, peradventure, we might escape. But a man met us there, and seizing on me, called to his fellows, who in one instant mastered our feeble resistance. 'Be still, and struggle not,' I said to Edward; and we were carried, or rather dragged, to the shore, and through the waves, into a boat, at the bottom of which they laid us, fast bound with cords. Methought there were other persons in the boat, but it was too dark to discern aught. Then we began to toss on the waves, and to distance the shore. Ever and anon I spoke to Edward, cheering him not to be afraid; and I could hear him saying his little prayers, and calling on Jesus and Mary to save us. The darkness would never cease, I thought. Like the crew on St. Paul's ship, I longed for the day with passion, albeit it should prove more dreadful than the night. It seemed as if it would never come; but at the last the faint grey hue in the horizon harbingered the morn. I glanced at my son. He had fallen asleep. Bound, wet, pale, like a fair lily he lay motionless on the hard planks. Then painfully raising myself a little, I looked before me, and—with what feelings I pray you to imagine—perceived that the Sénéchal and

Barville were in the boat in the same plight as ourselves. Mine eyes met those of Messire Pierre. O, what a recognition that was! I watched him with an intensity which hath no parallel; for it seemed to me that such fidelity as his would snatch us even from the jaws of death. If eyes can speak, his did so then. They said '*Courage*,' and mine answered '*Hope*.' The sea rose, and the wind also. Edward slept on, and I gazed alternately at the Sénéchal and at the men, five of them in number, which were rowing. I heard one say to the others, 'We shall be made men if we land in England with this freight, dead or alive. The York king shall guerdon this prize more than if it were a Spanish galleon.' Then I perceived they were no common pirates, with whom composition could be made, and for a moment despaired. I looked at the Sénéchal, and he smiled. The next instant— O God, how speak of it! how describe it!—he and Barville were on their legs. There was a terrific assault,—blood-chilling groans, death-screams; a splash —a cry; another, and another. Blood streamed in the boat over Edward and me. The bark rolled, heaved, lurched—nearly foundered. Two men were struggling at my feet. I could not discern friends from foes. A drowning wretch caught hold of the boat side, dragging it to destruction: a blow cut off his hand. He fell back and sank. I closed my eyes. When they oped again, Pierre de Brézé was cutting my bands; Barville, Edward's. Two dead bodies were in the boat; three engulfed in the sea. Then they seized the oars, and, more dead than alive, I turned my back to the corpses, and shielded Edward from their sight."

Here the Queen paused, and hid her visage in her hands.

"Great God!" the Duchess of Bourbon cried, "is is possible to witness such events and exist?"

"Ah, Pierre de Brézé," cried his friend George Chastellain, embracing him, "let all former heroes, let all the knights of old rise from their graves to do thee homage! For where in ancient or in modern history shall be found more glorious exploits than thine, friend of my heart, flower of chivalry, champion of fallen greatness!"

"Relate yourself, Messire Pierre," the Queen then said, "in what a marvellous manner you effected our escape." Whereupon the Sénéchal thus spoke:

"Those wretches had bound us with cords, which were themselves fastened to an iron hook, fixed so firmly at our end of the boat, that no hope of deliverance seemed to exist. Nevertheless, urged on and fortified by desperation, and conscious of the prodigious strength with which God hath endowed me, I set myself with all my might to pull at the cord held by the said hook. After long and fruitless efforts, at last I felt it giving way. And then I contrived to extricate myself from my shackles without visibly shaking them off, so that when I chose I could set myself free; and under favour of the obscurity, I in a like manner liberated my companion, and whispered to him to be in readiness at a given signal to cast off the cords, spring on the rowers, master the oars, seize their weapons, slay or thrust them overboard. When the dawning light revealed the presence of the Queen and the Prince, I doubted how to act—the peril of oversetting the boat in the projected struggle was so imminent; but the despaired look of her majesty resolved me on that point; and I thank God the issue was successful, albeit fraught with incredible dangers. We threw overboard the two corpses, and set to rowing with all our might. For seven weary hours we tossed in the Gulf of Solway. Towards evening the wind changed, and drove the boat with terrific speed back to the coast of Scotland, and on to a sandbank at the mouth of the bay of Kirkcudbright, on the opposite side to the town, the waves beating against it with so great violence, that each moment we thought to see it dashed to pieces. Howsoever, we neared the shore sufficiently that, leaping into the sea, I could walk knee-deep in the water and the sand, carrying the Queen on my back; and Barville conveyed in like manner the Prince. I leave your Grace to judge what a *Te Deum laudamus* I sang when we once more stood on dry land."

"Alas," the Duchess exclaimed, "Sir Knight, the bravest of the brave, what words can justly sound your praise, or testify sufficient compassion for this sweet Queen! for although she hath escaped with her life, never assuredly before had fortune brought a princess of her high rank into such frightful perils. If a book were to be written on the vicissitudes of royal and unfortunate ladies, she would be found to exceed them all in calamity. Say, fair cousin, gentle Queen Margaret, what followed that unlooked-for landing on an inhospitable coast."

"Madame," the Queen replied, "we remained *perdu* in a small hamlet in a desolate district, where the people were so simple that we feared not discovery. They could not believe any one to be a queen except they saw her with a crown on her head and a sceptre in her hand. I would fain have parleyed with the Queen Regent; but the Sieur de Brézé reported to me that my presence in Scotland occasioned no small uneasiness to my cousin Marie, who offered to furnish me the means of repairing to the fortress of

Bamborough; where I rejoined my dear ladies and faithful servants, and thence sailed for Flanders, whither in a good hour God's providence hath led me."

Then the Duchess embraced the Queen with great affection, and with many tender speeches and tears parted with her. The last part of the evening Messire Chastellain spent with her majesty. She willed him to seat himself near her, and took pleasure for some hours to discourse with him of her troubles. "Sir," she said, "you see a lady well-nigh distraught with grief, and on whom fortune hath inflicted cruel wrongs;" and bewailing herself more than was her wont, she wrung her hands with such excess of sorrow that his own tears could not be restrained for very pity of her case; which perceiving, she said, "Sir, if you are at leisure for such devices, I beseech you write for my consolation a little treatise on the inconstancy of fortune, setting forth mine own calamities, with those of other noble ladies who have suffered signal adversities."

"Madame," he replied, "since I had the honour of conversing with your majesty at L'Ecluse, and learnt some part of your unexampled misfortunes, I have purposed to compose a poem, entitled 'The Temple of Ruined Greatness.' The great master Boccacio planned and began a similar one for the commemoration of the calamities of great men, from Adam to King John of France. And methinks, great Queen, that in the frontispiece of my designed temple shall be seen the tomb of the great poet, beside which your majesty shall stand, calling on him to awake and record your misfortunes and your wrongs. He will rise at your piteous voice, and console you by the many instances he will cite of the vicissitudes of others." The Queen said this project liked her well, and then she added, "Sir, I assure you there have been moments when I was tempted by the desperation of my circumstances to convert mine own hand into an instrument of self-destruction; but happily the fear of God and His restraining grace have prevented me from so deadly a sin."

Alas, I thought, God's grace, and the sentences of Holy Writ touching the blessedness of those who mourn, and that everyone God loveth He most chastiseth, should minister more true comfort than all the temples of ruined greatness in the world. Since we have been in Flanders, I have admired that the Queen sets so much store on this sort of consolation, and the discourses of learned and ingenious persons; but I ween the air she breathed in her young years was scented with this poetic perfume, and so she finds a sweetness in it which our English minds cannot discern.

CHAPTER XXXV.

The Queen's Lady in England.

Islington, January 27th, 1464.

I CAME here eight days ago, having, by the mercy of God, made a safe journey, and a fair passage over seas from the harbour of Grace to Southampton, and thence travelled to Winchester to see the Bishop, who received me with exceeding kindness, and entertained me and my companion with his wonted hospitality. Methinks there is not a greater servant of God now in existence than this prelate. I never met with any one which could forbear to love him when once he had seen and conversed with him; and albeit he hath lived much in courts and with persons of high rank, he hath an almost incredible simplicity of manners, joined with so much good breeding and nurture as can be thought of. He was right glad to see me, and yet he said he misliked the Queen should be deprived of the services of one which so truly loved her, and who had been her companion in so many dangers.

"My lord," I replied, "your grace may assure yourself that naught could have resolved me to quit her majesty even for a time, unless her own expressed desire that I should for her ends visit this country and report to her the state of men's minds in London and other places. She deigned to say that, whereas she could rely on some of her servants touching zeal, and on others touching discretion, there were but few had both these qualities, which she saw in me. My lord, it would well-nigh have broken my heart to part with my sovereign mistress when her life was daily threatened, and her necessities pressing; but now that she is amongst her own kinsfolk, and her father hath given her the castle of Queniez, near St. Michel, with two thousand livres yearly for her maintenance, I am not so disquieted about her as heretofore."

Then his Grace asked me if it was true the Duke of Burgundy had entertained the Queen right royally at St. Pol, and treated her with great kindness. "Yea," I replied, "with exceeding good cheer; and when we left St. Pol it was under the escort of the Duke's archers; and some of his knights—the Lord de Moreuil, Messire Francisco of Ferrara, the Sieur de Renty, and Guillaume de Saux—rode by the side of the carriage all the way to Bruges. At the gate of that city, which she left disguised as a poor woman in a covered cart, the Count de Charolais met her, and in the name of his father paid her his compliments, and with as much homage as could be rendered to any queen in the world he conducted her to her lodgings; and all the time we abided in Bruges we lived at the Duke's expense, and banquets were held in honour of her majesty and the Prince. The good people of the town could not now make too much of their Highnesses. Every day they brought presents of wine and gifts very rare and precious; so mutable is the temper of men, and easily swayed by example."

"The Count of Charolais," the Bishop said, "was always, I ween, well disposed towards his English kinsfolk; but his father and himself have been often at strife, report saith."

"Ay, my lord; but your grace will be contented to learn that the Queen laboured to become a peacemaker betwixt the Duke and his son, whom she regards with no small affection. By her means, Messire Pierre de Brézé hath mediated betwixt them on disputed points, and favourable hopes are entertained of the issue."

"The Holy Trinity be praised!" my lord of Winchester exclaimed. "Blessed be the peacemakers, for they shall be called God's children! Her dear majesty hath, then, wholly forgiven her cousin of Burgundy?"

"O, my lord, she saith she hath received so many marks of affection and honour from this prince, that she fears she can never show herself thankful enough; that she hath found him the best among the good and the gentlest, and possessed withal of better sense than any one on earth."

His Grace smiled, and said again, "God be praised! To lose an enemy and gain a friend is so good a hap, that it may well cause an over-partial judgment in a grateful heart."

"When we travelled from the Low Countries to the Duchy of Barr, a detachment of Burgundian troops guarded the Queen all the way, and only turned back when she had passed the frontier of her father's dominions. The King of Sicily was so moved by this generous behaviour to his daughter, that he wrote a letter to the Duke of Burgundy, his ancient foe, wherein he gave him many thanks, and declared he could not have expected, and did not merit, such attentions."

"Glory be to God!" the Bishop cried; "one good action leads to another; like when one throweth a stone into the water, each circlet formeth a wider one, so each proof of good will betwixt men reacheth others, and goodness widens its sphere. But, I pray you, gentle Lady Margaret, or rather Dame Agnes Clere,—since it is under that name you disguise yourself,—how was her majesty received in her own land and by her own people?"

"Warmly and tenderly," I replied. "Her kinsfolk lavished on her gifts and endearments, and the peasants and townspeople acclaimed her joyfully. Flowers were scattered on her path; bells were rung and songs composed in honour of the daughter of King René. But, O my lord, how sad were these rejoicings, how bitter these greetings to King Henry's wife! She bore herself loftily and proudly; she smiled, but in an unsmiling fashion. On her father's bosom she wept abundantly, and during their short interview I think she poured out her heart's hoarded sufferings in that paternal one which loves her so well. But his majesty was soon forced to leave her; he is involved in a load of cares and troubles touching the disputes betwixt King Lewis and his feudatories, of which Monseigneur Jean, his son, is one. But at the Castle of Vaudémont, and in Monseigneur de Calabre's palace, and at Amboise, where her aunt, the widowed Queen Marie, is lying sick, she concealed her emotions under a cold severe aspect, which chilled some and pained others of her kinsfolk. The day I took leave of her majesty, she said to me, 'When you see the Bishop of Winchester, tell him to pray for me.' Therefore, my lord, to move you the more assiduously to besiege Heaven for her I will relate somewhat touching the suffering of that noble but ulcered soul. Some time before I came away she spoke thus: 'God forgive me for what I feel when I see Yolande with her lord in so great happiness and glee that nothing can be compared to it. For nineteen years her wedded life hath flowed in an even current of contentment which seemeth almost incredible. Contrast, I pray you, her fate with mine. Ferry is noble, valiant, and loves her well. No contrary fate hath barred her from the enjoyment of that love. My lord is more than noble: he is royal. If Ferry de Lorraine is handsome, King Henry is more so; if he is brave, so is my lord. He hath never shrunk from danger or avoided it, save when fell disease hath smitten him. His natural courage is indomitable, shown in endurance like in action. If Yolande is beloved by her husband, I dare to say I am worshipped by mine. But see she lives in the sunshine of conjugal affection lavished upon her each day and each hour. If her lord goes to the wars, they are not civil brawls, and he returns crowned with laurels. My gentle lord is hunted from one hiding-place to another like a wild beast; and lands and seas lie between us, so that I cannot hear sometimes for months what hath befallen him. And when have I ever rested peacefully in his arms? When have I even for a few days together enjoyed certain content? When hath the long thirst for happiness which consumes me been slaked? When shall it be slaked? If I had wedded a deformed or a wicked prince, or married one I hated, my misfortunes would be comprehensible; but all that should be sweet in my life turns to gall. The loves which fill my heart breed poison. My son! O Meg! my poor faithful Meg! God only knoweth the suffering which maternal tenderness causeth me! Look at my sister with her children. Her fair-haired René, her little Yolande, the small Marie, the babe Amélie, the infant Ferry; she smiles upon them all—kisses, caresses, chides with careless fondness. All are dear to her, all are winsome; a light whipping hath been the worst trouble of their young lives. Think you her love for these children is the same impassioned vehement love

as mine for my one beautiful royal boy? For me painful thoughts mix with each mother's joy. If I kiss his noble forehead, I think of the crown which rebels seek to deprive him of; if I hear his gay laughter, of the day when assassins were like for ever to stifle his voice; if I see him eat, I call to mind the hour when he vainly hungered for a morsel of food; if he showeth his early wit, youthful courage, and greatness of soul, then I call to mind the speeches of our enemies. "If," say they, "the heir of Lancaster was a deformed imp or a fool, he might be suffered to live; but seeing the promise in him of future greatness, he must perish." This is the direst thought of all; but besides dagger-wounds, my heart endureth a thousand needle-pricks. Hast noticed the rich attire of these young Vaudémonts, these children of Lorraine as they be styled, and how mean Edward's garb shows by the side of all this splendour? And then Yolande, poor simple soul, offers to bestow on him the like gear as her son's, and says sisters should share all things alike, and that she oweth all her joys to me. Can she share with me her untroubled nights, her peaceful days, her light heart, a husband's daily company? Nay, nay; sisters share not alike. God maketh His sun to rise on the evil and on the good, and His rain on the just and on the unjust; but the sunshine of happiness beameth not alike on His creatures, and the winds of adversity blow not on them with the same rigour. One sister of the same house is submerged in grief, whilst another basks in prosperity.'
— My lord, what could I say? what comfort give to this afflicted lady? Hope? Alas! fevered, restless hoping is the cancer which consumes her life. Resignation? Ah! those which have learnt like your grace and others less holy and less learned than yourself, but yet scholars in the same school, to love God not with

a distant homage, but a personal ardent love, find in the worshipful adoration of His will consolations unspeakable in the darkest clouds of calamity. But to those which with their whole feeble strength repel His mighty hand there is no more bitter speech than to bid them to be resigned."

The Bishop sighed, and said, "This noble lady's prayers have ever been akin to Rachel's, when she cried, 'Give me children, or else I die.' With this unresigned and passionate persistency she asked for this son; and now she cries to God, 'Give this child a crown, or else I die.' These threatening petitions seldom are blest. May the Lord Jesu comfort her now! for the last news of the King must have needs plunged her into despair, as far as this world is concerned."

"Heavens! my lord," I exclaimed, frighted at these words, "what hath befallen his majesty?"

"Alas," the reverend prelate replied, "I feared you were ignorant of this last hap. I would fain have had better news to greet you with. Did you not hear the King's capture spoken of at Southampton?"

"He is taken, then? O, my poor mistress! my sweet Queen! God help you when you receive these tidings. Nay, my lord, I heard naught at Hampton, for I drove straightway in a hired conveyance from the port to your palace. O God, I did not think to hear the King was taken. I pray your grace to tell me how it came to pass."

"He was at Waddington Hall, where, on the approach of any strangers, he had been used to retire into a concealed chamber, where he was safe, until a monk of Abingdon discovered the secret passage to it, and revealed the same to Sir James Harrington, which, with his servants, invaded the house and arrested his grace in the name of the present king." The Bishop spoke with more composure than I could see he inwardly possessed, for the tears stood in his eyes.

"Where is he now?" I asked in a dejected tone, for verily I felt utterly cast down.

"In the Tower," the good prelate said. "In sooth, Lady Margaret, this holy monarch's, this dear prince's calamities are so repeated and so great that they work in me a reverent belief that he hath been appointed by God to suffer the penalty of others' crimes. We wit well from Holy Scripture that the sins of the fathers are visited on the children, even unto the fourth generation; and what so like as that this pure, saintly, and innocent victim carries in his person the chastisements which others have earned from the Divine Justice?"

"Alas, must the innocent," I exclaimed, "suffer for the guilty?"

"O daughter," I was answered, "is not the Passion of our Lord a reply to this query? Shall the disciple be above the Master, and not rather tread in His footsteps and be conformed to Him in this life, so that he may be with Him in His glory? I thank God that this sweet prisoner, my holy and dear example, who of all men doth most need to hold this faith, doth so cordially embrace it, that when some days since I fell at his feet weeping—"

"O my lord, my lord!" I exclaimed, "you have seen him."

"As soon as I heard he was at the Tower I went straightway to London and to the door of his lodgings, and none dared refuse me admittance. If there had been any to witness that meeting, methinks they should have deemed William of Winchester to be the hapless prisoner and King Henry the consoler. Yet his injuries had been of no common sort. All show of old respect, of reverence for an anointed king, of pity for fallen greatness, had this time been lacking in his treatment. Mounted on a sorry nag, his legs tied to his stirrups, with an insulting placard on his royal shoulders, he was brought to London, and — yea, I will tell you the worst, Lady Margaret; for if others informed you of it, I fear you should offend God by the utterance of such words as indignant passion too often exhales. Look at that crucifix, daughter; yea, take it in your hand. Think on the manner the Lord God was used in the streets of Jerusalem. Think of His blows and revilings; and then, armed by such showings, list to the recital of His true disciple's entry into London. The Earl of Warwick — stay, daughter; no flashing of the eye, no clenching of the hand; pray God to forgive him who hath been so unhappy as to commit so grievous a sin, — the Earl of Warwick met the King at Islington; and after issuing a proclamation forbidding all persons to show him any respect, he led him three times round the pillory as if he had been a common felon, crying aloud, 'Treason, treason!' and 'Behold the traitor!' A poor man which stood in the crowd, and which hath since discoursed with me, said with many tears, 'I warrant you, my lord, the good Saviour must have looked on the Jews as this our poor King did on his enemies that day.' When a brutal person, stepping out of the crowd, struck him in the face, he rebuked him with these only words: 'Forsooth and forsooth, you do foully to smite the Lord's anointed.' Yea, weep, gentle lady, for the full heart needs relief in these moments wherein those we do love and honour fall a prey to the evil passions of men. But, good Lord, after a little thought, we become reconciled to good men's sufferings, and are more ready to weep over their persecutors than themselves."

"Yea, yea, right reverend Father," I cried, when I could speak.

"I grieve not for that holy saint the King, but O, the Queen!" he gravely answered. "God knoweth there is not a greater well-wisher to her majesty than my unworthy self; but if the future could be unfolded to our eyes, dame Margaret — if we could look into that next world, in which so many mysteries shall be solved, we should, it may be, perceive that the heaviest strokes of adversity are instruments of a great mercy towards the soul which they appear to sift like wheat. Cease not to pray that by these means it may be cleansed from present alloy, and come out pure at the last day."

I joined my hands and bowed my head; for thinking of the Queen's sorrow pierced me to the heart despite this good counsel.

"The Prince, my sweet pupil, gives tokens and hope of future excellence?" the Bishop said, seeking, I ween, to rouse me from my dejection. I assured him that his grace was most toward and gracious in all his actions and behaviour. And for an example thereof I related that at one of the banquets at Bruges given by the nobles of Burgundy in honour of the Queen, the water for the ablution of hands was offered first to her majesty; upon which she called to herself the Count of Charolais, praying him to come and wash with her. But he refused to come forward, and would have the water next offered to the Prince of Wales, who of his own accord, and in the most pretty wise imaginable, drew back, and said he could by no means wash unless his fair cousin the count would wash with him. And in a childish, caressing manner, when the count waved his hand and denied his request, tried with all his little strength to pull to himself his tall burly kinsman and constrain him to it. When he could not succeed, and the truly noble Prince of Burgundy declared it was but loss of time, for that he should never consent to equal himself to the Prince of Wales, our little prince said, " But, fair cousin, these honours are not due to us from you; neither ought precedency to be given in your father's kingdom to such poor and unfortunate persons as we are." The Count de Charolais replied, " Unfortunate though you may be, you are, for all that, the son of the King of England; whereas I am only the son of a ducal sovereign, which is not so high a vocation as that of a king."

" Alas, pardon me, my lord, if my tears flow again when I think that the hopes which I entertained up to this hour, that at St. Omer the Duke of Burgundy and the King Lewis should have obtained the King's restoration, are now dashed to the earth."

" No foreign aid, Dame Margaret, could unseat the Yorkist dynasty, even if King Henry was at large. The people love him with a secret, tender, faithful love; but the great earl, the most powerful nobles, and foremost of all, the citizens of London, hold the throne in their hands; and for the nonce the present King is the sovereign of their choice."

" And how," I said, " have you fared at his hands, my lord? for I see by your recent visit to King Henry that you disguise not your fidelity to him."

He smiled, and replied,

" At first I was in great dedignation with King Edward, and my friends obliged me to fly into secret corners for fear of his anger; but I have been lately restored to my flock and to his favour."

" You have the art, my lord, to win the hearts of the

most adverse, and to command the esteem of the most opposed parties."

"If this be true," he replied, "it is an artless art; for it consists in so much rusticity, that I use no disguises with any one, and try as far as in me lies to be my Lord's messenger to all. God hath not set me as a judge over contending parties, but rather to move all to the observance of His law and the practice of virtue. Our holy King commends this moderation, and is glad I can plead with those now in his place for poor oppressed persons and his loved College of Eton. 'Ah, Master William,' quoth he, in that more comfortable than sad interview of last week, 'I pray thee, if thou lovest me, befriend Eton.' And when I told him that the Pope's bull for its dissolution, which had been obtained by false representations at Rome, had been revoked—thanks to Master Westbury's courageous efforts—he smiled with his wonted sweetness and said, 'St. John, but this is good tidings, Master William. I would be led round the pillory more than three times if that could save Eton.'"

After some further discourse with this holy man, which strengthened me not a little at the outset of a mighty and perilous office to be discharged in behalf of my lady the Queen, and furnished guidance in my dealings with others, I craved the Bishop's benison, and retired to rest. On the morrow some further talk passed betwixt us, and I thanked God, which had suffered me to see this apostolic man, who lives in a palace like a poor person himself, albeit hospitable and free to others. Amongst other things he showed me his plans for the erection of his designed College of St. Magdalen at Oxford, which he had intended to make the noblest and richest structure in the learned world, with stately towers and lofty pinnacles, and a most tunable and melodious peal of bells; and the scholars thereof to be persons of good morals and manners, and an aptitude for learning which should make them famous men of letters as well as religious men. Master Tyborde, who was with us in the library, exclaimed,

"Ay, my lord, when will this all come to pass which you had so generously conceived and so admirably designed?"

The Bishop smiled, and answered,

"Like other and yet greater things, good master Tyborde, when God pleaseth, how He pleaseth, and not at all if it shall so please Him."

"Your grace is the most resigned man in the world," said the other; and then the Bishop replied,

"Nay, I have a secret, Master William, by which I have in all things always my will, and this is no other than making God's will mine; and so nothing can happen to displease me, save to see Him offended."

Then condescending to the curiosity of a seely woman, these great and scholarly men exhibited to my amazed sight a book not written with a pen by a man's hand, but in some kind of manner stamped, which is called printing. One Caxton in London hath imported this new art from Germany; and the Bishop told me, if it extended and should come into general use, it would multiply books and diffuse learning to an incredible degree. This book which he showed me was Cicero's work *De Senectute*, done into English, and was dedicated to himself by the ingenious contriver of this singular mode of writing. I said jestingly, that if books should multiply so fast, I should look in mine old age to have myself a library. The Bishop laughed, and said what he most feared printing should effect would be to turn ladies from good housewives into

readers of romances and idle tales, and that some
check should be devised to keep them from it. His
friend Anthony Woodville, he told me, spent whole
days in the press at Westminster, and the present king
had been to see it. This made me ask him if it was
true that the so-called king had married Lady Gray.
He told me there was no doubt of it, albeit no open
acknowledgment thereof had yet been made; that the
espousals had taken place at Grafton, near to Stony
Stratford, none being present save the spouse, the
bride, her mother the duchess, the priest, two gentlewomen, and a young man to help the priest to sing.

"But report saith that the so-called king hath been
twice betrothed before—and in the last place to Elisabeth Lucy."

"It is the common report," the Bishop answered.
"I pray God it may not to be true, for then these
ladies have been grievously injured."

"Bessie Woodville married to the usurper!" I exclaimed. "Verily, my lord, I begin to think they do
not err which say the Duchess of Bedford is a witch."

He smiled.

"Verily, Dame Margaret, genealogies affirm she
counts amongst her ancestresses the fairy Melusina,
and hath inherited all her bewitching arts. In my
opinion that great fairy was a lady of incomparable
cunning and seductive manners; and fairies and
witches of this sort are not like to be lacking here and
there in this poor world as long as it lasts."

Aught more severe than these words I could not draw
from the good Bishop's lips. I had more ado to be tem-
perate in my resentment towards this new-fangled queen
than against more guilty persons. But I could not ex-
hale my wrath before his grace, and so held my peace;
and on the morrow of that day travelled to London.

CHAPTER XXXVI.

Dame Katharine Bugdon.

To behold again, after many years' absence, a once-familiar scene—be it a lone cottage on a bare heath, or a crowded and populous city—worketh either a pleasing sadness or a profound melancholy in a reflective mind. But how greatly doth this feeling increase when the memory of tragical events, the loss of many friends, or of those which either natural affinity of blood or a more than common affection have made more dear than ordinary friends, is added to it! As I rode through the streets of London, these oppressive vapours swelled in my breast like a gathering cloud; and when at last I reached the house at Cheapside where I was to lodge, they broke loose, and resolved themselves into a plentiful rain of tears. It was with Katharine Strange, the wife of Mr. Bugdon, that I was to spend the time I should be in London. She had once belonged to the Queen's household, who had given her a portion, and procured her father's consent to her marriage. Dame Katharine had not, like so many others, lost the memory of her majesty's benefits, and would have gone through fire and water to serve her grace. She folded me in her arms when I arrived, and clung to me, weeping; and when she had conducted me to my chamber, we kissed again, and then cried afresh, and for some time could not converse without new bursts of tears. Howsoever, when the

first emotion of this meeting was past, I marvelled to
see how young and sprightly this little lady seemed.
The years which had set on me the stamp of middle
age had passed lightly over her pretty head. She was
little changed since the time when she was called at
court "Mischievous Kate;" and when, after I had
taken some rest and refreshment, we began to talk of
past and present hopes, I soon found she was the same
loving, wilful, passionate damsel as of yore, when she
proved the torment of twenty lovers, and the plague
of all her friends, by her odd humours. Not to be
fond of Katharine Strange had been an impossible
thing; but patience was a needful quality for her
admirers of both sexes. I had no small curiosity to
see the husband which had for nearly ten years endured
her varying moods; but he was not in London when I
arrived. Even in our first conversation I perceived
that we should be like to quarrel on some points. She
had the most critical spirit imaginable; and even
touching the King and Queen her bold tongue must
wag. It was always with her, "Wherefore this? and
wherefore that?" "Marry! what a witless thing this
is!" or, "Good Lord! how should such a mad scheme
succeed?" or, "Is the Queen demented, that she
should do in this wise or in that?" And then she
must needs take offence at the King's patience, and
call it tameness.

"He was served right by the Earl of Warwick," she
cried; "for if a king doth not resent injuries, he
deserves to have them heaped upon him."

I was so angered that I would fain have given her a
box on the ear; but I perceived she was all the while
crying with vexation, which made me pardon her
tongue. And when she ended her speech thus: "Men
are wont to say, 'enough to provoke a saint.' For

my part, I declare saints are enough to provoke poor common persons," I could not choose but smile. Then she began to commend the Yorkists:

"Lord, they do as far surpass our friends in wisdom as the children of this world the children of the light, as saith the gospel; and yet I can neither call the red-rosers children of light, for such stupid blind persons never existed in my opinion. For now, I pray you, why was not the Prince of Wales long before now betrothed to Margaret of York or Isabel Neville, and then there should have been a hope of peace? If the Queen—God save her!—had, with all her wit, but possessed one half of the skill of the witches of Grafton, I warrant you matters should not have come to this pass. Ah! good Lady Meg, think you, when she is crowned, that that brave Queen Bessie will call to mind the day when you sued her mistress to portion her that she might marry John Gray?"

"It was at Dame Maud Everingham's request that I made that petition," I replied; "for, I promise you, I never liked or admired that placid lady."

"O, for my part," quoth Kate, "I like her cunning. Verily, it doth honour to our sex. Come, you must needs commend that fine speech of hers to her kingly wooer, 'My liege, I know I am not good enough to be your queen,' and the rest of it."

"O, pardon me," I answered impatiently; "this should be all very fine, if we had not all our lives known Bessie Woodville and her sweet humility. I never thought but that she was virtuous; but I thank God that is not so rare a thing that one must needs throw up one's hands in admiration thereat. And as to lealty and gratitude, she showeth herself as ignorant of these sentiments as if they did not exist."

"Well, they are out of fashion, dear Dame Margery;

and Bessie was always constant to that divinity, if to no other allegiance. But all this time there are folks which say she is not consoled for the loss of her first husband, and doth sacrifice her buried love to this Yorkist wedlock for the sole welfare of her children."

"Ay; and I doubt not of her fine brothers also, which but a short time ago professed to be King Henry's most faithful subjects."

"I' faith," Kate cried, "they will soon feather their nests, these accomplished gentlemen, if report is to be believed, and in a right Woodvillish manner. Of all the sacraments, matrimony is I ween, the one most prized by Madame Jacquetta's offspring. You are fresh from foreign parts, my lady, and your wit is, I doubt not, sharpened by the air of France; so now, I pray you, guess who is to be the bride of the eldest of these sweet brothers?"

"Is it Isminia Scales?" I said. "She hath more wealth than any marriageable damsel I wot of."

"Ah! the younger brother, Master Anthony, is to have her," Kate replied. "But the eldest hath a more noble ambition. He cannot stoop to wed a chit of thirteen. Nothing but a duchess will serve his new Highness."

"A duchess!" I said. "What duchess is there widowed and rich which he can marry?"

"Well, I marvel you are so dull. I pray you should not the Dowager Duchess of Norfolk be a seemly bride for a young gentleman of the Melusinian lineage?"

"This is foolish jesting," I said petulantly.

"Nay, but I verily promise you," cried Kate, "it is no jest at all. The gentleman is wise—the lady fond. He was eighteen not long ago, and she only just turned eighty. Nay, look not so incredulous. I warrant you this diabolical marriage is no invention of mine, but a thing very like to happen, and which is openly talked of at Grafton. Since the gentle Bessie's spousals 'tis an admirable thing how fair her sisters have grown in the eyes of the Yorkist nobles. Those tocherless damsels had been some years out of their teens, and none had thought of doing them worship in the way of marriage; but, Lord! they are not now numerous enough for these good suitors. Lord Maltravers will have Mistress Margaret; Lord Essex sighs for Jacquetta; his Grace of Buckingham for Katharine; Lord Herbert's heir wooes pretty Mistress Mary."

"So the tide turns," I said sadly. "God's will be done; but of all things the most bitter to witness is ingratitude."

When, after this converse with Kate, I was alone in my chamber, I repented of my irritable words and sharp resentment touching the new so-called queen. The remembrance of my promise to Jeanne at Nantes to aim at perfection came remorsefully to my mind. Alas! how much outward changes affect the soul and make us misdoubt the progress we seemed to have made in virtue! When I was following the Queen amidst great afflictions and dangers, I was in nowise tempted to those venial sins which thrive not in the soil of weighty calamities, but rather in the daily chafing of small contradictions. The spectacle of her courage and daring, her vehement resentments and pathetic sorrows, the virtues of several of her followers, my grief for my dear father's dishonoured—but O, how honourable!—death, raised me above small evils and temptations. I did not hate as the Queen did, and to curse an enemy would have been an impossible thing to me. . But when I was at London (and here I speak not of that first day only, but of all the time I remained there), and had to witness day by day the meanness of some, the treacheries of others, the abandonment of a fallen cause by those which had sworn on the Blessed Sacrament to be leal to it; when I heard outrageous falsehood uttered with shameless audacity, and those who had ruined the Queen and her adherents seeking to blacken their fame by foul slanders; then, as I have not the gay spirit to laugh like Kate at their crimes, I find it difficult to forbear sharp and scornful language. It is not the ignorant brutality of the mob nor the open violence of lawless men which stirs up angry passion in my soul, but the wise malice, the covert attacks, the well-devised inventions of insidious foes, whose triumphant villany is gilded by specious pretexts and dissembled with profound cunning. This none but a saint could meet with equability.

Another source of trouble to me at that time lay in the uncertainty of right and wrong touching certain matters. Till then the path of duty had always been clear to me and evident. To follow my mistress in her perilous journeys; to minister to her comfort; to soften, cheer, or at the least console her in her troubles, had been my chief, constant, and lawful end. But when I found myself concealed in the city under an assumed name, yet known to many as a secret mover in their majesties' righteous, but, as some deemed it, desperate quarrel; when I had to go with messages to persons whose deaths might be occasioned by the receipt of them if discovered; when others employed by me as messengers were arrested and tortured, to force them to reveal who were the Queen's agents in England, like poor Mark the shoemaker, who was pinched to death because he would not betray my name,—then I was sorely pricked in conscience, and sometimes wrung my hands in anguish, being uncertain how to act. The good Bishop of Winchester, albeit he would gladly have shed his blood to procure King Henry's restoration, misliked these secret dealings, not that they in anywise partook, he said, of the nature of treason, but because they exposed men's lives with little or no hope of a good issue. But I was the Queen's servant, and what was I to do when I received by any certain channels her commands to go hither or thither and communicate with persons she designed to me? More than once I craved her license to return to France, but was denied; for these private manœuvrings, which I build little on, her grace highly esteemed. They were not always without danger. This reminds me that one day Kate came to my chamber in a great passion, her eyes flashing like a pussy-cat's in the dark, her hair escaped from her head-gear and bristling in all directions.

"I am resolved," she said, stamping her foot, "to leave Mr. Bugdon's house."

"Heyday!" I exclaimed; "why Kate; what hath he done!"

"Refused to admit a person who produced a token which showed he came from Queniez. He may shut his door on the Queen's friends, but he shall shut it on me also, will he or nill he, for I am one of them; and I vow I will not stay here another day, but go to my father at Islington; and you shall come with me, Lady Margery. This untoward, ungentle, cruel man shall tarry by himself in his great dull house, and shut its door on whom he pleases; but he shall never so much as see or hear of me again. I thank God I am not a

Yorkist. He may when I am gone, an it pleases him, stick a white rose in his doublet, ay, and in his bonnet too, for aught I care. Only I won't see it."

"Come, come, sweet Kate." I said. "Prithee be reasonable. This poor husband of thine—"

"My poor husband! Marry! is it come to this? He is to be pitied for being my husband. Well, your ladyship may stay behind to console him, if such is your pleasure. Was ever a woman so ill-treated? I perceive that fidelity to their majesties is an offence in your eyes, Lady Margaret; and you like that Yorkist man Bugdon better than your poor friend."

"O Kate," I cried, "listen to reason."

"O, if it is reason to be mean; if it is reason to be ungrateful; if it is reason to curse and swear at one's wife because she loves the King and the Queen—"

Then I could not forbear to smile; for this cursing swearing husband was the most good-humoured, quiet gentleman imaginable, and endured with the philosophy of Socrates the assaults of his wife's tongue. A low knock was heard at my door; and when I said "Come in," lo and behold, this violent man stood in the passage, his round complacent face shining with kindliness. Before he or I could speak, Kate began:

"Sir, I am not going to stay here to be reproached and foully entreated; nor will I abandon Lady Margaret, because forsooth she wishes well to your rightful sovereigns. I am going to Islington."

"O Lord, sweet wife, if thou hadst gone thither as often as thou hast threatened it I should be more affrighted; but the boy which cried wolf—"

Then the rage of the little mistress had no bounds.

"I am not a boy, and I am not a wolf," she cried amidst her sobs. "I wish I was a boy, for then I could not have been your wife; and if I had been a wolf—"

"Thou wouldst have eat him up instead of marrying him," I said, which made her suddenly laugh; but she hid her face in her kerchief, that we might think she was weeping. Mr. Bugdon seized the opportunity, and said,

"Lady Margaret, one Hawkins hath been here—"

"Ay," groaned Kate.

"Heavens!" quoth I. "Well, I know who he is. We must needs use great caution in his regard, for I have been advised it is by no means certain that he is a reliable person."

"There, Kate," cried Mr. Bugdon, trying to pull her hands from her face. "Did I not tell thee I was frightened to let him in? and before the words had hardly passed my lips, thou didst bounce out of the study in such a tantram as never was seen. Belike thou hadst been at Islington by this time."

"O yes, Mr. Bugdon; it is a well-known thing you can always turn the tables on me, and always make yourself out to be in the right. It should be more like a generous person, which you call yourself—"

"Lord, Katy, when did I call myself so?" he exclaimed, with an amused countenance.

"And if you did not," she rejoined, pouting, "others say it of you. There's Lady Margaret there, who pities you because you married me."

"O Kate," I cried, "how can you tell so great a—I know not how to call it?"

"Well, you called him my poor husband, which cometh to the same thing."

This made Mr. Bugdon shake his sides with laughter; and Kate ran down the stairs, though he tried to bar her passage. I began then to perceive that if she had been less unreasonable he would not have been one-half so happy. One man's meat is another's poison. This day's dispute was a sample of their conjugal differences. They are well-matched in the main; for his placid good-humour and her inflammable vivacity, like unto two opposite substances which fizz and make a pleasing draught when joined together, by force of contrast produced an agreeable result. They were always of one mind on one point, and that was in their kindness to me; and also despite her accusations, in devotion to their majesties.

It was well Mr. Bugdon had evinced prudence touching that said Hawkins; for he was soon afterwards seized, and on being racked in the Tower, confessed that he had attempted to borrow money for the Queen from the wealthy knight Sir Thomas Cook; and though he had refused to lend it, for not having disclosed Hawkins' designs therein he hath been accused of treason, and fined eight thousand marks.

In the course of the year I received a letter from the Queen, written soon after she had learnt the King's captivity. I think her father encouraged her to support this trouble with greater resignation than was her wont in trials wherein she was compelled to remain passive. Sir John Fortescue let me also to wit that for the present she was more calm, and fixed all her thoughts on the time when her son should be of an age to act in his father's name.

"She knoweth," he wrote, "that there is no possibility at this day for any new emprise; and for my part I thank God for this impossibility, which affords opportunity for my lord the prince to be exercised in learning and trained to habits of good nurture, which are uneasily acquired in a mode of life full of perils, hairbreadth scapes, and adventures unbefitting his young years. Howsoever, I deny not that he hath profited by the early teachings of adversity; for when I compare his age, I thank God he doth far exceed any I see in this country. Blessed be God, as he groweth in stature, he also increaseth in all virtuous dispositions; but he is now of an age wherein discipline and assiduity to his school are of import to his advancement. I have begun to write for his highness's use a digest of the laws of England, wherewith to exercise him when he is older in sad thought and reasonable studies. He inherits much of his father's gentleness and fondness for study; but light poesy, martial pageants and field sports, are like most to engage his fancy in this country, where men are as a rule, I think, more witty than wise, more brave than constant, more quick than profound. I pray you, my good lady—as I doubt not you can do much towards it—to dissuade the Queen from any rash attempts; for who knoweth that any untoward step should not prove fatal to the King, who, I doubt not, even in his dungeon finds a heaven in his sacred thoughts and virtuous resignation. The minstrels of this country, and yet more the Provençal bards—troubadours, I should say—excite her grace by their songs to take up arms, and exhort their king to espouse her quarrel. At a banquet at Aix his favourite poet thus addressed the King of Sicily:

> 'Arouse thee, arouse thee, King René,
> Nor let sorrow thy spirits beguile;
> Thy daughter, the spouse of King Henry,
> Now weeps, now implores with a smile;'

and much more of the like stuff. But that poor monarch's affairs are in so distracted a condition, that one should as wisely ask him to invade the moon as England. Even the Sénéchal sees this to be true, and, like a good and a brave man as he is, hath resolved to quit the Queen, and resume the service of his natural sovereign, the French king. God reward him for his faithful sticking to her majesty in a needful time, and his no less faithful retirement when his presence at her small court is best dispensed with. Heaven speed him wherever he goeth! If anything could cause me to esteem the fooleries of knight-errantry, it would be the gallant spirit of the Sieur de Brézé, which hath been nurtured by its tenets. I commend myself to your ladyship, and very heartily desire to hear of your welfare."

When tidings reached London that the so-called new Queen had been publicly proclaimed at Reading, and great honour done to her even by the Earl of Warwick, Kate was so angered that she would not eat or speak all the day. At the last she burst forth:

"Well, thank God there is one person in England more displeased and melancholy than I this day."

"Who is it, sweetheart," Mr. Bugdon asked.

"Why, proud Cis," she answered, "the rose of Raby, Madame the King's mother. She is almost mad, I hear, to be forced to give place to Master Richard Woodville's daughter."

"Ay; I remember he was the handsomest man in England, and the Duchess Jacquetta likewise an exceedingly handsome gentlewoman," said Kate's luckless lord.

"My patience!" she exclaimed; "it is enough, sir, that a woman should have long yellow hair falling down to her knees for you to think her handsome! But handsome or not, that pair could never go beyond seas till now, or her brother, the Count Lewis of St. Pol, should have slain them; and a good thing it should have been."

"Alas," I said to them, "what think you I have heard to-day? The Count of Charolais, after all that passed at Bruges not so much as one year ago, hath answered the so-called King's request that his new wife's foreign kinsfolk should attend her coronation by an assent. It makes my blood boil to think on it. Before long we shall hear, I ween, of a so-called Prince of Wales; and I warrant you this bold prince will not so much as wash his fingers in the same basin as that urchin."

"Master Dominic," Kate said, "hath promised the usurper that Mistress Bessie shall have a son. He is his favourite astrologer, and the most unsupportable old idiot in the whole world."

There our talk ended; but when five months later the birth of the so-called Queen's daughter took place, Kate was so pleased at the discomfiture of Master Dominic, that it made her quite merry.

"Ah, Lady Margery," she cried out, "my Lady Peacock, as we used to call her, that long-necked Isabel Butler, which hath shifted her allegiance, but not her lodgings, hath not, it seems, lost her sharp tongue. Ah me! I love her for that retort."

"What retort, sweet Kate?" I asked, well disposed to be entertained; for I was light of heart because the usurper had not a son.

"This one," quoth she. "Master Dominic craved to stand nigh to the door of the Lady Bessie's chamber, because he was resolved to be the first to spread the news of the birth of a prince. So when he heard the new-born child a-crying, he put his visage close to the keyhole, and asked, 'What hath her grace?' Then Lady Isabel's dulcet voice—don't you call its melodious tones to mind, Lady Margery?—cried through the hole, 'Whatsoever the Queen's grace hath here within, sure 'tis a fool she hath standing without.' The poor man ran away, and hath not been seen at the palace since."

"'Tis a like speech for the Lady Isabel to have made," I said, laughing. "Persons are more constant to their humours than to their affections."

CHAPTER XXXVII.

Warwick Lane.

IN the year 1467, when I was still at Dame Katharine's house, where, after the first few weeks of my stay, I lodged and tabled, not as a guest, but a pensioner, I met with a singular accident, which I will now relate. Having one day gone to the Blackfriars, to speak to a monk who was about to travel into France, and had offered to carry letters for me to Verdun, I was returning alone on foot through the City; for on these occasions I would neither expose myself to be betrayed, nor bring others into danger by procuring anyone to accompany me. I lost my way somewhere near to St. Paul's Church, and found myself in a street I was unacquainted with, and in the midst of a great confusion of persons coming and going, or else standing about gaping at the passers-by. Many of them wore red jackets, and others were carrying huge pieces of meat on prongs. I heard some one behind me say, " I swear this part of the town is naught but a bear-garden since this great earl hath returned! From St. Paul's to Newgate-street the taverns are filled with ox-flesh from his kitchens." Then it crossed my mind this must be Warwick-lane, and for more reasons than one I sought to retrace my steps. But as I turned round with that intent, a troop of horsemen came riding along the narrow street, and the crowd falling back suddenly, I was thrown with great violence against a heap of stones. The suffering was very great, and I must have fainted soon afterwards; for, except the first moment of that sharp pain, I can call nothing to mind, save that I opened my eyes in an unknown chamber, and found myself lying on a bed with two or three strangers round me. I felt confused; and when I tried to move, a portly dame told me I must lie still, for my leg was broken, and the surgeon had been sent for to set it.

"How hath it happened?" I faintly said; "and where am I?" I was beginning to feel I could not move without sore pain.

"You have been knocked down in the lane," the same person replied. "This is Warwick House. The Duke of Clarence commanded you should be carried here; and I'll warrant you, mistress, you could not have desired any thing better, for the Countess hath appointed me to the care of you; and, albeit I say it that should not, there is not the likes of me in all Yorkshire for the tending of wounds. Laws me! after the bloody Lancastrians took Sandal Castle—which I thank God they soon lost again— I had no end of dying persons on my hands, so that I am used to them, you see, and I can lay out a corpse as fairly as any woman in England. And I shall be right glad, mistress, to render you every service in my power."

"Thank you," I answered. "But what I most desire is that a litter should be sent for to carry me to my lodgings. I would not for the world stay here to give trouble."

"It is not possible for you to move, mistress," that terrible woman rejoined. "The surgeon hath been sent for, and it should offend him mortally to come and find no leg to set."

"Is my leg really broken?" I exclaimed, unable to restrain my tears, for to abide under that roof seemed at that moment a dreadful torment to me.

"Yea, as truly as I stand here," quoth the burly dame.

I closed my eyes, and murmured, "My good God, Thy will be done! I would the suffering I endure was twice as great, but not endured here. Howsoever, not my will, but Thine be done!"

The door opened then, and I heard some one say in a low voice, "Mistress Joan, how fareth that poor lady?"

In another moment I knew, though I opened not my eyes, that the Countess of Warwick was standing by my bedside. I remained as if insensible, and mentally prayed that she should not know me again. It was now many long years since we had met who had been once close friends. I felt her hand gently feeling my pulse. Then it was laid on my forehead. She said to the nurse, "Open the casement;" and light and air were let into the chamber. Then into my ear were softly breathed these words, "Margaret de Roos, is it you?" I opened my eyes, and they met hers. She sent every one out of the room. Then her arms were thrown round my neck, and my head leant against her bosom. This hath been one of the most unlooked-for passages in my life, and to explain what I then felt I must go back to the time when Anne Beauchamp and I were young, and our hearts linked together by one of those early womanish friendships, which, like wild spring-flowers, are sweet, brief, often crushed in the bud, but which leave behind them in our memories a lingering scent, which survives long years of absence and apparent indifferency. Other loves—deeper, stronger, fraught with passion, or linked with duties—arise, and we no longer think on those frail blossoms of youthful affection as on aught that should count in our lives; and yet they die not wholly. When, weakened by suffering and agitation, confused by a singular accident, suddenly prostrated on a bed of pain amidst strangers, I saw that sweet, noble countenance, which I once loved so well, bent upon me with a compassionate tenderness, I could not forbear from greeting it with a passionate caress. I had been with Lady Warwick at Middleham in the first years of her marriage, and witnessed her excellent domestic virtues and her great qualities, which I doubt not conspired to extend and confirm the boundless and fatal influence her husband exercised in England. If he was, in the eyes of the people, the picture of a great English lord, bold, warlike, generous in giving, albeit ungenerous in soul and a desperate traitor, she had all the comeliness, the modesty, the virtues most beseeming a noble English lady; and when our poor Queen was cruelly defamed by her enemies, because of her French birth and her French manners, I doubt not that she was often unfavourably compared with the Countess of Warwick. But, howsoever blind in her worship of her husband and obedient to his will, she had never herself that I wot of maligned the Queen, or shown any active enmity towards her and the King. I marvel even now that, after all that had passed, I could feel so softened a heart towards her; but this I must further say to excuse it: I have had few loves and friendships all my days, and of these most have faded in a sudden, fatal, or leastways final manner. And the one abiding earthly affection, now the first and greatest I entertained—that one which binds me to the Queen—there is in it no reciprocity, no mutual tenderness, no sweetness of retrospect, no possible gentle endearments which soothe the heart and minister to its weakness. With my whole soul I have clung of late years to the true, sole, never-forsaking love, to which the deepest and strongest earthly one is but as a drop from a Divine and eternal fount. My good Father in heaven, my loving God, knoweth I would not now exchange the joys of His love and service for the fairest earthly lot. But the echo of an old music was in Anne Beauchamp's voice, the ghost of a past happiness in her fair face, and for this it was that I rested my head on her bosom and wetted it with my tears.

After a long expressive silence she said,

"Sweet friend, how should I call you, and whither send to say you are here?"

"I am Dame Anne Clere," I answered, looking fixedly in her face.

"That is well," she replied. "No other name shall pass my lips."

"Of your charity," I then said, "give me wherewith to write to my lodgings, that no search should be made for me; and let him who carries the missive not disclose where I am."

I wished to conceal from Kate my forced residence at Warwick House, and only wrote to her that urgent reasons impeded my return for a short time, and that she should on no account seek to discover my abode. This letter the Countess assured me should be delivered without delay, question, or explanation. From that moment she nursed me like a tender sister.

When my limb was set, she stood courageously by my side and held my hand. She had set before me at the foot of the bed a devout image of our Lord crucified, for this she thought would best help me to bear my pain. She brought curious books and painted Missals to entertain my solitary hours, and came every day afterwards several times to converse with me. She spoke of the old days at Middleham—our rides and hawkings, the fair vestments we embroidered for the chapel, and our sports with her two little wenches on the grass-plat under her windows. These pleasant scenes came back before me like the visions of a dream; it seemed as if all the terrible haps since then had been only nightmares. We neither of us spoke of them any more than as if the civil wars had not existed; or as if all evil passions were laid, and the whole world at peace. She never so much as once named her husband (for which in my secret heart I blessed her), nor any person whatsoever of that party, nor did I mention their Majesties. Nor did she inquire when I had come to London, or put to me any like question. I often begged her to suffer me to return to my lodgings; but she declared—which was true—that the leeches forbade it, and she would then gently add, " Sweet friend, has Anne Beauchamp in any thing caused thee to lament this brief suspension of a long separation? And wouldst thou leave me in uneasiness touching thy cure?—for when once we part God knoweth when we shall meet again."

So I continued at Warwick House, which, when I think of it, seems an almost incredible trick of fortune. One day she said to me, " Should it like thee to see the wenches which so often sat on thy knees when I was nursing them?" I must needs confess I had a great desire to do so, partly from revived affection for their mother, and also from curiosity, so much talk was ministered as to their marriages even amongst the few persons I saw in London.

So, later in the day, behind Lady Warwick there came in the two damsels her daughters. Both were fair. Lady Isabel, the eldest, then about fifteen, was the handsomest at the first sight; but no sooner had you spoken with them than you would set no more store on her beauty, as compared to that of her young sister Anne, in my opinion at least, than on a peony compared with a rose. Lady Isabel had a bright, somewhat bold look. She laughed a great deal in speaking, and was like her father, which, I fear, indisposed me a little against her. Lady Anne, then in her thirteenth year, had a pretty coyness in her manner, and seemed a little afraid of the sick lady she had been brought to see; but as I looked at her I could not but think of my dear lord the Prince saying some years ago, "Anne Neville is very winsome;" yea, winsome is the word which paints her.

Lady Warwick said that, if it would like me, Lady Anne should come and keep me company on the morrow, and bring me flowers, for that she and Isabel were forced to go into the country for two days. So about noon, after I had dined, she came and brought with her large bunches of flowers, which she said she would make posies of for the porcelain vases in my room. She was still very timid, and kept her large fawn-like eyes bent on her pretty task, only now and then glancing at me in a shy manner, and answering Yea or Nay when I spoke to her. I liked to look at her, and by degrees she grew a little bolder. Amongst other things, after we had been talking of what flowers we loved most, she said,

"Dame Clere, I am very fond of roses. I wish—

don't you also wish it?—there had never been any wars about them."

"Sweet Lady Anne," I answered, "I wish there were never any wars at all, and assuredly that those called of the roses had never happened."

"Ah, there we are of the same thinking," she said. "I am so glad; Bella is not like us. She says, if there had not been these wars, George should not have been Duke of Clarence, and she likes to be a duchess. She is to marry George, you know."

"And you Lady Anne, would you not like to be a duchess?"

"O no," she said, lifting up her head quickly. "George's brother Richard would fain marry me; but I will not for all the world marry him if I can help it." Then in a very low voice she added, "I want to be a princess."

"Indeed!" I said, "and what prince would you marry?"

She became a little red, and then said,

"If I tell you, Dame Clere, will you be sure and not tell anybody?"

"Is it such a great secret?" I answered smiling.

"Well, you see, I never told any body but Bella, and she was very angry; and my sweet mother once I said it to."

"Was she angered?" I asked, with a foolish beating of heart at this childish talk.

"She is never angered with me; but she put her finger on my lips and shook her head. But I should be affrighted to tell the earl my father. Peradventure, you, Dame Clere, mislike that poor prince?" Then she looked up in a determined manner from her flowers and said, "It is Prince Edward of Lancaster!"

O, how unreasoningly glad I was! "God bless thee,

sweet Lady Anne!" I cried; and being weak—I am ashamed to tell it—I burst into tears.

She came close to my couch, and putting her pretty young cheek on the pillow close to my old one, she said,

"Do you know him?"

"Yea, of yore I did," I cautiously replied.

"And was he not the sweetest, gentlest, fairest little prince in all the world?" she asked.

"He is good and brave also," I rejoined, much moved.

"O, I am so glad he is brave! I like brave men. Look, Dame Clere; when I was very young at Calais, some Lancastrian prisoners were brought there, and one of them which Joan nursed, when he was a-dying, gave her this little silver swan. After he was dead she asked to speak with my father, and showed it to him. 'I would not keep it,' she said, 'for all the world, for it is the badge of the so-called Prince of Wales. I pray your lordship, what shall I do with it?' 'Throw it into the sea, good Mistress Joan,' quoth my father, laughing; 'or give it to Anne to play with.' So she let me have it as a plaything, and I have kept it ever since."

I could not help saying, "Prince Edward hath never forgotten his little playmate."

"O, is that true?" she said. "I am well pleased he remembers me. Then you have seen him not a very long time ago, Dame Clere?"

"Ay," I answered, "not a very long time ago."

"If you shall see him again I wonder if you will tell him that I have not forgotten him. You must not say, Dame Clere, that I would like to marry him, for he would think me very bold. I should be ashamed that he should hear I said so. But methinks you might say, 'Lady Anne hath never forgotten her little playmate.'"

"Well, if it please God," I replied, "that I should see the Prince again, I will e'en tell him so."

She had now finished filling the vases, and, after giving me a kiss, went away.

On the morrow she stole again to my chamber. This time she brought in her arms a chessboard, and the men to play with.

"Dame Clere," she said, "can you play at chess; and will it like you to do so?"

"Very much," I answered; for verily it pleasured me to see her sitting opposite to me, knitting her pretty brow when she was puzzled, or smiling gleefully when she had made a good move. All her shyness with me had now vanished; and when the game was over she entertained me with her sweet prattle. I asked her who had learnt her to play at chess.

"One whom I mislike very much," she answered,— "Prince Richard of Gloucester. He was at Middleham with us last winter, and also at York, when my uncle the archbishop was enthroned. Nothing would serve him but that Bella and I should sit with him at his table on the banquet-day; and then he would teach me all the evening to play at chess. He angered me not a little in this way: he had taken my queen, snatching her from the board like this. He threw her into the box, and shut down the lid with a malicious look. 'So I would serve that flying French Margaret,' he cried, 'if I could but catch her. She is as mischievous as a chess-queen. Her idiot husband in the Tower is as helpless as your king there.' I said I was tired of playing, and would not finish the game; I was so vexed with him.—Dame Clere, do you hate the late King and Queen as some persons do?"

"Far from it," I replied.

"Methinks, Dame Clere, that King Henry is a better man than King Edward. Bella will not say so; but that is because this present King is George Clarence's brother. You do not know how cruel Richard is. If he wants any thing, he does not care how much he hurts others, so he can have his will. He hates the Prince of Lancaster more than you can think of. I am sure if he was to come to London, he would try to kill him."

At that time of the sweet young girl's visit to me a knock at the door of the chamber was heard, and was soon followed by the entry of Lady Isabel in very gay attire, who, after saluting me, said, "I thought Anne was here, and so that I might come. I did so want to talk to somebody, for London is so dull after these two days at Shene!"

Then I perceived Lady Warwick had been to the court, but, with her mindful fear of wounding me, had not spoken of it. Howsoever Lady Isabel had no like restraint, and I rather set her on to talk than otherwise, for I had a painful curiosity concerning those so-called majesties. She said the first evening they were at the palace was spent in the Queen's withdrawing-room, where some of the ladies played at Marteaux and others at Closheys, and then ended with dancing, and that she had danced with the King.

"And how many times with the King's brother?" quoth Lady Anne.

"O, not more than once," Lady Isabel replied. "On the morrow, when Matins were done, we heard Mass in the palace-chapel. It was the Mass of our Lady, and most melodiously sung. Then after breakfast we went into the little park, where we had great sport, and I rode one of George's hobbies. Dinner was ordained in the summer-house; and afterwards we went to see the garden and vineyard of pleasure. Before supper we all bathed; and when we had been in the bath as long as was our pleasure, the Queen sent us green ginger and divers comfits. In the evening we danced again, and some of us played at games. The chambers have been all newly furnished, and nothing more dainty can be thought of. I told George that when I am married I would have a pleasaunce chamber like unto the one I had at Shene, all hanged with white silk and linen-cloth, and the floor covered with a carpet. And mostly I am resolved to have a bath, covered with a tent of white cloth. But now I must tell you what happened on the second morning. After we had been at Mass, all the ladies of the court environed Sir Anthony Woodville, and tied above his left knee a band of gold furnished with precious stones, and figured with S's, meaning *souvenance*, and to this band was hanging a noble sprig of the flower Forget-me-not. He laid his hand on his heart, and said in an agreeable manner, 'Ladies, this comes nigher to my heart than to my knee.' And Isminia, who was spokeswoman, said full sweetly, smiling on her new lord, that he should take a step befitting the times. He answered that he was abashed at this adventure; howsoever he did not look one wit abashed, but thanked these ladies for their rich and honourable present; and in his cap he found a letter written on vellum, and bound with a gold thread. Therein he was told of the emprise which the flower of souvenance was intended to move him to undertake. He went forthwith to the King, to crave his leave and license to hold the emprise at the Queen's coronation, and bring the adventure of the flower of souvenance to a conclusion. The King read the articles and permitted the jousts; and Sir Anthony hath sent a herald to the Count de la Roche, inviting him to touch the flower, 'in token of acceptance of his challenge.' It is expected he shall be one of the knights the Duke of Burgundy will send with her uncle the Count of St. Pol to do honour to the Queen's coronation. I hope George will practise tilting before that time. It would please me if he should unhorse that fine Sir Anthony. There is but one thing I hate at the court, and that is the much talk about the Woodvilles. Verily, one should think there were no other knights and no other scholars in England. It is Sir Anthony here, Lord Rivers there, Sir John at every turn; and those sisters and their lovers, I am weary of their names. What think you of the Queen's two sons—the young Grays—sitting higher at the banquet than the greatest lords of the kingdom? I promise you this shall cause no small stir. But maybe, Dame Clere, I weary you with my talk. I fear you look fatigued."

"Nay, Lady Isabel," I replied, "I am in no wise weary in body."

"But a little in mind," she said, laughing, "with my foolish talking. Hath Anne been good company to you?"

"Yea," I said tenderly, taking in mine the hand of the sweet child; "the dearest comfort to me imaginable."

"But she is a little rebel, Dame Clere. I assure you she sometimes talks rank treason. We call her the Lancastrian.—Come, get thee gone, Pussy. Thy lover Richard was so peevish that thou wast not carried to Shene, that he had not a word to throw to a dog, much less to a Christian."

Little Lady Anne frowned, and said Richard was always peevish.

"Nay, nay," cried her sister; "see, he hath sent thee this pretty carkanet."

"I will not have it," quoth the little lady.

"O, who is peevish now?" cried the other.

Methought this savoured of the beginning of a quarrel, and I was well pleased that Lady Warwick then came in, having put off her courtly gear.

In a few days I had so far amended that I could be carried from Warwick House to Cheapside. Lady Warwick would have fain sent me in her own litter and with her men; but I besought her to let me hire a conveyance, in which I rode to Mr. Bugdon's house at an hour when only one servant was astir, who let me in. The parting with that generous friend and her sweet little daughter Anne cost me some tears. When I found myself again in my old lodgings with Kate and her husband, only a feebleness in my leg, which was very palpable, could convince me the last month had not been one long dream. To this day no one, I ween, but Lady Warwick and I know who was the sick dame Clere, so carefully and lovingly tended in the south chamber at Warwick House.

CHAPTER XXXVIII.

An Arrival and a Departure.

ONE evening, more than a year after my accident and constrained abode at Warwick House, I was sitting at work in Kate's withdrawing-room, while she was looking out of the front-parlour window at the passengers. My thoughts had been all day concerned, I know not wherefore, with the imprisoned King. I received tidings of him now and again from persons—chiefly religious, or else scholars and artists—which had licence to enter his apartments; and whatsoever I could hear in this way I transmitted, as occasion offered, to the Queen. Kate and I often walked in a street near the river, whence we could see one of the windows of his chamber. We could discern through the grating the cage of his favourite bird, a starling, which had learnt to say, "Poor Henry! poor King!" The Abbot of Westminster told me the first time he heard this compassionate cry of the poor fowl, it almost moved him to tears. Once I observed the King's dog, an old friend of mine at the court, standing with his paws against the bars. One day it seemed to me that I perceived the King himself. "Of a surety," I said to Kate, "there is a figure leaning against the casement with a book in his hand." But the very thought that it was himself dimmed my eyes with blinding tears, and Kate had too short a sight to see so far. On the evening I write of, this said Kate disturbed me from my fit of musing by this question: "Dame Margaret, hast heard the last news from the court?"

"What news?" I said—"good or bad?"

Then she: "Why, good for the good, I suppose; and bad for the bad. The saying is, 'When rogues fall out, honest men get back their own.' By that same token, the news should be good for honest folk. The great earl is so enraged with his puppet's wife, that some think in his choler he will knock down the puppet himself."

"Ah," quoth I, "what is his present cause of offence?"

"This," she said. "It seems he had set his heart on marrying the daughter of that excellent princess, Anne of York, the little heiress of Exeter, to his nephew, George Neville. But he counted without his host, or rather without his new queen. For, lo and behold, Lady Bessie on the sly gives four thousand marks to her virtuous sister-in-law for to contract the damsel with her own son Lord Dorset. It is reported that the so-called king-maker foamed at the mouth when the news reached him. Some hope the cunning lady will prove the truth of the saying that biters are bit; for the girl is sickly, and not like to live, and so her four thousand marks shall have gone for nothing. The Woodvilles are more hated every day. Lady Bessie wrote so sharp a letter last week to Sir William Stonor, touching his hunting and slaying her deer in Exhill and Barnwood Forests, when all the time he had her lord's commission for the doing of it, that he hath vowed to be revenged on the whole brood of the Bedford witch. 'Set beggars on horseback,' quoth he, 'and you shall see the end thereof.' Talking of beggars reminds me of robbers—"

"For shame, Kate!" I exclaimed. "Begging is a

lawful and often a Christian action. Our Lord hath appeared to some in the shape of a beggar, and—"

"O, content thee, Dame Margery, content thee!" she cried. "I thought of those lusty beggars which carry a good uplifted stick in one hand the better to move your charity. I am not sure your ladyship doth not resemble them a little, for you are somewhat prompt to oblige persons to be virtuous after your own fashion with a good knock on the head."

"Pardon, good Kate, pardon!" I cried. "I was over-quick in interrupting thee. What robbers wert thou about to speak of?"

"Peradventure, your ladyship sees no affinity between robbers and outlaws, and will be displeasured if I say that a man which hath been here more than once seeking to speak with you is, I am assured, no other than a noted freebooter of the name of Robin of Redesdale, and that you should be careful what dealings you have with him."

I told her that, albeit I had never yet spoken with this person, I had asked Lord Beaumont, who is secretly one of our friends, if I should see him, as he wished, touching the Queen's affairs. He replied that this Robin is said to be a ruined nobleman of our party, which conceals his name, and under the semblance of a common outlaw, is assembling forces in Yorkshire. But the truth of this report he could by no means ascertain. Whosoever he is, for some cause or other the man abhors the Woodvilles. But in these times a man's hatreds are as little to be counted on as his allegiance.

"Ay," Kate answered; "yet I should trust one more than the other. And for that reason I am not without hoping that the great earl's detestation of the King he hath set up may so increase, that good shall come of it which we may live to see."

"But what shall he do for a king," I said, "if neither York nor Lancaster serve his turn?"

"Why, is there not fair George, his son-in-law, which he holds in his sleeve like a conjuring man doth a mouse or a kitten, ready to be let out when the right time cometh? I always thought, when the usurper crowned that widow-woman, leaving Isabel Neville for his brother, and flouting likewise that greater Isabel of Spain, which would have fain been his queen, that he played himself a foul trick. The earl is, I ween, gathering up the strings behind the scenes, and before long we shall witness a new performance."

"Alas," I said, "there is this evil in these days for us who, being virtuous conspirators, must hide our lawful efforts as if they were criminal acts,—that we needs must get accustomed to rejoice in the faults and dissensions of others as good haps to ourselves, and not to look upon them as they are, that is, offences against God."

"Tut, tut, Dame Margery!" Kate replied; "you have too nice a conscience in these matters. The crimes of our enemies are stepping-stones to our friends, and I am not going to lament them. Here is supper. Where, I marvel, is Mr. Bugdon?"

She opened the door, and cried out: "Sir, shall you never come down to your meals till an hour after they are served?" No answer coming, she repeated the summons, and that time stamped her foot. This not availing, she ran up the stairs and burst into the poor man's study, who is writing a treatise on the harms printing will bring upon the world. He was so engaged in his work that for all the noise she made he never heard her at all, or took notice of her presence, until she snatched the paper from before him, and bounded down the stairs with it in her hand. I had much ado to prevent her from throwing it into the fire.

Whilst this scuffle was taking place, a serving-man came into the parlour and said there was a reverend man at the door, and another person with him, who craved to speak with Dame Clere.

"Is the reverend man a begging-friar?" Kate asked.

"No," the servant replied; "he is a priest. French-like, I ween, by the looks of him. He says his name is Tavernier."

"Bid them come in," Kate said, before Mr. Bugdon, who had followed his piece of writing down the stairs, had time to speak, or I either. He misliked nothing so much as the sudden letting in of unknown persons into the house, and, to say the truth, so did I. For one true friend the Queen had in England, there were twenty unsad persons to be found of desperate fortunes and doubtful fame, which proffered their services and disgraced our cause. But Kate's wont was to suffer her actions to outrun her own thinking and the counsel of others; so, before we could prevent it, two strangers entered. The priest wore on his head a French ecclesiastic's hat, which concealed the most of his face, and a cloak wrapped round him. His companion was an elderly man of ordinary appearance. They bowed two or three times and looked back to see if the door was shut behind them. I had no defined thought in my mind, and could not have said what I feared, and yet I shook like one in a fit of the ague. There was somewhat in the look of these persons, and their not speaking at first,—one standing stock-still and the other bowing in an embarrassed manner,—which affrighted me. Mr. Bugdon bowed, and cleared his throat. Even Kate looked a little amazed. When the servant withdrew, the secular gentleman said, "Mesdames," and turning towards Mr. Bugdon, "Monsieur, this reverend man hath a message of importance to deliver to the Dame Anne Clere, and for that reason would desire to see her alone." He looked at Kate and me, doubting which of us to address. The Priest moved towards the door of the withdrawing-room. Inspired with a sudden courage, I stepped forward and opened it; upon which he darted into the aforesaid room, which had no light in it, save that of the fire. I followed him, shut the door, and said with an affected boldness,—for there was something unnatural to me in this muffled priest's appearance,—" I beseech you, sir, let me know at once who you are and whence you come. I misdoubt you are not what you seem," I added with increasing uneasiness, as I felt my hand laid hold of. Then followed the words, "*Marguerite, c'est moi,—la Reine.*"

"*O mon Dieu!*" was all I could utter, I was so entirely surprised. Instead of kneeling or expressing any welcome, I stood still, staring as if I had seen a ghost.

"Calm yourself; collect your senses; do not you know me—the Queen?"

Tears came to my relief. "O madame, madame! you here?"

"Yea, I myself. But first tell me—can I entirely confide in Katharine and her husband?"

"O, fully," I answered. "But, for God's sake, show me your face; take off that hat! Let me see your eyes, madame, that I may be assured it is you."

She lifted up the hat, which half covered her visage, and smiled; then I passionately kissed her hands. She drew me to her bosom and embraced me.

"Go now," she said, "and tell our friends I am here."

When I went into the parlour, if I had had leisure or inclination to laugh it would have been risible to see the distressed looks of the three persons in that room, and how quickly they turned towards me when I entered for to be relieved from their embarrassment. A foolish doubt if the Queen's companion was in her confidence checked the words on my lips. As I stood hesitating, she came in. I seized Kate by the hand, and cried, "Kate, don't you see who it is?" The astonished dame gave a little scream, and fell at her majesty's feet. Mr. Bugdon turned white, and then red, ran to lock the door, and in his bewilderment shook hands with the Queen's companion before making his obeisance to her grace's self.

I must confess that when I look back to that evening I admire how the most, as we should think them, incredible things, when they do come to pass, seem natural, and also how apparently thoughtless persons in an emergency will sometimes evince unsuspected qualities. I could not but marvel at Kate's presence of mind. She behaved as if the Queen's sudden appearance in her house had been a very joyful, indeed, but in no wise astonishing event. She straightway conducted her to the best armed-chair in the room, and placed a foot-stool for her feet. The supper lately set on the table she spread before her with many, yet not too many, excuses that it should be no better than it was; I the while could only stand mutely gazing at the Queen, whilst a number of questions kept rising in my mind,—why had she come? with whom? for what end? with what hopes? When the noises in the street recalled to me that we were in London, and at a short distance from her mortal enemies, I began to tremble again with a more defined terror than before. I dare not say to her, "Wherefore have you come?" or address to her during her repast any other questions, save for to hope her health had not suffered in the crossing of the sea, and that she had left my lord Prince well, and such-like common inquiries. "Monsieur Duluc," she said to the gentleman who had come with her, "will you not taste of this good English dish?"—which made me know he was the merchant from Nancy which she had once greatly served, and who in return had furnished her in Scotland with money, and fitted out the ship in which we sailed to Flanders. After her meal was over, the Queen commanded me to sit down by her side, and would have Kate do the like; but nothing would serve Kate but to sit on the floor at her feet. Mr. Bugdon and Mr. Duluc she likewise commanded to be seated; and then she spoke to us as follows:

"My trusty and well-beloved friends, is this not a surprising—nay, as it should have seemed beforehand, an incredible—thing that thus suddenly I should arrive amongst you? Doth not truly the danger appear excessive, not to say desperate? Are you not all affrighted to death of me, and, indeed, if you were not so generous and good, for yourselves also? Yet, believe me, the very excess of the risk tends to safety, as I hope in God you shall find. To be brief, this is the case: I heard in Paris, whither I have been to meet some of our partisans, that this good friend of mine was about to travel to London, with no other companion save a priest from Aix, who has relatives in this country, and that they had their passes in order for any English port they should land at. An impetuous, irresistible desire to see the King took possession of me. This seemed the fairest occasion in the world to accomplish it; and I prevailed on the said ecclesiastic to lend me his name, his dress, and his safe-conduct, putting off his own journey to another season. It so happened that he could help me yet further to compass my object. For he hath a brother here in London, a quaint carver of wood, which often works for the King, and hath frequent access to his chamber. 'What so natural,' he said, 'but that when his own brother cometh to London, and he a priest, he should crave license to bring him unto his majesty, who is well known to like the converse of ghostly persons?' These words quite resolved me to tempt the enterprise, and this is my project. If, my good friends, you can conceal me here this night, M. Duluc will seek this artificer, and deliver to him his brother's letter, wherein he prayeth him, for the love of God and the House of Anjou, to assist me in this matter."

"God will prosper you, madame!" Kate exclaimed.

Mr. Bugdon, poor man, cast a dismayed look towards me, and I must needs confess that my apprehensions ran alongside of his; but after her majesty had already braved the terrible danger of coming to London, how could any one persuade her to return without the accomplishment of her great and natural desire? So I could but look down and sigh, which gave him small comfort.

"Now, madame," said Kate, "this should be the plot: let your majesty put on once more your hat and cloak; and when I have called the servant and desired him to open the door, with many *congés* and bows, and Dame Margery and I craving aloud your blessing, and that you should be mindful of us in your Mass to-morrow, pass into the street, and tarry out of sight for the space of a Credo and ten Pater nosters or so, the while I shall despatch the serving-man and the two wenches to bed. Then Mr. Bugdon shall gently open the door, which, when your grace shall see it, you will then quickly return and enter. There is a bed in a closet within Dame Margery's chamber most concealed and quiet, wherein your majesty can spend the night, and to-morrow we shall receive your further commands. As to the monsieur, he should be less conveniently lodged; but if—"

"*Grand merci, madame!*" cried M. Duluc. "With her majesty's permission, after I have seen M. Tavernier, I will seek a hostelry. The openness of my showing in London shall rather hinder than promote suspicion."

"Yea," said the Queen, "I am of the same thinking; and at the dawn, before their serving-folk bestir themselves, these good friends shall let me out, and I will repair to St. Paul's Church, whither, at a convenient time, such as he shall propose, you will come to me with M. Tavernier, who in a good hour, I pray, will conduct me to the Tower."

The exit and return of the Queen was effected as Kate had devised. When she had withdrawn into her closet, she took off her disguise, and, putting on some night gear of mine, lay down on the bed to take some rest. To sleep seemed impossible; so I sat down by her side, and then could more clearly discern the changes which three years had wrought in her yet beautiful visage. Dark lines surrounded her eyes, and silvery hairs had begun to mingle with her black tresses. Her cheeks were no longer smooth, and her hands had grown very thin. She thanked me for the poor services I had rendered to her since we had parted. Upon which I prayed her to suffer me to return to her in France, for that I was not cunning enough for the responsible dealings which I had been charged with of late.

"In good sooth," she replied, "albeit I am well con-

tented with thy services here, it would like me now, I
own, to have thy care and company at Queniez. Alas,
England hath rejected me! and I am a stranger in
France; or rather—for this doth sound ungrateful to
my kinsfolk and others for the much love they have
shown me—France hath become strange to me. The
French air aggravates my heart sickness, or else maybe
there is no remedy for a disease which is restless, and
causes me to loathe successively each place of sojourn.
When characters are dissimilar, kindness often misses
its aims. I thought my father's great sorrows and
mine should have found in these years mutual relief.
But his resignation is one I cannot conceive or imitate:
by the same token he finds solace for my mother's loss
in ingenious devices every where painted of turquoise,
bows with ruptured strings, and poetic comments on
this theme; and for the death of Anne, his youngest
born, in the construction round her tomb of the Castle
of Garde-Anne, adorned with various learned conceits.
Then the gardens of La Reculée, the processions at
Aix, his pastoral retirements at Tarascon, his pleasure
orchards and artistic pastimes, console him for the loss
of kingdom after kingdom. The writing of a lay or
the limning of a picture obliterates the pain of fortune's keenest strokes. I tried for a time these philo-
sophic contentments. For a few days the converse of
poets and the incense of praise ministered a brief dis-
traction to my cares; but either I am endowed with a
less acquiescent mind than King René, or this English
air, so long imbibed, hath changed my nature. I soon
sickened of this comfort. Even the pious diversions
of my dear father distaste me. I am too sore of heart
to enjoy holy plays and pastimes, and Christian teachings veiled under heathenish symbols. I have another
image before me of devotedness than this artistic one."

Then, lifting up her hand, she pointed towards where the Tower stands, and said, "*There* is an example of holiness such as I can worship, albeit never emulate. The purity of a soul never stained by mortal sin; God loved and served by a royal wight from the early dawn of reason; humility surviving flattery; resignation to a most cruel malady that touches both body and mind; forgiveness never withheld of the direst injuries; matchless tenderness towards one whose fiery spirit doth often chafe at virtue's self. O, Henry, my lord and husband! my Christ-like king! if I may see your face again, and carry back your blessing to your son, I care not how soon after I die. It may be that an endless doom of sorrow is mine, that my star is fatal."

"O, speak not, madame, of stars!" I exclaimed. "Leave that unchristian fashion of speech to King Lewis or this usurper here, and the Duchess of Bedford."

At that name, which the moment it had passed my lips I would fain not have pronounced, the Queen's whole countenance changed. Like a roused lioness she started up.

"Bedford's duchess! Ah, that false woman shall surely rue the day when my maid-servant, her cunning daughter, dared to ascend her mistress's seat, and, like a painted image of royalty, occupy my throne! But the sorceress Jacquetta shall not always triumph. Even now I hear that Warwick abhors Elisabeth and her kin."

"It is so reported," I replied; "and, moreover, that he begins to meditate the overthrow of the King he hath set up, and the elevation of Clarence, his own son-in-law."

A gleam of terrible joy flashed in the Queen's eyes.

"They will destroy each other!" she cried, clasping

her hands exultingly. "O, I should die of happiness the day York fell by the hand of Warwick, or Warwick by means of York!" She looked not the same person in this mood as she had done a moment before when speaking of the King's virtues.

The whole night was spent in questions and answers, the Queen investigating every point concerning what I had seen and heard touching the condition of men's minds and the dissensions in England. I feared to see the morning's dawn, and would fain have still persuaded her to forego her rash enterprise; but as soon as the first light was seen in the sky, she rose and disguised herself as on the foregoing day. Kate brought her some food she had herself prepared in the kitchen, and then I went with her to St. Paul's Church, walking on the opposite side of the street, that, in case any were stirring, I should not seem to be accompanying this apparent priest. The doors were not yet opened when we arrived, and for more than an hour her majesty had to stand on the steps waiting. When at last we could go in, she sat down on a bench near the entrance, with a book in her hand, feigning to be saying office. I knelt at a little distance, not taking my eyes off her. At about nine of the clock I saw M. Duluc come in with another person and whisper to the Queen, who straightway followed them out of the church, and, after a brief parley with the stranger, walked away with him. He had a package in his hand, which I concluded should be a piece of his workmanship, to carry to the King. I went up to M. Duluc and said, "Are they now going to the Tower?"

"Yea," he answered with an expressive shrug; so much as to say, "What a mad attempt!"

"Let us go," I said, "where we can watch what happens."

We kept them in sight, and crossing London-bridge, went to the street where Kate and I often walked. We saw them stand for a moment at the gate of the Tower, and then, which caused me a sensation of mingled joy and terror, enter its precincts. I know not for how long a time we stood in the same place gazing at the window of the King's chamber, and discerning nothing but the bird's-cage through the bars. The river was lined with persons waiting, I heard it said, to see *the King and Queen* and all the Court embark in a state barge. Presently the usurper rode by with a great company of courtiers, and his wife followed with her ladies in richly-adorned cars. Ah, Lady Elisabeth! fortunes go by turns. Yours was in the ascendant then. A great change, indeed, since the time you humbly sued for a marriage-portion at the Queen's hands! There were shouts of " Long live the King!" and " Long live the Queen!" when the *cortège* went by, mixed with some groans, which increased when Lord Rivers and Lord Scales came in sight. But when one tall figure on horseback, the most noble-like imaginable appeared, surrounded by a bevy of knights, which almost resembled an army, the cry of " A Warwick! a Warwick!" rose with such deafening cheers that the air seemed to vibrate with them. I marvelled if they could reach the Queen's ears where she was, and shuddered to think of her nearness to these mortal enemies. Before long I became so fatigued as to be hardly able to stand. The minutes seemed hours; the pale wintry sun too hot, albeit I was shivering all the time. The light pained my strained eyes; each sound hurt mine ears. At last M. Duluc whispered to me,

" They are coming out."

"Are you certain of it?" I asked, with a beating heart.

"Yes," quoth he. "Come quickly, and we shall overtake them."

We hurried across the bridge, but were delayed by some carts, and lost sight of the Queen and her companion. Howsoever, when we reached Kate's house she met me at the door, and said, "All is right."

I found the Queen in her secret room, sitting with her head leaning on her hands. She looked up when I came in, and said: "I have seen the King. When I first discovered myself to him, he was so amazed that he would not be persuaded it was not a vision. At the last he awoke, as from a trance, and opened his arms to me." This was all she said at that time, and seemed unwilling to be disturbed from the thinking over this brief interview. In about two hours' time after her return, Kate came in, and whispered to me that there was one at the street-door seeking to speak with me. I went thither, and found a man in a common dress, who said to me, without any preamble: "The Queen is here, and I must see her without delay."

"Sir," I replied, trembling all over, "the Queen is on the river with the King. This is a private person's house."

"It is Queen Margaret I must see. She is here, and, as I live, I must have speech with her. I pray you, let her wit Robin of Redesdale is here."

I then called to mind what I had heard some time ago touching this man, and I bade him wait where he was, for that I was too simple to comprehend what he meant, and would fetch the mistress of the house. I went straight to the Queen, and gave her this person's message. She started up from her musing posture, and commanded me to bring this Robin of Redesdale to her. She conversed a long time with him; and if I judge by her burning cheeks, cold hands, and feverish light in her eyes after this interview, it was one of no common interest to her cause.

Before nightfall M. Duluc came to say that the Queen's presence in London had been bruited and her disguise suspected. One of the guards at the Tower had said to a comrade: "I'll be shot if that priest hath not the eyes of the banished Queen." This was taken hold of by a third, who reported the speech to the governor, and he to the King. Constables were on the alert, and the only chance of safety was in flight before scent could be got of her abode.

Coarse female gear was procured for her majesty, and a common cart, in which alone with me and a friar she travelled to the coast; M. Duluc staying behind to delude the search by false information, trusting afterwards to make his own escape. I thanked God I could once more share the Queen's dangers, and attend on her in person. Kate declared she should come to the coast with us, if she had to run alongside the cart; but Mr. Bugdon waxed desperate then, and swore if she left the house he should betray the Queen. What he shall have suffered for this after our departure can easily be surmised. But, howsoever, his threat and the Queen's commands forced her to stay behind; and in a good hour we left London before her grace could be tracked, and safely reached the French coast in another day and night.

CHAPTER XXXIX.

The Comte de Queniez.

THIS is a letter which the Queen wrote from Tours to her brother, the Duke of Calabria, in December, 1469:

"MY ENTIRELY AND WELL-BELOVED BROTHER,—Although you are engaged in the glorious troubles of a war which, I pray God, shall fix on your head the crown of Catalonia, at once your natural heritage and rightful conquest, I doubt not but that the affection you have always shown to me, by your actions as well as by your words, shall 'cause you to rejoice at the approaching change in the fortunes of the House of Lancaster, and the hopes, which daily increase, that our calamities shall soon find an end. I have come to Tours for to meet the King of the French and the King of Sicily, our own dear father, who hath hastened thither to concert with the said King and our sister Yolande, and the Count de Vaudémont, the most expedient means whereby to hasten the recovery of our kingdom of England.

"Your highness's heart would have been deeply moved if you had witnessed this meeting between your poor sister and that tender father, who has ever loved us all with so incomparable an affection. It was the first interview since my young years in which tears of joy and not of sorrow were elicited from mine eyes by his tender paternal embrace. His sensibility could not restrain itself; and this emotion proved so contagious that, at the sight of our tearful joy, the like tokens of it rolled down the cheeks of King Lewis. His Majesty is wholly changed in his behaviour both to his uncle and to me. He lavishes proofs of his favour on the King of Sicily, even so far as to desire him to use henceforward yellow wax in the sealing of his letters; a privilege which hath never yet been conceded to any but the Kings of France. He gives him hopes that he will soon assist your highness with an army in Spain, which I pray God he fail not to do. As to my son, he behaves to him in the most friendly and honourable manner imaginable, and says to all who will hear it that the Prince of Wales surpasseth in merit all the young princes of his age. And verily, my dear brother, I who have as good a right as any princess in the world to show myself hard to please touching youthful excellence—for were not my brothers heroes even in childhood, and men in virtue at an age when so many others are hardly weaned from the follies of infancy?—I must confess that the sole bud which hath blossomed amidst so many storms on the shattered tree of England's royalty is worthy of his father's ancestors and of his mother's race. All who see him love him. Methinks, Monseigneur, that not having a son of your own,—which God knoweth I, like every one else in the world, do lament,—it hath pleased God to endow mine with a share of your virtues. Ah, how few princes could exclaim, as you did on hearing of the Roman emperor who was wont to say he had lost a day if therein he had done no good action, 'Well, I thank God, in that wise I hope I have never lost a day!' But I delay over-long the relation of those singular events which have happened in England, and on which the tower of our future hopes is built.

"A deadly feud hath arisen betwixt the usurper and the puissant earl which lifted him to the throne. Various causes are assigned for this virulent hatred of foes which once were friends, the most dire which can exist. Warwick hath vowed to be revenged, God knoweth for what dark secret injury, on the Earl of March, and designs his son-in-law, the brainless Clarence, for his successor. Already he raises troops against the Yorkists, in which many of our partisans, out of hatred for the usurper, have enrolled themselves under the cognisance of the bear and ragged staff. But I leave your highness to judge if these recruits will prove faithful to that leadership when the banner of the Red Rose is again unfurled, and the cry of 'A Henry!' resounds through the land. Then, an outlawed nobleman, once counted as a common robber, hath levied on his side no small force, and defeated the usurper's troops in a pitched battle, and, which pleases me most, caught the husband and the eldest son of the false Duchess of Bedford and cut off both their heads. She is publicly incriminated for witchcraft, and it is said proofs of her evil practices have been discovered. The usurper is at this moment in some sort in durance at the palace of the Archbishop of York, Lord Warwick's brother, and treating with him for the marriage of his daughter with George Neville, the son of Lord Montague. But I am assured Warwick will never consent to it, nor pardon him. There are deeper causes for his resentment than even the shedding of blood. So good hopes exist that they will destroy one another. King Lewis is of opinion that our triumph is at hand, and that the King, my husband, will reascend his throne in less than a year. He caresses both Edward and me with singular affection. I pray he prove sincere.

"I would to God your highness had not a kingdom of your own in need of your presence, for if I had your aid I should be certain of success. But God wills it otherwise; and I must be content with less puissant defenders. The brave and leal Pierre de Brézé is dead, who fought in my cause when it seemed hopeless. I have seen my most valiant friends perish in greater numbers than I can recount. But I hope in the justice of my quarrel and the zeal of those partisans which yet remain to me.

"I commend myself, Monseigneur and most dear brother, to your good prayers, and I pray God to have you in His holy keeping.
"MARGUERITE."

On the same day on which I copied this letter from the Queen to her brother, I received one from a youthful writer, which I will likewise transcribe; but first I must relate what led to my receiving it.

On my return to Queniez, three years before the time I am now speaking of, nothing could exceed the kindness which my lord the Prince showed me. He always was and is, without doubt, the most gracious creature ever born. Where shall one see any one more fair to behold, more pleasant to converse with, —so merry without folly, so gentle without effeminacy, of an excellent understanding and lively parts, truly virtuous in all his actions? Methinks even his mother cannot love him more tenderly than I do. I am glad he is good, for my weakness towards him is so great, I should find it hard to refuse to do any thing he asked me, howsoever unreasonable.

One day soon after my return to France, he led me

aside and said, "Come now, Lady Margaret, I pray you to tell me if, during these past years in London, you have seen the lady of my thoughts?"

"Who should she be, my lord Prince?" I answered, feigning not to understand him.

"O, Dame Margaret!" he exclaimed, opening wide his eyes with the same look in them his mother's used to have when she came as a young bride to England, "think you I am become inconstant to my sweet little lady-love, that winsome Anne Neville, who, if report is to be believed, hath become the fairest maiden in all England? Now, if you have seen her, you can tell me if report is a truth-teller."

I tried to put him off with excuses, but in vain. With his pressing questions and pretty coaxing ways, he forced me at last to confess I had seen her, and that her looks were not amiss. Then followed the "Where, Dame Margaret?" and the "How?" and the "For what space of time?" and more questions, one after another, than could be answered at once, till at the last, bit by bit, this cunning young prince drew from me the whole narrative of my accident in Warwick-lane, and what ensued from it. I prayed him to keep it secret, as, with the exception of Sir John Fortescue, I had not revealed this hap to any one. He was the most discreet person imaginable for his years, and I had no fear he should bruit it.

But when once he had gained this piece of knowledge from me, nothing would serve him but to hear, over and over again, what Lady Anne was like,—the exact colour of her eyes and of her hair, and her precise height when I had seen her; what she was wont to do and say when she came to my chamber; what was her head-gear and the shape of her gowns. And then further, if she had ever spoken of him, and did she hate him very much; because, sweet lady, she had been taught to esteem the Yorkists, and he feared she must needs hold in abhorrence the heir of Lancaster.

When I assured him she had expressed no unchristian sentiments towards him, he said, smiling, "Come, Dame Margaret, let me hear the very words she used touching Prince Edward of Lancaster."

And when I repeated what the little lady had said, that she had never forgot her old playmate, tears sprung in his eyes. "Lady Margaret," he said, "if I am moved by these kindly words, think it not all foolishness. This fidelity to an early fondness betokens, methinks, a nobleness of soul in this young maiden which I cannot think of without emotion." After a little silence, he asked me if Lady Anne had spoken of the brother of the so-called king, Richard Plantagenet.

"Yea," I said, "she did; but as it was not to commend him, it should be more charitable not to repeat her words."

"O the heavens!" he exclaimed. "This is good tidings, that she did not commend him. That same wicked babbler, report, said some time ago she was to be married to that Richard; and this should be the worse hap in the world for that poor wench to have such a foul, ill-natured husband as that prince is said to be."

"He would fain have married her," I said, "but she assured her father she would rather die a thousand times than have him."

"There is a brave girl!" he exclaimed joyfully. "I wish now more than ever I did that my father was on his throne again, for then I would make her Princess of Wales."

"Ah, my lord Prince," I replied, "the sons of kings

marry not according to their likings; so I pray you let not your fancy run fondly on this Lady Anne. Is not your cousin Marie of Lorraine as fair a princess as can be seen? and the demoiselle Jeanne d'Harcourt, is she not likewise very beautiful?"

"Yes, faith, Lady Margaret," he rejoined, "they are both very comely, and so are twenty other ladies I have seen in Paris when I was last there; but, for all that, they have not the bashful, innocent, pretty look of the Lady Anne, which I remember as I had seen her yestereve. And you do not deny she hath it still; so, until I find the like expression in other damsels, I will not wed them if I can help it."

This conversing about Anne Neville was often renewed, and I perceived that the Prince took note of every thing I said touching the young lady, by that same token that he learnt to play at chess, because I once mentioned she was fond of that pastime.

When he was in his fifteenth year he sojourned for a while with his grandfather at his castle of Reculée, and on his return he showed me a painting on vellum, which was an excellent likeness of Lord Warwick's daughter.

"How now, good my lord Prince," I exclaimed, "how came you by this portrait?"

"O verily, then, I see it is her portrait," he cried, laughing; "I was sure I had guessed aright the form and colour of my sweet mistress's winsome visage and her bashful look, which well becomes a saint's picture. The King was portraying St. Delphina, to whom he is very devout, and I sat by his side while he was limning. He took my counsel and painted as I told him. I said he should make her like a little maiden I had seen in England, and I painted her in words whilst he used his brush. When the picture was finished, I prayed him to give it to me. Those were pleasant days with my good grandsire. He is so gracious and so good, every one must needs love him. His tales and songs are most delectable. There is a rare and excellent wit in all he doeth; and albeit no one hath experienced more bitter griefs, he is always of good cheer and most *débonnaire.*"

Thus praising his grandsire, my lord the Prince carried back his picture to his school; and who can describe how often he stood gazing on it, and writing verses to this portrayed mistress? At a tournament at Angers, where he broke his first lance at the age of sixteen, he entered the lists as the champion of Garde-Anne, an ingenious device which made me smile.

I felt some disquietude touching this boyish flame, built on fancy and nurtured by romance, fearing that the delight I took in pleasuring this beloved prince had led me to minister to its vagaries, and that I should therein have failed in my duty to the Queen. But Sir John Fortescue, to whom I disclosed my apprehensions, bade me not to be concerned thereat. "For who knoweth," quoth he, "that this fantastic passion for an innocent absent girl shall not defend the Prince from other dangerous allurements? It is not very like that he shall see this Lady Anne before he is engaged in more serious devoirs; and moreover who can warrant—" Here the good knight paused awhile, and then added: "Yea, who can warrant that these two pure streamlets of childish affection may not one day unite the brawling torrents which now flow asunder? More incredible things have been seen. To none but you, Lady Margaret, would I utter this thought; but events in England are shaping themselves in strange ways, and we may yet see more singular haps that at present are dreamed of."

All these years the Queen was plunged in ceaseless correspondence with foreign princes and her partisans in England. She seemed to live only in the expectation of the future; and albeit her love for her son was more vehement than ever, it took at that time but one form. The resolve that he should one day reign, and the means to be pursued for that end, robbed her of the pure enjoyments which she then might have found in his pleasant converse, sweet gaiety, and tender love for her. Well, a short time before that meeting at Tours, which her majesty speaks of in the above letter, the Prince, who is now eighteen, had been to Paris under the name of the Comte de Queniez, which thin disguise constrained him to a less costly display of apparel and equipage than if his rank had been proclaimed. He travelled with us to Tours, and I took heed that his manner and countenance were somewhat changed. He was at one time very mirthful, then all of a sudden pensive and almost sad. His moods were as variable as the lights and shadows on a breezy day. He was for ever talking of Paris; and I misdoubted that his fanciful love for the Lady Anne had been succeeded by a more real passion for some lady at the French court.

I had heard from the Queen before we left Verdun that the Earl of Warwick had landed in France, having openly raised his standard against his mock king; but not being prepared for the sudden contest therein involved, had sailed for Calais, and narrowly escaped being captured by the so-called royal troops. The favour he had always enjoyed with King Lewis had doubtless procured him a welcome in his dominions. The Queen's terror was lest the said King should espouse the cause of Clarence; but of this till this time there is no sign, for he hath marvellously caressed his cousins since their arrival.

But to return to the Prince. I saw he was watching for an occasion to speak to me alone, which intent accident defeated several times. At last I met him in the corridor leading to the Queen's room, and he said to me in a hurried manner, " Hist, Dame Margaret! quick, take this letter, and let no one get wind of it.. I have seen and several times conversed with her. She is divine! the most graceful, the most witching noble wench in the whole world! I am madly in love with her. O Heavens, there is some one coming! Try and speak to me after the banquet, there's a good dame."

This is the letter he then gave to me:

"*The Lady Anne Neville to the Lady Margaret de Roos.*

"My Lady Margaret,—I greet you; and forasmuch as I hope you have not forgot the little companion you had at Warwick House when you lay there sick four or five years ago, I write you this letter, which will be carried by one I little forecasted should have been my messenger to you, or any one else. At first, dear lady, I thought to leave you to guess how I came to discover the true name of sweet Dame Clere; but if you mislike guessing as much as I do, this should be an ill return for your past goodness to me, and should also lead you to suppose that my good mother had betrayed your secret, which I wit she hath never done to any one. And so I will, as briefly as I can, relate what caused me to know you to be what you are.

"I misdoubt you have already heard we are in France, my father having been forced to take refuge in this kingdom by the ungrateful conduct of King Edward, which hath caused indignation to all well-disposed persons, and compelled even his brother, my sister's husband, to turn against him, and espouse my said father's quarrel. We were very much tempest-tossed at sea, and not suffered to land at the poor little town of Calais, which loves us so well, by the present cruel holders of it for that bad king; albeit my sister was at the time in a very perilous condition, which sea-sickness enhanced. But I thank God neither she nor her fair little son suffered serious damage therefrom; and when we landed at Dieppe, there was one more Christian soul in the ship than when we sailed from England. When she was sufficiently recovered to travel, we came thence to Paris, where the King hath appointed to us very convenient lodgings, near to his own palace. For mine own part, I have never in my life been one half so happy.

"And now I would have you to wit that I have seen Prince Edward of Lancaster more than once—yea, many times—since we came here. The King of France gave us a banquet four days after our arrival, —that is, he invited my mother and me; for my father had tarried on the road to confer with Lord Oxford, and Isabel was still too weak to stir abroad. O the heavens, sweet lady! what a great hap did that banquet prove to my poor self! For, I pray you, who should his Majesty appoint to lead me to the dining-hall but one he styled his fair cousin, the Comte de Queniez? I had no suspicion this was the Prince of Lancaster; but even in those first moments I thought this gentleman more noble in form and visage, and gracious in his haviour, than any prince I had ever seen.

"When we were seated at the banqueting-table, I was somewhat abashed, for I felt afraid to speak French, which is yet strange to me; but my diffidence was soon eased by this pretended count addressing me in excellent good English. 'Lady Anne,' quoth he, 'doth this city of Paris like you?' 'Exceedingly well,' I replied, glad to speak in mine own tongue; 'it hath an incomparable pleasantness of aspect and a lightsome air which chaseth away melancholy.' 'Is it superior to London, in your opinion?' he asked. 'O, sir,' I replied, 'London is my native city; if I should commend my birthplace, it should be no praise to it.' 'Think you, then,' he said, smiling, 'that the praises we give to what we love have no value?' 'Much.' I answered, 'as a token of affection, but little in the way of commendation.' 'Ah, one ounce of affection,' he exclaimed, 'is of greater worth than a pound of commendation.' 'Sir,' I said, 'if you despise commendation, I will not say what I was thinking of.' 'O, I pray you say it,' he cried; 'I despise not commendation, only I set a higher store on affection.' 'I was going to say,' quoth I, 'that I marvelled how you, sir, a French person, should speak English so well.' He turned round, and said with a smile, 'You think I am French?' 'You have a French name,' I answered, blushing not a little at my mistake. 'O sweet Lady Anne!' he softly whispered, 'question your memory, I pray you. Nay, look not on your plate, nor at yonder pasty turret, nor on your own fair little hand; but, if you would assist remembrance, look at me.'

"I was ashamed to seem ashamed to raise mine eyes to his face, and so I gave one fixed look at his visage, and then my heart began to beat very fast, for betwixt remembering and guessing, I suddenly bethought me who he was. 'Come, what doth memory say?' he pleasantly asked: 'have you ever seen one like me before?' 'Methinks,' I replied, my cheeks waxing more burning every moment, 'that I have

seen eyes like yours before.' 'When and where?'
asked he, smiling. 'A long time ago, sir,—in a little
child's face. But maybe I am mistaken.' 'Shall I
tell you,' he said, 'what memory tells me when I gaze
on your face, Lady Anne?' 'Yes, sir, willingly, if it
will assist mine own.' 'Well, this is what she por-
trays: a state-room in a palace hung with red damask
silk, and tall windows looking on a river with many
barges on it; and in the casement of one of those
windows stood a little wench, dressed in a white
kirtle, holding a doll in her arms. Memory says this
little wench had the softest blue eyes in all the world,
and the most incomparably lovely face. She counted
the barges as they went up the river, and the boy at
her side those which went down it. They played in
this way for some time; and then the boy fetched his
hobby-horse, to show it to his little playmate, and
they both rode on it, laughing; he kicking it with
his feet and she clinging to him half afraid. And
they said they were riding to be married—' 'At
Westminster Abbey,' I said in a low voice. 'Ah,
now, by St. John,' he cried joyfully, 'we have good
memories. Yes, sweet Lady Anne, that was the so-
called love-day in London; alas, a very false or fleeting love it proved! But the two children's love was
of another sort, I ween—it was not leastways false
or fleeting in the boy's heart.' These last words were
said in a very low voice, I could only just catch the
sounds of them. A pause ensued, and then the Prince
said: 'Methinks, Lady Anne, I have a dear friend
whom you know.' I could not think who this should
be, and he said, 'One Dame Clere, which broke her
leg, and sojourned at Warwick House, some years
ago, in London.' 'O heavens! doth your highness
know that good sweet dame?' I exclaimed. 'Call

me not highness, Lady Anne,' the Prince said, with a heightened colour. 'It is only the Comte de Queniez, not the Prince of Wales, who may sit at the same board with Lord Warwick's daughter.' This confused and pained me. 'Do you, then, hate my father, sir?' I said; 'if indeed I am to address you in that plain fashion.' The Prince's face flushed still more deeply as he replied, 'Inasmuch as he is *your* father, I should esteem him the most of any man in the world; but, alas! King Henry's son must be Lord Warwick's enemy, or at least his adversary.' Then hastily changing this painful discourse, we talked of dear Dame Clere; and the Prince discovered to me her real name, and that she is his mother's most faithful friend, the companion of her travels and dangers, and her comforter in sorrow, and he himself, he says, dearly affections her. Ah, dear Lady Margaret, methought at the time there was some mystery touching your stay in our house. I am right glad to learn the truth, and I love you more than ever.

"You must wit that after that day at the palace the Comte de Queniez often walked in the public gardens, near which we live, and wherein my mother and I took the air every day. She was very willing he should join us, and hath suffered him freely to converse with me, which has made the time pass very agreeably, and I wish I could live that month over again. She never said one word of these meetings to my father when he arrived, anyways in my hearing, nor hath she nor I so much as named the Prince to Isabel or Clarence.

"Howsoever I must now end this letter, for I must give it to the Prince to-day, for nothing will serve him but to carry it to you himself. I therefore pray your ladyship to commend me to God in your good prayers, and to be no worse a friend to me than in times past, for I am your loving Anne Neville as in the days when you let me know that Prince Edward had not forgotten his playfellow. I obliged him to confess you had said the like to him of me. May the good Jesu have you in His keeping!—Your humble loving servant,

"ANNE NEVILLE."

CHAPTER XL.

The Struggle.

AFTER I had read the Lady Anne's letter I was afraid to speak with the Prince, for now that, through his meeting with her, his imaginary attachment had changed into a veritable bewitchment, I misdoubted if, being in his confidence, I should act rightfully towards the Queen in fostering a liking which was unknown to her, who, of all persons in the world, was most concerned therein, and most like to be averse to it. I kept all the day out of his way, and after supper in the withdrawing-room played at Marteaux with some of the other ladies to avoid conversing with him.

Any one that evening should have supposed he had been in love with old Lady Margaret de Roos, so closely did he hover about her, watching for an occasion to catch her eye or whisper in her ear. Albeit disquieted at these his efforts to talk to me, I could not but inwardly smile at their ingenuity.

Each time a game was finished, he either said, "I fear your ladyship is a little tired with playing : there is a fresher air in the next chamber ; will you move to it?" or again : "Will it please you, Lady Margaret, to taste of the conserves the King hath sent us? They are set down with the wine in the adjoining room;" and finally: "Come, Lady Margaret, let us play at cards. I will teach you an excellent good game I learnt in Paris."

"Ay indeed, fair cousin," cried the young Count René of Lorraine, who overheard him; "one in which, if I mistake not, the suit of hearts taketh precedency of all others."

The Prince blushed to his temples, and replied he should be glad to learn the game his cousin spoke of, but for his part he had not heard of it at Paris or any where else.

This jest of that young Monseigneur made me suspect that talk was ministered at Tours touching the meeting at the French King's palace of the Prince and Lord Warwick's daughter; but I could not discover that the Queen had heard of it.

Howsoever, two days later, when I was walking with her in the pleasure-garden, there came there King Lewis, and my lord the Prince with him. The Queen advanced to meet his majesty, and they walked together in one of the alleys, the Prince and I keeping behind at a discreet distance. There was no help now for it but I must converse with him; and he spent no time beating about the bush, but as soon as we were out of hearing of the Queen and the King, began in this wise:

"Well, madame, you have read that fair creature's letter. I pray you now be my good friend and tell me the truth. Is she like, think you, to love me as I love her?"

"My lord Prince," I answered, "if you will pardon my boldness, methinks there is a question you should ask of yourself before you put that one to me."

"What question?" quoth he, a little chafed.

"This one, my lord—Should the Prince of Wales love the Lady Anne Neville? Should the son of King Henry desire to be loved by the Lord Warwick's daughter?"

I saw the shoe pinched. The comely face of the Prince waxed crimson, and he hastily replied, "I want *my* questions answered; not to have any put to *me*."

"I crave your highness's pardon," I said; "I had forgot my duty, and had best repair that fault by a humble silence."

"O cunning Lady Margaret," he exclaimed, with his sweet smile—the sweetest smile in the world, bright as his mother's, and mild as his father's—"who knoweth as well as she to chide by artful respect and rebuke with lowly courtesy? But prithee, dear sweet Lady Meg, forgive my rude speech, and listen to me. 'Tis very well to say, '*Should* you love,' but if I am horribly in love already, what can I do?"

"Love," I replied, "should not play the tyrant over reason and duty, but prove subservient to them, my lord Prince."

"*Should* again!" quoth he, shaking his head; "I promise you, whether he should or not, love doth play the tyrant in a very absolute manner when it is a true love such as mine for sweet Anne Neville. O, Lady Margaret, I love her distractedly; but, believe me, if her father persists in his rebellion against my father, his rightful king, then, albeit I must always love her who never for one day faltered in her allegiance to our house,—by the same token that in her home she was called Lancastrian, as you very well know, and yourself have told me before now,—I know I cannot wed her. But you are not privy yet to all the state secrets, Lady Margaret. Great changes are at hand. The

King Lewis hath told me to-day that he hath been in correspondence with the Earl of Warwick and Lord Oxford since they landed in France, and hath plainly told them that to set up another Yorkist king in the place of the present usurper should be a most impolitic, nay an impossible, thing, and the only attempt to do it ruinous. These noblemen have replied in terms which hold out hopes, his majesty saith, that they should only too gladly seek for reconcilement with our house, if such an issue was to be looked for. Lady Warwick, with whom he conversed thereon in Paris, said she should be the most overjoyed person in the world if this long breach should be healed, which she confessed to the King had cost her more tears than any one could wot of; and that if any gentle offer from her husband was like to be embraced, she should go down upon her knees to him to make it. She declared her eldest daughter's royalty should be to her the greatest grief imaginable, for it would lack every semblance of lawful right. The king then said: 'But, madame, should it be to you an equal sorrow if your youngest daughter should one day wear the crown of England?' Then her colour heightened; and albeit she only replied with a smile, that a soothsayer had once told her Anne should be a queen, he thinks that never was a lady better pleased than she was at this question. Now, Lady Margaret, though I do confess my love to be a tyrant, methinks it overrules not duty and reason, for it should seem duty and reason are on its side; and if sweet Anne loves me, and my sweet mother is persuaded by the King to entertain these peaceful thoughts, what shall be lacking to make love, duty, and reason agree together, like faith, hope, and charity? And now, will you tell me so much, and I will ask no more of the contents of that letter which I carried to you from

Paris, with as great a temptation to read it as ever I had in my life to offend against honesty,—so much, I say, as if the writer saith she mislikes me not?"

"Alas, my lord Prince," I answered, "I should slander the Lady Anne if I should say she had written to me one word which argued she liked not your highness well; but you well know, good my lord, that young damsels of her rank and virtue yield their hearts only where their parents bestow their hands."

"True, Lady Margaret; but if—"

"O, my lord Prince, that little word *if* doth often prove a deceitful lure. There are, I fear, more cold winds than you wot of like to nip the blossom of your hope before it can turn into fruit."

"Think you, then, my mother should be vehemently opposed to this alliance? Will she not be persuaded to pardon the Earl of Warwick?"

"*Can* she pardon," I exclaimed with emotion, "the wrongs she has suffered from him? My lord Prince, you know not the bitter memories which his name awakens in those who love your parents." Then I bethought me I should not speak in this wise to the Prince; for if a reconciliation should be possible—and who was I, that I should dare to forejudge this weighty question?—it were well to bury past resentments in the shroud of silence, if oblivion was not possible. So I checked myself, and said: "I pray you, my lord, to forget my hasty words. God defend I should speak aught against forgiveness, or any peace He shall put it in men's hearts to make. But this much I must needs say: if the Queen your mother—"

At that moment her majesty and the King turned suddenly round, and we stood face to face with them. I can call to mind as if it was but yesterday how they looked as they passed us. The Queen's visage was convulsed with passion. She seemed to tread the ground as if disdaining it. The King's countenance was not in the least moved. One of his hands was laid on his breast, and with the other he held his beads. When they reached the door of the Queen's *pavillon*, which opens on the pleasaunce, the King made a very lowly obeisance. I could not hear what he said, nor what her majesty replied; but I saw by her gestures and countenance that it was some sort of vehement denial. I misdoubt the Prince watched them with a beating heart; and when they disappeared, he exclaimed: "I am certain the King has broached the matter. How angered the Queen looked!"

"You had best soon see her yourself, my lord," I said. "If any one can move her to any concession, it is your highness."

"I will," he said.

"My lord," I cried, calling him back, "if you will heed my humble counsel, let not the pardon to the earl be joined to any other matter, howsoever near your heart. Let that come afterwards."

He made a sign of assent, and left me.

When I reëntered the palace, I met Sir John Fortescue, who stopped me, and said: "Lady Margaret, doth the Queen know the Earl of Warwick hath arrived here?"

"Heavens!" I cried; "it is not possible!"

"Yea," he said; "and moreover he is by this time, I ween, closeted with King René. God grant good may come of it! Our Prince is head over ears in love with the Lady Anne."

"She is not here?" I asked.

"No; she is with her mother and sister at Angers. Let me know, if you can, how the Queen is minded touching the earl. It should be a hard struggle to her to see and to forgive him; but I pray God she may do so, for the King's and the Prince's, and most for England's sakes."

"The Queen asketh for you, Lady Margaret," said the Prince to me, coming out of his mother's chamber. He was as pale as death, and his lips quivering.

I found her majesty alone. I was almost afraid to approach her. She said nothing for two or three minutes. All at once she uttered a kind of cry, and opening her arms clasped me to her breast.

"Thou hast heard what they ask me to do? O God, O God! was this to be added to all the rest? But no, no—a hundred thousand times no! I am not so degraded yet. That man!—the author of all my woes, the persecutor of my husband, the traducer of my fame, he who hath pierced my heart with wounds which can never be healed, which shall bleed till the Day of Judgment, when I shall loudly appeal to God for justice against him—that I should see and pardon him! O, never, never! Bid the grave give up its dead. Let him return to me all my friends he hath slain; let youth, joy, and love be mine again, which he drove from me before I was eighteen; and then, it may be, I can forgive him. Every hair of my head, every nerve in my body, every vein in my heart, seems to rise and protest against this meeting. I am afraid to see him. I have not lost my senses in many terrible haps; but I know not what the sight of that man might work in me of frantic passion and furious hate. Let him not approach me, Margaret. Stand at the door, and keep him from me. Stay with me to-night. I am afraid to dream that I have forgiven him. And Edward—Edward asked me to pardon Lord Warwick! I could have laughed to hear him. He whom he branded as base-born, whom he proclaimed the child of crime and shame! Poor boy! I scared him with my anger; but he should not have dared to speak to me of Warwick. *Warwick!* O, that a name should have the power to raise such a tumult in the soul! Give me thy hand; put it here. Dost thou feel how my heart beats? I tell thee I think it would kill me at once to meet that man. I to forgive Warwick! Can such a thought have entered his own brain?"

"My own thought," I said, "if I may dare to speak it, is that he should never have conceived such a hope, if the French King had not held it out to him in the first place."

"Ah, that heartless fox!" she rejoined, clasping her hands together as if she would have crushed her delicate fingers in that convulsive gesture,—"that hypocrite! Is he to play the peacemaker, and preach to *me* forgiveness? This it was which maddened me just now. If one should come to me and say: 'Margaret of Anjou, your husband is a helpless captive—your son's fate is in your hands: if you pardon not the Earl of Warwick, you ruin them both;' I could listen, albeit not consent; for never, never shall I yield that point! But this dry, hard, fierce reasoning I cannot give heed to without raving; and if by pardon is meant I should stand still, and let that man kneel to me and kiss my writhing hand, and with parched and fevered lips utter the words, 'Lord Warwick, I pardon you'—no, Margaret de Roos; no! even that I never will do. Let no one dare to speak to me of it again. I am not fallen so low as to belie by a shameful deed the justest, deepest, wildest resentment which ever burned in the heart of a woman and of a queen. Go to, go to! Let all the world deceive and mock, if it lists. Let my cousin, this artful king, insult God's majesty by his abominable piety, his saintly hypocrisy;

I am not made of such stuff. Another spirit my mother bequeathed to me. O, my mother, my mother! I thank God you died before ever you heard that your daughter's honour had been assailed by the slanders, the public slanders, of the wretch they would have me pardon. Heavens! even pagans said Cæsar's wife was not to be suspected; and I, the wife of a Christian king—"

"Ah, madame!" I exclaimed; "*there, there* you yourself point to the difference. To forgive is Christian—"

"Margaret de Roos, dare not—dare not to utter that word! King Lewis hath poisoned for me every religious thought. I loathe the very sound of pious sayings. It sickens me; it curdles the blood in my veins. I could have torn his beads from his hands and trodden them under foot, when he muttered betwixt *Aves* his cunning speeches! O God, forgive me! Sweet Mother of God, pardon me! Pardon, pardon, O God of heaven and earth! Why have they made me abhor that word, so that I hate to utter it?"

Then she sank exhausted on a couch, and lay a long time silent, whilst I knelt beside her, and bathed her forehead with cold water. Ever and anon her lips murmured, "Pardon Lord Warwick!" and then her hands clenched themselves again, and her brow contracted as if with a sudden pain.

The night was passed much in the same manner as the day. Little sleep did her majesty get; if she slumbered a moment, then I could see her dreams still ran on the same theme. Once she awoke, and calling me—for I had sat up with her—she said, "That man is not here, is he?"

"Who, madame?" I said, uncertain of her meaning. For no one, I was sure, had told her of Lord Warwick's arrival.

"Warwick," she whispered; "I dreamt he was under the same roof with me. If I thought so, I would rise and, if needs be, on foot leave this palace."

"Content you, madame, content you," I said. "In the hours of night all kinds of strange imaginations haunt the brain."

Then another time she sat up in her bed and counted on her fingers. "Margaret de Roos," quoth she, "I am reckoning the score of offences they call upon me to forgive in the Earl of Warwick. My peace destroyed; my honour defamed by public proclamation; my husband dethroned, cast into a dungeon, loaded with chains, led round the stocks, jeered at, and mocked; my son and I barely 'scaping death more than a score of times, made outlaws, beggars, fugitives, abject wanderers on the face of the earth—all by that man's prompting, devising, doing, for twenty long years of unmitigated, persistent, malignant enmity; and now—now, forsooth, when, stung by the serpent he fostered in his bosom, he turns despaired to me—shall I play the hypocrite, and say I forgive him? O, cursed would be the hour, cursed the day, in which I should utter that falsehood!"

Thus she raved and moaned alternately the livelong night. At last the morning dawned; and when she had risen and was dressed, then began a marvellous display of that calm cunning which is more than a match for the most resolved and impassioned will. The French King, like a skilful angler, played with consummate art, and by means of various instruments, for many successive hours, with the impetuous impulses of my hapless Queen's poor struggling heart. First, a letter from her father was placed in her hand, which I saw powerfully affected her. She read these words aloud: "Beware, my daughter, if, after having saved all by your noble firmness, you lose not all by wilful obstinacy." She let the missive drop, and covered her face with her hands.

Then Madame Yolande ran in to her chamber weeping, and falling on her neck cried out: "Sister, sweet sister, I deny not that that English lord hath been most like the devil in his actions of any man in the whole world. But the good God, I have heard say, would forgive the devil himself if he could repent; and I am assured that when Milor Warwick was asked the first time if he would sue for pardon to the Queen Marguerite, tears rolled down his cheeks, and he replied, yea, of a surety, he would do so, and on his bended knees, if he thought there could be a woman in the world of so noble and godlike a spirit as to forgive slanders against herself, even as Christ Himself pardoneth blasphemies when repented of."

"Pardieu!" exclaimed the Comte de Vaudémont. "Methinks, madame my sister, you have it in your power to taste the rarest sweetness of glory which can be known on earth; for here is your greatest enemy and worst slanderer ready to fall this day at your feet, and to confess his falsehoods before the whole world, than which greater amends to your honour cannot well be conceived."

The Queen fastened on one word in the count's speech, and said: "*To-day*, said you, monseigneur my brother? In the name of God, was my nightly prescience true? Is Lord Warwick here?"

"Yea, yea, madame," the count hastily replied. "He came yesterday, and hath since conferred with the King of France, and seen many of your kinsmen. He is as passionately set on the restoration of his majesty your husband as ever he was on his dethronement; and his hatred of the Duke of York excels your own by so much as the ingratitude of a friend exceedeth in blackness the malignity of an enemy."

With more or less of skill and of cunning all the French princes held the same language in turns to the Queen, who listened to their words with her eyes fixed on the floor, ever and anon murmuring to herself: "Warwick here, Warwick at hand, Warwick suing for pardon! Is this an insane comedy, or an unparalleled trick of fortune bringing that to pass which sober reason cannot credit?"

Lastly, the king himself came to visit her; and after his wonted religious speeches, which she heard with an almost undisguised impatience, he made his final attack on the fortress of her resolve by a well-skilled insinuation that whereas if she forgave the earl, whom he affectioned, and for whom he would do more than for any man living, he should zealously befriend her cause; so, if she would not pardon him, he should think her quarrel too hopeless to espouse it.

Upon this she said to him, wringing her hands: "God is my witness, sire, that if none but myself were concerned I should rather lay my head on the block, or be tied in a sack and thrown into the Loire, or, worse yet, beg my bread at a church-door, than yield in this matter. No, sire; never, never of my own spirit can I forgive this man, nor be contented with him, nor pardon him. And I would have your majesty to wit that I and my son have in England certain friends and parties which we are like to lose by this means; and this will be a greater hindrance to us than these new unnatural allies shall do us any good."

"If it be so, sweet cousin," the king answered, "I am most contented thereat, for then the shrine of our Lady of Embrun shall be all the richer for the gold offerings in which we may then more piously expend the sums which your war should else have cost our treasury. My fair young cousin, your son, shall thus owe his crown not to any foreign aid, but to his English subjects, which all parties should most desire. And if the Earl of Warwick leaves Tours this day without having obtained an interview with your majesty, he will be, I ween, all the better received by his fair daughter Madame de Clarence, whose ambitious hopes shall then revive."

I saw the Queen writhed at this speech; but yet she yielded not. Two opposing tides, like eddies, in her mind swayed her backward and forward in this internal conflict. First she thought there should be ruin, and not gain, in this compromise; and on this ground fought against it. Then, if the reasonings of her friends and the king's artful discourse showed the policy of a reconciliation with this maker of kings, as he is called, the swelling surges of indignant pride arose, and she protested she could sooner forgive the earl, after her own victory, if he should stand before her a chained and doomed prisoner, than now, when he came, as it were with the crown in his hand, on bended knee, but with a proud heart, to sue for pardon at her hands.

But towards evening, after further parleys with the Dukes of Guyenne and Alençon, Monsieur de Maine, and some others, a change came over her. The Prince never said so much as one word to her touching Lord Warwick that day; but there was a wistful expression in his countenance which I think she took heed of. She sent for Sir John Fortescue late in the afternoon; and after a brief conversation with him, she wrote to the King that she would see the earl that evening in his majesty's withdrawing-room, but only on one condition, which was that, in his royal presence, and before all the princes then at Tours, her own kinsmen, the English lords of his and of her parties, he should unsay all the calumnies he had ever uttered against her, and declare their falsehood to have been known to himself even when he framed them, and to promise he would do the like in England in as public a manner as he had defamed her. Unless this was promised, she swore that she would never see or speak to the said earl.

Presently came the King's answer, wherein he affirmed that these conditions were accepted. A smile —if aught so sad and scornful can be called a smile— curled her lip, and she bade her women dress her for this interview. She sat motionless whilst they plaited her hair, the blackness of which was now tinged with gray; and when they put on her royal mantle, it seemed as if they were robing a marble image—she looked so cold and rigid. The Prince stood at the door of her chamber, and offered her his hand to conduct her to the king's apartments. She took no notice of him, and walked straightforward with as pale a visage as one going to the scaffold.

When she entered, the princes were already assembled. She greeted the king, who stood awaiting her, with a silent obeisance, and then craved that the chamber should be darkened. I ween she desired that none should watch her countenance during the interview with the earl. All the French princes and princesses which were akin to her stood on one side of the room, and the English lords and esquires of her party on the other; the King Lewis at her right, on one side of her armed chair, and the lord Prince on the left. I was behind her, holding the back of the seat, or peradventure my limbs would not have supported me. When the door opened, and Lord Warwick and Lord Oxford entered, the King advanced to greet them, and led them towards her majesty.

CHAPTER XLI.
Love's Victory.

Tours, June 13th.

THE Queen and the Earl of Warwick—the two proudest hearts on this earth, I ween—have met face to face, and discharged in vehement words their impassionate resentments. It was like when contrary torrents dashing against each other produce foaming eddies, as I have seen when a great river rushes into the sea. But albeit, when the earl was reproached by the Queen for his treasons and foul slanders, he broke forth in retorts charging her counsellors with having plotted his destruction, body and goods, and saying that no nobleman, outraged and despaired as he had been, would have done otherwise than oppose force to force and enmity to enmity, his emotion was not anyways comparable to hers. Methought he rather assumed that great anger than felt it, and was resolved at any cost to achieve the reconcilement in hand, swayed thereunto by a masterful passion of present revenge more powerful than all former resentments. When he spoke of the so-called King Edward, a paleness overspread his visage, which is the most sure token of the direst rage. It made me almost tremble to see that man at the feet of the Queen. It seemed so incredible he should be there; and the change in him so sudden and unnatural. This is, I think, what he said to her.

"Madame, I unthroned you and your lord the King,

but I have now been the means of upsetting your enemy; and I would have you to know that for the time to come I will be as much his foe as I have heretofore been his friend and maker. So take me, noble lady; so repute me. Forgive all I have done against you. I offer myself and I will bind myself in all manner of ways to be your faithful subject from this time forward, and a true liegeman to this your son, and I will set the King of France for my surety."

"Yea, that I will be," cried the King. "Sweet cousin, pardon the earl, and he will be to you the most true servant in the world."

Whether the Queen was silently tasting the strange bitter joy of seeing this her famous enemy sue for forgiveness, or that the conflict yet continued in her soul betwixt contending passions, I know not; but half raised from her chair of state, her hands resting on the arms thereof, her face averted from him, and her eyes fixed as if gazing on some vision in empty space, she remained motionless and speechless for well-nigh one quarter of an hour. At last the earl said,

"Madame, pronounce my sentence."

She turned her eyes full upon him with a singular, mournful gaze.

"Have you unsaid *all?*" she asked him.

"Yea," he replied; "not with my lips alone, but with my heart also."

"You hear him?" she exclaimed, her ashy pale cheeks suddenly flushing. "Sire and princes and lords, English and French, you hear him? The Earl of Warwick confesses that wittingly, maliciously, and falsely he charged me with foul crimes which I disdain here to rehearse. Before God and before you, he owns to have been a slanderer and a liar."

A silence deep as death followed these words. There

was not one present, methinks, who did not feel an
almost unsufferable confusion. I glanced at the earl.
He had not changed his posture, but I could see that
the veins in his forehead were swelled to bursting. A
sudden change passed over the Queen's countenance.
I ween the fulness of her triumph softened her. She
laid her hand on the earl's shoulder, and said in a loud
distinct voice,

" Lord Warwick, I forgive you."

Shouts of gratulation burst on all sides. The Prince
threw himself into the earl's arms.

" Edward ! " the Queen cried, as if wounded to the
heart. I thought she would have fainted. But the
Earl of Oxford at that moment came forward, and falling on his knees before her, uttered these words:

" Pardon me also, my liege lady."

She instantly replied,

" My lord, *your* pardon is right easy to purchase;
for I know you and your friends have suffered much in
King Henry's quarrel."

She then made an obeisance to the King and retired
to her chamber. When she was alone with me and
had cast off her regal mantle, she sat down on the
rushes in a kind of hopeless mood which I had never
seen in her before.

" Think you," she said to me in a hoarse voice, and
with a troubled look in her eyes, " that there will be a
benison on this day's work? No, no, Margaret de
Roos. If there be such a thing as unholy reconcilement, then I fear me this is one."

What she said pained me, for verily betwixt the royal
peace-maker's hypocrisy, the earl's new hatreds, and
the Queen's unforgiving forgiveness, I saw small virtue
in this sudden alliance. The Prince's innocent joy,
the radiant hopes which beamed in his eyes, seemed to

me like flowers blossoming on heaps of blackened ruins and desecrated tombs.

Since the day of the reconcilement King Lewis ceased not to urge the Queen to proceed to her father's court at Angers, whither he offered to accompany her. The Countess of Warwick and the earl, the Lady Anne Neville, and also the Duke and Duchess of Clarence, were in that city; and nothing would serve his majesty but that they should all meet there, for what purpose it is easy to think. So we travelled thither on the day after the Feast of the Holy Apostles Peter and Paul. The Prince had had much to do to disguise his impatience. I cannot choose but smile at the many wiles he used to draw me during those intervening days to talk of the Lady Anne. On the day before our departure he showed me a poem of King René's, from which he had transcribed these lines, and set them to a fair tune:

> "Par la dame Vierge du pays,
> Quand je vous vis,
> Ah! par lieu de Paradis,
> Tout autre vouloir perdis,
> De penser ailleurs!"

and added: "That is truly my case, Lady Margaret; I can never turn my thoughts to any other damsel than my sweet Anne, who is

> 'Mon doux amour, mon recomfort,
> Et mon espérance outre bord:
> Seule au monde! j'aurais tort
> Si autre j'aimais.'

But I will never love another or marry one I do not love. Now be a good lady to me, sweet Lady Margaret, and tell me what mean the words which since yestereve my mother hath let fall touching a certain royal bride which should be a meet consort for the

Prince of Wales. I see not the princess in Europe which I could wed if I was free to choose, which I am not. Come now, I pray you, and tell me who she hath in her mind, that we may forthwith carry on a siege to dislodge her from it."

I answered him not directly, but took from a vase of flowers near to which we were standing a red rose and a white one, which I joined together, and showed them to him.

"Heavens!" he exclaimed, amazed. "Blows the wind from that quarter? By my troth it cannot be. You do not mean Elizabeth of York?"

"None other," I replied. "The proposal cometh through the so-called king's brother, prudent Gloucester."

"O that man, that Richard!" the Prince exclaimed, stamping his foot. "He is the evil genius of our race. The wretched hunchback loves, or leastways covets, my Anne, I know. Doth he offer me, then, his puling niece in exchange for her? I will no more wed that little pale prickly rose than I will yield my Anne to him; no, not if ten thousand kingdoms should be the guerdon. But hath my mother, think you, lent her ear to this base proposal?"

"Methinks," I replied, "it proved not wholly distasteful to her. She says her reconcilement with the earl hath shaken her pride, and thrown open the door to thoughts opposed to those hitherto cherished. But to my thinking, my lord Prince, and I say not this to flatter your desires, this insinuated offer of the Yorkists is but a wile to detach the Queen and your highness from your new powerful ally and subject."

"Ay," he exclaimed. "Give me the brave earl and his fair daughter, and let the Yorkists go hang!"

I smiled at this speech, and advised him at once to open his heart to the Queen.

"No," he replied; "let her first see Anne, and then on the morrow King Lewis and my grandsire will propose the match to her."

Angers, July 15th.

In this old palace of the Queen's father, on the most fair summer evening imaginable, a notable assemblage of royal and princely personages have met and embraced, which little thought once this new amity should have arisen betwixt them. The noble King René folded his daughter in his arms when she arrived, her head rested awhile on his bosom, and when she raised it and gazed on his face his tears fell fast on her brow; joyful ones, I ween, for he was right glad her prospects were mended. The Queen Jeanne welcomed her guests with her wonted goodness of heart and grave courtesy. The King of the French showed so great a contentment with the good cheer made for him by his uncle and aunt, that nothing could exceed it. He caressed every one in turn, but most of all our Prince, whose colour went and came as the hour approached when the Countess of Warwick, with her daughters, was to visit her majesty. When they came in, methinks his heart and mine were beating alike fast. The countess, whose noble visage it gladdened me right well to see, knelt to the Queen, who raised and kissed her. Then the Duchess of Clarence made her obeisance, if the bending of the knee can be so called when no other sign of homage doth appear. The duke, her husband, likewise performed this ceremony with a constrained, embarrassed air, which gave it an ill grace. Then the countess took her youngest daughter by the hand and said, "Your majesty hath,

I ween, to pardon us all save this little wench, which never swerved from her allegiance to King Henry." The Queen looked intently at the lovely face of the Lady Anne, which was timidly raised to hers, and whose mantling blushes made it yet more sweetly winsome. She smiled and said, " Lady Anne, I could have guessed you had always been loyal; I read it in your eyes."

A beautiful flush overspread the pretty creature's face, and she falteringly said, " Madame, this is the most happy day I have known."

"God give you many happy days to come!" the Queen kindly replied.

I leave those who read to think if the Prince was not all eyes and ears during this brief colloquy. At the banquet that day he was seated by the Duchess of Clarence, and opposite to the Lady Anne. Whenever he spoke to the duchess, she replied with an ill-disguised haughtiness which opposed an icy barrier to all his gracious courtesy. I noticed that the Earl of Warwick twice or thrice glanced frowningly towards his daughter, as if to recall her to her duty; upon which she forced a smile and addressed some remark to the Prince, who for his part seldom took his eyes off her sister. In sooth this Lady Anne is the fairest maiden imaginable: of so delicate a complexion and refined loveliness, that she as much surpasses every lady at this court in beauty as the rose doth all the other flowers of the garden. The sweet bashfulness of her countenance, its thousand graces over and above the marvellous perfection of her features and form, make her more witching than my poor pen can portray. I do not marvel that the Prince is in love with her; but O, what will the Queen say to this strange alliance?

I would give one thousand pounds, if I had them,

that the Duchess of Clarence had not brought hither my old companion at court, now become her favourite lady, the long-necked and sharp-tongued Isabel Butler. Alas, methinks she looks like a bird of ill-omen; and I cannot choose but wonder at her boldness in appearing before her royal mistress, which she suddenly abandoned in the midst of the wars. But shame hath fled, methinks, nowadays into remote corners, and is not in fashion as heretofore.

The King of France danced in the evening with the Queen of Sicily, and the Comte de Vaudémont with the Duchess of Clarence, the duke with the Lady Anne, and then the Prince of Wales with his cousin, Madame Marie de Lorraine. Whilst these danced, Lady Anne kept her eyes, for the most time, fixed on the ground; yet I could see now and again the beautiful truants break loose from that constraint, and watch for a brief moment the graceful movements of the Prince. Afterwards she came to my side, and after some talk touching the time I was sick at Warwick House, she said agreeably: " Lady Margaret, I wot well it is breaking God's commandment to covet a neighbour's servant, but think you it is a sin to covet any one's mistress? I am sorely tempted to this envy; for beshrew me if I would not fain be the servant of your mistress."

The Prince had come and stood behind my chair, eavesdropping, he said, and straightway they began to talk together in a low voice. This dialogue ensued between them:

"Sweet lady, what treason are you hatching with this great plotter, Lady Margaret?"

"I was seeking ghostly counsel from her, my lord, for the satisfying of my conscience."

"Wherein is it troubled, sweet Lady Anne?"

"I cry you mercy, my lord Prince; I had as lief not turn your grace into a ghostly adviser."

"Well, there is one sin for which I ween you should do penance, Lady Anne."

"What should that be, my lord?"

"Why, the breaking of a promise. You never sent me a token of remembrance in your letters to this lady —no, not so much as one word, if she is to be believed; and yet in Paris—"

"O, good my lord, it was your grace which promised yourself that token. I uttered not one word of assent when you asked for it."

"Therein you condemn yourself, sweet lady; for doth not silence signify consent?"

"O, not all kinds of silence, my lord. I shook my head when you condescended to make that request."

"But I took no heed of that crafty denial, sweet Lady Anne; and I will by no means confess that you have not ill used your poor servant, who vainly hoped, day after day, to receive some little proof he was not quite forgotten."

Lady Anne cast down her eyes and answered nothing. She had not a very ready tongue; but her confusion was so pretty when she lacked courage to speak, that one loved her the more for it. The Prince seemed of that opinion. He looked at her in silence for a moment, and then, to ease her embarrassment, I think, he said: "Have you been yet to La Reculée, Lady Anne, and seen the fair gardens my grandsire hath planted, marrying nature with art by a thousand graceful devices?"

"Yea, my lord; they are the most beautiful imaginable."

"Nay, not so perfect as those at his country palaces

near Aix and Marseilles, or at his favourite St. Remy. There you see the orange-trees, with their gold fruit and white blossoms shining amidst the pale olive-groves, and birds which bear all the hues of the rainbow on their wings flying about their gilded cages. Fishes too, in estuaries, leaping in the sun; and so many flowers and fruits, that methinks a greater variety was not to be seen in the garden of Paradise. O, Provence is the land of sunshine, poesie, music, and love. If I had a sorcerer's wand, I should at this moment wave it, and straightway we three should now be sitting on a fair terrace overlooking the blue sea, the scent of the orange-blossom perfuming the air, and a band of minstrels singing a welcome to a northern flower, more fair than the rose, more delicate than the mimosa, sweeter than the jasmine; and as the day declined, and the music ceased, and the fire-flies danced around us, and the stars appeared one by one in the dark-blue sky, I would say, Thank God, who hath made this world so beautiful, and mostly that He hath created one being in it dearer to me than all the kingdoms of the earth."

I was surprised at the suddenness of this poetic but grave speech, and so methinks was Lady Anne. Her colour went and came, and she said in a half-playful, half-serious manner: "Well, if it were lawful, my lord Prince, I could verily wish you were a sorcerer, for you would then conjure up a very beautiful enchantment. But even Anjou is, in mine eyes, a piece of fairyland. Not to speak of that bright blue sky, the like of which is rarely if ever seen in England, what fair manors and singular comely pleasure-houses are scattered over this province! not frowning towers and fortresses like elsewhere, but pastoral palaces and sweet hermitages."

"Ah, that is my grandsire's taste, which mingles poesy and religion in all he builds or plants in his realms. Methinks Nature hath been too lavish towards him. She hath given a king talents which should have made a famous poet, a great limner, and a minstrel; piety meet for a saint, courage for more than one hero, and wit for many philosophers. Jealous Fortune despaired of her ability to rival Nature, and abandoned Nature's favourite. Thus the most virtuous, learned, admired, and passionately-loved monarch in this world hath been likewise the most misfortunate."

This speech of the Prince pleased me not wholly, and I was so bold as to say to him: "Piety, my lord, is not a gift, but a virtue."

"Nay, good Lady Margaret," he replied, "is it not a gift of the Holy Ghost?"

"But not of Nature," I objected.

"Dear Lady Margaret," quoth the Prince, "you are no poet."

"Truth, my lord Prince; and you are too much of one."

He laughed at my testy humour; and Lady Anne then said that King René had carried the Duchess of Clarence and herself on St. Peter's day to La Baumette, which she declared was the sweetest spot in the world, and one where she would like to spend her days.

"If you told my grandsire so," said the Prince, "you proved unwittingly a most ingenious flatterer, for La Baumette is as dear to him as the apple of his eye. You saw there the gracious devices and fair paintings wherewith his own hand adorned its walls. It is the sanctuary of the Knights of Los Croissant, the memorial of my holy grandam, and a miniature copy of the famous cave of La Baume, in Provence, where the great lover of Christ, blessed Mary Magdalen, ended her days. Said you a prayer, dear lady, at her altar?"

"Yea, a little prayer; a very short one."

"O, I pray you, what was it? What did you ask for?"

"You are too curious, my lord."

"Will you tell Lady Margaret?"

"Nay, nay; she is very discreet; but —"

"Well, tell me this only, sweet Lady Anne: do you sometimes pray for me?"

"Well, good my lord, I pray for the King, the Queen, and the Prince of Wales."

"Ay, but I would rather you prayed for Edward of Lancaster."

"Anne," cried a sharp imperious voice, which startled us all,—"Anne, the countess our mother is rising to depart. Are you forsooth going to keep her waiting?"

The Lady Anne blushed deeply, and moved forward with the Duchess of Clarence, who did not so much as make an obeisance to the Prince as she passed him. I was more grieved for this lady than angered with her. There was an unnaturalness in her husband's espousal of her father's new allegiance which sat uneasily on them both.

This peaceful evening was the forerunner of a more desperate, or at the least longer, encounter than even the one at Tours. Heavens, what a fortnight ensued! The French king, after Mass on the Feast of the Visitation, proposed to the Queen this alliance, prefacing it with many singular commendations of the Lady Anne, which she, unwitting what was to follow, gave a ready assent to, praising her beauty and modest haviour. When she discovered the purport of his discourse, in her first emotion she exclaimed: "Ah! What, will my Lord Warwick indeed give his daughter to my son, whom he so often branded as the offspring of guilt or fraud!" Then, when that momentary triumphant feeling had passed, she recoiled with a violent indignation from the thought of this marriage. "Has every one but me," she cried, "forgotten the past? Because I have forgiven a rebellious subject, must I needs take to my bosom his daughter and caress the child of a pardoned traitor, who, if he had met with his deserts, should have hung on a gibbet? If he had been the most virtuous and leal Englishman in existence, his daughter should have been no befitting match for the Prince of Wales; but being what he is, I would as lief my son married the child of the meanest esquire in the land as ally himself with this repentant rebel." She would not again leave her chamber after these overtures had been made to her, and was almost sick with anger and vexation. Every day she grew more melancholy. At last one morn she said to me, "I am surrounded by importunate counsellors; they compelled me against my will to this unnatural reconcilement; and now they force upon me with relentless persistency this marriage, which I mortally mislike, nor, as I live, can I see honour or profit in it for me or for my son. I shall and I will find a more profitable parti, and of more advantage, with the so-called King of England. If I had treated with him in place of pardoning that earl, it should have been more politic; but that royal fox my cousin holds me in his power, and uses all my kindred like tools in his hands—my father and my son included."

"Madame," I said, "God defend I should presume to advise your majesty; but thus much I will dare to say: any overtures which pass through the young Duke of Gloucester's channel are like to be most false and fatal, and such as the most inveterate malice can devise."

"There is not one honest man in the whole world," she cried, with a wild look, "save one or two, and those God hath made witless."

After that she would see no one for a while. When the Prince came to inquire after her health, she refused to speak to him, except that once she burst forth: "My son, if these vile proposals have been made to you touching a marriage with Anne Neville, God defend you should have lent an ear to them; for with your mother's consent that alliance shall never take place." The Prince's countenance changed, but he uttered not a word. "Take this letter," she said, "which I showed yestereve to the King of the French. Read it, and see that one nobler than Lord Warwick's daughter, royal in some sense, is offered to your acceptance."

"By whom, madame?" the Prince said, glancing at the signature.

"In sooth, by the villain Richard."

"Sweet mother, if all the kings in the world should urge me to wed against your will, I never would fail in my duty to you; but O, mother and queen, by your most noble motherhood and royalty of heart; by all you have endured and achieved since I, the great cause of your trouble, came into the world, I pray you abhor and disdain the offers of those wicked brothers, —in whom vice hath choked all greatness of soul, and fling from you as an accursed thought that of matching your son with the child of that bad man. Mother, Lord Warwick hath been guilty, very guilty, towards you; I know it, I feel it; but there is in him another spirit than in these men, Edward and Richard of York. My father, my good, my holy father, would say so."

There were tears in the Prince's eyes, and his cheeks glowed like crimson as he uttered these words. It was not possible his mother could look unmoved on his beautiful face, all agitated with strong emotion.

"Edward!" she gently said. He fell down on his knees beside her, and laid his head on her lap. It well-nigh broke my heart to see her bend her pale haggard face towards that fair young head, loved with a greater maternal passion than can be conceived by quiet souls. She laid her thin hand upon it, and looked up to heaven with a glance of so great misery, that I could not bear to see it. He raised his visage —his sweet comely visage—and gazed on her sadly and fondly. She took his head betwixt her hands, as she was wont to do when he was a little child, and looked into his eyes most wistfully. "Lovest thou Warwick's daughter?" she said in a faltering voice.

"More than my life," he answered. "O mother, my life may haply be a short one: let it be happy whilst it lasts."

Poor Queen! A shiver ran through her at these words; they seemed to pierce her heart; but they did their work. A few hours later I saw the Countess of Warwick and the Lady Anne pass into the royal chamber; and on the morrow the marriage contract was signed in the presence of the two kings and Monseigneur de Guyenne. And in the church of St. Mary Lord Warwick swore on the True Cross always to hold the party of King Henry, and always serve him and the Queen and the Prince as a true and faithful subject oweth to serve his sovereign lord. The King of France and his brother swore they would help and sustain to the utmost of their power the

Earl of Warwick in the quarrel of King Henry; and the Queen swore to treat the earl as true and faithful to King Henry, *and for his deeds past never to make him any reproach.* Her voice trembled not a little when she pronounced this oath, which she will without doubt religiously observe. After the recovery of the kingdom of England, the Prince is to be regent of all the realm, and the Duke of Clarence to have all his lands and those of the Duke of York. From this time forth the Lady Anne Neville is to remain in the hands and keeping of the Queen Margaret; but the said marriage is not to be concluded till the Earl of Warwick hath been with an army over into England, and recovered the realm for the most part for King Henry.

God send all these promises are performed! The betrothed are the most joyful lovers which can be seen. The Queen hath taken the Lady Anne into her own lodgings, and doth set great store by her. The Duchess of Clarence is, I ween, mortally offended, because at the banquet to-day the Queen would have the Lady Anne, by reason of her betrothal to the Prince, pass before her sister. I saw Isabel Butler whisper in the duchess's ear a moment afterwards, and her grace bit her nether lip almost through as she listened to her. The French put about that the duke carouses more than is fitting. I like not the mood of this lady, nor the haviour of her lord.

CHAPTER XLII.

An Idyl of Anjou.

How like unto a dream have been these months! After so many reverses and scenes of blood and horror, the world seems to have turned into a scene of enchantment. Since the day of the betrothal of our young Prince and his fair Anne, as soon as the Queen gave her consent to it, the French king lavished honours on her and on her son, by that same token that he chose them to be joint sponsors to his new-born heir at Amboise; and the words "sweet cousin" and "gentle kinsman" were never out of his mouth on the day of the christening, or on the morrow when the Prince and his bride plighted their mutual troth, which ceremony was followed by great feasts, banquets, and rejoicings. But, despite his love and new happiness, the bridegroom would fain have accompanied the Earl of Warwick and his brave followers to England. He chafed like a restrained courser at the denial which the Queen and the earl opposed to his ardour.

"Sweet Prince and son," quoth the earl (and this speech of his methinks conquered at last the Queen's resentment towards him), "let not your hand stain itself with English blood. Let your name be the pledge of peace, the sign of hope, the heart's comfort of every bosom in our torn and bleeding country. Land not in England as the Lancastrian, but only as the English king, with—may I dare to say it who should not?—your fair Saxon wife by your side, as a token of reconcilement, an omen of peaceful days."

Then was seen the nobleness which was in the Queen's character, the love stronger than pride, which in fiery natures doth sometimes exist. These words, which would have angered a meaner soul, caused her to lay her hand on Lord Warwick's arm, and to say:

"Yea, in Edward and in Anne let all enmity die. She shall not be branded, like me, as a Frenchwoman, nor mistrusted by reason of a foreign accent. I thank God for it. Ah, my Lord Warwick, how marvellous a trick fortune hath played us that you should love my son and I affection your daughter! Who shall disbelieve any change on earth to be possible who hath witnessed this hap?"

Yet the Prince pleaded that he should hurry to release his father, and fall at his feet from whom he had been so long parted. But the earl would by no means hear of it, to the no small contentment of the Queen, who was tremblingly frightened lest he should leave her.

"No, gentle Prince and son," quoth the said earl, "it cannot be. I have a pledge to fulfil, and must needs acquit myself of it alone. If you thrust yourself into this enterprise, God is my witness I will not hold to my bargain."

It needed all the Princess Anne's pretty endearments to smooth the brow of her frowning young lord. He had to be contented to play the lover, not the husband, for a while; for albeit contracted, they were not to be married until what time tidings came from England that the King was free and the country returned to its allegiance.

In sweet pastimes, sports, and diversions the summer

weeks passed by. The King of Sicily and his good
queen made of each day a festival for these young
lovers. In sooth it was a fair sight to see their mutual
affection and great happiness. In the gardens of La
Reculée, or the hillside of La Baumette, at the old
palace of Saumur, or by the still waters of the Loire,
or those of the bright Mayence, enchanted hours sped
by, I ween, as they wandered side by side, loving
glances following them, music floating in the air, soft
breezes wafting perfumes from the sunny slopes and
clovered fields, his dark blue eyes fixed in enraptured
gaze on hers, which are, he says, like the little flower
the French peasants call *les yeux de la Vierge*. Exceedingly pretty it was to watch them reading together his
favourite lay, which he steals from his grandsire's
chamber,—the royal pastoral of Regnauld and Jeanneton, *le berger et la bergerette*, which is a picture of the
loves of the King and his young wife Jeanne, when
retiring for a few days from their court they lived in
disguise, tending their sheep and working in their
garden like poor happy country folk. It is a comely
painting in verse of nature's woodland bowers, fresh
gushing streams, and flowery meads, all peopled and
alive with little denizens plying their sportive crafts.
You behold therein the painted fishes at play, their
enemies the birds which watch them furtively, then
grow tired and fly away, but soon return again to wage a
mortal war, shaking their pretty feathers and spreading
their wings in the sun, or, fighting with the wind, make
campaigns against the little flies. These disports of
the birds, fishes, and flies, their wars and mutual loves,
furnish ingenious comparisons to the enamoured pair.
In the fidelity of the doves, in the translucent waters
and the fresh verdure, they discover images of the
faithfulness, truth, and hopefulness of their conjugal

affection. I ween it liked well the lady Princess to hear the Prince read these passages of love ; as when the Shepherd says,

> " Ne pensons qu'à bien aimer
> Et délaissons mélancolie."

And nothing would serve him, she told me, but that she should recite the speech of La Bergerette :

> " Car en l'aimer dont je t'aime
> Il n'y a rien d'amer,
> T'aimerai très parfaitement
> De tout mon cœur et loyaument.
> (Et en le baisant dit), ma joie
> Est quand tu es où que je soie."

"And then, good Lady Margaret," she added, " it was but reason that he should answer like the Berger :

> " Plus de dix fois disant, Ma mie,
> Je n'aimerai autre que toi,
> Mon bien, mon conseil, mon attente
> Si très parfaite en loyauté,
> Qu'au monde il n'y a royauté
> Pour qui changeasse."

But the most joyful of all these playful days was one on which the whole court assembled on the hillside near La Reculée to gather the muscat grapes which King René had been the first to implant in Anjou. All these royal and noble persons were dressed as vintagers, and each one carried a light osier basket trimmed with gay ribbons, into which they stored the purple bunches with lightsome labour and frequent laughter. The sun was hot, and the delicate ladies full soon grew weary of the work, and with their swains sat down to rest in a pleasant orchard near the vineyards. Then a strain of sweet music floated in the air, and a band of shepherdesses approached the company and invited them to a rustic repast in a fair pavillion, hung with wreaths of purple, blue, and red corn-flowers. Very mirthful and pleasant pastimes followed the rural banquet, in the midst of which a messenger arrived, bearing letters for the Queen, which at the first glance I could see came from England, for she turned pale, and her hands trembled so that she could not cut the string herself. Lady Warwick was likewise changing colour; for as yet it was only known that the earl her lord and the Duke of Clarence had landed at Dartmouth with their puissance and proclaimed their intention of delivering King Henry from durance, and that many thousands had gathered round their standard. Since then various reports had crossed the Channel; but the birds must have carried them, for adverse winds had impeded the passage of ships from England to France; and amidst the feastings and disports of King René's court and the pleasant entertainments of this autumn, there had been more weary watchings and secret suffering in the hearts of those three dissimilar ladies, the Queen, the countess, and the duchess, than was known to the more lightsome spirits that surrounded them.

As the words "Tidings from England!" flew from mouth to mouth, there was a general stir amongst the company.

"What news, my daughter?" cried King René.

Alas, his noble heart hath been more accustomed to receive intelligence of disasters than joyful announcements! And there is a resigned cheerfulness in his countenance which betokens one habituated to suffering, and possessed of a mastery over his inward self which nothing can conquer, or else a lightsomeness which no weight can crush. The Princess Anne ran to her mother, and the Duchess of Clarence sat down, her head leaning on her hand, which concealed her face.

"God be praised!" the Queen uttered in a faltering voice.

"Then all is lost!" my quick ears heard the duchess murmur.

The Prince caught up his mother's words and repeated them aloud, upon which a prolonged "Et vive!" burst from the crowd of kinsfolk, courtiers, and servants in the tent, and was reëchoed by the peasants outside; for it was soon bruited that King René's daughter, the idol of his people, had met with some great good fortune. It was a strange medley of sounds. The English cried "Hurrah!" Some fell on their knees, praying aloud; others waved their kerchiefs. When silence was obtained, the Queen rose with a letter in her hand. She held out the other to Lady Warwick, and said in a clear voice in French,

"Madame, your lord hath redeemed his pledge. The King is free and in his palace of Westminster."

"Say, then, 'God bless Warwick!' madame," the countess exclaimed, with tears running down her cheeks.

"Yea, God bless Anne's father!" the Queen cried, holding our her arms to the Princess, who fell weeping on her bosom in the fulness of her joy.

The Prince turned with his bright kindly smile to the Duchess of Clarence and said,

"My sweet sister, may God also bless your husband, whom I almost envy his share in your noble father's triumph!"

Like a ray of sunshine is suddenly obscured by meeting with a dark cloud in the sky, so the beaming countenance of the Prince was saddened by the gloomy displeasured look of the duchess. She made him a stiff obeisance in return for his gracious speech; and when it was announced, and renewed shouts acclaimed the tidings that the usurper himself—unable to keep his ground in England in the face of the earl's influence, which day by day rallied thousands to King Henry's standard—had been constrained to fly to Holland, she suddenly rose, and leaning on Isabel Butler's arm, walked away down an alley of sycamores, where I could see them through the branches conversing together, the one with a pallid and the other with an inflamed visage. It grieves me to see the ill counsels of that lady fanning the jealousy of that poor duchess, till the sparks of ill-will turn into a flame of enmity against her sister. Each time the Princess, by the Queen's ordering, doth take precedency of the duchess, I observe Lady Isabel's malignant glance or poisonous whisper calling on her mistress to resent this humiliation; and when she plays with her babe in her presence, she must needs break off with a deep sigh, as if compassionating the infant, with many a "Heigh-ho!" and an "Ah me!" uttered in a dolorous tone, which chases away the mother's smiles and awakens in her resentful thoughts.

When I could approach the Queen to wish her joy of the good news she had received, her majesty said to me,

"It was the Bishop of Winchester which conducted the King from his dungeon to the palace. Think how joyful this meeting must have proved. But a yet more joyful day, I ween, will be the one when I reach London."

At that moment the sky became suddenly overcast, and as the Queen uttered these words there was a flash of lightning, followed by a loud clap of thunder —the loudest methinks I ever heard. A deluge of rain followed, and we all took refuge in the pavillion. The Countess of Warwick drew me aside and showed me a letter she had received from her lord, and which it would like her the Queen should read, for it spoke of the love which was showed by the English people for King Henry, which was greater, he said, than could be thought of; for no sooner did the tidings spread that he should rejoice the country again by reigning as heretofore, than the men of every class and in every shire arose, and the cry of " A Henry ! a Henry !" flew from place to place, filling the air with acclamations. " Would to God," the earl said, " I had earlier known this King, or been acquainted with one-half of his virtues. What I have now witnessed of his goodness surpasseth what I should have thought possible in a mortal man. It is as if a living picture of Christ was daily before mine eyes. I remember, sweet wife, to have heard thee speak of a saint who called the crucifix his book. Well, this King, which I once scoffed at and evil treated, is now a book to me, and his example and company learn me more of religion than any preachers ever did. But albeit a sad and virtuous people should be happy in such a monarch, and, as I said before, the most of the common people hold him in marvellous great affection and reverence, the tumultuous Londoners and dissipated nobles shall soon weary of his reign, if the Queen and the Prince come not soon to lend to the court the lustre of worldly splendour, which was not lacking in the last years. Therefore, methinks the progress of their highnesses should not be long delayed; for, on the one hand, the ceremony and state which must attend it must needs cause slowness, and also, I fear, the want of money, though I hope in God the King of Sicily, out of his great generosity and love to their graces, shall therein assist them as much as in him lieth or even beyond his ability, for his power is much less, I ween, than his will to do it.

"Sweet wife,' I thank God for the King's deliverance, and the full, merciful, yea loving pardon which he hath granted me for all the injuries and insults heaped upon him in past times; but I find in myself a singular kind of dejectedness since my return to England, and chiefly since the day when I came to London. The daily sight of this my sovereign's sweet humility, and his detachment from earthly things, works in me a contagious misesteem for this brief life, a loathing for bloodshed, and an awful sense of the nearness of the day when he who hath been styled the Kingmaker on this earth must stand before the throne of One Who judgeth kings in His wrath. I charge thee, dear and true and very beloved wife, to pray for me very much, and get religious persons to do the like; for, in sooth, I have heretofore been too little careful of my soul's health. And now regarding worldly matters: methinks it were time now, if it should please the Queen's majesty, that the contract betwixt the Prince and Anne should take effect, and I pray God to bless them both in this world and the next; and if it please Him my life should be prolonged, I hope to have greater comfort in this son-in-law than in Isabel's husband, who hath shown less wit and spirit since our coming hither than I had thought he possessed, and that was not much either. But I doubt not he is displeased at her absence whom, to do him justice, he worships with a singular affection. The King hath ratified all the Queen and the Prince conceded in his favour, and this should be enough for any man's ambition who was not born heir to a crown."

The latter part of this letter Lady Warwick retained, but gave me the first pages thereof to show to the Queen, which I did when I waited on her grace at her bedtime. She read it, and after a long thoughtful silence said, "I have always thought the King's example casts a spell on those about him. I have witnessed this effect and felt it likewise. When in his company I lost the bold venturesome spirit which thinks of nothing but achieving its objects. This dejectedness of the earl, after a signal triumph, is a bad omen. The King hath infected him with his scruples, and robbed him of the strength which should have served us. How can one live with one who counts riches and greatness and life itself as nothing, and continue to fight for them with the vehement will which wrings success from the hands of fortune! See, this man, which feared neither God nor man when he was against us, is now cut to the heart, talks of his sins, makes ready for death! O, that I had the wings of an eagle to fly to London! Leave me now, but let the Prince know that I would see him early to-morrow."

Some days have passed since the writing of the last pages. The Princess Anne hath been with me this morn: she and the Prince have become from the most fond betrothed lovers the most happy wedded pair in the world. She said they had found the Queen to-day not so merry as the good tidings from England should make her; but by tender caresses and playful talking they had caused her dear grace to be of better cheer. Sitting both at her feet, they jested together, and then discoursed of the future, and built in fancy a cottage in England whither they should retire, like the King and Queen of Sicily, far from the gay court and busy world, to enjoy their love, which would never change as long as they lived.

"Where shall our cottage be?" quoth the Prince.

"O, I pray you, good my lord," she replied, "let it be on the banks of the Thames, not far from the palace at Sheen, for the meadows there are more green and fair than any others in the world. And then our sweet mother the Queen shall come and visit us disguised; and I shall make with mine own hands sweet cakes and preserves to set before her. My mother hath an excellent receipt-book, which I shall then borrow. Thou shalt always call me Nancy in our retreat, sweet Prince, and shalt suffer me to call thee Ned."

"Ay," answered the Prince, smiling; "but who shall write a poem styled 'Ned and Nancy'? Perhaps the blind poet Audleigh, or the old Welsh bards I remember at Harlech. It would like me well to be near London, and sometimes to go in secret into its streets to console poor wretches whose woful cries reach not the ears of princes, and to cause glad surprises to miserable debtors enchained by usurers, as my grandsire is wont to do here in Provence."

The Queen said, "Fair son, you must likewise entertain as he doth the nobles of the land with tournaments and banquets; for benefits are weak engines wherewith to win the hearts of a proud people, when knightly splendour and warlike repute are not added to them. A king, alas, may be adored by the poor, as hath been too well seen in England, and yet dethroned by ungrateful men."

"O, I will live as a Christian, sweet mother, and fight like a Turk when there is occasion," quoth the Prince, laughing. "And as to tournaments, we will hold an emprise at Westminster which shall astonish the whole world. It shall not be my fault, I promise you, if the English do not love me."

The Princess, who was repeating to me this dialogue, stopped short, and clasping her hands together, exclaimed, " O, Lady Margaret, is there any one on earth who would not love him, except —" She hesitated a little, and then told me how it pained her that the duchess her sister betrayed a determined mislike of the Prince.

"Your grace must remember," I replied, " that the disappointment of a crown is one which few women could endure with patience."

"Well," quoth the Princess, " I would as lief be a servant-maid in a kitchen as marry a king if I loved him not."

"But doth not the duchess love the duke?" I said.

The Princess shrugged her graceful shoulders and answered, " If I must speak the truth, she would have loved the duke more an he had been a king, and loves him a little by reason of his being a duke. If he had no royalty of birth, no nobility of lineage, no large possessions, if he were only plain George Plantagenet, I warrant you she would set small store on him. O, I pray you think me not too unsisterly ; but how can one like Isabel love a man so weak and so drunken as George Clarence ? It maketh me sad to see her which was so long my fond playmate thus unworthily mated. I would rather have died than have married one of these Yorkist dukes. Now my sweet lord every one must needs admire. He hath the most generous disposition in the world. His soul is like a clear lake in which the hues of heaven are reflected. When we were speaking of the secret cottage we shall build, he said for his part he should like to discover the spot in Hexham Forest where he and the Queen were hidden in an outlaw's cave, and erect there an hermitage, and not far off a religious house, where God should be always praised. And then he bethought himself of the good outlaw, and said he should seek him out, and, if it pleased God, make him as happy as a prince; 'yet not so happy as the Prince of Wales,' he added, smiling, 'for there is but one Anne Neville in the world, and he cannot have her.'"

"I am ashamed, Lady Margaret," added the sweet Princess, blushing, "to be so boastful of my lord's praises; but, heavens, do I not know it is his goodness, not my poor merits, which adorn me in his eyes? In sooth, dear lady, I am too happy. The Queen, which I feared so much should flout me, is so indulgent to her poor daughter-in-law that I am amazed at her condescension. She listened this morning to our foolish talking with a half-sad but wholly loving countenance, ever and anon calling me by some endearing name, or holding my hand in hers, as it is not her wont to do with her nieces, or any one else that I can see."

"Her love for her son," I replied, "is so passionate, that it must needs overflow towards you, dear lady, who so entirely worship him."

"Yea," she exclaimed with a bright smile lighting up her fair visage,—"yea, Jeanneton did not idolize her Regnaud more, I promise you, than doth Nancy her sweet Ned. But, by the way, my Lady Margaret, you are reported to have the pen of a ready writer. I pray you, if this be true, and you love me, write a poem on *nos amours*, as these French people say."

I assured the Princess I had no ability for this task; at which she pouted, and vowed she should apply to the King of Sicily, who never refused her requests, and would not be so churlish of his muse, only she was so much of an Englishwoman that verses in her own language would please her best; and so, in a pretty huff, she left me.

The tidings from England continue to be most cheerful; and in a few days the Queen is to proceed to Paris, where the French King hath already caused a *Te Deum* to be sung in the |church of Notre Dame for the liberation of King Henry. He hath appointed the Counts of Eu, of Vendôme, and of Dunois, and Messire de Chatillon to escort her majesty thither as a guard of honour. The Prince and Princess, the Countess of Warwick, and the Duchess of Clarence travel with her. I fear me I shall have to ride in the company of Lady Isabel Butler, and will hear naught but taunts and ill-natured comments on her grace and the Prince. Howsoever, those that are losers should be treated with patience; and I pray God I may keep my temper, and not think of this lady worse than she deserves. She is a most desperate Yorkist; but Heaven defend she prove not treacherous also, or, at the least, a dangerous spy.

CHAPTER XLIII.

The Abyss.

WHAT followeth was written by the Queen at Harfleur in the month of February 1471:

Once more I look on that Channel sea which I have grown to think my enemy. Once more I scent its salt savour. Again the roaring of the wind, the hoarse booming sound of the billows breaking on the shore, and the sharp rattling noise of their retreat, besiege mine ears. O sea, adverse, disquieted, stormy sea! never one whole day at peace, how meet an emblem thou art of my heart and my life! There is a little fishing-smack tossing outside the harbour, the setting sun gilds its sails; but that hugh rolling mass of clouds which will soon swallow up the golden orb shall rob the vessel also of its reflected light. So hath it been with me more times than I can number. In the midst of the rejoicings at Paris, where nothing was left undone to do us honour, and the Hotel of St. Pol was constantly filled with the highest persons in the State and in the Church, all vying to pay homage to our recovered royalty, how dismal were the tidings which reached me! The Duke de Calabre, my sole brother, the idol of King René, the glory of our race, the model of knights, the example of princes, died, alas, from a fell disease in Spain, where fortune was raising him to a throne. I should once have wept torrents of tears at this miserable hap; and now it hath killed my joy, but left me visibly unmoved. Yet when I am alone, and the thought of Monseigneur Jean forces its way into my mind, I find myself more sensible of his loss than I appear. O sweet brother, I loved thee well! God knoweth it, albeit I have not shed many tears for thee.

A slow fever consumes me. I should not care to live if once I could see Edward sure of his throne. My love he no longer needs, but my aid is more needful to him than ever. His Anne dotes upon him with all the passion and tenderness which can be imagined; yea, even my hungry heart is satisfied with the worship she pays him, and he is more enamoured of her now than when they were married six months ago. But he is nineteen, she seventeen. How should they steer their bark alone amidst the shoals of a dangerous sea? and what is yon dreadful England but a treacherous ocean of deceits and perfidies? God help them! How happy they look! I can see them on the shore gaily pacing up and down, and ever and anon stopping to look into each other's faces with an incredible contentment. Well, they have both fair visages worth gazing on. How kinglike is his attitude! How graceful her figure! She is no disparagement to him. Any monarch in the world might glory in her loveliness. How they laugh when the rough uncivil waves drive them back with their white foam! She tries to stand her ground, and plants her small foot on the sand, as if to defy the advancing tide. Ah, the foam hath touched the border of her dress; they retreat. How prettily she smiles at what he says! I ween he tells her the story of King Canute, and reads her a lesson on the impotency of monarchs. Now they have sprung up on the jetty, and are fighting with the blustering wind. Happy, careless wights, they see no evil omen in those frowning surges; they hear no dismal prophecies in the howling of the winds! They turn back; ay, I thought he would go into the church and give alms to all those beggars. He hath inherited all his father and his grandsire's proneness to prayer, and their bountiful spirits towards the poor. I, alas, take less and less comfort in devotion. Since my childhood a battle hath been waged within me betwixt two opposing spirits. If it were not heresy, I should think I had two souls to whom by some freak of nature one only body had been given, so fierce hath been the strife I speak of. Or else I am possessed, or God Himself fighteth with me. These waitings have been my life's curse. When in action the inward contest ceases, or I mark it not; but to sit still is horrible.

The last letters of the earl are imperative. The fate of the kingdom and our house turns, he says, on our speedy arrival. We must soon join him, or our cause is imperilled. "Only let the English see the Prince," he writes, "and all shall be secured. The King entertains no hopes for the future; and as he is by many deemed to be a prophet, they are dismayed at his silence. Clarence is useless and morose, my brother Montague dejected; but if the Prince was here, I should then fear nothing."

We must put to sea to-morrow. I care not what those cowardly sailors say. I will cross that hellish sea, though all the demons of the abyss should be conjured against us.

March 23d.

Well-nigh two months have passed of weary suspense. The story of my youth is rehearsed again with deeper and more acute suffering. Heart-sickening delays; obstinate winds; adverse elements fighting against me. Thrice we have embarked, thrice dared a raging sea; thrice been driven back, each time with loss to our ships, on this detested coast, and the fools about me cry out, "Witchcraft! witchcraft!" and talk of spells and sorcery until I go mad at their folly. And then devout persons say, "Give in, give in. 'Tis not God's good pleasure you should cross the sea; yield to these visible tokens of His will;" and this angers me alike. It hath not been known or heard, or been on record in any past age, that this opposing wind should blow for more than seven weeks without ceasing, and with this violence. Each day I vainly look to its falling, each night I listen to its wailings in this ill-built house, until I think I hear it uttering distinct words, intermingled with fiendish screams. Once it was Clifford crying, "I am doomed for your quarrel;" and then close to mine ear, as if in a whisper, the word "Rutland" seemed to be uttered. Another time during the whole night the names of Lord Bonville and Sir Thomas Kyriel sounded to me as if repeated by the blast, and the word "Perjured, perjured," seemed driven by the hurricane through my brain. But the worst of these delusions—for I am not mad, and in the daytime I know them to be such—was when I saw the white bloody head of Anne's grandfather pass along the sky pillowed by black murky clouds. I fixed mine eyes upon it, transfixed with terror. Before it disappeared Lord Salisbury's features changed to those of Edward's wife; but in lieu of its wonted sweetness, I saw in her visage a look so melancholy and despaired that it was more horrorful to me than the gory head of her grandsire. And since that night, sometimes when I am looking at her, this expression seems to me to take the place of her own, and I turn affrighted away. It happened thus this morn; she and Edward came into my chamber to show me a great store of primroses which the March sun had caused to blossom in a sheltered valley behind the town. She had woven them in a pretty fashion, and said she should send them to the church for our Lady's image against the second morrow, for she had been wont to give her flowers on this feast in all her past years. Then she added, "Ah me! sweet Mother Queen, I marvel where we shall kept it next year?" Then I suddenly perceived, or thought I did perceive, that afore-said change on her fair visage, and turned shuddering away. I heard her say sadly, "Sweet Prince, take these flowers away; the Queen mislikes them." Ay, take away all the brightness and bloom from their young lives! I mentally exclaimed. My wretched doom is upon them. No joys can thrive nigh to me. Like the shade of a poisonous tree, my destiny darkens their dawn and withers their happiness.

March 24th.

I will embark to-morrow. Better perish in the waves than die of misery on this detested coast. But we shall not die. One more struggle with fate, one more defiance hurled at fortune, and the fight shall be done. Lady Warwick is like-minded; so is the Duchess of Clarence. Both have declared this life of expectancy is not to be endured. Only Anne turns pale, foolish wench, and fears to embark. "O, sweet Harfleur," she cried, "sweet Harfleur! dear shore, lovely sands, quiet nooks, which have been witnesses of my sweet Prince's love for his poor wife; and I pray God he shall love her as well in a palace as in this plain hostelry and mean fishing village." She hath not the spirit of a queen; but God knoweth it is of little help in these times, and she may fare better than those whose hearts are set to a more lofty key. That sister of hers is made of another metal, I trow. The pale proud lady visibly doth hate us sorely. Albeit she pineth to embark, yet she hath persuaded her mother to sail in another ship. Suspicious thoughts cross my mind that that fool her husband hath cunning enough to be false. Moroseness is an evil sign in small-brained, gibbering sots like Clarence. I have not drawn one free breath since that alliance with Yorkists and ancient traitors. Ah, the clouds are dispersing this eve; the sea is waxing calm. Would we were on it! If the wind keep straight this night, we shall sail at dawn. How short may the passage prove which shall end this torment!

April 12th, at sea.

Will none have so much pity as to cast me into the waves? I am the Jonas of this ship. None shall prosper which serve or sail with or cleave to me. The wind was fair when we embarked, the sea smooth, the skies sunny. But in less than three hours the horrible whistling began which presages a storm. The demons of the deep were on the watch. For fourteen days and fourteen nights they have buffeted us with unceasing fury. Nothing keeps me alive, I think, but the fever which burns my veins; for I can neither sleep, eat, nor drink, except when Edward forces me to it. I am supported by his caresses more than by the loathed sustenance of a loathed existence. Time! time! O, I pray you, ye wise ones of the earth, what is time? Is there, in sooth, an end to all things visible? I once heard a preacher say that one moment in hell should seem endless to the damned. A wretch which had been dead only an hour appeared to one on earth, and asked how long he had been in the flames. He could not credit it should have been so brief a time;

it had seemed to him like unto a thousand years. Methinks since I have been in this ship time hath ceased to advance. The storm abates not one jot. God only knoweth whither we are drifting.

The Abbey of Cerne, Easter-eve.

Once again we are ashore! Once more in England, O land sighed for and so hard to reach! At Weymouth no tidings could we learn, save that the usurper is marching to meet Warwick. A strange stillness seemed to reign in the air as we rode hither. The damp moistness thereof chilled my limbs, but quieted my brain. Here I have stretched myself on this poor pallet, and I write these lines as if I was not Margaret the Queen, but only a shipwrecked, poor lonely woman cast on a foreign shore, without hope or cares or friends.

Easter Sunday.

Here the Queen ended her writing yestereve, as the bells were ringing for the feast. She let the book fall out of her hand. I thank God we are landed and in a religious house on this day. The monks and the peasants which came here for shrift last night are ignorant of all late haps, and Sir John Fortescue and Sir Henry, my brother, have vainly sought for news in the neighbourhood. We have kept the festival in a singular peaceful manner, half-way, as it were, betwixt the raging sea and the turmoil of impending strife. After the Prior of St. John had said Mass, the Prince and Princess sat on a tomb nigh to the cloisters with a book on their knees, in which they sometimes read a little, and then stopped to converse. How sweetly he seemed to discourse to her, and with what a pretty reverence she listened to him!

Easter Monday.

The Princess called me after Evensong to stay with her whilst the Prince was with the Queen.

"Lady Margaret," quoth she, "I am a little sad. The Prince said to me to-day, 'Sweet wife, we have had happy days in France—more blissful and delectable than can be thought of. Yet if it pleased God soon to take my life away, I should not grieve thereat only for thee.' I am frightened he is too good. When he had received this morn,—I cry God mercy for it, —but I could not choose but gaze on his face, it was so like unto an Angel's. But yet I cannot think he will die before he is a king, for the most cunning woman in Yorkshire foretold long ago I should one day be a queen. And so with that I comfort myself."

Methought this was poor comfort; but this sweet lady is more winsome than wise. God ha' mercy on her if she should fall on evil times! Hark! there are quick footsteps in the cloisters. I write on, afraid to move. I ween news have come. I must needs go to the Queen. . . . .

I went, and what a spectacle met mine eyes!—her majesty swooned away, lying in her son's arms, and the Princess, with a white face and trembling limbs, stood weeping beside them. My brother whispered in mine ear, as I remained aghast, "Lord Warwick is slain and the King again a prisoner."

We all gathered in silence around the Queen's motionless form. We feared, I ween, to see her open her eyes. When she did so, her countenance became so wild I cannot describe it. She reviled the calamitous temper of these dreadful times, and said in an incredibly bitter manner, "O vain past useless labours, turned only to present deeper misery! I had rather die than live longer in this state of infelicity." And as she uttered these words she fell back again, looking so white and corpse-like that we were affrighted. The Prince, with the most tender caresses, revived her. One should have thought he had been an Angel more than a man in this sad hour; and she was guided by him in all things, as if living only on his sight. When she was a little restored to herself, he gave orders that our whole company should travel to sanctuary in Beaulieu Abbey, where we arrived this evening. Alas! here we have found Lady Warwick, who had landed at Portsmouth, and thence came to Southampton with intent to join the Queen at Weymouth; but on the road, hearing of her husband's defeat and death, she fled across the New Forest, and betook herself also to the protection of this sanctuary. When the Queen and the countess met, they seemed at first unable to speak. The widowed lady hid her face in the folds of her majesty's robes, who laid her hand on her bowed head, uttering these words: " God have mercy on you, Lady Warwick! Who should have forecasted your lord would have perished in our quarrel? I pray God to assoilsie him." Then she added, "Where is the Duchess of Clarence?" A low moan was the answer.

"O mother, sweet mother!" cried the Princess, throwing her arms around the countess's neck, "hath my sister left you?"

"O mine Anne," she said, "I have no daughter but thee. The wife of perjured Clarence hath fled to her false lord. God forgive them! My husband's death lieth at their door. God have mercy on them!" And those were all the angry words she said; but thenceforward her hair became grey, and she looked an aged woman.

G G

The Duke of Somerset, his brother, and many of the Lancastrian nobles have arrived this morn, and found her majesty drowned in so great a sorrow that she would hardly give them welcome, or raise her head from her pillow, say or do what they would to comfort her. The duke told her they had already a good puissance in the field, and trusted the presence of her grace and of the Prince should soon draw all the northen and western counties to the banner of the red rose. But her eye kindled not as of old at these speeches. She was as one that hath been struck to the heart. I could see a singular change in her haviour. The only thought in her mind was the Prince's safety, for which cause she said she had sought sanctuary.

"O, my lords," she cried in an impassioned manner, at last lifting up her head, "I pray you of your loyalty, provide for the Prince's security. In my opinion no good can be done in the field this time, and therefore it will be best for me and the Prince, and such as choose to share our fortunes, to return to France, and there to tarry till it please God to send me better luck."

"Heavens, sweet mother!" the Prince exclaimed, "this is a new thing that you should counsel retreat, when we have braved so many dangers to come hither. These noble lords look for other words from your lips than those ill-sounding ones touching safety, when honour and knighthood beckon us onward to victory or death."

"Victory or death!" the Queen repeated in a dejected tone. "God knoweth I have often uttered those words. Methinks I knew not what they meant. Warwick used them when he took leave of me at Angers Clifford before the rout at Towton; the Lord de Roos on the eve of the fight at Hexham. O, it hath always been death and never victory for the friends of Lancaster. If you are my friends, my lords, force us not from sanctuary, or else suffer us to return to France."

A burning flush overspread the Prince's visage.

"Good my mother," he cried, "have you forgot that the King is once again in vile durance? Have you lost courage when courage is most needed? O, be yourself again; and if you abide in sanctuary, which none can blame, let it be to pray for your son, who will not tarry for one hour longer in this Beaulieu, which is no Beaulieu to one who pineth to measure himself with the tyrant of his people and the sworn foe of his king and father."

She listened to these words without one spark of the wonted fire which used to burn in her whole aspect when the like sentiments were expressed before her in bygone days.

"There will be no good done this time," she kept repeating, till a heavy gloom fell on the lords who had come with Lord Somerset; and he himself exclaimed at last, greatly displeased, "There is no occasion, madame, to waste any more words, for we are all determined while our lives last still to keep war against our enemies." And so said they all, and the Prince made them great cheer. So she then arose from her couch in a staid manner, and said in an unnatural constrained voice, "Well, be it so." Since this moment, methinks she moves like one in a dream, or that walketh in sleep

We travel this night towards Bath, and these noblemen affirm that the western counties be so loyal to the King, that a great army shall be in the field before the usurper knoweth whither his danger doth lie. If we but cross the Severn at Gloucester, and join Jasper Tudor's forces in Wales, victory is certain. The

Countess of Warwick will hide here in sanctuary, but nothing will serve the Princess but to follow her lord. She hath a brave heart, albeit not an over strong mind, this fair Anne.

Tewkesbury, May 3rd.

The Queen cannot sleep, and she hath commanded me to bring unto her her journal-book and write what she shall tell me. I have sat here, pen in hand, well-nigh one half-hour, and yet she speaks not. We are all right weary with travelling, for we have journeyed night and day twenty-six long miles in a foul country, all in lanes and stony ways, betwixt woods, without any good refreshing; the other part of our host could not have laboured any further. Yet the Queen would have fain, I know, pushed on towards Wales, but Lord Somerset saith he will here tarry, and take such fortune as God shall send. Taking his will for reason, he hath pitched his camp in this fair park, and entrenched himself, sorely against the opinion not only of her majesty, but of all the most experienced captains of the army; so whether it be of election or no, we are verily compelled to abide, and the usurper with his forces is but distant one mile from us, the scouts report. At Gloucester the men would not suffer us to cross the bridge, which was as a death blow to her majesty. Neither threats nor fair words availed. They were under the obeisance of the Duke of Gloucester, they said, and bound to defend her to pass. The Princess waxed as white as as a sheet when that duke's name was uttered. "God deliver us from Richard!" she said, trembling; "I dreamed last night he killed my lord." "Dreams," I answered, "go by contraries; so it shall happen that your lord will slay the duke." Then she would open her office-book, a rare one which King René gave her, and therein she read these words: " Abroad the sword destroyeth, and at home there is death alike." When the Prince said, " What aileth thee, sweet wife?" she pointed to them; he crossed himself, and answered, " Though He slay me, I will trust in Him."

I write on, and the Queen speaks not; she hath forgotten her intent. I pray God she forgets all, for verily the thought of the morrow is more than can be endured; albeit I can yet pray, which I fear she hath ceased to do. O morrow, what shalt thou bring forth? O morrow, when thou shalt be to us yestereve, how shall we feel towards thee? What shall future chroniclers relate of thee? What shall this pen of mine record touching thee? O unknown, slow-advancing, resistless morrow, thousands of throbbing, watching hearts are awaiting thee. Their fast beating hurries not thy measured approach. The hours pass, the shades of night deepen, the horrorful stillness increases. I can ill brook even so much as to look at the Queen's visage. The Prince and the Princess, after saying their prayers, like two tired children have retired to rest. She sobbed awhile; but he kissed away her tears, and told her he had been so happy with her for eight months that nothing could exceed it, and that he had prayed God to accept his life and give England peace, if it should please Him. She chided him for this prayer, and said she hoped God would not hear it. Then he said, " Yea, sweet Anne, death for me, peace for England, and for my mother and for thee—" I could not hear the end, for she stopped his mouth with her kisses, and hung about him and wept. Now I think they are both asleep, for there is no sound in the next room. The Queen hath ordered me to close the book and to lie down. God have mercy on us! Twelve of the clock hath struck; four hours more and the day will dawn.

The gray light of the morn doth now appear, and every one is astir. I write these words whilst the Queen is putting on her riding gear. At the door do wait the Prince, the Duke of Somerset and his brother, Lord Wenlock, Lord Devonshire, and the Prior of St. John. They are to ride with her grace about the field and cheer the men. Ah, now the Queen is apparelled, her cheek is flushed and her eyes sparkle again. The Princess seemeth scarcely able to sit her horse. Heavens! what a scowl is on Lord Somerset's visage! O God! what hath the Prior whispered in his ear which makes him glare like a tiger at Lord Wenlock! I must shut up this book, and hide it in my bosom till to-night. Where shall I open it again?

CHAPTER XLIV.

"Out of the Depths I have cried unto Thee."

FROM THE LADY MARGARET DE ROOS TO THE COUNTESS OF VAUDEMONT.

The Tower of London.

MADAME, now that the misfortunes of the Queen, your most dear sister and my most loved mistress, have arrived at their final extremity, and every spark of earthly hope is extinguished in her breast, I call to mind the promise I made you at Angers, that whensoever opportunity served I would inform you without disguise of the haps which should befall her majesty. Evil tidings travel swiftly, and I doubt not you have already been consternated by rumours and bruits touching the sinister events which have succeeded one another with so great and terrible a speed that I am

astonished to find in myself any sense or memory left
wherewith to describe them. A religious man who
visits us in this dungeon will send this letter across
seas, and I pray God it shall safely reach your grace's
hands; albeit if the tidings it contains could be for
ever concealed from your knowledge, then I should
contrariwise pray it should never meet your eyes.
Know then, noble lady, that one fortnight ago a fatal
battle was fought at Tewkesbury, in which the Queen's
forces were defeated with great slaughter, and one life
lost of greater price than a thousand or ten thousand
others of inferior value. The causes of this rout God
only knoweth. It matters little now if madness or
wicked treason led to this disastrous issue. The com-
manders of the Queen's army, the Lords Somerset and
Wenlock, turned their weapons against each other in
the most important period of the day, upon which
their affrighted troops fled in wild confusion. The
Prince, alas, with a desperate but inexperienced valour
in vain sought to rally these disbanded disheartened
men; and when the Queen saw how the day went, and
her most loved unique son plunge into the *mêlée* with a
handful of followers, she waxed frantic, and would
have rushed after him. But the violence of her agitation betrayed her courage, and she fell insensible from
her horse. We carried her to a religious house in
which she took refuge, as also did the Countess of
Devonshire and her daughter. There she spent some
hours in so great terror and weariness that it seemed
as if nothing worse could ensue than this suspense.
But let no one surmise that their misery cannot increase, for none may foresee what he shall yet endure
before he dies. Towards daybreak a report came from
a peasant that the Prince had been taken and murthered in the usurper's tent. None durst breathe this

to the Queen or the Princess; but outside their lodging the rumour spread, casting every living soul in the convent into despair. I went in and out of the royal chamber with a composed visage and a breaking heart. Each time I entered, one or the other said, "What tidings?" or, "In God's name, is aught known?" and the like questions, which I could ill endure; for as the day went on the horrorful news of the Prince's death became confirmed by more certain reports; and if it were not an abominable sin for one to die by his own hand I would fain have laid violent hands on myself, sooner than awaited the hour when the Queen should learn the truth. Alas, it should have been well if with virtuous courage we had informed her gently of what she was soon to be told most ungently; for whilst we all stood transfixed with grief and apprehension, of a sudden Sir William Stanley, the most brutal man in the world, broke forcibly into the house and into her majesty's presence, and made her and the Princess his prisoners. The Queen asked him if her son was taken. "Yea," he savagely replied, "and despatched too." "Whither?" gasped the Queen. "To the other world," cried the caitiff, "by means of a dozen good Yorkists' swords plunged in his breast." The cry which burst from the Princess was not so horrorful as the Queen's silence. Her eyes started out of her head, and her hair stood on end. "Is this certain?" I said, striving to draw the cruel man aside; but he would not stir, and with a dreadful joy in his visage answered, "As true as I am alive; by the same token that I saw with mine own eyes the corpse of your so-called Prince with more gashes in it than would have killed twenty men. Sir Richard Croft captured and carried this traitor before the King, who gazed on him awhile, marvelling at his audacious haviour, and then asked him how he durst presumptuously to enter his realm with banners displayed against him. Upon which the graceless knave answered that he came forsooth to recover his father's kingdom and his own inheritance. His majesty struck him on the face with his gauntlet, and six loyal swords straightway leapt from their scabbards to stifle treason in his blood. Clarence first stabbed him—" At these words the Princess gave another terrific shriek and fell, fainted, at the feet of the miserable mother, who, not reft of her senses by a benign swoon, but distraught by a most acute agony, fixed her eyes on that foul messenger with a gaze which forced him to turn away. Then there burst from her livid and foaming lips maledictions mingled with groans and cries, of which none which did not hear them could so much as imagine the horror; the pierced heart exhaling its anguish with a supernatural strength, as if through that frenzy Heaven spoke its own malison. Her arms were extended, her eyes dilated, her voice of so singular a loudness that it was heard outside the convent walls. We all listened trembling to those dread curses. "Edward Plantagenet" (these were her words), "the blood of my son be upon thee and on thy born and unborn children! Mayst thou have sons, that they may be butchered in cold blood and their groans haunt thee in thy unblest grave! Clarence, perjured, loathsome wretch, may thy end be as shameful as thy life! Bloody Gloucester, may thine be violent as thy deeds! If a child call thee father, let it perish miserably, and the woman which shall bear it die of a riven heart! The malediction of a despaired mother shall cleave to you, brothers of an accursed race; your doomed souls will sink deeper and deeper into guilt, and your fierce hands tear each other to pieces. May no priest shrive you in your dying hour! May your eyes close without a benison, and open in the lowest depths of hell, where fiends like yourselves await you." "Silence, foul-tongued blaspheming Queen!" Sir William cried, clasping his poniard; "add not treason to treason. Tremble for your own life." O, what a convulsive derisive shriek broke from the livid ashy lips of her poor majesty when this threat was uttered! "My life!" she cried. "O, man, if the monster you call king hath bid you kill me, peradventure I may yet have to thank that murtherer. But no; I am mad; I mistook your speech. It is not possible my son is dead. There is no one on earth so cruel that he could have killed him. The sons of kings perish not thus. You have always detested me; you said it but to torture me. Unsay it, and I will unsay all those curses; I will pray for the Yorkists, I will resign the crown, and return to France." "Ah, ah! resign the throne!" exclaimed the caitiff. "Madame, I tell you your son is dead and buried also by this time. My master is now your master, and you and this so-called Princess my prisoners: you must e'en prepare to travel to Coventry. If the King spares your justly forfeited lives, then you shall, I ween, grace his triumphal march to London." So saying, without more ado, he turned on his heel and departed without any token of respect from the Queen's presence.

O madame, where could a more piercing sight of sorrow be met with than was witnessed after the cruel herald of that matchless grief had left her? The Queen sat on the floor, whence she would suffer none to raise her. She fixed on me, whose own heart was riven, her large tearless, lustreless, dark eyes. "Is it true he is dead?" she said in so strange and wistful a voice, as if praying for God's sake I should say no, thall all present began to weep. And the Princess opened her eyes and cried: "O sweet mother, sweet mother, he was too good to live! Would to God I was also dead!" But the Queen said nothing more. We laid her on a bed, where she remained, looking more like unto a corpse than a live person, till she was forced into a chariot and carried to Coventry. There we heard the victor had been so enraged by the reports of his ungenerous servant touching the distraught bereft mother's maledictions that he had well-nigh resolved to put her to death; but either from policy or compassion he changed his purpose, and the royal prisoners followed in his train to London. The Princess clung to the Queen like a Ruth to a Noemi, and well should the miserable lady have said like that other mourner: "Call me not Noemi—that is beautiful; but call me Mara—that is bitter; for the Almighty has quite filled me with bitterness." I think she would have more keenly resented the shame and bitter humiliation of that dreadful journey, if her internal agony had not wrought in her an almost insensibility to outward circumstances. As we passed through the towns and villages many flocked to gaze on that fair ruin, that shipwrecked glory, that hapless sport of cruel fortune: some, I could discern, felt an ill-concealed resentment of her woes, which led them to cross themselves as she passed, and some of the women to wipe their eyes; but others of the viler sort hooted at her. She either did not perceive, or was indifferent to, these tokens of compassion or of scorn. Nor did she once notice the country through which we passed. The Princess shed many tears, and mostly when a fair scene or a joyous group met her eyes. It was pitiful to see one so young submerged in such a sea of woes; but the Queen's grief—what can be likened to it? She spoke only two or three times during this journey; once she said that if she should be with the King in London, she should be more of one mind with him than heretofore. Another time, when I essayed to whisper in her ear some comfortable words of prayer, she shuddered as if it pained her. When she had seen the King, she said, then peradventure she should pray. He seemed much in her thoughts; not in the same manner as in former times, but as if she looked to find in him some kind of help in her almost intolerable agony. For once again she said, "If I can but creep into his prison and hide me there, perhaps I shall sleep;" she had not once closed her eyes for many nights and days.

Well, at the last, madame, we came to London, and were conducted straight to this Tower, in which a dark and dismal lodging received the Queen. From the window thereof I could, howsoever, discern the King's apartment, and with comfort perceived his majesty's bird in its wonted place. I was most afraid of the effect which the news of the Prince's death should have produced on the poor King; for if his mental malady had returned, then how miserable should be that meeting for the Queen! It was six of the clock when we arrived, and soon afterwards the governor of the Tower came to the Queen's chamber. She asked if she could go to the King her husband, and if his majesty was in good health. He replied that King Henry was well and of good cheer. Thereupon a piteous cry broke from the Queen, as if she augured from those last words that his majesty was yet ignorant of the Prince's death. "Let me go to my husband," she cried; "my sole request is to share his prison; none but barbarians can refuse it." The governor said he durst not conduct her grace to King Henry's apartments without the king's license, but that the Duke of Gloucester was expected in a few hours, and perhaps he would give warrant for it. The Princess waxed very pale when she heard that duke named, and craved of the governor that he should send to her sister, the Duchess of Clarence, a brief letter she then wrote to her. When he had taken it and departed, she told me she had prayed her sister, if she loved God, to have her removed from the Tower, and concealed in the most humble place which could be thought of; yea, even disguised as a servant-maid, if needs should be, so that that duke should have no knowledge of her abode. "For, Lady Margaret," she added, "the devil himself is not more cunning or more powerful than that Richard; and one half of my present misery, even more terrible than the loss of my sweetest Prince—which God knoweth is sufficient anguish—lieth in my fear of his devices." Not long afterwards an order came for the removal of the Princess to the custody of the Duchess of Clarence, who bestowed her, as I have since heard, in an obscure house in the suburbs of London. The Queen took scanty heed of her departure, though the Princess hung about her sobbing and weeping. "Your majesty knoweth why I go hence," she timidly said. The Queen raised her head and answered, "God help thee; all thy happy days are over, nor hast thou seen the worst which shall befall thee." I wot not if she thought much or understood what she said.

Towards eleven o'clock at night there was a rumour in the building like of several men hurrying along. A singular tremour seized me,—strange, unexplainable, overpassing all terrors I had hitherto felt. It was as if a mysterious intimation was yielded to me of some great hap at hand. Once again, in about an hour's time, I heard the same noise again, and then a death-like silence reigned in our dungeon. I climbed unto the casement at about one of the clock, and looked towards the King's window; but the night was dark, and no light to be seen any where. The Queen was lying still, not asleep, but in a kind of stupor. When the light began to dawn, I heard steps again in the vaulted passages; and towards five o'clock the gaoler set on guard over us unlocked the door, and beckoned to me to come outside the inner chamber, where I had been lying beside the Queen. One of the officers of the Tower, he said, craved speech with me. I looked up and saw a man with an exceeding pale and haggard face, who said, when he had motioned away the gaoler, "You are the Queen's lady?" "Yea," I answered, trembling like one in an ague-fit. "Then, in God's name," he said, "so deal with your mistress that she look not out of the casement at any time this morn, lest a ghastly sight meet her eyes." "O God!" I cried, "what have they done?" "Slain King Henry," he whispered. "May God give them time for repentance who laid sacrilegious hands on the Lord's anointed!" he added, shivering. I stood gazing on him like one stupefied. I could neither move nor utter. "For five years," he said, "I have waited on that King who now lieth a corpse. A more sweet saint was never seen, nor a more foul murther ever committed." "How came it to pass?" I cried, ready to faint with horror. He replied: "The Duke of Gloucester came at midnight and asked if King Henry had been informed of his son's death and the Queen's capture. When he was answered nay, 'Then,' quoth he, 'we shall now see if this saintly fool will bless God like Job when he findeth himself stripped of all.' So saying he entered the chamber wherein the holy king was at his prayers, and, wantonly disturbing him, began

to jeer at his poor clothes, and his bird, and the few
flowers he had nurtured through the winter, as if he
had desired to draw from him some impatient words;
but failing therein, he said it greatly marvelled him to
see one so occupied with trifles when mighty events
had come to pass in this land; 'for,' quoth he, maliciously eyeing the poor king, 'the false-named Prince
of Wales is dead, and the proud Queen which would
have drowned England in blood captured.' I shall
never forget the King's visage when he had heard
those cruel tidings—no, not if I live one hundred years;
a grief so angel-like, so Christian a patience, never
before was seen in one so afflicted. He looked up to
heaven meekly, so much as to say, 'God's will be
done;' uttered twice in a wistful manner his son and
his wife's names; and presently baring his bosom,
presented it to the murtherer." "He killed him
then?" I cried aghast. "Yea, at once pierced his
heart; and when he fell back dead, wiped his dagger,
and left the chamber without more ado than if he had
cut the throat of a deer. I would not be in that man's
place at God's judgment-seat, not if I was to be made
a king to-morrow. He that killed King Henry killed
a saint. And now they will carry his body to St. Paul's
church to lie there in every one's sight, that all the
Queen's party may be assured of his death. Ah, even
now I hear the gates open!" I ran affrighted into the
inner chamber. The Queen was standing on a bench,
with her visage leaning against the iron bars of the
window. I sprang to her side to draw her away, if
needs had been, by force. It was too late. She had
seen her husband's corpse carried forth, without singing
or saying, uncovered on an open coffin. She uttered
no word or cry, nor shed a tear, but raised her hand
to heaven, and stood like a carved image of woe,

henceforth insensible and mute. I called for help; a leech was sent for, and her women came to succour her. An irresistible desire then seized me—not without some thought of future comfort to her poor grace—to follow this lamentable cortège which had issued from the Tower. By the aid of a friendly gaoler and the aforesaid officer I found no impediment thereunto, and overtook its march at a short distance from the gates. O God, methought I should have died when I first perceived the noble corpse lying bareheaded on the bier; but when I approached close unto it a singular joy filled my soul, and it seemed as if I could have intoned the *Magnificat*, so great was that gladness. A very delectable perfume appeared likewise to scent the air. Yet it was a pitiful sight that royal body, in which two gory wounds were visible, whence the fresh-flowing blood cried murther as plainly as if they had tongues wherewith to proclaim it. But the kingly brow, the meek, restful, holy visage, breathed so sweet a peace that it is not credible what comfort it gave me. So Christlike was its aspect, that as the corpse was carried through Cheapside to St. Paul, surrounded by more glaives than torches, its passage became like a procession when holy relics are translated. Some bent the knee or crossed themselves as it went by. Women wept aloud; many struck their breasts and cried, "God ha' mercy on us!" A few at first, and then others, growing bold by example, furtively approached the coffin and touched the dead limbs. At Blackfriars, where the wounds bled again, efforts were made to collect the blood from the stained pavement; and deep-mouthed curses on the murtherers were heard. When the body was exposed in St. Paul's Church, it is incredible how great a number of those persons who hastened thither to gaze knelt down to pray, and albeit most adverse to the Lancastrian king during his life, invoked him after his death. When the bruit of his violent death spread amongst the people, so great a resentment of his sanctity and horror of his murther arose, that King Edward and the Duke of Gloucester left London in haste, fearing some outburst from the citizens. And as the church continued to fill with devout mourners, orders were given to remove the fair corpse, which was done with unseemly speed by a party of soldiers from Calais. I followed the sacred relic to the river-side, and, by a singular hap, was suffered to enter the barge which was to carry the kingly body to its resting-place. As the shadows of evening were falling, and the melancholy moon beginning to shine on the quiet waters and fair banks of the Thames, the silent barge glided along with its saintly freight till it reached the Abbey of Chertsey, where, in an obscure manner, King Henry was that night buried. I knelt and kissed the mould which covered the poor grave, even as if a martyr had therein rested. Ah, madame! the honours which men denied to that tomb God hath showered upon it; and a more noble homage is rendered to Henry the Saint than was refused to Henry the King.

When I returned to the Tower I found the Queen sunk in the same silent despair. I told her of the singular ghostly beauty of the King's dishonoured and yet how greatly honoured obsequies; but she would not hearken or cross herself, or yet say "God's will be done;" but ever and anon wrung her hands like one to whom life is insupportable, and essayed to tear her hair, which is turned wholly gray since the fatal day of Tewkesbury. Night succeeded day, and day followed night, and no change was seen in her grace. Stupor succeeded to frenzy, and reviving memory renewed frenzy. Even her enemies were frighted at this living death, and the reigning queen sent her physician to report on the Queen's condition; but no leech howsoever learned could mend that disease of the soul, or yield one hour's relief to a riven heart.

One day, when she had repulsed all offers of prayers or priestly ministrations, and with a resolved anguish thrown herself on the ground, to lie there, she said, as became one whom God had crushed and whose hell was begun on earth, I left her presence almost brokenhearted. And as free passage was now allowed to the Queen's attendants in the Tower, I went to pray at the church of St. Saviour, seeking comfort from God, Who alone can give it in such straits. As I was coming out of the said church, there met me in the porch one brother Thomas, a simple holy man whom I had known in former years. With many signs of joy he greeted me; and when I said nothing could exceed the sorrows we had seen, "O my lady," he cried, "there is comfort enough for the sorest heart in Christendom in the great mercies received at our holy King's tomb at Chertsey. O, I promise you more miracles have been wrought at his grave than should suffice to prove him a saint. The people flock thereunto from all the neighbourhood, and a store of sick persons are cured through his prayers."

As he uttered these words a thought came into my mind, for the which I shall bless God all my days. I took leave of that good friar, and walked quickly to the river-side. There I hired a boat to carry me to Chertsey. The day was very fair; a cool breeze rippled the water, light fleecy clouds coursed athwart the sky, the beauteous woods and green meadows cheered my sight, and the thought of God's goodness stole into my parched soul like a refreshing dew.

"O my God!" I cried, "Thou who hast made this world so fair, Thou hast not doomed any soul to endless misery. Out of the depths save her for whom I pray; save the most lone and bereft creature in this world from despair."

Then for weeping I could make no more audible prayer. But when I reached Chertsey, and came to the place where the holy King is buried, a blissful sadness filled my soul,—nay, a holy joy, transcending and overpowering grief. I knelt down and bathed the sod with tears of incredible sweetness, whilst one of the friars related to me how great had been the cures there obtained. Then I raised my voice and invoked that blessed departed soul which had been so virtuous and godly in life, and with many urgent entreaties besought the holy King to intercede for the loving and miserable wife he had left on earth. I doubt not that this prayer was heard, and a great miracle of grace wrought in that hour; for, let those who read this believe it or not as they list, when I returned to the dungeon where I had left my mistress so resolved against prayer and haughty towards God, I found her with a changed visage, down which tears were flowing, her eyes closed, and her hands clasped. The Bishop of Winchester was kneeling by her side, weeping likewise; but when I entered he smiled and signed to me to approach.

"Behold," he said, gently pointing to the pale haggard face of my poor Queen,—"behold a great battle hath been fought here. God hath conquered, His child hath bowed to His will."

Then the Queen raised herself, and slowly in broken accents, very solemn and mournful, she spoke these words:

"My God, I have fought against You from my youth

up. Against You, You only, I have sinned. From the depths I cry unto You now,—from the lowest depths of an incredible misery, for You are more mighty than I. The might of Your judgments is upon me. O heavens! they are crushing, resistless, agonising "—her lips quivered, and she added, "and just, my God." She took my hand and said, " I have been shriven, dear friend. When my lord of Winchester first spoke to me of confession, it sounded to me like mockery, for I was resolved for ever to hate and curse those murtherers ; but, Nathan-like, that man of God hath shown me mine own sin, and God in that hour changed my heart. I can forgive now; I have forgiven them all. O my lord of Winchester, I am no more the Queen—no more Marguerite of Anjou, but the most poor, lone, weak, sinful creature on earth, from which God hath taken all He once gave her."

" For the one sole end," he replied, " that the heart which He created for Himself, and which hath so long fought against Him, should love Him at the last, and turn to Him like a penitent child."

" My lord Bishop," she then said, " are you assured that my lord the King and my sweet son are in heaven ?"

" I firmly credit it," he answered with emotion.

" Then," she exclaimed, a gleam of her old expression passing over her face,—" then, so help me God, I will be there one day also, even though I should have to pass through a fiery furnace to reach it ! Yea, I will pray for and cherish all the sufferings which shall speed me on that road. I will fight with myself as I have fought against mine enemies. I will love this dark prison, its poor fare, its lack of every comfort. I will thank those which shall insult and ill-use me, for they will be my props and succours in this enterprise.

O my lord, the most defeated, abandoned, betrayed woman in this world, Marguerite the widow and the reft mother, shall yet be a conqueror!"

CHAPTER XLV.

Per Crucem ad Lucem.

The passages which follow are transcribed from the book in which, from time to time, the Queen wrote during her captivity, but with so trembling and feeble a hand that the most part of it was illegible. Only here and there at intervals I deciphered what I now copy.

(This was written in the last days of June, of the first year of her imprisonment:)
The sight of this book causeth me a mortal sickness of the heart; but with an effort like unto that of a patient who receives from a physician's hand a loathsome remedy, I constrain myself to trace a few lines on these blank pages, of which yet a few remain unsoiled by the recording pen of bygone years. For since I noted old triumphs over earthly foes, and defeats sustained at their hands, I would now also set down the various haps of the great fight I waged of late with Satan, and his ally mine own proud breaking heart.

O God, what fierce torments I endure! what surging tides of revengeful hatred, billows of impotent rage, mighty currents of despair, loaded with defiant curses, do batter and undermine the new-made walls of recent resolves! I should ere now have died by mine own hand, and rushed unbidden, doomed by mine own act, to hell, if through an opening in the sky, visible through the grated bars of this prison, I had not often seen, or thought I saw, a hand stretched out holding a cross, on which these words were scrolled: *In hoc signo vinces.*

Time goes on. There is a barrier betwixt me and all human love and care. Even my father hath forsaken me. I shall perish, and none shall weep or pray, save a few poor servants, for Marguerite d'Anjou, once the most loved and praised princess in all the world. I look round on this dark chamber at mine own self, at the gloomy sky and sullen river, and wonder if these should be the pains of purgatory which I endure. O God, even so let it be! Is not the fiery agony in my bosom a flame sufficient to cleanse from sin? I welcome it, then. Suffering, be thou my balm—misery, my solace—hopelessness, my hope!

(Some time afterwards the Queen received this brief note from the King of Sicily by the hand of one Montrobert, who obtained access to her chamber:)

"My child, may God help thee with His counsel, for rarely is the aid of man tendered in such reverses of fortune! When you can spare a thought from your own sufferings, think of mine. They are great, my daughter; yet I would fain console thee."

(She wrote beneath the copy of this letter:)

My father, are these the only words of comfort thou canst give me? Poor aged man, poor broken-hearted king, thy gray hairs are going down with sorrow to the grave! Griefs have been thy companions all thy days; but pitying angels have marched alongside of them; and I ween the least of mine have gone deeper into my soul than the worst of thine into thy gentle heart.

Yea, Isabel de Lorraine died, and Jeanne de Laval took her place. Yea, thy first-born, Jean de Calabre, is no more, and René de Vaudémont and Blanche of Anjou are dead; but devotion, and music, and poesy, and limning, and the gay *savoir* of the sunny South take their place, and enshrine their images in wreaths of roses and reliquaries adored with gems. Forget, poor father, forget her who was once the joy of thy soul and the light of thine eyes; picture not to thyself the pale spectre, the despaired prisoner, which was once thy Marguerite. Wouldst thou console her? Ah, you cannot recall the past—you cannot, King René, bring back the days when she sat on your knees at Tours, and you called her for the first time " La petite Reine d'Angleterre!" O youth! O hope! O life! you were wondrous fair, but deceitful traitors, every one of you!

(Later on, after a most singular visit received in the Tower of London :)

Strange, passing strange, hath been this day's meeting! O, very strange is this world, with its justices and injustices, its hatreds and its relentings! Was it that painted queen, vain flourish of my greatness,[1] which was truly here an hour ago, weeping at my feet, and I, O heavens! weeping with her? I must needs set down what passed in this interview, or to-morrow I may wake and think it is a dream.

The Governor of the Tower opened the door of my chamber, ushered in a veiled person, dressed in black, and then hastily withdrew. I gazed in silence on this motionless figure; at last she uncovered her visage, and said:

"Madame, I am the unhappy one who is what once you were, but who can never forget what you were and what she was."

[1] Shakespeare.

Verily this was the wife of the usurper, mine own servant in past days. I fixed my eyes upon her as she stood before me, and did not rise, but crossing my arms on my heaving bosom, I said,

"What seek you here, Elisabeth?"

She fell down on her knees, nay, rather threw herself on the ground at my feet, and cried,

"The repeal of that curse!"

"What," I exclaimed with all the rushing passion of repressed but now loosened fierceness; "what, have curses power to fright you on your blood-stained throne? Does the voice of Edward's mother, of Henry's wife, ring in your ears as you lie by the side of the assassin? And when you bend over the beds of your doomed children do you see blood flowing from their breasts? Do you see an avenging angel of darkness hovering by their side?"

She gave so dreadful a shriek that it struck me dumb.

"O, repeal that curse!" she faltered.

I did not answer, and then she grew eloquent. This is, methinks, what she said, all the while clutching my gown, as if a hopeless prisoner could escape from her:

"Madame, for the sake of God and His holy Mother, pity me! If to have known the extremity of human agony teaches one to feel for another; if the most God-like thing on earth is to forgive; if none can enter heaven but such as pardon even an unrepentant enemy; if you would ascend whither two angelic spirits have preceded you,—O, greater in this dungeon than ever on a throne, more powerful to doom and to absolve than the sovereign of this realm, O, injured, broken-hearted, terrible Queen, grant my prayer; repeal this curse, which is spread like a pall over my innocent children! Set your feet on my neck; I lie at your feet; tread on me, spurn me, but recall that curse!"

As her words fell on mine ear, contrary passions swayed my soul. It seemed as if I held in my hands the doom of the abhorred race of Edward of York; and demons whispered, "Curse them again; call down upon them God's judgments." But then, with her old cunning, or else a mother's instinct, she exclaimed, "O sainted king, O holy Henry, pray for me!" And before me rose (perhaps with her witchcraft she evoked it) the patient, meek, noble face of my slain husband; and at the same time came a sudden singular softening of heart, which was like unto the calming of a stormy sea through the prayers of a saintly soul, or the driving away of foul spirits from a possessed person. I raised that mother from the ground, and made her sit by my side. A strange sadness stole over me, different from any I had hitherto felt; a singular compassion, albeit unmixed with any esteem for her.

"God have pity on you," I said in a tremulous voice, which sounded to me not like unto mine own; "God have pity on you, Elisabeth Woodville; God have pity on you, widow of the Lord Grey; mostly, God have pity on you, wife of Edward of York! I pray the good God to pardon me that, in an hour of sorrowful despair, I pronounced a curse on your innocent children, and prayed that they might perish as my son perished. I cry mercy to Him, and that He may show it to me; I cry also mercy to you, that in that unchristian passion of grief I desired this doom for the sons of my son's murtherers. Listen, I will retract that prayer."

"God bless you, madame!" she murmured. Then

I knelt down, with the crucifix in my hand, and said, "O Lord God, visit not on the children the iniquity of the father. Spare this woman's sons, whose husband spared not mine. Let not my bold, rash words avail against them in this life, nor against myself at Thy dread judgment-seat!" Then as I rose again a mournful feeling seized me, as if I had forecasted this present prayer should not be heard, and that my lips had uttered in their agony a true doom and inevitable prophecy. "Now go," I cried to this poor usurper of my former state; "now go, and carry with thee these words, which methinks God impels me to say to thee. If the sincere prayer I have now made hath no avail; if the divine justice, despite those I shall continue to put up, pursues thy children; if thou shouldst taste one day the horrible anguish I have known,—then bethink thee, miserable successor of my throne and of my woes, that there is but one plank of safety to which an agonised soul can cling in the midst of an ocean of unutterable misery—the Cross of Christ!"

(This which followeth was writ some months later, after the Princess of Wales, the Duchess of Clarence, and others, had been suffered oftentimes to visit the Queen.)

"I will see no more these two young fair women which glide into my dungeon like memory's emissaries and the world's deputies. Anne, with her wistful blue eyes, which, like the forget-me-not flower, seem ever to speak of a dead hope and a buried love; and Isabel, whose indignant soul since her father's death loathes the house of York and the mean idiot her husband: who, like a vision of mine own young self, kindles the embers of passionate resentments, and, with one flash of her proud eye, relights the expiring flame, well-nigh

extinguished in my breast by hard penance. No; I
will bid farewell to those fair types of old loves and old
hatreds. They stir mine heart too deeply. They picture to me my sorrows, my passions, my dreams, and
my despair. I will have no other company but my
God; no solace but my crucifix; no comforts but my
prayers; no joy but penance long and sharp."

When I told them I would see them no more, both
wept. They have a singular love for this fallen piece
of greatness, which I am. Anne looked sorrowfully in
my face and said, "Sweet mother, take not from me
the living though aged portrait of my lord." Isabel
spoke not at first; her bosom heaved as mine was
wont to do in days of yore. Then she broke forth:
"O Queen worthy of the name, Queen greater in this
dungeon than on the throne, wherefore do you banish
me? I would fain learn from you to conquer fate."

"Learn from me," I replied, "that fate is a vain
word, which, if it meaneth aught, doth signify God's
will. Take this lesson from one who would not bend
before that will, till it shattered to pieces the whole
fabric of her hopes. Go to—go to, poor noble
wenches; prepare your souls for suffering far from me,
in whose breast storms have too lately raged for peace
to flow from it into yours. Leave me to God and
solitude; leave me to pray and to atone. Would my
hands were as clean as yours from blood-guiltiness!"
Then the voice of my guardian angel, I ween, whispered to me, "Make atonement now. Bow down and
confess." "Before you depart," I said to the two
weeping sisters, "I will do penance at your feet;" and
falling on my knees before them, I exclaimed,

"I cry you mercy, Isabel and Anne, that I ordered
the death of your grandsire, old Lord Salisbury!"

"O Queen!" cried Isabel passionately, straining

me to her breast, "God forgive my father his sins against you; and, O, God forgive me who betrayed him and you!"

Anne kissed me several times; and now I shall see her no more. She goeth to the archbishop her uncle, who will defend her against Richard Gloucester,—the cruel hawk which ever hovers over the poor fluttering dove.

(When the Queen was moved to Windsor by the strenuous efforts thereunto of the reigning Queen, she wrote at night these words:)

"O ill-devised kindness! O miserable compassion, which hath wrought this exchange from the dark befitting dungeon of the old Tower to this seat of sweet memories and past glory! Fatal fair Windsor, where, under an evil star, my murthered King was born; whither I came a bride, where I now return a desolate captive widow, the prisoner of my subjects, the forsaken of men, and I pray God not of Him also! The fane of Eton meets mine eyes from this window where I now sit, and the sound of its bells reaches mine ear like a long unheard voice. O verdant meads, and soft-flowing waters! how long shall you flourish—how long flow? How many hundreds of years shall witness the sports of children and the pageantries of kings? How long shall mass be said for the just and for the unjust, for the evil and for the good, in yonder hallowed fane devised by my sweet saint? O that they had borne me to that other shrine of Chertsey, in howsoever mean a place, to dwell by those sacred remains, which I pray God one day to remove where kingly honours shall be paid to them! For this I live, and for the hope that ere I die the meekest king which ever sat on a throne shall be placed by the Church on her altars. He is e'en now one of God's and of the people's saints; his name in their prayers, his tomb a pilgrimage. Alas! I have dwelt on this thought in the long, sleepless hours of the night; but yestereve a painful fear arose in me, that, as David was not suffered to build a temple to the Lord God because his hands were stained with blood, mine shall not be found pure enough to engage in this holy pursuit. O God, my God, most benign and merciful! since the day on which I recalled that curse on my enemy's children, wholesome agonies have pierced my soul. Before me rise in dread array those whose deaths I ordered or caused, righteously I thought until now, but presently showing like foul murthers. The anger which heretofore was vented on my foes now turns against mine own self, because I have not a pure heart and clean hands for the task and end I pursue. But shall I then despair? No; for sorrow cleanseth, penance restores innocence, alms redeem sins. So, welcome kind helpful sorrow; and penance, do thou befriend me! Iron that is rusty may be scoured; and, as I have through pride lifted up myself, so will I pluck down my heart through humility, and willingly become a mocking-stock unto the world. Money, alas! I have none to give; but if God again yields moisture to mine eyes and some poor share of pelf to my keeping, I vow to make atonement for my evil deeds; and then peradventure He shall suffer me to sue for my lord's honour beyond the grave who was so little honoured in his life. And touching tears, it is not said, my Lord Jesus, that You shed any in Your agony, but yea, that You sweated blood therein. Behold, sweet Lord, the source of tears is dried up within me, and nought save a miracle like unto that in the desert, when Moses struck the rock, can bid them again to flow. But I have blood yet in these veins. Take it, my God; let it corrode and change! Let it be no longer healthful, but poisoned! Let it disfigure this outward form—once a fair one. Let Marguerite d'Anjou become a sight of horror, from which men shall turn with loathing; so that her soul is saved as if through fire, and, clean in the sight of angels, her prayer be heard at Rome on earth and by God in heaven!"

(At Wallingford Castle, whither the Queen was quickly removed from Windsor and placed under the keeping of the good Lady Surrey, she heard of the persecution of the Princess of Wales, and that she was compelled to marry Lord Richard Gloucester; upon which news she wrote *this*:)

I thank God that He hath instructed me to look upon the most keen thrusts of fortune as treasures wherewith pardon for the past and hope for the future may be bought. For otherwise how should my soul revolt in this hour, and break the bounds of human patience, at the loathsome hap which forces Anne into the arms of the killer of her life, the murtherer of her love! In vain hath she fled from his detested suit, in vain hid herself under the disguise of a poor serving-wench, or taken refuge in the sanctuary of my Lord of York's palace. I have ever been fatal to all who loved and cleaved to me. Through the accusation of correspondence with my friends this prelate hath been cast into a dungeon, and the Ruth of a most miserable Noemi falls a prey to brutal force and detestable love. O ill-omened nuptials! O blood-stained festivities! Miserable Anne! More terrific is thy fate than mine own, and mysterious God's dealings with thee; I thank Him, even in the extremity of my woes, that a like trial befell me not, for my brain would have been maddened, and I should have been like to murther the wretch in his sleep.

(A few days later the Duchess of Suffolk, willing to divert her majesty's thoughts from that new painful theme, carried her across the boundaries of the park to her own manor of Ewelm, and that night the Queen wrote what followeth :)

More liberty is now allowed to the hapless she-wolf of France than heretofore. Methinks they perceive that she no longer wageth an earthly warfare or detests her foes, as in past days. The poor wolf—if such she ever was—has lost its fierceness, and, like the one at Gubbio which St. Francis made a peace with, is robbed of all its terrors. She hath a work to compass, and her enemies help her to it. Lady Suffolk learnt this lore many years ago, and tutors me now in this new school. We talked thereon to-day the while we walked under the trees nigh to the parish church which her slain lord rebuilt. It is a comely piece of work, standing on a fair hill, and hard adjoining to it is founded a pretty hospital for two devout priests and thirteen poor men to dwell and be sustained in it for ever. It is a fair little God's house, which it liked me well to see; and we passed by the school, which is such a one as this lady's grandsire Master Chaucer described in his poesies:

"Little scole of Christen folk that stood
Down at the further end in which there were
Children in scores that came of Christen blood,
And learned within that schoolhouse, year by year,
Such kind of doctrine as men uséd there;
That is to say, to sing and to read
As all small children do in their childhood."

Ah, me! is it credible, when one has suffered and

sinned for well-nigh fifty years, that once it was a child's heart which throbbed in a frame now so worn-out and shattered?

(Montrobert's arrest in Brittany, and the misunderstanding of the Queen's letters to her father, to which hidden meanings were falsely ascribed by the council in the king's absence, who then was in France, and treating with King Lewis for her liberation, caused her majesty to be brought back in haste to the Tower, where she wrote thus:)

Once more in this old prison of kings and princes! I would not exchange it for any other lodging, save only a religious cell, where the whole world should forget me! What sights these walls have seen and yet shall see! for men are alike in all ages, and there is little mercy in their hearts—not even in a woman's, if God's Spirit doth not guide her. O that I had never been a queen!

(Some time afterwards she wrote in cipher:)
I have seen Pembroke, who is concealed in London, and hath young Richmond with him. He sought to awaken in me thoughts of revenge and new ambitions. But his efforts, like unto spent shafts, took no effect on the dead surface of my heart. They go to Brittany this night, and he carrieth with him a letter from me to my father, which I pray God may reach him, and that I may obtain freedom to exchange this prison for a convent, where God is served by pure spotless souls and likewise remorseful sinners.

(And she added shortly afterwards:)
O my God, will blood for ever flow in this land by reason of my poor name and life! Falconbridge and

Oxford, and now poor Exeter, have perished. I
thought my heart was dead; but these violent, and
one of them unhallowed, deaths pierce and prove it
alive.

(And then further on:)

I stand accused in the absence of the king (I take
for my sins the pain of that word's writing) of a plot
with the lords in Brittany. My afflicted letters are
distorted, and each word of sorrow reads as conspiracy
to Hastings and his creature Nash. Be it so; I will
stand a poor prisoner at their bar, and answer their
charges gently; gently as one who hath sinned and
needs forgiveness at the great judgment-seat of God.
And yet—I, Marguerite! the Queen!

O my God, the conflict deepens! Give me the victory!—old familiar words.

No, I am not to stand before the council. One has
defended the cause of Margaret d'Anjou; one has
pleaded for King Henry's wife, King René's daughter;
one has been her friend. O heavens, this schooling is
strange, these lessons severe! Who should have forecasted this new trial of royal and womanly pride? I
owe this grace to the king's mistress, to the courtesan
Jane Shore! Well, be it so. I kneel and bow my
head and my heart in the dust. Yea, let the public
sinner befriend the fallen queen. God knoweth! she
may yet take precedency of her in heaven, and her
prayers help the guilty Marguerite at that great bar
where many first shall be last, and many last shall be
first.

(When the Queen's liberation was announced to her,
which had been procured by the good, albeit not disinterested, efforts of the French king, she wrote:)

And so it hath come at last, this freedom long deferred and not greatly desired. These four long years are ended : so will life terminate one day, and the soul be set free as now the body. My prison hath become too sweet for a penitent. Time there was when despair haunted my solitude ; when sleep was dreadful, and waking terrible ; when the ghosts of those I had doomed to death, and the more gentle ones of such as had perished in my quarrel, were wont to pass before me at night in sad horrorful array; when spectral battles were fought in this chamber, and dead men came and sat with me, looking alive, and yet with gory wounds in their breasts, or else headless. But Margaret de Roos bethought her of sprinkling holy water about my bed, and prompted me to call on Christ and cross myself when these visions came. Since then they seldom haunt me; and if they do, I give them a gentle welcome, and pray if they be not lost, but only suffering souls, that they should pray for me; and so they depart in peace.

(At Greenwich palace, where the Queen resided three days before her departure, and license was given to all who craved it to kiss her hand and take leave of her grace, of which many persons, and some which were once her enemies, did with great zeal take advantage, she wrote these sentences :)

O singular sojourn! O new method of suffering! O more perfect humbling than could be easily devised of a proud heart! here in this mine own palace I have once again played the queen. Princes and nobles have come to gaze on the banished Queen : some pitiful, some curious, some peradventure with an old fidelity yet alive in their hearts. I would fain have stolen away like a thief in the night, veiled this changed visage and withered form, stood alone on the English shore, and cried to it a last farewell from the depths of a broken heart. But other counsels prevailed, and in the state-chamber of this old palace I received my whilom subjects, showed them my gray hairs, my sunken cheeks, and my eyes no longer bright. The most of them were young; for death, like a ruthless mower, had cut down their fathers in their prime. Those who had seen me young were mostly in their graves. One or two there were who had survived the civil wars. In their aged eyes methought tears were to be seen. We learn lessons insufficiently when alone and untempted. I had often conned at my prie-dieu the one which teaches to kill resentments, and thought I had been perfect in it. But when Clarence came with his wife into my presence, that hard-earned lore forsook me for an instant. The struggle was fierce and brief. When his lips touched my hand, I shuddered, but did not recoil. The poor soul, his wife, looketh the picture of misery. Alas! the most miserable on earth are not always those which have lost all.

(This is the copy of a letter which the Queen received from the Duchess of Gloucester the night before she left England:)

I dare not, madame, call you *mother*. I dare not approach your majesty, even in this final hour of your doleful English sojourn, to press a last kiss on your royal hand, for the sight of the poor Anne, which was once so welcome to you, must needs be abhorrent now. Yet on my knees, alone in God's presence, I bid your majesty a last farewell. She who was once Edward's wife from the depths of her singular misery crieth, "God bless you!" Neither for your highness nor for me can earth smile again. Long I struggled; long delayed my wretched fate; long hid myself in low disguises; and finally dragged my Lord of York, my poor uncle, into disgrace and death. But at the last force triumphed, and to preserve my honour I became what I am. O Queen, O mother! you did not curse me nor my unborn children?—you did not pray God to visit on them the crimes of their father? O, if you did, unsay that curse, for I am about to be a mother; and may the love and the grief and the passion of my heart, which hath lived in it all these years, stamp on my infant's face the likeness of my true lord, and Richard's child have Edward's visage! May the likeness of my worshipped prince live in my hapless babe! O mother Queen, I must needs love my child! Hate me not for it. I made a wild prayer in those days when I first saw my lord the Prince in Paris. I vowed if I might be his wife, if only for so much as one day, that I should gladly suffer afterwards the most horrorful fate life could inflict. Methinks God took me then at my word. Madame, when you behold again fair Angers and the river Mayence, and the palaces near it, mostly Reculée, think of me, I pray, with pity; for albeit my name is changed for a detested one, I am yet Anne Neville, and the love which began on the love day in London hath never flitted from my breast for one hour. It is a sacred and a buried one. Thank God there is another world, where those who, like your majesty and your poor servant, have been the chosen marks of adversity shall meet and no more suffer.

ANNE.

THE END OF THIS BOOK.

Convent of the Poor Clares at Vannes.

I am now, in mine advanced years, a postulant in the religious house which Jeanne de Kersabiec entered in her youth, and where Monseigneur Gilles de Bretagne is prayed for every day. God hath, I hope, given me a true vocation to this life, and in a few days I shall put on the habit of St. Clare. Methinks, before I take this solemn leave of the world, of which few have seen greater ups and downs, it should be well to write somewhat of the last years of my dear royal mistress, whose eyes I closed, and whose memory I venerate with a singular admiration. She did not write any more in her Journal after we landed in France at the beginning of January 1476; but she would sometimes ask me if I had set down aught touching her sufferings, and the peace she had found since I had prayed for her at her husband's tomb. O God! what a change was wrought in that Queen since, as she was wont to say, One more mightful than herself had conquered in the strife she had waged with Him since her childhood! Yet she was not so wholly altered but that some traits of her old character were sometimes visible; only its force was turned against herself, and she showed as great an eagerness to endure a suffering or a humiliation as heretofore to gain a triumph or crush a foe.

On the day when Sir Thomas Montgomery took her to Rouen and resigned her to the French ambassadors, she was called to sign a renunciation to the crown of England, which she did with so meek a grace that it drew tears from the eyes of the witnesses. She would by no means be styled the Queen Marguerite. "Nay," quoth she, "I am no queen now, but only 'Marguerite, formerly in England married.'" And when she had to name the king, she styled him the present King of England, with only a glance to Heaven, the source of all her hope; for it was now nothing to her, she said, who reigned or who despoiled her. She renounced likewise to King Lewis all her future rights to her father's dominions; and I heard her say, as she laid her head that night on the pillow, "God hath given and God hath taken away all earth can supply; now He hath given what neither earth nor Himself will take away." Then, as the chimes of St. Ouen fell on her ears for the first time for many years, a tear rolled down her cheek. "Methinks," she murmured, "I have got a little child's heart again, to be so pleased with those bells. I seem to hear them repeating rhymes:

> 'Adieu, bonheur !
> Salut, malheur !
> N'ai plus d'espoir
> Plus de déboire !
>
> Amour au ciel
> Et jamais fiel.
> O doux revoir !
> Plus de déboire.'"

As long as the bells rang she sang these words in a low voice.

The Queen had purposed to pass through Paris to thank the King her cousin for his good offices touching her liberation; but he sent her a discourteous advice not to come thither, and to proceed straight to her father's dominions; and he offered her an escort on the way, which she refused, and was like to have perished in consequence. For as we passed through a district where there was a settlement of English in a miserable plight, they got wind that she was the Queen Marguerite returning to her father. Loud murmurs rose against them, and they cried she was the cause that England had lost France, and sought for to kill her. This danger moved her not in the least. Fear had no access now to her heart. She said death at these ruffians' hands should have been welcome as the best ransom she could offer for her sins, which now were ever uppermost in her thoughts. She thirsted for penance as she had once done for greatness. When some soldiers had rescued her from this peril, she looked on these malcontents with an angerless eye, and from her ill-filled purse sent them some relief.

The meeting betwixt her and the aged King her father at the castle of Reculée drew many tears from him and tokens of tenderness. But after a while, albeit a great mutual love did bind them, a diversity of character, which was chiefly to be observed in their manner of sorrowing, led to a partial separation. The castle of Queniez, which he gave her, again became the Queen's habital residence. Once she said to me, after spending some days at Reculée: " My father seeks to reawaken in me the love of music and poesy and sculpture, in which he finds his great solace. He would fain lead me to the contemplation of Nature's beauties and Art's wonders. But the chords are broken, the notes are dumb which once responded to these themes. What are the sunset's hues and the glow of the early dawn to one whose eyes, when raised at all, can rest on nothing nearer than God's throne? What are carved images or rare paintings to one who ever sees before her two royal, princely, pale visages, with fair beautiful eyes waxed dim, white naked breasts, and bloody red sides? What is music to her ears who listens through long sleepless nights to the imagined cries of the wounded and the dying, or to the harpings of angels driving away those discordant sounds? I look at my father's aged gentle face, untouched by stormy passions, serene and fair in its decay, and albeit I sometimes long to crouch at his feet or hide myself in his arms, as in my childish days, pouring forth the untold sufferings of a lacerated soul, I still forbear from this cruel solace, and leave him to his gentle works of mercy, seasoned with ingenious art and poetic gracefulness. O, my poor friend! thank God with me that there are not many of the hearts which He hath made who have needed like unto mine to be saved as if by fire!"

At Queniez she spent all her time in prayer, fasted much, and gave alms of her poor means. Twice she went to Paris to the Séjour d'Orleans, a house King Lewis had given to her. This was to procure the sending of a petition to Rome for the King her husband's beatification. She was visited in her solitude, I think, two or three times by the young Earl of Richmond. She wished him well, I ween, and gave him always her benison; for the holy King, her lord, had prophesied, she said, he should one day be the King of England, and she doubted not it would so happen, since it was a saint foretold it.

The Queen often said her life was not hard enough to please her, that she longed for a yet heavier cross, and spoke of a prayer she had made in London for a singular suffering which she looked for before her death. And verily it came, in the shape of a fell disease which affected her whole frame, and turned that visage, once so peerless, into a spectacle of horror to all save those who loved it too much to be frighted by it. Then was seen a touching instance of God's grace overcoming nature (which rebelled at this infliction, and en-

dured a cruel martyrdom therefrom). She exulted in
this token that her long prayers had been heard and
this hard sign thereof granted. O, my Queen! in your
disfigured aspect, to any eyes but mine utterly changed
—in your sunken hollow eyes, in your livid visage, in
your holy gladness and peace—methought I saw, day
by day, Christ's Passion rehearsed and His meekness
copied. Since by much tribulation heaven is won ;
since singular misfortunes are needed to hallow fiery
souls; since this world is but a school for a coming
one,—we should not weep for you, my Queen, or for
the like royal or obscure sufferers of this or any other
age. But as by your death-bed I stood, and closing
your eyes uttered the words, *Requiescat in pace*, so we
may say them of all who, after long fighting in the
world's service, grow weary thereof, and then, yielding
themselves to God, find rest unto their souls.

This, my mistress, who had known the extremities
of greatness and humiliation, of joy and of sorrow, of
beauty and disfigurement—who had been so loved
and so hated—one while exalted to the skies, then
cast into an abyss—she, this royal wight, this great-
hearted lady, made this last bequest to the heiress of
her name and of her loveliness, Marguerite her niece.
In her own Missal, which she gave her, Marguerite
d'Anjou wrote with her dying hand these words:

Vanité des vanités, tout la vanité !

THE END.

NOVELS BY
LADY GEORGIANA FULLERTON

(Six Shillings each.)

ELLEN MIDDLETON.
LADY BIRD.
TOO STRANGE NOT TO BE TRUE.

(R. Bentley, New Burlington Street.)

GRANTLEY MANOR.
A STORMY LIFE; QUEEN MARGARET'S JOURNAL.

(Burns and Oates, Granville Mansions, W.)

TO APPEAR SHORTLY—

CONSTANCE SHERWOOD.
MRS. GERALD'S NIECE.

www.ingramcontent.com/pod-product-compliance
Lightning Source LLC
Chambersburg PA
CBHW031944290426
44108CB00011B/666